BOOKS BY

RALPH KORNGOLD

ROBESPIERRE
and the FOURTH ESTATE

SAINT-JUST
(*in French only*)

CITIZEN TOUSSAINT

TWO FRIENDS OF MAN
The Story of William Lloyd Garrison and Wendell Phillips
and Their Relationship with Abraham Lincoln

Two Friends of Man

Wendell Phillips and William Lloyd Garrison

Two Friends of Man

The Story of
WILLIAM LLOYD GARRISON
and WENDELL PHILLIPS
and Their Relationship with
ABRAHAM LINCOLN

by
RALPH KORNGOLD

Little, Brown and Company · *Boston*
1950

*Published simultaneously
in Canada by McClelland and Stewart Limited*

PRINTED IN THE UNITED STATES OF AMERICA

DEDICATED
With Profound Appreciation
to My Friend
RAYMOND THOMAS MOLONEY
Who Made This Book Possible

. . . Public sentiment is everything. With public sentiment nothing can fail; without it nothing can succeed. Consequently, he who models public sentiment goes deeper than he who enacts statutes and pronounces decisions. He makes statutes and decisions possible or impossible to be executed.

— ABRAHAM LINCOLN

Contents

PART FOUR — *War and Reconstruction*

PART FIVE — *Separate Ways*

Illustrations

PART ONE

Garrison

CHAPTER I

Boyhood

THERE was excitement at Maugerville[1] in the province of Nova Scotia, as New Brunswick was then named. A meeting had been called at the meetinghouse and hardly a family in the parish but was represented by one or more of its members. The occasion was indeed an extraordinary one. Word had reached the settlers on the St. John River of the uprising of the Colonies, and they were deeply stirred. Most of them had come to the province some dozen years before from Essex County, Massachusetts — from Rowley, Boxford, Byfield, Ipswich, Marblehead and adjacent towns — and their hearts beat in unison with those of their distant relatives and friends. The meeting was for the purpose of expressing solidarity with the rebels.

The bell tolled. The meetinghouse filled quickly. The chairman called the meeting to order, and there followed bursts of perfervid rustic oratory that were vigorously applauded. A committee was chosen to draft a manifesto and adjournment was taken until three o'clock. When the meeting reconvened the manifesto was read. The Declaration of Independence was still to be born, but even without that lofty pattern to guide them, the committee had managed to produce a creditable document. Its reading heightened the enthusiasm, and one after another the settlers stepped forward to affix their signatures.

One hundred and twenty-five eventually signed, twelve refused. Nine of these lived at the river's mouth, three belonged to the parish. One of the latter was Joseph Garrison, grandfather of the famous Abolitionist.

Joseph Garrison was an Englishman, presumably of French origin. The name, with slight variations, is fairly common in the Department of Tarn-et-Garonne, in Southern France, and signifies "little oak." When the New England colonists arrived, he was al-

[1] Pronounced *Majorville*.

ready established on the Jemseg, a tributary of the St. John, and made a tolerable living growing hay, raising cattle and "stripping" coal in a bituminous surface deposit he is credited with having discovered and which later became known as the Grand Lake Coal Mines. The arrival of the Massachusetts colonists had brought about a profound change in his life. One of the new settlers, a certain Daniel Palmer, had obtained a land grant a few miles down the river. He was a man of reckless courage and Herculean strength. It was told about him that once, in Massachusetts, when three armed Indians had invaded a house, he entered alone and threw all three out of a window "as though they were so many straws." Garrison went to call on him and found the visit rewarding, for Palmer's daughter Mary was fair to look upon. One who knew her in her old age described her as "a jolly sort of person — portly, with round face and fair hair, of a sanguine temperament, and a great favorite with children, whom she amused with quaint stories." It is not difficult to visualize her in her youth — pleasingly plump, fair-haired, rosy-cheeked and even more jolly. Garrison's visits to his neighbor became increasingly frequent, and on August 14, 1764, when he was thirty and Mary twenty-three, they were married.

We know little about Joseph Garrison's appearance, except that he was dark, became bald prematurely, had a slight congenital lameness, and a birthmark that swathed his chin from ear to ear and was "sometimes as red as blood." He must have had considerable firmness of character, since he refused to sign the manifesto, of which his redoubtable father-in-law was one of the authors, and defied the threat of ostracism voted at the meeting. It may well be that, less emotionally involved than his fellow settlers, he was able to foresee that the British Government would have little difficulty in stamping out the isolated spark of rebellion on the St. John.

The Government took its time about it, but a year later the sloop of war *Vulture* (destined to fame as the refuge of Benedict Arnold following his betrayal) came sailing up the river from Halifax, armed with fourteen cannon and crowded with redcoats. The soldiers disembarked, occupied the meetinghouses; word went forth that all settlers on the St. John must come and swear fealty to the King. If a man failed to put in an appearance, a platoon of soldiers came to fetch him; and if, warned of its approach, he took to the woods, the soldiers terrorized his family, smashed furniture, drove off his cattle, ruined his crops. A number of the fugitives were caught and taken aboard the sloop. Maugerville never saw them again.

2

Joseph Garrison died in 1783, aged forty-nine. Nine children had been born to him and Mary — the youngest William (after whom the Abolitionist editor was named), posthumously. Shortly after Joseph's death, Mary remarried, outlived her second husband by many years and herself died in 1822, aged eighty-one. Her fifth-born, Abijah, who saw the light of day in 1773, was destined to become the father of the Abolitionist leader.

Abijah grew up tall and well-proportioned. He had the reddish-blond hair, ruddy complexion and gray-blue eyes of the Palmers and had fallen heir to their sanguine, easygoing ways, love of companionship and jollity. From his father he inherited the disfiguring birthmark, "red as raw beef," which, as he grew older, he managed partly to conceal by growing a beard. Notwithstanding the facial blemish he is said to have been a handsome lad. He managed to acquire a rudimentary education, liked to read, wrote exuberant letters and even tried his hand at poetry. He went to sea when a boy and in his early twenties became a sea-captain.

One day his ship cast anchor in Passamaquoddy Bay, at Deer Island, New Brunswick. He was strolling about in the evening when a girl passed him of such uncommon appearance as to engage his instant attention. Tall and athletically built, she walked with litheness and grace, her blue dress setting off her superb figure to advantage. Her features were a trifle severe, but finely chiseled. Abijah followed fascinated. He hesitated for a moment when he saw her turn off the road into a barn, but noticing others enter, concluded that a public gathering was in progress and went in. It proved to be a religious meeting of the Baptist denomination, a sect frowned upon by those who valued their social standing. Abijah's mother had, however, been a Baptist, so he did not feel out of place. During the service he did not take his eyes off the girl, and at the conclusion of the meeting hastened outside. When she appeared he accosted her with the words: "May I see you home, Miss Blue Jacket?" She walked on without replying.

The rebuff did not discourage him. He made inquiries and learned that her name was Frances Maria Lloyd and that she was the daughter of a pilot named Andrew Lloyd, who had come to Deer Island from Ireland more than a quarter of a century ago. She lived with an uncle — her parents, who were Episcopalians, having disowned her for joining the Baptists. She had gone to a meeting of the sect with a number of young people expecting to be amused, but had found herself deeply stirred and had insisted on joining.

Abijah went to a tavern, called for pen and paper and wrote her a long letter in his most florid style. He had a fair knowledge of the Bible and was fond of quoting it in his correspondence, which may have impressed the young woman. Anyway, he succeeded in making her acquaintance and eventually they were married. The marriage date is not known with certainty, but December 12, 1798, appears the most probable.

3

The first year of their marriage Abijah and Fanny (as her intimates were wont to call her) had difficulty getting settled. For a while they lived among his people on the Jemseg, then in St. John, after that in Granville, Nova Scotia. A girl was born and died, then a boy, James Holley, then again a girl, Caroline Eliza. Abijah was away at sea most of the time. Six years after the marriage he wrote to Fanny: "I know of nothing in this life that wou'd augment my happiness more than to be at Home with my Family and Free'd from a Tempestuous Sky and Enraged Ocean." A year later, finding himself without a ship, he found staying at home not altogether satisfactory. In a letter to his mother and stepfather he complained about the drought and the hard times, owing to the war with Napoleon and the absence of trade with the United States. He told . of his decision to move again, this time to Newburyport, Massachusetts. That same spring he made the move, and rented two rooms in a frame house on School Street, between the First Presbyterian Church, where Whitefield had preached and lies buried, and the house in which the great preacher died. There, on December 12, 1805, William Lloyd Garrison was born.[2]

Abijah found employment as a sailing master and sailed to the West Indies. "It seems years since I saw you last," he wrote to

[2] This is the date given in the town records. Garrison's sons, in the biography of their father, give December 10 as the date of his birth.

Fanny in 1806, "I cou'd with pleasure this moment give up all I shall earn on this voyage to be present with you and my children." He was to have that satisfaction sooner than he expected, for the following year came the embargo. Ships from Newburyport lay moored in Boston, New York, Philadelphia. Wharves were deserted, warehouses closed. Coopers, blacksmiths, sailmakers, calkers, seamen did not know how to feed their families. When men got together they cursed Jefferson and the "Jacobins," as the New Englanders called the Jeffersonians, and there was talk of leaving the Union.

Abijah found the enforced idleness hard to bear. He would leave the house, spend an hour or two at the "Social Library," wander aimlessly about the streets and usually wind up at the tavern. There, over a glass of grog or ale, men forgot their worries and were merry again. It was with reluctance that he would finally start for home, where he knew Fanny would reproach him for spending on drink money that might soon be needed to keep the children from starving. He still loved his wife, or thought he did. When she unloosened her dark hair, it fell about her rich and luxuriant, covering her like a veil, and she had preserved her queenly bearing. If only she were less pious and more jolly! Their landlady, Martha Farnham, happened to be a Baptist, and not content with going to church at every opportunity, the two women held prayer meetings at the house. Abijah had no quarrel with religion, but felt he was getting more than his due.

One day in June, 1808, the second year of the embargo, he came home from the tavern and found Caroline in bed. The child had eaten some flowers in a neighbor's garden and had come home complaining about pains in the stomach. Fanny and Martha administered the usual household remedies, but the girl died before evening. It was a cruel blow and did not bring husband and wife closer together. She found consolation in praying with Martha; he sat alone and brooded.

A few weeks later Fanny gave birth to a girl, christened Maria Elizabeth. She saw God's hand in giving her a girl-child to take the place of Caroline, but to Abijah the presence of a baby made the house even less habitable. He had lately stayed away from the tavern, but a few days after the birth of the child went again. Several of his seafaring friends were there and when he told them about the new arrival there was back-slapping and several rounds of drinks.

Abijah forgot his troubles and when they were leaving the tavern a reckless mood came over him. He suggested that all come home with him: he would buy a couple of bottles of rum and they would celebrate.

Fanny must have been at a neighbor's and have tarried there for some time, for the party was in full swing when suddenly the door opened and she appeared on the threshold. The merriment ceased; the men felt like guilty schoolboys. The wrathful woman strode to the table, picked up a bottle by its neck, swung it against its mate, breaking both, upset the glasses with a sweep of her hand and not only ordered her husband's friends to leave the house, but speeded their departure with an occasional vigorous push.

Abijah did not interfere and remained silent when Fanny emptied the vials of her wrath over him, but the following day he left home and she never saw him or heard from him again. He went to New Brunswick, made a few voyages, taught school for a while. In 1814 his cousin Joanna Palmer received a letter from him — a lonely man's letter in which he begged her to write to him, but made no mention of his family. "When you answer this I will write you a Sentimental piece," he promised, meaning one of his poetical effusions.

4

William Lloyd Garrison, whom his mother called Lloyd, was not yet three when his father disappeared. Fanny was thirty-two and so healthy and vigorous that people used to say: "Only a cannon ball can kill Fanny Garrison." Martha Farnham proved a good friend and took care of her brood while she hired out as a nurse. In 1809 the embargo was lifted and for a while Fanny managed fairly well, but two years later came the great fire that wiped out part of the business district and the following year war broke out. It was to last three years and almost ruined the town. "Everything was old and rusty and dead," wrote a local historian. "Nobody thought of painting a building, and there were so many of them empty that rent was nothing, and the purchase price of anything was less than that. If an old fence blew down, there it lay, unless it was picked up to burn, and when a pump-handle broke, no more water came from that well."

The boy was then not yet seven and never forgot the hardships and humiliations of that trying time. On court or fair days he would circulate among the crowd, a basket on his arm filled with molasses candy his mother had made. Most humiliating of all was his daily pilgrimage with a covered tin pail to the rear door of a rich man's house on High Street, to receive the leavings of the one-o'clock dinner. Boys who suspected the purpose of his errand would maliciously ask what he had in the pail and would sometimes attempt to look, when there would be a fight.

He and his little sister attended the primary or "writing" school. He was not an apt pupil, making slower progress than his sister, and was left-handed. This last the schoolmaster managed to cure by rapping him on the knuckles with a ruler. Ultimately he developed a beautiful handwriting, but all his life he wrote slowly and laboriously.

The time came when Fanny was no longer able to earn a living in Newburyport and decided to move to Lynn. Only James was to accompany her. Martha offered to look after Elizabeth, while Ezekiel Bartlett, a deacon of the small Baptist church, agreed to care for the younger boy. Bartlett, who was married and had two daughters, made a meager living sawing wood, sharpening saws, making lasts and selling apples from a little stand in front of his cottage at the corner of Water and Summer Streets. He sent the boy to grammar school for a trimester, but at the end of that period felt he needed his help to make ends meet.

5

Fanny had apprenticed the thirteen-year-old James to a shoemaker in Lynn and now sent for Lloyd, whom she placed with Gamaliel Oliver, a Quaker, to learn the shoemaker's trade. He lived with his employer and was well treated, but he was only nine and too frail for the work. To sit for hours with a heavy lapstone on his knees, hammering away at sole leather, made him ache all over; waxing thread cut the tender skin of his fingers. He had, however, learned to make a tolerable shoe when a Lynn shoe manufacturer who wished to set up in business in Baltimore hired Fanny and her two sons. They went there by boat. The journey lasted twelve days and the weather was stormy. Lloyd was so seasick that yearnings for the sea, which he had had occasionally, left him never to return.

Slavery had been abolished in Massachusetts towards the end of the eighteenth century, but in Baltimore Lloyd saw the South's "peculiar institution" at its worst. The city was a shipping point for Maryland and Virginia slave breeders, and every day one saw coffles of manacled slaves led through the streets towards the harbor. Fanny and her two sons lived with their employer. She did housework, James worked at the last, Lloyd ran errands and swept floors. But the business did not prosper and after a few months the manufacturer returned to Lynn. Fanny decided to remain.

She rented a small cottage and went out to nurse, while the boys found work at their trade. Her tribulations had only served to increase her piety. She went to church three times on Sunday, held prayer meetings at home and received callers in need of spiritual guidance. James, who was now fifteen and resembled his father in character as well as appearance, felt restless and dissatisfied. In Lynn, where boys as well as men were served with rum at their work, he had acquired the drinking habit, and his mother's reproaches worried him. One day he disappeared. He had gone to sea.

Lloyd, too, felt far from happy. In 1816 Fanny wrote to Martha Farnham: "He is so discontented . . . that he would leave me tomorrow and go with strangers to N.P. [Newburyport]; he can't mention any of you without tears. He is a fine boy, though he is mine, and every Sunday he goes to the Baptist church, although he has so far to walk. I expect he will be a complete Baptist as to the tenets."

Poor Fanny! She was undoubtedly an excellent woman, but nobody enjoyed living with her. Her younger son showed his displeasure so plainly that she decided to let him return to his native town and live with "Uncle" Bartlett. This time she must have been able to pay something towards his keep, for he was sent to grammar school.

He loved Newburyport. The town, which then had a population of between seven and eight thousand, is built on the sloping bank of the Merrimack. The river reaches far into the forests of New Hampshire, whence came the sturdy oak timber for the town's shipyards. Louis Philippe, who visited the region before he became King of France, wrote that all Europe did not afford a more delightful drive than could be found on the north bank of the river. President Dwight of Yale waxed enthusiastic about the town's fine mansions, clean streets, air of elegance and luxury. The mansions, along the elm-shaded High and Water Streets, had been erected by the town's wealthy shipowners, who at one time made money at such a rate that one of their number, Joseph Marquand, is said to have exclaimed: "Lord, stay Thy hand; Thy servant hath enough!"

Lloyd went swimming and huckleberrying with his playmates, or they gathered pennyroyal and other herbs, bunches of which hung in every attic. Sometimes he and his friends would go to a wharf opposite one where there were barrels of molasses, remove their clothes, swim across, and with the aid of a flat stick inserted into the bunghole sample the contents of each barrel. If surprised, they dived into the stream and swam back to their starting point.

When winter came there were skating and snow battles with the North Enders. The future advocate of nonresistance proved so adept at fighting that for a time he was the leader of the South Enders against their traditional enemies. He joined the choir of the Baptist church and a singing school "where there were lots of boys and pretty girls." At home he had a female cat of which he was very fond and which early one morning arranged her newborn kittens around his head on the pillow and patiently waited for him to awaken and admire them. In short, he was happier than he had ever been.

This carefree existence lasted two years. He was thirteen when he received word from his mother that she had apprenticed him to Moses Short, a cabinetmaker at Haverhill. So to Haverhill he went and sawed and planed and felt homesick for Newburyport and took little interest in the work. Taking French leave appears to have been a family trait, for before six weeks were over he got up one morning long before dawn, bundled up his few belongings, dropped them out of the window into the garden and followed noiselessly. Soon he was walking along the highway and when the stagecoach passed he swung onto the rack behind. When the coach would stop he would pursue his way on foot only to swing aboard again when it caught up with him. He had covered a good part of the way when suddenly, at a relay, he found himself confronted by Moses Short, who had taken a short cut.

Apprentices were not unlike indentured servants, bound for seven years. Their treatment often left much to be desired and when one was caught trying to escape he usually received a flogging. Short, however, was more aggrieved than angry. He told the boy that he could leave if he wished, but it must be done properly. If he would return quietly, a legal release would be arranged. It was a fair offer. Lloyd returned and a few weeks later was back in Newburyport.

6

Ephraim W. Allen, editor and publisher of the Newburyport *Herald*, advertised for a printer's apprentice. In his office appeared Deacon Ezekiel Bartlett in charge of the thirteen-year-old Lloyd. Allen liked the boy's appearance, the boy thought he would like the printer's trade. So the papers were signed, young Garrison moved over to Mr. Allen's, and in October, 1818, began a seven years' apprenticeship that proved the prelude to his career. In his old age he was to say: "Had I not been a practical printer — an expert compositor and able to work at the press — there had been no *Liberator*."

To form pieces of metal into words, words into sentences and paragraphs, to see the metal magically impart its message to sheets of paper — it fascinated the boy. What if that printing press were to disseminate ideas that had germinated in his own brain? But to have ideas worth communicating one must know and understand. He began to read avidly. He read the exchanges that came to the office, especially articles dealing with politics. He read Scott, Byron, Moore, Pope, Campbell, Milton, Coleridge, Shelley, Shakespeare, Junius, and the now almost forgotten Mrs. Hemans, whose poetry Emerson believed to be immortal. He tried his hand at literary composition, but it was not until he was sixteen that he attempted to break into print. What fixed his determination was indignation at a young woman's success in obtaining seven hundred and fifty dollars from a Boston dandy for breach of promise. After declaiming at length against the verdict he thus castigated the sex:

"The truth is, however, women in this country are too much idolized and flattered; therefore they are puffed up and inflated with pride and self-conceit. They make the men to crouch, beseech and supplicate, wait upon and do every menial service for them to gain their favor and approbation; they are, in fact, completely subservient to every whim and caprice of these changeable mortals. Women generally feel their importance, and they use it without mercy.

"For my part, notwithstanding, I am determined to lead the 'single life' and not trouble myself about the ladies."

The phillippic was in the form of a letter addressed to the editor of the *Herald*. He wrote it in a disguised hand and signed the epistle "An Old Bachelor." Allen found it sufficiently entertaining to merit reading aloud to his employees. Then, unsuspecting, he handed it to young Garrison with instructions to set it up.

During the succeeding twelve months the boy sent fifteen communications to the editor, most of them initialed A. O. B. [An Old Bachelor]. Not only did all appear in print, but the correspondent was invited to persevere and to call at the office to make the editor's acquaintance. The letters covered a variety of subjects. A description of a shipwreck exhibited an ignorance of things nautical that does not appear to have troubled the editor. One letter dealt with the grievances of American shipowners and captains against certain South American countries. "The only expedient to command respect and protect our citizens will be to finish with cannon what cannot be done in a conciliatory and equitable manner, where justice demands such proceedings," wrote the future advocate of nonresistance. He championed the candidacy of Harrison Gray Otis for Governor and took the Holy Alliance to task for wishing to restore Ferdinand on the throne of Spain.

7

Letters he received from his mother were disquieting. She had contracted consumption. Her son, exhibiting a faith in patent nostrums that remained with him through life, recommended that she take "Balsam of Quito." She replied that she wished for nothing more than "the Balm of Gilead, the great Physician of Souls, to heal the wounds that sin had made." She sent for her daughter Elizabeth, who all these years had been living with Martha Farnham, not realizing that in so doing she was signing the child's death warrant. The twelve-year-old girl promptly contracted the disease and died two years later. She was still living when her brother began sending his anonymous contributions to the *Herald* and jubilantly announced their acceptance. Fanny was not impressed and wrote: "You must write me one of your pieces so that I can read it on one side of your letter, and I will give you my opinion whether you are an old bachelor, or whether you are A.O.B., as A may stand for Ass, and O for Oaf, and B for Blockhead." He did not comply, feeling no doubt that since the "pieces" were of a secular nature she would not approve. Eight months after his sister's death, he could not refrain from doing some further boasting. "It is now about a year since I commenced writing for the *Herald* — and in that time I have written about fifteen communications. . . . When I peruse them over, I feel absolutely astonished at the different subjects which I have discussed, and the style in which they are written. Indeed, it is altogether a matter of surprise that I have met with such signal success, seeing I do not understand *one single rule of grammar*,[3] and having a very inferior education."

A "signal success" that had not brought him a dollar seemed to Fanny a vain and foolish thing. She replied: "Next your turning Author. You have no doubt read and heard of the fate of such characters, that they generally starve to death in some garret or place that no one inhabits; so you may see what fortune and luck belong to you if you are of that class of people. Secondly, you think your time wisely spent while you are writing political pieces. I cannot join with you there, for had you been searching the scriptures for truth, and praying for direction of the holy spirit to lead your mind into the path of holiness, your time would have been more wisely spent, and your advance to the heavenly world more rapid."

In March, 1823, he received a letter from his mother begging him to come and see her. Although still an apprentice he had been appointed foreman and was in complete charge of the printing office. His employer having gone on business to Alabama, it was not until June that he was able to comply with his mother's request. He sailed from Boston, and after a two weeks' journey arrived in Baltimore. He had not seen his mother for seven years and was expecting a great change, but was hardly prepared for what he saw. He found her in bed, under the care of a woman friend, and so weak that she was unable to raise herself from her pillow. "I found her so altered, so emaciated, that I should never have recognized her, had I not known that there were none else in the room," he wrote to Allen.

They had much to talk about and during the three weeks he remained in Baltimore he seldom left her bedside. Unable to prolong his stay any longer, he finally tore himself away. Both knew they would never meet again on earth, but both believed in a meeting in another world. A few weeks after his return to Newburyport he set up his mother's death notice. She was forty-five when she died.

[3] Italics in quotations appear in original text.

8

After his mother's reprimand Garrison had stopped his journalistic work. He now began to write again. The Salem *Gazette* became his principal medium of publicity. Under the pen name "Aristides" he took sides with Pickering in his quarrel with John Adams and championed William Harris Crawford for the Presidency against John Quincy Adams and Andrew Jackson. He was already a man of parts. Formerly when Allen was out of town Caleb Cushing was wont to take his place; now the editorial responsibility devolved upon the nineteen-year-old apprentice, who acquitted himself well. One who knew him at that time wrote: "He was an exceedingly genteel young man, always neatly and I might say elegantly dressed, and in good taste, and was quite popular with the ladies." About this time he began wearing glasses, which he would remove when reading or writing.

It is interesting to note that his ideas were almost the exact opposite of what they were to be in his maturity. The "No Government" man, who was to abstain from voting, was now preoccupied with politics. The religious liberal, accused by his clerical opponents of infidelity, was now "a complete Baptist as to the tenets." The scorner of a pharisaical observance of the Sabbath was now a strict Sabbatarian. The champion of Woman's Rights was now opposed to women exercising even the right of petition. The advocate of nonresistance was seriously considering entering West Point and becoming a professional soldier, and toyed with the idea of going to Greece to fight the Turks. As for slavery, which was to engross his life, he now gave it scarcely a thought.

CHAPTER II

Youthful Editor

A YOUNG printer named Isaac Knapp, with whom Garrison had struck up a friendship, had become editor and publisher of the *Essex Courant*. Knapp's predecessor had championed Jeffersonian democracy with scant financial success; the new editor steered an independent course, but did not find the new policy more rewarding. When Garrison would visit him he usually found him downcast and regretting his journalistic venture.

After concluding his apprenticeship, Garrison had gone to live at Martha Farnham's, but had remained on the *Herald* as a journeyman printer. He now proposed to his employer that he lend him the money to buy out friend Knapp. Allen was willing, and so, at the age of twenty, Garrison became an editor and publisher — the youngest in the United States. He changed the name of the weekly to the *Free Press*, and thus announced his policy to the public:

> As to the political course of the *Free Press*, it shall be in the widest extent of the term, *independent* . . . It shall be subservient to no party or body of men: and neither the craven fear of loss, nor the threats of the disappointed, nor the influence of power, shall ever awe one single opinion into silence.

The first issue contained so spirited a polemic concerning the State's long overdue claim against the Federal Government, for the defense of the Massachusetts coast during the war with England, that ten subscribers canceled their subscriptions. Garrison reported this together with the information that more than an equal number had been added to the list, which he confessed to be "unbecomingly stinted, considering the magnitude of the town." That he meant to spare neither friend nor foe became evident when John Adams and Thomas Jefferson died on July 4, 1826. Allen, forgetting that in the past he had been wont to refer to Jefferson as the "Great Lama of Infidelity," eulogized the dead statesman. His former apprentice took him to task for his inconsistency, professing himself nauseated by the "disgusting, irreverent, and puerile panegyrics, all of them inflated and reprehensible." Slavery received attention for the first time in an article concerning Fourth of July orations. He expressed his impatience with the meaningless "rhapsodies upon the deeds of our fathers" and declared: "There is one theme that should be dwelt upon till our whole country is free from the curse — it is SLAVERY."

2

One morning when Garrison entered his office, he found an envelope under his door containing a poem signed *W*. He was about to throw it unread into the wastepaper basket, when something restrained him. He read the lines, found them far above the average and decided to print them. When a second and a third contribution arrived from the same source, he questioned the post rider and learned that the poet was a Quaker lad named John Greenleaf Whittier, who lived with his parents on a farm outside East Haverhill. He was by this time sufficiently interested to decide to visit the poet and induced a young woman of his acquaintance to accompany him. He rented a chaise and they drove the fourteen miles to Haverhill.

Arrived at the farm, they were admitted by Whittier's sister Mary into the roomy colonial kitchen the poet has described in *Snowbound*. It was she who without her brother's knowledge had sent the first poem to the *Free Press*. Whittier was working in the field and needed considerable coaxing before he would show himself. The visitors beheld a tall, rangy youth, with large, luminous dark eyes and an oriental cast of countenance. "He came into the room," Garrison wrote, "with shrinking diffidence, almost unable to speak and blushing like a maiden." Soon after, the father entered; Garrison addressed himself to him, trying to convince him that his son should be given every opportunity to develop his talent. The Quaker listened gravely, then said: "Sir, poetry will not give him *bread*." Garrison wrote: "The fate of Chatterton, Otway, and the whole catalogue of those who had perished by neglect, rushed upon our memory — and we were silent."

But in almost every issue of the *Free Press* now appeared a poem by Whittier. A. E. Housman has remarked that "poems very seldom consist of poetry and nothing else; and pleasure can be derived also from their other ingredients." While "other ingredients" predominate in Whittier's poetry, few will deny him the title of poet. That Garrison was responsible for Whittier's interest in the slavery problem, the poet has acknowledged in a letter to his friend. "I cannot be sufficiently thankful to the Divine Providence," he wrote in 1863, "which, in a great measure through thy instrumentality, turned me so early away from what Roger Williams calls 'the world's great trinity, pleasure, profit and honor,' to take side with the poor and the oppressed."

3

Garrison was a born crusader. As a boy he had seldom hesitated to take the part of a smaller lad against a bully, even with the odds greatly against him. As a man, when something appeared to him evil or unjust, his impulse was to smash it regardless of consequences. He was in fact the most combative of men and Nature must have wished to shield him from harm when she made him espouse nonresistance early in his career. As editor of the *Free Press* he did not care a whit to what party or clique a man belonged whom he set out to castigate, or whether his influence was great or small. The result was that people were constantly canceling their subscriptions, and while others were added to the list one is inclined to doubt his statement that the latter outnumbered the former. The fact remains that when after six months a purchaser presented himself, he decided to sell.

In December, 1826, a few months after the sale of the paper, he moved to Boston. Bronson Alcott wrote of the Boston of that day: "There is a city in our world upon which the light of the sun of righteousness has risen. . . . Its influences are quickening and invigorating the souls which dwell within it. . . . It is the city that is set on high. 'It cannot be hid.' It is Boston. The morality of Boston is more pure than that of any other city in America." The Boston where Garrison had decided to try his fortune was not quite the shining metropolis Alcott imagined it to be. It had adopted a city charter seven years before the rhapsody was written, and had not over thirty thousand inhabitants. It had its share of vice, poverty, corruption, complacency, class and race prejudice. But it had considerably more than its share of the country's intellect. Harriet

Martineau was to write a few years later: "I certainly am not aware of so large a number of peculiarly interesting and valuable persons, living in any near neighborhood, anywhere else but in London."

Garrison's only acquaintance in the city was a printer named Bartlett, whose wife kept a boardinghouse on Scott Street. He rented a room at the boardinghouse, but work was slack and Bartlett could not employ him. For nearly a month, in fair weather or foul, he tramped from printing office to printing office, always receiving the same answer. His money ran out, his boots became badly worn and the city was beginning to take on a hateful and hostile aspect when his luck changed and he found employment as a journeyman printer.

Now that he had regular work his interest in politics revived. When the Federal Party called a caucus at the Exchange Coffee House, he decided to attend. The caucus was for the purpose of nominating a candidate for the House of Representatives to take the place of Daniel Webster, now a senator. The party leaders had agreed on a Boston attorney named Benjamin Gorham, but Garrison had other plans. Gorham meant nothing to him, but there was Harrison Gray Otis, whom as an apprentice he had championed for governor and whom he still greatly admired. He prepared a speech and committed it to memory. On the day of the caucus he dressed in tightly strapped trousers, a skirted coat, a frilled shirt, a stock and a stand-up collar, put on his tall beaver with spreading crown (not, however, before depositing in its interior the manuscript of his speech for use in an emergency) and went to the Coffee House.

All went as the leaders had planned. Speaker after speaker sang the praises of Benjamin Gorham. There was no mention of any other candidate. But then the unknown young man arose and to the consternation of the leaders proceeded to deliver a eulogy of Mr. Otis. What if he lost the thread of his discourse? Unabashed he removed his hat, produced the manuscript and went on to the end. When he placed Otis's name in nomination there was applause and several electors seconded him. The machine was thrown into disarray. Otis was too important a man to be treated lightly. There were whispered conversations among the leaders and then the motion was made and carried to adjourn for three days so Mr. Otis could be consulted.

Nothing came of Garrison's ambitious incursion into Boston politics. His hero declined the nomination. But there followed a lively polemic in the Boston *Courier* between an indignant elector and the political interloper. The elector wrote that he had experienced considerable difficulty in learning the name of the brash young man who "possessed the impudence to take the lead and nominate a candidate for the electors of Boston." This gave Garrison the opportunity he craved. Polemics was his specialty. "I sympathize with the gentleman in the difficulty which he found to learn my cognomination," he wrote with revealing self-assurance. "Let me assure him, however, that if my life be spared, my name shall one day be known to the world, — at least to such extent that common inquiry shall be unnecessary. This, I know, will be deemed excessive vanity — but time shall prove it prophetic." His faith in his destiny was indeed so profound that he did not feel he was exceeding the bounds of modesty when a year later he wrote during a controversy: "You declare you have never heard my name before. . . . I have only to repeat without vanity, what I declared publicly to another opponent . . . that, if my life be spared, my name shall one day be known so extensively as to render private inquiry unnecessary; and known, too, in a praiseworthy manner. I speak in the spirit of prophecy, not of vainglory, — with a strong pulse, a flashing eye, and a glow of the heart. *The task may be yours to write my biography.*"

His friend Whittier, commenting on some of his own youthful boasts, has written: "There is a period in life — a sort of tadpole state between the boy and the man — when any sort of pretense, egotism, and self-conceit may be expected."

4

Garrison had changed his boardinghouse and had gone to live at Number 30 Federal Street, at the Reverend William Collier's. Collier, an enterprising Baptist minister, preached the gospel, kept a boardinghouse and still found time to engage in the publishing business in partnership with his son. They published two weeklies and a monthly. Garrison's roommate, Nathaniel H. White, did their printing; it was with him our friend now found employment. One of the weeklies was the *National Philanthropist*, believed to have been the first periodical devoted principally to the cause of temperance, a forlorn cause at that time. Excessive drinking was a legacy from colonial days. In 1763 Boston merchants estimated that nine hundred thousand gallons of rum were consumed annually in Massachusetts — four gallons for every man, woman and child! In Garrison's time Irish workmen received three "jiggers" in addition to their daily wage of seventy-five cents, and rum or gin was served at ordinations, weddings, births, funerals, in fact on every conceivable occasion. A "sober" man was one who carried his liquor well. Under these circumstances a temperance paper could hardly have been expected to draw much support. The Colliers soon got tired of paying the deficit and disposed of the publication to their printer, who appointed Garrison editor.

In the course of his career Garrison changed his mind about several of the causes he championed, but never about temperance. In 1832, when he had adopted Abolition as principally meriting his devotion, he nevertheless was to write: "God is my witness that, great as is my detestation of slavery and the foreign slave-trade, I had rather be a slaveholder — yea, a kidnapper on the African Coast — than sell this poison to my fellow-creatures for common consumption. Since the creation of the world there has been no tyrant like intemperance, and no slaves so cruelly treated as his." As editor of the *Philanthropist* he did not, however, confine himself to the advocacy of temperance. He championed world peace and assailed gambling, imprisonment for debt, desecration of the Sabbath, infidelity and irreligion. The transportation of mail and persons on Sunday especially provoked his editorial ire. "He would no sooner have gone to the post-office on that day to mail or receive a letter than he would have stolen the contents of a contribution-box," —wrote his friend Oliver Johnson.

One article from his pen foreshadowed his future career. The House of Assembly of South Carolina had passed a bill forbidding the teaching of reading and writing to people of color. Garrison commented: "There is something unspeakably pitiable and alarming in the state of that society where it is deemed necessary, for self-preservation, to seal up the mind and debase the intellect of man to brutal incapacity. We shall not now consider the policy of this resolve, but it illustrates the terrors of slavery in a manner as eloquent and affecting as imagination can conceive."

5

Those were the palmy days of Unitarianism in Boston. The gospel according to Harvard Divinity School was being preached by William Ellery Channing, Henry Ward, Francis Parkman, John Pierpont, Charles Lowell, N. L. Frothingham and others almost equally famous. But Garrison at that time was no religious liberal. His favorite exhorter was Lyman Beecher, pastor of the Hanover Street Church, whom Robert Ingersoll has called "one of the wardens of the Puritan penitentiary." There was no nonsense about Dr. Beecher. He never boldly declared, like the Reverend Jonathan Edwards, that children are "young vipers, and infinitely more hateful than vipers," but he believed in infant damnation, election, total depravity, eternal punishment and the divine inspiration of the Bible from Genesis to Revelation. He was opposed to baptism of infants, toleration, democracy and the separation of church and state. He did not believe in slavery, but considered it as nothing compared with such horrors as Romanism and Unitarianism. About these two heresies he could manage to work himself up into such "upheavings of passionate emotion" that he thought it advisable to keep a pile of sand in the basement of his house, so he could shovel it back and forth and thus regain his composure. The Catholic Church he referred to as a "ferocious beast" and "the mother of harlots" and Unitarianism as "modern infidelity." What Garrison found inspiring in these fulminations is difficult to understand. To the modern reader they seem empty froth. Beecher's own daughter, Harriet Beecher Stowe, found them unintelligible. Yet there must have been power in the man, for he influenced Phillips as well as Garrison.

Garrison often attended the Federal Street Baptist Church, but not because he particularly enjoyed the sermons of the pastor, the Reverend Howard Malcom. There was another, more potent attraction whose name was Miss Emily Marshall. Edmund Quincy, son of the President of Harvard, wrote of her in his old age: "I well know the peril that lies in superlatives, — they were made for the use of very young persons; but in speaking of this gracious lady, even the cooling influences of more than half a century do not enable me to avoid them. She was simply perfect in face and figure, and perfectly charming in manners." Garrison had to worship at a distance, for Miss Marshall belonged to Boston's aristocracy and eventually married a son of Harrison Gray Otis.

CHAPTER III

The Forerunner

ITINERANT clergymen and travelers with a social mission often stopped at "Parson Collier's." In March, 1828, the clerical host ushered in a diminutive, slender man whom he introduced as Benjamin Lundy, editor of *The Genius of Universal Emancipation*. Garrison knew the *Genius* to be the only anti-slavery paper in the United States and had often marveled at the editor's courage in publishing it in a Slave State. So intrepid a man he had imagined to be "a Hercules in shape and size."

Lundy was born in 1789, at Hardwick, New Jersey, the son of Quaker parents. His mother having died when he was five, he left home at an early age and wandered about the country. At nineteen he apprenticed himself to a harness maker at Wheeling, Virginia, where for the first time he saw coffles of slaves on their way to the South. "Their coffles," he wrote, "passed through the place frequently. My heart was deeply grieved at the gross abomination; I heard the wail of the captive; I felt his pang of distress; and the iron entered my soul."

When he finished his apprenticeship he set up in business in St. Clairsville, Ohio, married, begot children and prospered. But he could not forget the sights he had seen at Wheeling and talked about them to his friends. Most of them being Quakers, they listened sympathetically and helped him organize the Union Humane Society, whose avowed purpose it was to combat slavery. It soon counted five hundred members. In John Woolman's *Journal* Lundy read how the saintly Quaker had sold his dry goods store so he might devote more time to combating slavery among his coreligionists. He decided to follow Woolman's example and even to improve upon it by consecrating all his life and fortune to the slaves' cause.

It was a momentous decision. He had a wife and children to support. He was hard of hearing and had a delicate constitution. He had no great talent as writer or speaker and there was no burning

passion or flaming indignation in him as there later was in Garrison.
But he had a quiet sincerity and an indomitable will. These sufficed.
Leaving his family behind, he loaded his merchandise on a barge
and took it to St. Louis, where he disposed of it at a sacrifice. The
admittance of Missouri as a Slave State was then agitating the
country. So he remained in St. Louis and wrote innumerable letters
to editors, most of which found their way into print. When the
Missouri Compromise was an accomplished fact, he set out for home,
covering the seven hundred miles on foot, in the midst of winter.
In adopting this mode of travel he might have meant to follow Woolman's example, but it proved of practical value by giving him the
opportunity to meet people, learn their views and drop seed that
often sprouted.

He moved his family to Mount Pleasant, Ohio, and in 1821
launched an anti-slavery monthly — *The Genius of Universal Emancipation*.[1] It was not the first anti-slavery periodical in the United
States; that distinction belongs to the *Philanthropist*, publication of
which was begun in 1817 at Mount Pleasant by the Quaker Charles
Osborn — but that paper now had ceased to exist. There being no
printing shop in the town, the *Genius* was printed at Steubenville,
some twenty miles distant, and the editor usually carried the entire
edition home on his back.

In 1820 Elihu Embree had launched the *Emancipator* at Jonesboro, Tennessee, a Quaker settlement. Death having cut short
Embree's career, the Quakers of Jonesboro offered Lundy the use of
his printing equipment. Lundy accepted and left for Tennessee, again
traveling the greater part of the distance on foot, his family following later. He established himself at Greeneville, a short distance from
Jonesboro, and remained there four years — during which time, and
for several years thereafter, the *Genius* was the only antislavery
publication in America.

Lundy advocated "gradual, though total, abolition of slavery in the
United States." Believing that many slaveholders might be willing
to free their slaves if they had the assurance the freedmen would
be settled abroad, he traveled to Haiti, Texas and Canada to look
over the terrain with a view to colonization projects. When he re-

[1] "I speak in the spirit of the British law, which makes liberty commensurate
with, and inseparable from, the British soul — which proclaims, even to the
stranger and the sojourner, the moment he sets foot upon British earth, that
the ground on which he treads is holy, and consecrated by the Genius of Universal Emancipation." — JOHN PHILPOT CURRAN.

turned from Haiti, he found the door of his house locked, the shutters closed. With a foreboding of disaster he inquired at a neighbor's and learned that his wife had died and his children were being cared for at Jonesboro. The dauntless little man wrote in his Journal: "I renewed my vows to devote my energies to the cause of the slave, until the nation shall be effectually roused in his behalf"; he made arrangements for the care of his children and went on with his work.

By 1828 Lundy had traveled on foot or on horseback through nineteen of the twenty-four States. Wherever he could get a few people to listen he held a meeting and sometimes managed to organize an antislavery society. He organized fifty in North Carolina, with a membership of over a thousand, eight in Virginia — some one hundred and thirty altogether, all among Southern Quakers. On his travels he carried his type with him in his knapsack, set up his paper wherever he happened to find himself and got a printer to run off the edition. He was often in danger, but escaped personal violence until he moved to Baltimore. There one Austin Woolfolk, a slave trader whom he had criticized in his paper, assaulted him on the street, leaving him bleeding and unconscious. He recorded the occurrence in his Journal without a trace of resentment or self-pity.

Such was the man whom the youthful Garrison now met in the Collier dining room.

2

Lundy called on the Boston clergy and invited them to attend a discussion of the slavery problem in the parlor of Parson Collier's boardinghouse. Eight accepted and there is reason to believe that Dr. William Ellery Channing was among those present. The little man was not an effective speaker. His voice was too feeble and his manner of speech too rapid. His defective hearing made a discussion led by him somewhat trying. There was, however, such simple-hearted sincerity in his manner and argument, that listeners could not help being impressed. But to be impressed is one thing; to identify oneself with an unpopular cause, another. Garrison, who was present, wrote: "One or two only were for bold and decisive action; but as they had neither station nor influence, and did not rank among the wise and prudent, their opinion did not weigh very heavily and the project was abandoned. Poor Lundy! that meeting was a damper to his feelings; but he was not a man to be utterly cast down, come what might."

He was not cast down. He wrote in his Journal: "Philanthropists are the slowest creatures breathing. They think forty times before they act." Then he buckled on his knapsack, picked up his staff, and for six successive months went from town to town, village to village, in New England, scattering the seed that a few years later ripened into the Garrisonian "Anti-Slavery Society."

In August of that same year he returned to Boston and held a public meeting in the vestry of Dr. Howard Malcom's Federal Street Baptist Church — the same where Garrison so often sat entranced by the beauteous Miss Marshall. How was it that Dr. Malcom, who notwithstanding the unfashionable nature of his brand of Christianity had managed to enlist the patronage of some of Boston's respectability, lent his vestry for such a purpose? The reason was that Lundy, while not abstaining from criticism, supported the Colonization Society, an organization highly esteemed by the clergy. Its president was Washington's nephew, Judge Bushrod Washington, its vice president, Henry Clay. Both were slaveholders, as were three fourths of the Society's officers and many of its members. The organization's real purpose, which in the South it boldly avowed, was to rid the country of free Negroes by colonizing them in Liberia, they being considered a menace to the South's "peculiar institution." In the North, however, the Society sang a different tune. There the public was told that its main object was the gradual abolition of slavery and the colonization of the freedmen. By practicing this deceit the Society hoped to gain Northern support that would enable it to obtain congressional appropriations. How the Society succeeded in hoodwinking sincere opponents of slavery is somewhat of a mystery, since even a casual perusal of its official organ, the *African Repository*, leaves no doubt whatever of its intentions. The explanation probably is that people do not see what they do not wish to see. The illusion that slaveholders would give up slavery voluntarily was too pleasant to be easily relinquished. An antislavery society led by slaveholders — could anything be more desirable? And if slavery troubled your peace of mind, how comforting to be able to join a society reputed to favor emancipation and yet remain on good terms with Southern slaveholders and Northern respectability!

Lundy, however, did not hesitate to say in the course of his discourse that he would support the Society only "if it united with its policy that great work of justice and righteousness, the total extirpation of slavery from the soil of America." He went further and said that, judging by the Society's past performance, fifty years would not suffice to colonize in Africa one year's natural increase in the country's slave population. This was more than Dr. Malcom had bargained for. He rudely interrupted the speaker, harangued the audience on the danger of meddling with so delicate a question — and dismissed the meeting.

But enough interest had been aroused to enable Lundy to hold a second gathering, at which an "Anti-Slavery Committee" was formed. Garrison became its most active member, thus aligning himself openly with the movement for gradual emancipation.

3

In the history of American politics there are few pages as unsavory as those dealing with the Presidential campaign of 1828, when John Quincy Adams and Andrew Jackson opposed each other for the Presidency. Administration papers charged Jackson with being a drunkard, illiterate, a libertine and a bloodthirsty duelist. They called his wife a loose woman and a bigamist, basing this accusation on the fact that she had married Jackson while under the impression that her ne'er-do-well first husband had completed divorce proceedings, which proved not to be the case. Newspapers supporting Jackson were equally unscrupulous, accusing Adams of having plundered the public treasury and of having acted, during his ambassadorship in Russia, as procurer for a Russian nobleman, thus accomplishing the ruin of a beautiful American girl.

In the midst of this ferocious political struggle the citizens of Bennington, Vermont, for the most part partisans of Adams, were chagrined to see the only paper in their community, the *Gazette*, hoist the Jackson standard. Leading administration supporters held a meeting at which financial arrangements were made to launch a new paper. But who should be the editor? Their choice fell on the youthful Garrison, who a short time before, for reasons somewhat obscure, had resigned from the *Philanthropist*. A committee went to Boston to interview him and to offer him a six months' contract. It will be remembered that when a mere stripling of eighteen, Garrison had opposed the election of Adams and had favored Crawford, but now that the choice lay between Adams and Jackson, he preferred the former. He was not overenthusiastic, however, and accepted only on condition that he could also advocate gradual emancipation, temperance, peace and moral reform. "It was a very singular kind of political paper," he said later, "but they gave me *carte blanche*."

Garrison misjudged Jackson, but so did Thomas Jefferson, who four years before had told Daniel Webster: "I feel very much alarmed at the prospect of seeing General Jackson President. He is one of the most unfit men for such a place. . . . He is a dangerous man." Garrison's dislike of the General was based mainly on Jackson's high-handed procedure during the Florida campaign and on the fact that he was a slaveholder who, it was claimed, did not scruple to deal in slaves. His attacks on Jackson did not lack vehemence, but he evidently had little faith in Adams's ability to accomplish the General's defeat. Shortly before the election he wrote: "We care not how numerous may be his supporters: to be in the minority against him would be better than to receive the commendations of a large and deluded majority."

4

Garrison's interest in emancipation had not waned. Every issue of the paper (named the *Journal of the Times*) contained an article on the subject. He circulated a petition for the abolition of slavery in the District of Columbia, in which he said: "The District is the property of the nation; its internal government, therefore, is a matter that concerns every individual. We are ashamed, when we know that the manacled slave is driven to market by the doors of our Capitol, and sold like a beast in the very place where are assembled the representatives of a free and Christian people." When three New England representatives voted against a resolution for the gradual abolition of slavery in the District, the *Journal* took them to task in such vigorous language that they sent lengthy letters of explanation. Garrison scornfully rejected their excuses and branded them as "dough-faces" — the current term of opprobrium for Northern men with Southern principles.

The fact that he aligned himself with the Colonization Society made his antislavery propaganda acceptable to the community. Vermont, moreover, was the one State in the Union where slavery had never existed and had always been regarded with disfavor.

There is a legend of a Vermont judge who told the attorney for a Southern slaveholder wishing to extradite a fugitive slave that his "evidence of ownership" was insufficient. When asked, "What evidence does your Honor require?" he is said to have replied: "Nothing less than a bill of sale from God Almighty."

Garrison's persistence could not help attracting Lundy's attention. He wrote in the *Genius:* "The editor of the *Journal* has shown a laudable disposition to advocate the claims of the poor distressed African upon our sympathy and justice; and if he continue to do so, his talents will render him a most valuable coadjutor in this holy undertaking." Garrison replied editorially: "Before God and our country, we give our pledge that the liberation of the enslaved Africans shall always be uppermost in our pursuits. The people of New England are interested in this matter, and they must be aroused from their lethargy as by a trumpet call. They shall not quietly slumber while we have the management of a press, or strength to hold a pen."

He continued to advocate strict observance of the Sabbath, attended church regularly and was regarded as one of the town's leading citizens. Some Vermonters thought he gave himself airs, and called him "My Lloyd" [Milord], others found him too loquacious and referred to him as "Lloyd Garrulous." John S. Robinson, later the State's first Democratic governor, satirized him in the *Gazette* in this fashion:

"My Lloyd is a young man, and an immigrant from the 'Bay State.' A pair of silver-mounted spectacles ride elegantly across his nose, and his figure and appearance are not unlike that of a dandy. He is, withal, a great egotist, and, when talking of himself, displays the pert loquacity of a blue-jay. . . . In regard to the affairs of the world, My Lloyd labors under a strange delusion, insomuch that he has taken upon himself to abolish slavery in the District of Columbia, reform the judiciary and militia of the State, and last, though not least, to impart the graces of a Boston dandy to the unpolished natives of our happy State."

5

The printing office of the *Journal* faced the village green. Its front windows surveyed the valley, where nestled the village of East Bennington, and the rugged barrier of the Green Mountains.

The rear windows looked out upon towering Mount Anthony. In these pleasant surroundings Garrison was seated one day at his desk, when the door opened and there entered a familiar figure carrying a knapsack and supporting itself with a staff. Garrison jumped to his feet and hastened to greet Lundy. Where did he come from? From Baltimore. . . . On foot? Yes. . . . In January? In this cold? . . . Lundy dismissed the matter as of no consequence. He had come to make a proposal. A Maryland slaveholder had freed twelve slaves on condition that Lundy take them to Haiti and see them safely settled. This would require about six months. At the expiration of that time would Garrison join him in Baltimore? They would enlarge the *Genius*, now a weekly publication; Garrison would be the resident editor, while he, Lundy, would travel about the country, hold meetings and sell subscriptions.

Garrison's contract expired in April. He could undoubtedly have had it renewed, for the paper was doing well. Horace Greeley called it "about the ablest and most interesting newspaper ever issued in Vermont." But the crusader in him responded to the call. He accepted and in April of that year left for Boston, where he expected to remain until Lundy's return.

6

He had engaged a room at Parson Collier's, where he found his friend Whittier, who on Garrison's recommendation had been appointed editor of one of the Collier publications at a salary of nine dollars a week. From a letter written by the poet we learn of an affair of the heart that occupied Garrison during this period: "He goes to see his Dulcinea every other night almost, but is fearful of being 'shipped off,' after all, by her. Lord help the poor fellow if it happen so." And after Garrison's departure for Baltimore: "I had a letter from him the other day; he says he has been in low spirits ever since he left Boston; says he is home-sick, and what is worse, love sick, which last sickness he justly supposes will be immortal."

In the meantime, however, Garrison was invited to deliver the Fourth of July address at the Park Street Church under the auspices of the Colonization Society. It was to be his first appearance before a large audience and he set to work preparing his speech, when a matter intervened — the details of which we learn from a letter he wrote to Jacob Horton at Newburyport, son-in-law of Martha Farnham:

"I am very reluctantly obliged to solicit a favor of you, which, if granted, shall be canceled in a few weeks.

"On Wednesday, the clerk of a militia company, (a poor worthless scamp,) presented a bill of $4, for failure of appearance on May muster, and at the choice of officers. . . . I told the fellow the circumstances of the case — that I had never trained — that my sight had always excused me — and that, in fine, I should not pay his bill. He wished me a 'good morning,' and in the course of the day sent a writ by the hands of a constable, charging me to appear at the Police Court on the 4th of July, and show cause why I refused to pay the fine! Of course, there is no alternative but to 'shell out,' or to fee a lawyer to get me clear, which would be no saving in expense.

"The writ and fine will be $5 or $6. I have not a farthing by me, and I shall need a trifle for the 4th. Can you make it convenient to loan me $8, for two or three weeks. I am pained to make the request, but my present dilemma is unpleasant."

Horton sent the money and our Fourth of July orator was spared the embarrassment of spending Independence Day in durance vile, but the reason he gave for his failure to appear at the muster was not the real, or at least not the principal one. In a review of the case he gave two months later in the *Genius*, he wrote: "I am not professedly a Quaker; but I heartily, entirely and practically embrace the doctrine of nonresistance, and am conscientiously opposed to all military exhibitions. I now solemnly declare that I will never obey any order to bear arms, but rather cheerfully suffer imprisonment and persecution. What is the design of militia musters? *To make men skilful murderers.* I cannot consent to become a pupil in this sanguinary school."

7

In later years Garrison was to become an effective public speaker. Charles Sumner, in a letter to Judge Joseph Story, speaks of Garrison's "natural eloquence." James Russell Lowell went so far as to write to a friend: "It may interest you to know that I thought Mr. Garrison the most effective speaker among anti-slavery orators." At this time, however, he could not speak without manuscript, and (as he himself wrote) "to *read* is a slavish mode of *speaking*, if speaking it can be called." In a letter to Jacob Horton he confessed shortly before the meeting: "My very knees knock together at the thought of speaking before so large a concourse. What then will be my feelings in the pulpit."

The church was packed. The *American Traveller*, in its account of the meeting, informed its readers that the orator "was of quite a youthful appearance, and habited in a suit of black, with his neck bare, and a broad linen collar spread over that of his coat. His prefatory remarks were rendered inaudible by the feebleness of his utterance; but, as he advanced, his voice was raised, his confidence was regained, and his earnestness became perceptible."

He had at one time criticized Fourth of July orators who indulged in meaningless rodomontade concerning liberty and the deeds of the Revolutionary Fathers. If his audience was accustomed to that kind of Independence Day oratory, the following must have sounded like blasphemy in their ears:

"Every Fourth of July, our Declaration of Independence is produced, with a sublime indignation, to set forth the tyranny of the mother country, and to challenge the admiration of the world. But what a pitiful detail of grievances does this document present, in comparison with the wrongs which our slaves endure! In the one case, it is hardly the plucking of a hair from the head; in the other, it is the crushing of a live body on the wheel — the stings of the wasp contrasted with the tortures of the Inquisition. Before God, I must say, that such a glaring contradiction as exists between our creed and practice the annals of six thousand years cannot parallel. In view of it, I am ashamed of my country. I am sick of the unmeaning declaration in praise of liberty and equality; of our hypocritical cant about the inalienable rights of man. I could not, for my right hand, stand up before a European assembly, and exult that I am an American citizen, and denounce the usurpations of a kingly government as wicked and unjust; or should I make the attempt, the recollection of my country's barbarity and despotism would blister my lips, and cover my cheeks with burning blushes of shame."

Garrison's speech, however, harmonized with the pronouncement of the Colonization Society's official organ, which declared: "Admitting that the Colonization scheme contemplates the ultimate abolition of slavery, yet that result could only be produced by the slow and gradual operation of Centuries." If opponents of slavery were satisfied with such a program, it is hardly surprising that Samuel J. May was able to write: "We were solicited, we were urged, entreated by the slaveholders themselves to interfere." Indeed, what better way to render an emancipationist harmless than to invite him to companionship with slaveholders in a society dedicated to the abolition of slavery "by the slow and gradual operation of Centuries"?

8

In 1816, the Reverend George Bourne published *The Book and Slavery Irreconcilable*. "The Book" was of course the Bible. Bourne rejected gradual and advocated immediate emancipation. His reasons were ethical and religious. "The system," he wrote, "is so entirely corrupt, that it admits of no cure but by a *total and immediate abolition*. For a gradual emancipation is a virtual recognition of the right, and establishes the rectitude of the practice. If it be just for one moment, it is hallowed for ever, and if it be inequitable, not a day should it be tolerated."

Eight years after the publication of Bourne's pamphlet there appeared in a small Indiana town *A Treatise on Slavery* by the Reverend James Duncan, advocating immediate emancipation. That same year, Elizabeth Heyrick, a British Quaker, published a pamphlet entitled *Immediate and Gradual Abolition* in which she made so convincing a plea for the former that British Abolitionists adopted her view.

Several weeks after his Fourth of July address, Garrison wrote in the *Philanthropist:* "I acknowledge that immediate and complete emancipation is not desirable. No rational man cherishes so wild a vision." But when a month or so later he sailed to join Lundy in Baltimore, he had become convinced that immediate emancipation should be the battle cry of every opponent of slavery.

What had happened? There is reason to believe that Garrison had picked up a copy of Bourne's pamphlet on some Boston bookstall, and that the minister's arguments had released a train of thought that led him to adopt Immediate and Unconditional Emancipation as his program. Garrison was therefore not the first to advocate "Immediatism" in America, but while in the hands of Bourne and Duncan the idea had lacked vitality, in the hands of Garrison it was to leap into life, to breed, to multiply, to progress along every conceivable channel, to arouse furious hatred and unbounded devotion, to invade the family circle, religious and educational institutions, executive offices and legislative halls.

His demand for immediate emancipation he was to elucidate in the following statement: "Immediate abolition does not mean that the slaves shall immediately exercise the right of suffrage, or be eligible to any office, or be emancipated from law, or be free from the benevolent restraints of guardianship. We contend for the immediate personal freedom of the slaves, for their exemption from punishment except where law has been violated, for their employment and reward as free laborers, for their exclusive right to their own bodies and those of their children, for their instruction and subsequent admission to all the trusts, offices, honors and emoluments of intelligent freemen."

From a tactical viewpoint a demand for immediate abolition had something to recommend it. It is the usual bargaining procedure to demand more than one expects to obtain. "Urge immediate abolition as earnestly as we may," Garrison was to write, "it will, alas! be gradual abolition in the end. We have never said that slavery would be overthrown by a single blow: that it ought to be, we shall always contend." [2]

The same was true of his demand that there should be no compensation to the slaveholders. He was to repeat stubbornly that the slaves, not the slaveholders, had a right to ask for compensation, but at the same time he wrote: "We would rather, if this must be the alternative, that the most exorbitant pecuniary exactions of the slave tyrant should be complied with than that their victims should never be set free."

His belief in Colonization as a solution for the slavery problem went overboard with his faith in gradual emancipation. He was to write: "It [Colonization] may pluck a few leaves from the Bohon Upas, but can neither extract its roots nor destroy its withering propensities."

It was a greatly changed young man who sailed for Baltimore to join Lundy.

9

Six years had passed since Garrison had been in Baltimore, where his mother had died. Lundy had secured lodgings for them both with the Harris sisters, members of the Society of Friends, at 135

[2] Wendell Phillips was to adopt the same tactic. He wrote to his friend Dr. Sargent: "If we would get half a loaf, we must demand the whole of it."

Market Street. It was here Garrison told him to what extent he had altered his views. The older man listened thoughtfully, then said: "Well, thee may put thy initials to thy articles, and I will put my initials to mine, and each will bear his own burden." Garrison replied: "Very good, that will answer, and I shall be able to free my soul."

The paper, printed on contract, presented a creditable appearance. There was a woman's page styled "The Ladies' Repository," edited by Miss Margaret Chandler of Philadelphia. The junior editor was no feminist in those days. When several hundred women in Pittsburgh presented a petition to Congress on behalf of Indian rights, he reprimanded them in this fashion: "This is, in our opinion, an uncalled-for interference, though made with holiest intention. We should be sorry to have this practice become general. There would then be no question agitated in Congress without eliciting the informal and contrarient opinions of the softer sex."

The sincerity of slaveholding members of the Colonization Society was put to the test by an advertisement which ran for several weeks and addressed itself "To humane, conscientious Slaveholders." It read:

> Wanted, immediately, from twenty to fifty SLAVES, to remove and settle in the Republic of Hayti, where they will be forthwith invested with the rights of free men, and receive constant employment at liberal wages, in a healthy and pleasant section of the country.
> THE PRICE OF PASSAGE WILL BE ADVANCED, and everything furnished of which they may stand in need, until they shall have time to prepare their houses and set to work.

The advertisement — the result of an agreement Lundy had made with Haitian authorities — was copied by several editors friendly to Colonization. Not a single slaveholder took advantage of the offer.

The dual editorship was not favorable to the *Genius*. As sole proprietor of the paper, Lundy had received considerable support. An entry in his Journal reads: "If any person had told me when I commenced that I should be as successful under all my disadvantages as I have been, I could not have believed him." Most of his supporters, however, were Southern Quakers or confirmed Colonizationists. The first were frightened by Garrison's vehemence, the second resented his skepticism concerning Colonization as a remedy for the slavery problem. "Where Friend Lundy could get one new subscriber," Garrison was to write, "I could knock a dozen off, and I did so. It was the old experiment of the frog in the well, that went two feet up and fell three feet back at every jump."

10

Although urban slaves — for the most part house servants — were far better treated than field hands, Garrison informs us that it was "nothing uncommon" when walking down a street in Baltimore to hear "the distinct application of a whip and shrieks of anguish" coming from a house. Once a Negro came to his office, pulled off his shirt and exhibited a back that looked as if it had been raked horizontally with a currycomb. Garrison counted thirty-seven bloody gashes between neck and loins. The man had failed to load a wagon to the satisfaction of an overseer.

The *American Gazette*, published in Baltimore, while refusing to accept the advertisements of Lundy's assailant, Austin Woolfolk, known to treat his human merchandise with exceptional brutality, published those of other slave traders. Garrison took the editor to task for his inconsistency. True, he said, Woolfolk was a brute, but what were a few blows more or less compared with the horror of slave trading? Woolfolk read the article and, assuming it to be from the pen of Lundy, threatened dire vengeance. Hearing of this Garrison informed the slave trader editorially that he, not Lundy, had written it. "If he wishes to discuss the subject of slavery, or to complain of any slander of his character, I shall be happy to see him at my boarding-house, No. 135 Market Street, where I will endeavor to convince him that he is pursuing a wicked traffic. . . . Let me assure him, however, that I am not to be intimidated by the utterance of any threats, or the perpetration of any acts of violence."

Presumably Woolfolk did not know of Garrison's nonresistance principles, or thought it inadvisable to put them to the test, for he not only failed to put in an appearance, but carefully avoided him.

11

In his original draft of the Declaration of Independence, Jefferson had censured the African slave trade. The clause was struck out on demand of South Carolina and Georgia. In his *Memoir of the*

Convention Jefferson wrote: "Our Northern brethren also, I believe, felt a little tender under these censures; for though their people had very few slaves themselves yet they had been pretty considerable carriers of them to others."

The "Northern brethren" were still interested in the interstate slave trade. It was an important business. In 1836 the Virginia *Times* of Wheeling, Virginia, estimated that "during the twelve months preceding, forty thousand slaves had been exported from Virginia, to an aggregate value of twenty-four million dollars." The total annual export of Negroes from the slave-breeding[3] to the slave-consuming States has been estimated at ninety thousand. In 1829 the Baltimore *Register* declared: "Dealing in slaves has become a large business; establishments are made in several places in Maryland and Virginia, at which they are sold like cattle. These places of deposit are strongly built, and well supplied with iron thumbscrews and gags, and ornamented with cowskins and other whips, oftentimes bloody." Baltimore had several such establishments whence the slaves were transported in vessels usually belonging to Northern ship-owners. Garrison wrote to a friend: "It is a shameful fact, — and in private conversation it is thrown at me repeatedly, — that the transportation of slaves is almost entirely effected in New England bottoms!!! . . . I was very warmly conversing, the other day, with a slave-owner on the criminality of oppressing the blacks, when he retorted — 'Your preaching is fine, but it is more especially needed *at home*. I detest the slave-trade — it is cruel and unpardonable: yet your Eastern merchants do not scruple to embark in it.' "

It was not only cruel, but homicidal. In September, 1830, the New Orleans *Argus* thus commiserated with the importers of slaves: "The loss by death in bringing slaves from the Northern climate which our planters are under the necessity of doing is not less than twenty-five per cent."

12

One day while scanning a local paper Garrison read the announcement that the ship *Francis*, belonging to Francis Todd of Newbury-

---

[3] The slave-breeding States were Virginia, Maryland, North Carolina, Kentucky, Tennessee and Delaware, named in order of their importance as suppliers of slaves. In 1832, Professor Thomas Roderick Dew, future President of the University of William and Mary, wrote: "Virginia is, in fact, a negro-raising state for the other states."

port, had sailed from Baltimore to New Orleans with a cargo of seventy-five slaves. That a shipowner from his native town should be engaged in the traffic enraged him. If for the sake of Lundy he had hitherto kept himself reasonably under control, this time he applied the verbal whiplash with complete abandon. Having stated the facts together with the name of the culprit in black-faced capitals, he wrote:

It is no worse to fit out piratical cruisers, or to engage in the foreign slave trade, than to pursue a similar trade along our own coasts; and the men who have the wickedness to participate therein, for the purpose of heaping up wealth, should be ☞ SENTENCED TO SOLITARY CONFINEMENT FOR LIFE; ☜ *they are the enemies of their own species — highway robbers and murderers;* and their final doom will be, unless they speedily repent, *to occupy the lowest depths of perdition.*

He did not trust to chance for Todd to learn what he had written, but sent him a marked copy of the paper. Todd, a church deacon and a highly respected citizen, felt aggrieved and brought suit for the sum of five thousand dollars for defamation of character. But already the matter had attracted the attention of the Baltimore authorities. No young whippersnapper of an editor could be allowed to interfere with "large business." The Grand Jury promptly indicted Garrison for having written and published "a gross and malicious libel" against Francis Todd.

One who speaks out fearlessly against injustice appeals to the hero latent in most men. Charles Mitchell, one of the ablest lawyers in the city, offered to defend Garrison gratuitously. His offer was gratefully accepted. The only inaccuracy in Garrison's statement was found to be that not seventy-five, but eighty-eight slaves had been transported on board the *Francis.* Yet, in spite of Mitchell's eloquent plea, it took the jury only fifteen minutes to bring in a verdict of guilty. Judge Nicholas Brice fined Garrison fifty dollars and costs, the whole amounting to one hundred dollars. The young editor, unable to pay, was committed to Baltimore jail on April 17, 1830.

13

It was no chastened prisoner who entered the jail to the cries of "Fresh fish! Fresh fish!" with which the inmates traditionally greeted newcomers. He was in the best of spirits, and the Warden, whose feelings towards him were not unlike those of Charles Mitchell, did what he could to make his confinement tolerable. His cell door was left unlocked, he was allowed to visit fellow prisoners and to receive as many visitors as he wished. No restriction was placed on his correspondence and he was often invited to eat with the Warden and his family.

He set to work immediately writing a pamphlet about the case. Lundy rushed it to press and copies soon reached editorial desks. "Certainly the fact would astonish all Europe," he wrote, "if it were trumpeted in that quarter, that *an American citizen lies incarcerated in prison, for having denounced slavery, and its abettors in his own country.*" Judge Brice commented: "Mr. Garrison is ambitious of becoming a martyr." The young editor replied: "If his assertion be true, he is equally ambitious of gathering the faggots and applying the torch."

The pamphlet met with a phenomenal response. In the preface to the second edition Garrison wrote: "As the news of my imprisonment became extensively known, and the merits of the case understood, not a mail rolled into the city but it brought me consolatory letters from individuals hitherto unknown to me, and periodicals of all kinds, from every section of the Union, (not even excepting the South,) all uniting to give me a triumphant acquittal — all severely reprehending the conduct of Mr. Todd — and all regarding my trial as a mockery of justice."

He had been writing poetry ever since he was sixteen, and what fitter occasion to call on the Muse for company than when one is in prison? He was, it is true, but a mediocre poet. "Literary taste is not his forte," wrote his friend Edmund Quincy. His son Wendell Phillips Garrison found his father's poetry to be lacking in imagination and noted that "nearly every piece bore the stamp of the moralist." Yet Bronson Alcott wept with emotion when reading some of his poems, and his sonnet "Freedom of the Mind," which together with several other sonnets he inscribed on the dingy walls of his cell in Baltimore prison, was given a place in many anthologies:

> High walls and huge the BODY may confine,
>   And iron gates obstruct the prisoner's gaze,
> And massive bolts may baffle his design,
>   And vigilant keepers watch his devious ways:

Yet scorns th' immortal MIND this base control!
   ' No chains can bind it, and no cell enclose:
Swifter than light, it flies from pole to pole,
   And in a flash from earth to heaven it goes!

It leaps from mount to mount — from vale to vale
   It wanders, plucking honeyed fruits and flowers;
It visits home, to hear the fireside tale,
   Or in sweet converse pass the joyous hours:

'Tis up before the sun, roaming afar,
   And, in its watches, wearies every star!

Garrison made friends with his fellow prisoners, listened to their
hard-luck stories and wrote letters for them. He wrote a petition
for commutation of sentence for a highway robber, sentenced to
life, who had served many years and had been an exemplary prisoner. He had the satisfaction of seeing the petition granted.

14

Whittier, who had gone into politics and eventually was to be
elected to the Legislature, had written to Henry Clay requesting that
he intervene on behalf of the man who but recently had hailed him
in the *Genius* as "the champion who is destined to save the country
from anarchy, corruption and ruin." The Kentucky statesman was
preparing to pay Garrison's fine, but was forestalled by a wealthy
New York merchant and opponent of slavery, Arthur Tappan. The
merchant wrote to Lundy to draw on him for whatever money was
required to set Garrison free, and on June 5, after an imprisonment
of forty-nine days, Garrison bade farewell to the Warden and to
the prisoners. Todd pressed the civil suit against him and eventually
obtained judgment for one thousand dollars, but the young man
had then already left the State.

Garrison and Lundy decided to part company. The parting was
not altogether friendly. Lundy was of the opinion that Garrison
could have kept out of trouble by being more "guarded in his language." Garrison was to write: "The truth is Friend Lundy has a
very irritable disposition, which is easily roused; and he finds it impossible to forgive us for venturing to question the propriety of his
colonization scheme."

Nevertheless, when after many vicissitudes Lundy died at Lowell, Illinois — August 22, 1839 — Garrison acknowledged his indebtedness to him in these words: "Now, if I have in any way, however humble, done anything toward calling attention to slavery, or bringing about the glorious prospect of a complete jubilee in our country at no distant day, I feel that I owe everything in this matter, instrumentally and under God, to Benjamin Lundy."

CHAPTER IV

The *Liberator* and Its Editor

WHILE in prison Garrison had prepared three lectures. The first contrasted the program of the Colonization Society with his own; the second gave a vivid description of the slavery system; the third showed the extent to which the North shared responsibility for the "peculiar institution." After his release he left Baltimore for the North, intending to make a lecture tour of several months' duration and then launch an antislavery weekly in Washington. If he later chose Boston, it was because Lundy moved the *Genius* to the National Capital, Garrison had become convinced the North needed enlightenment even more than the South. In the first issue of his new paper he was to write:

"During my recent tour for the purpose of exciting the minds of the people by a series of discourses on the subject of slavery, every place that I visited gave fresh evidence of the fact, that a greater revolution in public sentiment was to be effected in the free States — *and particularly in New England* — than at the South. I found contempt more bitter, opposition more active, detraction more relentless, prejudice more stubborn, and apathy more frozen, than among slave-owners themselves."

He delivered his lectures in Philadelphia, where he was the guest of James and Lucretia Mott, whose influence was to be largely responsible for his abandonment of religious orthodoxy. "If my mind has since become liberalized in any degree, (and I think it has burst every sectarian trammel)," he wrote, "if theological dogmas which I once regarded as essential to Christianity, I now repudiate as absurd and pernicious, — I am largely indebted to them for the changes." When he reached Massachusetts he decided that his native Newburyport should be the first to hear his message. But he had reckoned without Mr. Todd, whose influence was sufficiently great to have the trustees of the Presbyterian Church intervene when the minister offered Garrison the use of the church auditorium. The pastor of the Second Congregational Church came to the rescue and he was able to deliver his first lecture. Then again Todd intervened. Garrison made no further attempt to enlighten his native town, and left for Boston.

2

In Boston Garrison took lodgings as usual at Parson Collier's, and then called on the Reverend Lyman Beecher, hoping to enlist his moral support. Dr. Beecher, however, was not the man to identify himself with an unpopular cause. ("True wisdom," he said in one of his Seminary lectures, "consists in advocating a cause only so far as the community will sustain the reformer.") He now excused himself, saying: "I have too many irons in the fire already."

"Then," replied the young zealot, "you had better let them all burn than to neglect your duty to the slave."

Dr. Beecher did not think so. "Your zeal," he said, "is commendable, but you are misguided. If you will give up your fanatical notions and be guided by us [the clergy] we will make you the Wilberforce of America."

When not looking for a hall in which to deliver his message Garrison wrote letters to public men imploring them to declare themselves for immediate emancipation. He wrote to Channing, to Webster and to several others, but received no reply. His search for a meeting place likewise remained unrewarded. Finally he inserted the following advertisement in the Boston *Courier:*

> *WANTED* — For three evenings, a Hall or Meetinghouse (the latter would be preferred), in which to vindicate the rights of TWO MILLIONS of American citizens who are now groaning in servile chains in this boasted land of liberty; and also to propose just, benevolent, and constitutional measures for their relief. As the addresses will be gratuitous, and as the cause is of public benefit, I cannot consent to remunerate any society for the use of its building. If this application fails, I propose to address the citizens of Boston in the open air, on the Common.
>
> WM. LLOYD GARRISON
>
> *No. 30, Federal Street, Oct. 11, 1830*

The advertisement attracted the attention of sexagenarian Abner Kneeland, founder of the First Society of Free Enquirers. Kneeland was an atheist, and his society made war on religion. A few years later he was to be indicted for having published in his paper, the Boston *Enquirer*, a "scandalous, injurious, obscene, blasphemous and profane libel of and concerning God." His society was the lessee of Julian Hall, on the northwest corner of Milk and Congress Streets. He had no sooner read Garrison's advertisement than he offered him the use of the hall.

It was only a couple of years since Garrison had written about "the depravity and wickedness of those . . . who reject the gospel of Jesus Christ," but he now saw no reason why he should "reject the co-operation of those who . . . make no pretense to evangelical piety" when "the religious portion of the community are indifferent to the cries of suffering humanity."

3

The hall was filled. Dr. Beecher and other notables were present. Three men were there who were destined to become Garrison's stanch friends and supporters. They had come together and were seated side by side. The eldest was Samuel J. May, a Unitarian minister from Brooklyn, Connecticut, who was visiting his father, Colonel Joseph May, a prosperous Boston merchant. His friends called him "God's chore boy," for while far less combative than Garrison, he was just as ready to rush to the succor of anyone in need of assistance. Sitting beside him was his brother-in-law, Bronson Alcott, whose daughter Louisa May Alcott was to become a popular novelist. He was a philosopher and a mystic who combined great profundity with great extravagance of thought. The Sage of Concord has called him "the most refined and the most advanced soul we have ever had in New England," and "the most remarkable and the highest genius of his time." Along with gems of thought worthy of Aristotle, Alcott propounded such absurdities as that the atmosphere surrounding the earth was the accumulated exhalation of mankind, and that the weather was fair or foul depending on whether good or evil thought predominated! He would say in all seriousness to a friend: "Men must have behaved well to-day to have such fine sunshine." The third man was May's cousin, Samuel E. Sewall, a Boston attorney and a direct descendant of the judge of that name who a hundred and thirty years before had written the first antislavery pamphlet in America.

When the speaker had finished, May turned to his two companions and said: "That is a providential man; he is a prophet; he will shake our nation to its center, but he will shake slavery out of it. We ought to know him, we ought to help him. Come, let us go and give him our hands." When they had done so, May said to the young lecturer: "Mr. Garrison, I am not sure that I can endorse all you have said this evening. Much of it requires careful consideration. But I am prepared to embrace you. I am sure you are called to a great work, and I mean to help you."

Alcott suggested that all come home with him. They accepted and remained in animated conversation until after midnight. Garrison told his new friends of his plan to launch an antislavery paper in Boston, which he intended to call the *Liberator*. Sewall thought the name too provoking and suggested the *Safety Lamp*. Garrison would not hear of it. "Provoking!" That was exactly what he meant it to be. Slavery in the United States had now lasted over two hundred years. During nearly three quarters of that time the Quakers had agitated against it in their inoffensive, conciliatory fashion. What had been accomplished? There were now more than four times as many slaves as when they began their propaganda. New Slave States had been added to the Union. The slave laws were more oppressive than ever. He meant to agitate. He meant to call hard names. He meant to make it impossible for any man to confess without shame that he was the owner of slaves. He was prepared for any sacrifice: "A few white victims must be sacrificed to open the eyes of this nation and show the tyranny of our laws. I expect and am willing to be persecuted, imprisoned and bound for advocating African rights; and I should deserve to be a slave myself if I shrunk from that duty or danger."

May was so fascinated by the young man's enthusiasm that the following morning, immediately after breakfast, he called on him at his boardinghouse and remained until two in the afternoon. Before the week was over he and Sewall had made arrangements for Garrison to repeat his lectures at Athenæum Hall.

The Sunday following, May occupied the pulpit at "Church Green," in Summer Street. So filled was he with Garrison's message that he interpolated his sermon with frequent references to slavery and finished with an appeal to the congregation to help abolish the institution before it destroyed the Republic. He was aware of the mounting uneasiness among his listeners, and having pronounced the benediction, said: "Every one present must be conscious tha the closing remarks of my sermon have caused an unusual emotio throughout the church. I am glad. . . . I have been prompted t speak thus by the words I have heard during the past week fron a young man hitherto unknown, but who is, I believe, called of God to do a greater work for the good of our country than has beer done by any one since the Revolution. I mean William Lloyd Garri son. He is going to repeat his lectures the coming week. I advise I exhort, I entreat — would that I could compel! — you to go and hear him."

The following day May's father, Colonel Joseph May, was walk ing down State Street when a friend rushed up to him and impul sively grasped his hand.

"Colonel," he said, "you have my sympathy. I cannot tell you how much I pity you."

The old man looked at him astounded. "Sympathy? Pity? For what?"

The other appeared embarrassed. "Well," he said, "I hear your son went mad at 'Church Green' yesterday."

4

In a small chamber, friendless and unseen,
    Toiled o'er his types one poor, unlearned young man;
The place was dark, unfurnitured and mean,
    Yet there the freedom of a race began.

Help came but slowly; surely, no man yet
    Put lever to the heavy world with less;
What need of help? He knew how types were set,
    He had a dauntless spirit and a press.

James Russell Lowell, the author of these lines, has availed himself of the usual poetic license. The room on the third floor of Merchants' Hall, in Boston, where on January 1, 1831, Garrison launched the *Liberator*, was not particularly small, being eighteen feet square, and not one, but two unlearned young men "toiled over the types," for he and Isaac Knapp of Newburyport had joined forces. Later they were aided by a Negro apprentice. The windows were grimy and spattered with printer's ink, as were the dingy walls. There was a press, picked up at a bargain, a couple of composing stands with worn secondhand type, a few chairs and a long table covered with exchanges, at which the editor attended to his correspondence. In a corner of the room was a mattress on which the two friends slept, for they could not afford the luxury of a boardinghouse. They lived on bread, milk and a little fruit, sharing the first two with a cat who, when Garrison sat down to write, would jump on the table and rub her fur caressingly against his bald forehead. Although the paper advocated temperance as well as abolition, Knapp found it impossible to wean himself from his craving for strong drink, a weakness which eventually led to his undoing.

In the literature of social protest few lines are more stirring than the following paragraph from Garrison's salutatory to the public in the first number of the *Liberator:*

"I am aware that many object to the severity of my language; but is there not cause for severity? I *will be* as harsh as truth, and as uncompromising as justice. On this subject, I do not wish to think, or speak, or write, with moderation. No! No! Tell a man whose house is on fire to give a moderate alarm; tell him to moderately rescue his wife from the hands of the ravisher; tell the mother to gradually extricate her babe from the fire into which it has fallen; — but urge me not to use moderation in a cause like the present. I am in earnest — I will not equivocate — I will not excuse — I will not retreat a single inch — AND I WILL BE HEARD."

The last statement proved prophetic. The *Liberator* never paid expenses, never had over three thousand subscribers, but its message became known from coast to coast and across the Atlantic. The paper had a fertilizing influence that caused the sprouting of various forms of opposition to slavery, of most of which Garrison disapproved, but for all of which he was directly or indirectly responsible. There were to be Abolitionists who formed political parties and others who abstained from voting; those who were orthodox churchmen and those who set out to destroy organized religion; those who believed in nonresistance and those who advocated armed intervention; those who wished to arouse the slaves to revolt and those who opposed this; those determined to remain within constitutional limits and those who scoffed at the Constitution. The Liberty Party, the Free-Soil Movement, the Republican Party — all, to a greater extent than their leaders cared to acknowledge, owed their existence to

Garrison. He was the sower who went forth to sow and whose seed fell onto fertile ground, blossoming forth in a variety of shapes. He was the spiritual father of innumerable children, most of whom disowned him. He shamed a reluctant nation into doing what it did not wish to do, and the nation has never forgiven him. In 1853, Wendell Phillips said:

"The community has come to hate its reproving Nathan so bitterly, that even those whom the relenting part of it is beginning to regard as standard-bearers of the antislavery host think it unwise to avow any connection or sympathy with him. I refer to some of the leaders of the political movement against slavery. . . . They are willing to confess privately, that our movement produced theirs, and that its continued existence is the very breath of their life. But, at the same time, they would fain walk on the road without being soiled by too close contact with the rough pioneers who threw it up. . . . If you tell me that they cherished all these principles in their own breasts before Mr. Garrison appeared, I can only say, if the antislavery movement did not give them their ideas, it surely gave them the courage to utter them."

5

"Why so hot my little man?" wrote Ralph Waldo Emerson; and at another time: "There is a sublime prudence which, believing in a vast future, sure of more to come than is yet seen, postpones always the present hour to the whole life." But now see Emerson, returning from Boston in 1850, a copy of the Fugitive Slave Law in his pocket, writing in his Journal: "This filthy enactment was made in the nineteenth century — I will not obey it — by God!"[1] What has become of the "sublime prudence"? To refuse to obey the Fugitive Slave Law meant to incur a thousand dollar fine and be liable to pay another thousand to the claimant of the fugitive, not to speak of a possible six months in jail. Was it that Emerson had come to agree with Whittier that a civilized man could no more obey the Fugitive Slave Law, even when a Lincoln set out to enforce it, than he could become a cannibal?

[1] This and other quotations from Emerson's Journal are from *The Heart of Emerson's Journals*, edited by Bliss Perry. (Houghton Mifflin Company, Boston and New York, 1926.)

Garrison never worried about keeping cool. He agreed with Burke that "To speak of atrocious crimes in mild language is treason to virtue," with Luther that "Those things that are softly dealt with, in a corrupt age, give people but little concern, and are presently forgotten." Samuel J. May once said to him: "O, my friend, do try to moderate your indignation, and keep more cool; why, you are all on fire." His friend replied: "Brother May, I have need to be *all on fire*, for I have mountains of ice about me to melt."

Was the method effective? That it made it well-nigh impossible to spread the gospel of emancipation in the South admits of no doubt. But except among Southern Quakers such propaganda had borne no fruit. Indeed, while at one time the slaveholders had been willing to concede that slavery was an evil and a curse, foisted upon the South by the mother country, after years of propaganda by Quakers and others they had arrived at the conclusion that it was the best of all possible labor systems, far superior to that prevailing in the North.[2] This change of outlook was clearly perceptible at the time of the Missouri Compromise, long before the appearance of the *Liberator*. It was due to the fact that the invention of the cotton gin had made slavery far more profitable.

When Garrison began publication of his paper nearly all opposition to slavery had disappeared, North as well as South. Albert Bushnell Hart, in a profound study of the subject, wrote: "When Jackson became President in 1829, anti-slavery seemed, after fifty years of effort, to have spent its force. The voice of the churches was no longer heard in protest; the abolitionist societies were dying out; there was hardly an abolitionist militant in the field. . . . In Congress there was only one anti-slavery man and his efforts were without avail." But in 1839 the managers of the Massachusetts Anti-Slavery Society were able to declare: "Ten years ago a solitary individual stood up as the advocate of immediate and unconditional emancipation. Now, that individual sees about him hundreds of thousands of persons, of both sexes, members of every sect and party, from the most elevated to the humblest rank of life. In 1829 not an Anti-Slavery Society of a genuine stamp was in existence.

[2] Governor George McDuffie of South Carolina was to call slavery "the cornerstone of the republican edifice." Senator James Murray Mason of Virginia said, "It is now almost universally believed, in the South, that slavery is ennobling to both races, white and black."

In 1839 there are nearly two thousand such societies swarming and multiplying in all parts of the free States. In 1829 there was but one Anti-Slavery periodical in the land. In 1839 there are fourteen. In 1829 there was scarcely a newspaper of any religious or political party which was willing to disturb the 'delicate' question of slavery. In 1839 there are multitudes of journals that either openly advocate the doctrine of immediate and unconditional emancipation, or permit its free discussion in their columns. Then scarcely a church made slave-holding a bar to communion. Now, multitudes refuse to hear a slave-holder preach, or to recognize one as a brother. Then, no one petitioned Congress to abolish slavery in the District of Columbia. Now, in one day, a single member of the House of Representatives (John Quincy Adams) has presented one hundred and seventy-six such petitions in detail; while no less than seven hundred thousand persons have memorialized Congress on that and kindred subjects."

Garrison was to say: "In seizing the trump of God, I had indeed to blow a 'jarring blast' — but it was necessary to wake up a nation then slumbering in the lap of moral death. . . . What else but the *Liberator* primarily, (and of course instrumentally,) has effected this change? Greater success than I have had, no man could reasonably desire, or humbly expect."

When in 1837 Dr. William Ellery Channing complimented James G. Birney on the reasonableness and moderation of his antislavery paper, in contrast with the *Liberator*, which he accused of being "blemished by a spirit of intolerance, sweeping censure and rash, injurious judgment," the former Kentucky slaveholder and Solicitor General of Alabama replied: "Our country was asleep, whilst slavery was preparing to pour its 'leprous distilment' into her ears. So deep was becoming her sleep that nothing but a rude and almost ruffian-like shake could rouse her to a contemplation of her danger. If she is saved, it is because she has been thus treated." He left no doubt about whom he had in mind when he said on another occasion: "My anti-slavery trumpet would never have roused the country — Garrison alone could do it."

Another former Kentucky slaveholder, the famous Cassius Marcellus Clay, who while a student at Yale heard Garrison speak and became a convert, wrote: "There is one saying of his [Garrison's] traducers, and the traducers of those who act with him, . . . that 'they have set back the cause of emancipation by agitation'! Nothing is more false. The cause of emancipation advances only with agitation: let that cease and despotism is complete."

6

Garrison did not expect to convert the slaveholders. He considered such an attempt a waste of time. In 1837 he wrote to Elizabeth Pease: "I have relinquished the expectation that they [the slaveholders] will ever, by mere moral suasion, consent to emancipate their victims." In 1840 he wrote to Elizabeth's brother Joseph: "There is not any instance recorded either in sacred or profane history, in which the oppressors and enslavers of mankind, except in individual cases, have been induced, by mere moral suasion, to surrender their despotic power, and let the oppressed go free; but in nearly every instance, from the time that Pharaoh and his hosts were drowned in the Red Sea, down to the present day, they have persisted in their evil course until sudden destruction came upon them, or they were compelled to surrender their ill-gotten power in some other manner."

Others were of the same opinion. Cassius M. Clay wrote: "The slaveholders have just as much intention of yielding up their slaves as the sum of the kings of the earth have of laying down, for the benefit of the people, their sceptres." In August, 1855, Abraham Lincoln was to write to George Robertson of Kentucky that the Tsar of Russia would abdicate and free his serfs sooner than American slaveholders would voluntarily give up their slaves. "Experience has demonstrated, I think, that there is no peaceful extinction of slavery in prospect for us."

Garrison feared, like Lincoln, that slavery would never be abolished except by force of arms, but he believed there was one other method worth trying. When Jesus of Nazareth called the Pharisees "fools," "hypocrites," "devourers of widows' houses," "serpents," "generation of vipers" — and asked, "How can ye escape the damnation of hell?" — he was obviously not using moral *suasion*, but moral *pressure*. This was the method Garrison had decided to adopt. Shortly after he founded the *Liberator*, he told Samuel J. May: "Until the term 'slaveholder' sends as deep a feeling of horror to the hearts of those who hear it applied to any one as the term, 'robber,' 'pirate,' 'murderer' do, we must use and multiply epithets when condemning the sins of him who is guilty of 'the sum of all villainies.' " [3] He hoped to arouse such a feeling of abhorrence and storm of disapproval in the North (and in fact throughout the civilized world) that the South would be forced to yield. That the method offered some hope of success was acknowledged by General Duff Green, who wrote: "We believe that we have most to fear from the organized action upon the conscience and fears of the slaveholders themselves. . . . It is only by alarming the consciences of the weak and feeble, and diffusing among our own people a morbid sensibility on the question of slavery, that the abolitionists can accomplish their object."

The method did not succeed any more than it had succeeded in Christ's time; but who will say that it was not worth trying? Nor can it be said that it produced no results. If Garrison failed to shame and intimidate the South, he yet succeeded in arousing such an aversion to, and fear of, slavery in the North that war seemed preferable to allowing it to spread. Archibald H. Grimké has well said: "The public sentiment which Lincoln obeyed, [Garrison and] Phillips created."

7

About a year before the appearance of the Liberator, David Walker, a Boston Negro who made a living as an old-clothes man, published a pamphlet entitled Walker's Appeal. He boldly called upon the slaves to revolt. "If you commence," he wrote, "make sure work — do not trifle, for they will not trifle with you — they want us for their slaves, and think nothing of murdering us in order to subject us to that wretched condition — therefore, if there is an attempt made by us, kill or be killed." There were three editions of the pamphlet, copies of which found their way into the Slave States. The consternation these produced in the South bordered on the ridiculous and was eloquent testimony of the fear that lurked under the South's brave exterior. Governors sent special messages to Legislatures. Repressive laws were hastily passed. Incoming ships and trains were searched. Colored seamen were taken from Northern ships entering Southern ports and imprisoned. "How much is it to

[3] The founder of Methodism, John Wesley, spoke of the slave system as the "sum of all villainies." Of American slavery in particular he said that it was "the vilest that ever saw the sun."

be regretted," declared *Niles' Weekly Register*, "that a negro dealer in old clothes, should thus excite two states to legislative action." Walker, however, died in June, 1830, and the South breathed a sigh of relief.

Then, in January, 1831, again in the city of Boston, appeared the *Liberator*, and in an early issue of the paper a poem from the editor's pen warning of the danger of a slave uprising if emancipation were delayed. One stanza read:

> Woe if it come with storm, and blood, and fire,
> When midnight darkness veils the earth and sky!
> Woe to the innocent babe — the guilty sire —
> Mother and daughter — friends of kindred tie!
> *Stranger and citizen alike shall die!*
> Red-handed slaughter his revenge shall feed,
> And Havoc yell his ominous death-cry;
> And wild Despair in vain for mercy plead —
> While Hell itself shall shrink, and sicken at the deed!

The slave uprising in the French colony of San Domingo towards the close of the eighteenth century proved there were reasons for the warning. Garrison, however, did not advise the slaves to revolt. He had condemned *Walker's Appeal* in the *Genius*, and the last stanza of his poem read:

> Not by the sword shall your deliverance be;
> Not by the shedding of your masters' blood,
> Not by rebellion — or foul treachery,
> Upspringing suddenly, like swelling flood:
> Revenge and rapine ne'er did bring forth good.
> God's *time is best!* — nor will it long delay:
> Even now your barren cause begins to bud,
> And glorious shall the fruit be! — Watch and pray,
> For, lo! the kindling dawn, that ushers in the day!

Shortly after the appearance of this poem, on August 22, 1831, there took place in Southampton County, Virginia, the most sanguinary slave uprising in the annals of American slavery. A Negro mystic named Nat Turner, a slave belonging to a small planter, gathered a band of followers variously estimated at from forty to two hundred, and after killing his master and the latter's family, moved from plantation to plantation, slaughtering between fifty and sixty persons, men, women and children. Bands of white men and the state militia finally subdued the rebels, but not without committing outrages upon innocent Negroes surpassing in cruelty anything of which Turner had been guilty. Finally, the Negro leader and nineteen of his followers were hanged. The uprising was responsible for a sensational debate in the Virginia Legislature during which slavery was condemned in language as violent as any Garrison had ever used. For a while indeed it seemed that what years of propaganda by the Quakers had failed to accomplish would come as a result of Turner's bloodletting. Governor John Floyd of Virginia noted in his diary: "Before I leave this Government I will have contrived to have a law passed gradually abolishing slavery in this state." But the people and the authorities eventually got over their fright and began looking about for a scapegoat. Walker was dead, but there was Garrison and his paper. Turner and his confederates had denied that they had read either *Walker's Appeal* or the *Liberator*, and no evidence to the contrary was introduced; but Governor Floyd wrote to Governor James Hamilton of South Carolina that black preachers had read from the pulpit the inflammatory writings of Walker and Garrison, which may or may not have been true. Anyway, Harrison Gray Otis, Mayor of Boston, received letters from the Governors of Virginia and Georgia "severally remonstrating against an incendiary newspaper published in Boston, and, as they alleged, thrown broadcast among their plantations, inciting to insurrection and its horrid results."

Mayor Otis was puzzled. Although the *Liberator* had now been published in Boston for nearly a year, he had never seen a copy or even heard of the paper's existence. "It appeared on enquiry," he wrote, "that no member of the city government, nor any person of my acquaintance, had ever heard of the publication. Some time afterward, it was reported to me by the city officers that they had ferreted out the paper and its editor; that his office was an obscure hole, his only visible auxiliary a negro boy, and his supporters a very few insignificant persons of all colors. This information, with the consent of the aldermen, I communicated to the above-named governors, with an assurance of my belief that the new fanaticism had not made, nor was likely to make, proselytes among the respectable classes of our people. In this, however, I was mistaken."

Neither the Mayor of Boston nor the Governor of Massachusetts felt he possessed the power to stop publication of the *Liberator*, though both regretted that shortcoming in the law. The South was indignant. The Columbia (South Carolina) *Telescope* believed the matter called for armed intervention. "They [the people of Massachusetts] permit a battery to be erected upon their territory, which fires upon us, and we should be justified in invading that territory to silence their guns," the editor declared. A Vigilance Committee in Columbia offered a reward of fifteen hundred dollars for the arrest and conviction of any person "distributing or circulating the *Liberator* or any other publication of a seditious nature." Georgetown, District of Columbia, passed a law forbidding any colored person to take the *Liberator* from the post-office on pain of twenty dollars' fine and thirty days' imprisonment. In Raleigh, North Carolina, the grand jury found a true bill against Garrison and Knapp in the hope of extraditing them. A correspondent in the Washington *National Intelligencer* proposed that the President of the United States or the Governor of Virginia demand Garrison's extradition, and in case of refusal by the Governor of Massachusetts "the people of the South offer an adequate reward to any person who will deliver him dead or alive, into the hands of the authorities of any State South of the Potomac." He did not have long to wait. On November 30, 1831, the Senate and the House of Representatives of Georgia appropriated five thousand dollars to be paid by the Governor "to any person or persons who shall arrest, bring to trial and prosecute to conviction, under the laws of the State, the editor or publisher of a certain paper called the *Liberator*, published in the town of Boston and State of Massachusetts."

Garrison was not in the least intimidated and wrote defiantly: "A price upon the head of a citizen of Massachusetts — for what? For daring to give his opinion of the moral aspect of slavery! . . . Know this, ye Senatorial Patrons of kidnappers! that we despise your threats as much as we deplore your infatuation; nay, more — know that a hundred men stand ready to fill our place as soon as it is made vacant by violence."

8

On his last visit to the United States, General Lafayette expressed his astonishment at the increase in racial prejudice. He recalled that in Washington's army, white and black had fought side by side and had messed together in harmony. Now, however, in the Free as well as in the Slave States, free Negroes were despised, persecuted, deprived of most of the prerogatives of the freeman, permitted to earn a living only at the most menial and ill-paid employments.

A glance at some of the laws governing the free people of color leaves no doubt concerning the tenuous nature of the freedom they enjoyed. In Maryland a Justice of the Peace could order a free Negro's ears cropped for striking a white man even in self-defense. A free Negro entering that State incurred a penalty of fifty dollars for every week spent within its borders, and if unable to pay was sold into slavery. In Georgia the penalty for teaching a free Negro to read or write was five hundred dollars if the offender was white, if colored he was fined and flogged at the discretion of the court. In Virginia and South Carolina any Justice of the Peace could disband a school where free Negroes or their offspring were taught to read or write, fine the teacher five hundred dollars and have twenty lashes administered to each pupil. In Louisiana a fine of like amount awaited the zealous Christian who taught a free Negro in Sunday School. In Mississippi and the District of Columbia a Negro unable to prove his legal right to freedom could be sold into slavery. In South Carolina a Negro who "entertained" a runaway slave by giving him as much as a crust of bread was fined fifty dollars, and if unable to pay was sold. In several Slave States free Negroes were not permitted to assemble for religious purposes unless white people were present, and they were forbidden to preach. In Ohio a white man who hired a Negro or mulatto even for a day made himself liable for his future support. In the Free States, Negro children could not attend public school and little or no provision was made for their instruction. In several Free and of course in all the Slave States, free people of color were denied the right of suffrage.

Custom solidified this edifice of injustice. It made it well-nigh impossible for an artisan, mechanic or shopkeeper to employ a colored apprentice. In the North as well as in the South, Negroes were required to travel in the steerage of a boat or on the outside of a stagecoach, when they were not barred altogether. When a convention of colored people in Philadelphia made a brave attempt to establish a manual labor school for Negroes in New Haven, Connecticut, the Mayor called a mass meeting of the citizens, and such a hue and cry arose that the plan had to be abandoned. When Noyes Academy, in Canaan, New Hampshire, admitted a few colored students, three hundred citizens with a hundred yoke of oxen dragged the building from its foundation and deposited it outside the town. In church, Negroes had to sit in separate pews — which in the Baptist Church at Hartford, Connecticut, were boarded up and provided with peepholes. When in Houghton, Massachusetts, a colored man acquired a white man's pew, the church authorities had the floor removed in that part of the edifice.

The case of Prudence Crandall, in which Garrison was involved, deserves special attention.

9

In 1832, Miss Crandall invested her small capital in a house in Canterbury, Connecticut, and established a "Female Boarding School." She was a capable teacher and had no difficulty in having girls entrusted to her care. One day a mulatto girl of seventeen, Sarah Harris, came to her with a humble request. If she boarded at home, would she be allowed to attend classes, "to get a little more learning — enough if possible to teach colored children"? Miss Crandall laid the matter before her pupils. Several had attended district school with Sarah and knew her to be neat, modest and well-mannered. They voted unanimously that she be admitted.

But they had reckoned without their elders. Tongues wagged. . . . A colored girl attending a private school for young ladies! What was the world coming to! . . . The wife of the Episcopal clergyman called on Miss Crandall to voice the disapproval of respectability. If Miss Crandall persisted in her course she would lose her pupils, she told her. "Then," replied the teacher, "the school must sink, for I won't turn her out." The minister's wife departed in a dudgeon, and soon after most of Miss Crandall's pupils were called home by their parents.

Miss Crandall, who occasionally read the *Liberator*, wrote to the editor: "I have been for some months past determined if possible during the remaining part of my life to benefit the people of color. Will you be so kind as to write by the next mail and give me your opinion on the subject; and if you consider it possible to obtain 20 or 25 young ladies of color to enter the school for the term of one year at the rate of $25 per quarter, including board, washing and tuition, I will come to Boston in a few days and make arrangements about it."

She came and met Garrison at the Marlboro' Hotel. He gave her letters to colored friends in Boston and New York and published her advertisement in his paper, with favorable comment.

A colored girl attending a school for young ladies was bad enough; but a private school for colored girls — it was too much! No sooner had Miss Crandall's intention become known than leading citizens of Canterbury called a mass meeting. Garrison wrote to his friend George W. Benson, in the neighboring town of Brooklyn: "If possible, Miss C. must be sustained at all hazards. If we suffer the school to be put down in Canterbury, other places will partake of the panic, and also prevent its introduction in their vicinity. We may as well, 'first and last,' meet the prescriptive spirit and conquer it."

Benson and Samuel J. May went to the meeting, which a thousand people attended. "Should the school go into operation," Andrew T. Judson, a Democratic politician and Colonizationist, roared from the platform, "our sons and daughters will be forever ruined and property no longer safe." Garrison's friends attempted to reply, but were shouted down. A committee called on Miss Crandall and informed her that "by putting your design into operation you will bring ruin and disgrace upon us all."

Garrison published an account of the meeting under the caption "Heathenism Outdone," and pilloried Judson and his fellow agitators in these terms: "We put the names of the principal disturbers in black letters, — black as the infamy which will attach to them as long as there exists any recollection of the wrongs of the colored race. To colonize these shameless enemies of their species in some desert country would be a relief and a blessing to society." So vehement was he that Miss Crandall begged him to moderate his tone: "Permit me to entreat you to handle the prejudices of the people of Canterbury with all the mildness possible, as everything severe tends to heighten the flame of malignity amongst them."

But for all her mildness she remained resolute, and the following month a score of colored girls arrived from Boston, New York, Philadelphia and Providence. Canterbury struck back. Shopkeepers refused to trade with her. The doctor declined to call. The church closed its doors against her and her pupils. Her house was smeared with filth and her well filled with manure. An old vagrancy law was invoked and her pupils threatened with ten lashes upon the bare back if they did not depart.

Miss Crandall's friends now rushed to the rescue. May and others gave bond for the pupils, making it impossible to invoke the vagrancy law. A local Quaker furnished water from his well; others helped to obtain provisions from neighboring towns. So Canterbury appealed to the Legislature. A law was rushed through forbidding schools in Connecticut to admit nonresident colored pupils. When news of its passage reached Canterbury there was rejoicing. The cannon, brought into action only on festive occasions, was noisily fired, church bells tolled; for had not Canterbury's sons and daughters been saved from "everlasting ruin"?

Not yet! Miss Crandall refused to obey the law. The case assumed national importance. Arthur Tappan wrote to May: "Consider me your banker. Spare no necessary expense. Command the services of the ablest lawyers. See to it that the great case shall be thoroughly tried, cost what it may. I will cheerfully honor your draft to enable you to defray the cost."

The courts were now asked to pronounce on Miss Crandall's guilt and the constitutionality of the law. At the first trial the jury disagreed, at the second she was convicted. Appeal was taken to the highest court in the State, which sidestepped the issue by dismissing the case on a technicality.

Canterbury's patience was now exhausted. An attempt was made to set fire to the school, but the flames did little damage. Then a mob assembled armed with sticks and stones and shattered every window. As the teacher herded her pupils where they would be safe from hurtling stones and flying glass, she decided not to put their lives in jeopardy and closed the school.

10

Garrison championed the free people of color as fervently as the slaves. "This then is my consolation," he wrote on one occasion: "if I cannot do much in this quarter towards abolishing slavery, I may be able to elevate our free colored population in the scale of society." Speaking before a colored convention in Philadelphia he said with feeling: "I never rise to address a colored audience without feeling ashamed of my color; ashamed of being identified with a race of men who have done you so much injustice and yet retain so large a portion of your brethren in servitude."

No matter how pressing his work, he would lay it aside when invited to address a colored audience. He did not flatter his listeners, but urged them to be worthy of liberty, to be temperate, industrious and to surpass the white man in virtue, which, he assured them, was no difficult task. They must not resort to violence, but should incessantly petition to be permitted to vote, to send their children to public school and to exercise every other right of the freeman. "If your petition is denied seven times, send it seventy times seven."

His influence was great among them. Once in Boston, when he had addressed them on temperance, they immediately formed a temperance society, which within a few days counted one hundred and fifty members. "Such acts as these, brethren, give me strength and boldness in your cause," he assured them. Henry E. Benson, in a letter to Isaac Knapp, described a scene that took place in Providence, Rhode Island, after Garrison had addressed a colored audience. "After the meeting," he wrote, "the poor creatures wept and sobbed like children — they gathered round him anxious to express their gratitude for what he had done for them, and tell him how well they loved him."

So persistent was he in their defense that some believed him to be colored, and when he advocated the repeal of the Massachusetts law against intermarriage, the rumor spread that he meant to marry a Negress. No resentment at the rumor is noticeable in this mild denial he published in the *Liberator:* "We declare that our heart is neither affected *by*, nor pledged *to*, any lady, black or white, bond or free."

11

If "the style is the man," then one might have expected Garrison in his maturity to have been a scowling, brusque, bitter, opinionated individual. Such in fact was the mental image formed by many. The reality confounded Buffon's maxim. Josiah Copley, editor of a religious paper in Pittsburgh, Pennsylvania, happening to be in Boston in 1832, called on Garrison after some hesitation. "I never was more astonished," he wrote. "All my preconceptions were at fault. My ideal of the man was that of a stout, rugged, dark-visaged desperado — something like we picture a pirate. He was a quiet, gentle and I might say handsome man — a gentleman indeed, in every sense of the word."

William H. Herndon, Lincoln's law partner, who visited Garrison in the latter's old age, wrote: "I had imagined him a shriveled, cold, selfish, haughty man, one who was weak and fanatically blind to the charities and equities of life, at once whining and insulting, mean and miserable, but I was pleasantly disappointed. I found him warm, generous, approachable, communicative; he has some mirth, some wit, and a deep abiding faith in coming universal charity. I was better and more warmly received by him than by any man in Boston."

Harriet Martineau, famous British authoress, who met Garrison in 1835, declared: "His aspect put to flight in an instant what prejudices his slanderers had raised in me. I was wholly taken by surprise. It was a countenance glowing with health and wholly expressive of purity, animation and gentleness. I did not now wonder at the citizen who, seeing a print of Garrison at a shop window without a name to it, went in and bought it and framed it as the most saintlike of countenances. The end of the story is, that when the citizen found whose portrait he had been hanging in his parlor, he took the print out of the frame and huddled it away."

The preponderance of opinion is that his conversation was the very opposite of his writing — mild, tolerant, disarming. Miss Martineau wrote: "Garrison had a good deal of a Quaker air; and his speech is deliberate like a Quaker's but gentle as a woman's. . . . Every conversation I had with him confirmed my opinion that sagacity is the most striking attribute of his conversation. It has none of the severity, the harshness, the bad taste of his writing; it is as gladsome as his countenance, and as gentle as his voice."

Harriet Beecher Stowe, who had confided to one of Garrison's sons that she was "dreadfully afraid" of his father, having made the editor's acquaintance, wrote to him: "You have a remarkable tact at conversation."

Ralph Waldo Emerson, who for a long time had been prejudiced against him, in 1844 wrote in his Journal: "The haters of Garrison have lived to rejoice in that grand world movement which, every age or two, casts out so masterly an agent for good. I cannot speak of the gentleman without respect."

12

In the first number of the *Liberator*, where appeared Garrison's immortal challenge to the slaveholders, one may read these lines from the editor's pen:

"An attempt has been made — it is still making — we regret to say, with considerable success — to inflame the minds of our working classes against the more opulent, and to persuade them that they are contemned and oppressed by a wealthy aristocracy. That public grievances exist, is unquestionably true; but they are not confined to any one class of society. Every profession is interested in their removal — the rich as well as the poor. It is in the highest degree criminal, therefore, to exasperate our mechanics to deeds of violence, or to array them under a party banner; for it is not true, that, at any time, they have been the objects of reproach . . . We are the friends of reform; but that is not reform, which, in curing one evil, threatens to inflict a thousand others."

The reason for this outburst was an attempt by Seth Luther and others to organize a Working Men's Party and to form labor unions.

In the fifth number of the paper a correspondent pointed out to Garrison that he was wrong in trying to discourage labor's attempts to organize:

"Although you do not appear to have perceived it, I think there is a very intimate connexion between the interests of the working men's party and your own . . . In the history of the origin of slavery is to be found the explanation of the evils we deplore and seek to remove, as well as those you have attacked. . . . We seek to enlighten our brethren in the knowledge of their rights and duties. . . . It is a duty owed by working men to themselves and the world to exert their power through the ballot-box."

Garrison replied: "There is a prevalent opinion that . . . the poor and vulgar are taught to consider the opulent as their natural enemies. Where is the evidence that our wealthy citizens, as a body, are hostile to the interests of the laboring classes? It is not in their commercial enterprises, which whiten the ocean with canvas and give employment to a useful and numerous class of men. It is not found in the manufacturing establishments, which multiply labor and cheapen the necessities of the poor. It is not found in the luxuries of their tables, or the adornments of their dwellings, for which they must pay in proportion to their extravagance. . . . Perhaps it would be the truth to affirm, that mechanics are more inimical to the success of each other, more unjust toward each other, than the rich are toward them."

Yet in 1831, and for a long time thereafter, the hours of labor in New England factories were from five in the morning until seven-thirty in the evening — the working day being thirteen and one half hours. The two half hours allowed for breakfast and midday dinner were as tiring as any, since the workers had to hurry home, bolt their food and hasten back to the factory to escape a fine. In 1849 a report submitted to the American Medical Association by one of its members contained the statement that "there is not a State's prison, or house of correction in New England, where the hours of labor are so long, the hours for meals so short, or the ventilation so much neglected, as in all the cotton mills with which I am acquainted." In Boston Irish workmen were forced to labor fifteen hours a day, including Sunday. The death rate among them was so appalling that it was claimed the Irish lived on an average only fourteen years after reaching Boston. The Cochee Manufacturing Company required its workers to sign an agreement to "conform in all respects to the regulations which are now, or may be hereafter adopted . . . and to work for such wages as the company may see fit to pay." Workers were commonly required to buy at the company store and were usually in debt to their employers. If they attempted to leave their employment without paying what they owed they were imprisoned. In 1831 there were over fifteen hundred people imprisoned for debt in Boston alone, more than half of whom owed less than twenty dollars. It may therefore be said that a system of veritable peonage prevailed.

Strikes were frequent, but prior to 1860 not a single strike was won in Massachusetts, and not until 1874 did that State have any legal restriction on the number of hours adult wageworkers could be required to work. Employers in other parts of the country often gave working conditions in New England as an excuse for not improving labor's lot.

In view of all this, how could a man ready for almost any sacrifice for the sake of the Negro have remained indifferent to the lot of white wageworkers?

Garrison was an individualist. In his opinion, if a man was not a chattel, he was master of his own fate. If he was poor the fault was his. In the days of handicraft, poverty had indeed usually been the result of shiftlessness; but the poverty of the factory worker was more often due to the greed of the employer. The handicraftsman, having finished his apprenticeship, looked forward to being his own master. If he worked long hours he was buoyed up by the hope of getting ahead in the world. But later, only the exceptional man could hope to become a factory owner or even a foreman. Garrison, grown to maturity in a transition period, failed to grasp that the average wageworker's only hope of improving his lot was to unite with his fellows.

When Garrison wrote "Mechanics are more inimical to the success of each other, more unjust toward each other than the rich are towards them," he failed to comprehend that fear was at the bottom of this. Yankee workmen feared the competition of Irish immigrants and sometimes rioted against them. White workmen were hostile to Negroes for the same reason and opposed emancipation fearing it would result in hordes of Negroes from the South invading the North and lowering their standard of living, already sufficiently low. Southern leaders shrewdly exploited this fear. In 1843, Henry Clay wrote to the Reverend Calvin Colton, urging him to prepare a popular tract whose "great aim and object . . . should be to arouse the laboring classes of the free States against abolition. The slaves, being free, would be dispersed throughout the Union; they would enter into competition with the free laborer; with the American, the Irish, the German; reduce his wages; be confounded with him, and affect his moral and social standing. And as the ultras go for both abolition and amalgamation, show that their object is to unite in marriage the laboring white man and the laboring black man, and to reduce the white laboring man to the despised and degraded condition of the black man."

The situation required shrewd and careful handling. Most of all it required a thorough understanding of the problem. Garrison lacked that understanding, and antagonized his natural allies. As a result American wageworkers remained indifferent, if not hostile, to Abolition. Some regarded it as a plot of the employers to lower wages. Others saw it as a scheme of professional philanthropists. The editor of the *Chronicle*, a Massachusetts weekly devoted to the interests of labor, wrote: "Philanthropists may speak of negro slavery, but it would be well first to emancipate the slaves at home. Let us not stretch our ears to catch the sound of the lash on the flesh of the oppressed black, while the oppressed in our midst are crying in thunder tones, and calling upon us for assistance."

CHAPTER V

The Anti-Slavery Society

THE evening of January 6, 1832, a fierce northeast wind drove snow, rain and sleet through the ill-lighted, cobbled streets of Boston. Garrison and Knapp emerged from their office in Merchants' Hall and struggled through the storm towards that part of the city then known as "Nigger Hill" — the North side of Beacon Hill. There, in the schoolroom under the African Baptist Church — on what is now Joy Street, but was then Belknap Street — the New England Anti-Slavery Society, devoted to immediate and unconditional emancipation, was to be born.

It had for some time been Garrison's ambition to organize such a society. With that end in view three meetings had been held in the law office of Samuel E. Sewall, who, however, believed that a society devoted to "Immediatism" was premature. As five of the fifteen who had gathered for the first meeting agreed with him, no action was taken, Garrison considering the "Apostolic number of twelve" indispensable. At the two subsequent meetings committees were appointed to prepare a preamble and a constitution, but it still remained to be seen if twelve men in Boston were willing to subscribe to these.

Fifteen had braved the inclemency of the weather and were assembled in the schoolroom. What manner of men were they who meant to throw down the gantlet to the slaveholders and their Northern allies in a cause not their own? They were for the most part young. The oldest was Arnold Buffum, a man of fifty, tall, gray-haired, with gold-rimmed spectacles and the broad-brimmed hat and severe, buttoned-up coat of the Society of Friends. He was a hat manufacturer, and was known as the "Quaker hatter," or the "Old-Hickory Quaker Abolitionist" — an indomitable man, descendant of an indomitable breed. An ancestress of his, Deborah Buffum, was tied to a cart in Salem and publicly whipped for having criticized the municipal authorities, while her brother was imprisoned and banished from Massachusetts on pain of death for spreading Quaker doctrine. Arnold Buffum's father had been a member of the Rhode Island Society for the Gradual Abolition of Slavery, and once gave shelter to a fugitive family of slaves on his farm at Smithfield, Rhode Island. The slaveholder managed to trace the fugitives and appeared on the farm to claim his property, accompanied by the sheriff and several deputies. But for all he was a Quaker, Buffum had armed himself and his farmhands and informed the sheriff that he would not give up the Negroes without a struggle. The sheriff, whose sympathies were with Buffum and the slaves, informed the owner that there would be no violence as far as he was concerned, and the disconsolate slaveholder departed.

Another of those present was Joshua Coffin, historian of New-buryport, a teacher by profession, who had had Whittier for a pupil. His readings from Robert Burns before the Whittier fire-place on winter evenings had aroused the young man's ambition to become a poet.

There was twenty-three-year-old Oliver Johnson, youngest of those present. He was editor of the *Christian Soldier*, in which he denounced the "heresy" of Universalism and the sin of slaveholding with equal gusto. Moses Thatcher, editor of the *Telegraph*, made war on the demon of alcohol and the imp of nicotine. William J. Snelling, editor of the *Amateur*, had been entrusted with the writing of the preamble. David Lee Child, husband of the famous authoress, Lydia Maria Child, was a lawyer and editor of the Massachusetts *Journal*, devoted to the fortunes of the Whig party. Two other law-yers were there — Samuel E. Sewall and the frail but able and cou-rageous Ellis Gray Loring. Robert B. Hall was a theological student, who when he became a minister was to abandon the antislavery cause. There were, besides, Stillman B. Newcomb, Benjamin C. Bacon and Henry K. Stockton — all worthy men. "No more than one or two," wrote Oliver Johnson, "could have put a hundred dol-lars into the treasury without bankrupting himself."

Yet in eight years their organization was to grow into a mighty host of a quarter of a million members, belonging to nearly two thousand societies scattered throughout the Free States. In Ohio alone there were to be three hundred, one with four thousand members. Within four years seventy agents would be touring the country, organizing an average of one society a day. This phenomenal growth was no surprise to the founders. In fact, they had expected a far greater rate of progress. "It seems ridiculous now," wrote Oliver Johnson, "but I remember that the least enthusiastic of our number thought it would not take more than ten years at the utmost to abolish slavery! With the Declaration of Independence and the Bible and God himself on our side, how could the contest be any longer protracted?"

Child was elected chairman, and called the meeting to order, after which Snelling read the following preamble:

We, the undersigned, hold that every person, of full age and sane mind, has a right to immediate freedom from personal bondage of whatsoever kind, unless imposed by the sentence of the law for the commission of some crime. We hold that man cannot, consistently with reason, religion and the eternal and immutable principles of justice, be the property of man. We hold that whoever retains his fellow-man in bondage is guilty of a grievous wrong. We hold that mere difference of complexion is no reason why any man should be deprived of any of his natural rights, or subjected to any political disability. While we advance these opinions as the principles on which we intend to act, we declare that we will not operate on the existing relations of society by other than peaceful and lawful means, and that we will give no countenance to violence or insurrection.

There was an animated discussion. The three lawyers, although they later joined the society, now were united in the belief that the call for immediate emancipation was premature, and declined to sign the document. But the "Apostolic number of twelve" was this time not wanting and the New England Anti-Slavery Society was born. Arnold Buffum was chosen its first president and was promptly "disowned" by the Society of Friends, which gave validity to the saying that time was when one Quaker could move the country for twenty miles around, but that now it required the country for twenty miles around to move one Quaker.

Outside the elements raged. Sleet, rain and snow assailed the windows, symbolical of the fury the pioneers would have to face. But they were of good cheer and as they parted Garrison was heard to remark: "We have met tonight in this obscure schoolhouse; our numbers are few and our influence is limited; but, mark my prediction, Faneuil Hall shall ere long echo with the principles we have set forth."

2

To make room for the growth of the new and genuine, the old and spurious must go. Garrison resolved to come to grips with the Colonization Society, whose existence paralyzed antislavery agitation. It was no mean antagonist he set out to combat. The society had the support of the churches and the endorsement of fourteen State Legislatures, some of which had voted it large subsidies. It counted among its members the most distinguished planters and almost every philanthropist and humanitarian in the country. It had managed to receive the seal of approval of the powerful British Anti-Slavery Society and its honored leaders, William Wilberforce and Thomas Clarkson. Yet, for all its apparent strength, it was highly vulnerable. In the sixteen years of its existence it had transported to Liberia 2162 Negroes, less than 800 of whom had been slaves whom their masters had freed on condition that they should be colonized. When one considers that an average of 15,000 Negroes were annually smuggled into the United States, and that the natural yearly increase in the slave population was 45,000, the society's claim of being engaged in resettling the Negro race on African soil appears absurd. Moreover, as Garrison was to point out, if the mulattoes had no business in the United States, what business had they in Africa? [1]

He went to work resolutely and compiled a booklet of two hundred pages, entitled *Thoughts on Colonization*. He took for his motto, "Out of Thine Own Mouth Will I Condemn Thee," and proceeded to do just that. From the society's annual reports and from its official organ, the *African Repository*, he collected a mass of evidence of the society's bad faith, the cumulative effect of which was overwhelming. As a result, the brothers Arthur and Lewis Tappan, Gerrit Smith, General Fessenden, Theodore D. Weld, Beriah Green, William Goodell, Joshua Levitt, Amos A. Phelps, and a host of other influential men who were to play important roles in the new organization, eventually resigned from the old society. He was, however, not content with mere victory; he wanted annihi-

[1] On his last visit to the United States, Lafayette expressed his surprise at the extent of amalgamation in the Slave States. He said that on his first visit nearly all the colored people in Virginia were black, but that now mulattoes appeared to be in the majority.

lation. Elliott Cresson, the society's principal agent, had gone to England to collect funds. Garrison meant to follow him and to deprive the society of its most formidable prop — the endorsement of men the very mention of whom sufficed to silence criticism. A lecture tour was quickly arranged to collect money for the journey.

The lectures were, for the most part, before colored audiences. The free Negroes had never trusted the Colonization Society. They realized from the beginning that its real aim was to rid America not of slavery but of the free people of color. Soon after its organization in 1817, they had declared in a manifesto: "Without arts, without science, or a proper knowledge of government, to cast into the savage wilds of Africa the free people of color seems to us the circuitous route by which they must return to perpetual slavery." They made this dignified pledge: "We never will separate ourselves voluntarily from the slave population of this country: they are our brethren by the ties of consanguinity, of suffering, and of wrong: and we feel that there is more virtue in suffering privation with them than in fancied advantages for a season." Again, in 1831, at their convention in Philadelphia, they had sent a manifesto to the society in which they said: "Many of our fathers and some of us have fought and bled for the liberty, independence, and peace which you now enjoy; and surely it would be ungenerous and unfeeling in you to deny us a humble and quiet grave in the country which gave us birth." Now Garrison was going to England to fight their battle. They flocked to hear him speak. They emptied the meager treasuries of their churches and benevolent associations to defray his expenses. They kissed his hands. They held up their children so they might see him. He was deeply moved and wrote to a friend: "Alas, that the value of my labors in their behalf bears so small a proportion to their unbounded gratitude and love!"

It was during this lecture tour that several attempts were made to kidnap him. When he reached New York the danger became so great that Arthur Tappan kept him hidden in an attic until it was time for him to sail.

3

On his arrival in London, Garrison was courteously received by the British Abolitionists. "Immediatism" had been their program in the campaign (now drawing to a successful close) for emancipation in the British colonies. William Wilberforce, ill and worn, lived in retirement on his estate at Bath and had ceded the leadership to Thomas Fowell Buxton, who no sooner heard of Garrison's arrival than he invited him to breakfast. Garrison was ushered into a room filled with a distinguished company, but to his embarrassment his host stared at him in amazement and asked: "Have I the pleasure of addressing Mr. Garrison, of Boston, in the United States?"

"Yes, sir, I am he," Garrison replied, "and I am here in accordance with your invitation."

Buxton threw up his hands. "Why, my dear sir," he exclaimed, "I thought you were a black man. And I have consequently invited this company of ladies and gentlemen to be present to welcome Mr. Garrison, the black advocate of emancipation from the United States of America!"

There was a general laugh. Garrison later commented: "That is the only compliment I have ever had paid me that I care to remember, or to tell of. For Mr. Buxton had somehow or other supposed that no white American could plead for those in bondage as I had done."

Elliott Cresson, the agent of the Colonization Society, had not been idle. He had ingratiated himself with Wilberforce, Clarkson and Buxton by telling them his Society had been offered one hundred thousand slaves gratuitously for settlement in Liberia, a statement devoid of all truth. To George Thompson, Agent of the London Anti-Slavery Society, he had said: "There is an incendiary paper published in Boston by a madman who is in league with a man by the name of Walker, who had recommended the slaves to cut their masters' throats." Thompson, however, was a reader of the *Liberator* and knew that Garrison had rebuked Walker for inciting the slaves to revolt.

Garrison began his campaign by challenging Cresson to public debate. Cresson declined, but was present at a meeting Garrison held at the Wesleyan Chapel. The young editor, equipped with copies of the Colonization Society's official organ and its annual reports, made out so damaging a case that the chairman interrupted him and asked Cresson if he cared to reply to certain specific charges. The latter angrily retorted that he did not care to do so "under existing circumstances, and with such a chairman, such a lecturer and such a meeting." Garrison then continued his indictment and finished by saying that "the Abolitionists of Great Britain should indignantly order Cresson back to his slaveholding employers, and bid him be thankful that he had not been detained on a charge of obtaining money under false pretenses."

He journeyed to Bath to lay his proofs before Wilberforce. The great leader, small, frail and broken in health, received him kindly and seemed anxious to get to the bottom of the matter. Garrison said to him: "I offer no document or pamphlet in opposition to the Society, upon which to form an opinion of its true character. Here are its Fifteenth and Sixteenth Reports; the former contains an elaborate defense of the Society by its managers, which in my opinion, is alone sufficient to seal its destiny. Read it at your leisure, and judging the Society out of its own mouth, let your verdict be given to the world."

Before Garrison left England, Wilberforce and all other principal leaders of the British antislavery movement, with the exception of Clarkson, signed a statement repudiating the Colonization Society. Clarkson later followed their example, but for the present preferred to remain neutral.

4

The culminating point of Garrison's first English mission was a meeting at Exeter Hall, at which he and the Irish leader Daniel O'Connell were the principal speakers. Garrison's speech at the Hall created great resentment in the United States. To him who believes in the maxim "My country, right or wrong," the speech, delivered before a foreign audience, must appear objectionable. It should be remembered, however, that Garrison's motto was "Our country is the world — our countrymen are all mankind." Moreover, it was not only his intention to exert pressure upon the South by arousing public opinion in the North, but also to exert pressure upon the North by arousing public opinion throughout the civilized world.

The speech read, in part:

"I accuse the land of my nativity of insulting the majesty of Heaven with the grossest mockery that was ever exhibited to man

— inasmuch as, professing to be the land of the free and the asylum of the oppressed, she falsifies every profession, and shamelessly plays the tyrant.

"I accuse her before all nations, of giving an open, deliberate and base denial to her boasted Declaration, that 'all men are created equal; that they are endowed by the Creator with certain inalienable rights; that among these are life, liberty and the pursuit of happiness.'

"I accuse her of suffering a large portion of her population to be lacerated, starved and plundered, without law and without justification, at the will of petty tyrants.

"I accuse her of trafficking in the bodies and souls of men, in a domestic way, to an extent nearly equal to the foreign slave trade; which traffic is equally atrocious with the foreign, and almost as cruel in its operations.

"I accuse her of legalizing on an enormous scale, licentiousness, fraud, cruelty and murder.

"I accuse her of stealing the liberties of two millions of the creatures of God, and withholding the just recompense of their labor; of ruthlessly invading the holiest relations of life, and cruelly separating the dearest ties of nature; of denying these miserable victims necessary food and clothing for their perishable bodies, and light and knowledge for their immortal souls; of tearing the husband from his wife, the mother from her babe, and the children from their parents, and of perpetrating upon the poor and needy every species of outrage and oppression."

Those who consider the indictment too severe should be reminded of the Abbé Grégoire's famous saying: "If the gentlemen were suddenly to turn black they would sing a different tune."

Garrison's *Thoughts on Colonization* and his British mission dealt a blow to the Colonization Society from which it never recovered. John Jay Chapman has written: "Nothing that Frederick the Great, Washington or Napoleon ever did in the field of war was more brilliant than this political foray of Garrison, then at the age of twenty-seven, upon the key-position and jugular vein of slavery." The society continued to linger a while longer in a greatly weakened state, but its influence was gone and Colonization ceased to be an issue in America until Lincoln revived it for a short time during the Civil War.

5

The packet boat *Hannibal*, on which Garrison had taken passage, cast anchor in New York on September 29, but remained in quarantine until October 2. The newspapers of the city, who had whipped themselves up into a frenzy concerning Garrison's Exeter Hall speech, took it for granted that he was on board. The Abolitionists evidently did not expect him, for no one was at the pier to greet him and an announcement of a meeting called at Clinton Hall for the purpose of organizing a local branch of the Garrisonian Anti-Slavery Society made no mention of the possibility of his being present. The New York papers felt certain, however, that the meeting and the arrival of the vessel were closely related and advised citizens to attend and voice their displeasure. A poster, addressed to "All Persons from the South," giving the same advice, appeared on the walls of the city.

Garrison, who had registered at a modest hostelry, called on none of his friends, but towards evening directed his steps towards Clinton Hall, on the Corner of Beekman Street and Theatre Alley. The poster presaged a mob, and when he neared the hall he saw that the street was packed with people.

An eyewitness has described the crowd as "a genuine, drunken, infuriated mob of blackguards of every species, some with good clothes, and the major part the very sweepings of the city." Lewis Tappan, prominent among the sponsors of the meeting, received his share of abuse: "The shouting, screaming and cursing for Tappan and Garrison defy all belief." No one recognized Garrison, who later wrote: "I regarded the rioters with mingled emotions of pity and contempt . . . as calm in my feelings as if those who were asking my life were my warmest supporters." He listened with amused interest to a well-dressed man, who was saying: "If I had my will, or if I could catch him, Garrison should be packed up in a box with air holes, marked 'this side up,' and so shipped to Georgia."

More than an hour passed, but the doors did not open. The trustees of the hall, fearful their property would be damaged, had intervened. Finally the rumor spread that the Abolitionists were meeting at Chatham Street Chapel. On to Chatham Street! Garrison trailed along. There fresh disappointment. The meeting had been warned of the approach of the mob and had adjourned. One man had remained — white-haired Isaac T. Hopper, a venerable Quaker, who sat with hands folded on the knob of his walking stick gazing meditatively before him. The invaders looked at him curiously, but left him in peace. The following day the *Commercial Advertiser* said Garrison "would do well to consider that his course of conduct in England had kindled a spirit of hostility towards him at home which cannot be easily allayed. He will act wisely never to attempt addressing a public meeting in *this* country again."

When he reached Boston and his arrival became known, a circular appeared in the streets calling on Bostonians to punish the traducer of his country. "He is now in your power — do not let him escape you, but go this evening, armed with plenty of *tar and feathers*, and administer him justice at his abode at No. 9 Merchants' Hall, Congress-St." Towards evening a mob gathered and for a while things looked ominous. But a leader was lacking and no attempt was made to storm the building.

Garrison remained defiant. He published his Exeter Hall speech in the *Liberator* with this comment: "To the charge made against me . . . of having slandered my country abroad, I reply that it is false . . . I did not hesitate there — I have not hesitated here — I shall hesitate nowhere, to brand this country as hypocritical and tyrannical in its treatment of the people of color, whether bond or free. If this be calumny, I dealt freely in it, and I shall deal, as long as slavery exists among us, or, at least, as long as the power of utterance is given to my tongue."

6

On September 12, 1834, Garrison wrote to George W. Benson: "By dint of some industry and much persuasion, I succeeded in inducing the abolitionists in New York to join our little band in Boston, in calling a National Convention at Philadelphia." Soon after his return from England, the call went forth for the convention to assemble in Philadelphia, on December 4, 1833.

Garrison arrived in what John Adams has called "the happy, the peaceful, the elegant, the hospitable and polite city of Philadelphia," on the morning of December 3. That same day some forty delegates met at the house of a local Abolitionist and decided to ask the Quaker philanthropist and prison reformer Roberts Vaux, one of the most respected men in the city, to preside over the gathering.

They hoped by this means to avert threatened violence, for notwithstanding Mr. Adams's handsome testimonial regarding the city's hospitality, the Chief of Police had found it necessary to notify the convention managers that meetings must be held in the daytime, as he could not undertake to protect the delegates after dark.

A committee of six, half of whom were Quakers, called upon Mr. Vaux, but received a frosty reception. They called upon one other leading citizen with no better result. This time, when the door had closed behind them, one of the committee, Professor Beriah Green of Western Reserve College, caustically remarked: "If there is not timber amongst ourselves big enough to make a president of, let us get along without one, or go home and stay there until we have grown up to be men." That settled it. No further attempt was made to place the convention under the aegis of local respectability.

Philadelphia was to become notorious for some of the country's worst proslavery riots, during one of which Pennsylvania Hall, built by the Abolitionists, was burned to the ground. This time, however, the crowd that had gathered before Adelphi Hall, on Fifth Street, where on the morning of December 4 the convention assembled, contented itself with making insulting remarks. A strong force of police guarded the entrance, near which a slaveholder's son kept repeating that he had come "to wash his hands in Garrison's blood." People whose intentions appeared peaceable were admitted as spectators and provided with chairs.

Of the sixty-seven delegates, representing ten of the twelve Free States, twenty-one were Quakers, four were women and three were Negroes.[2] The presence of women was little short of revolutionary. A few years earlier even Garrison would have objected. The women themselves realized that this was a momentous occasion and only one, Lucretia Mott, had the courage to take the floor during the proceedings. When she rose to speak her emotion overcame her and she became confused, but Beriah Green, who had been elected chairman, encouraged her by saying: "Go on, ma'am, we shall all be glad to hear you." Several others cried, "Go on! Go on!" whereupon she collected herself and did exceedingly well. Thus, unob-

[2] There is some difference of opinion regarding the number of delegates. According to May there were fifty-six; according to Whittier, sixty-two. The Declaration of Sentiments, signed by male delegates only, bears sixty-three signatures. Sixty-seven appears, therefore, to be the correct figure.

trusively, the woman question slipped into the arena behind the slavery question.

With Beriah Green on the platform were two secretaries — Lewis Tappan and John Greenleaf Whittier. Tappan has been described by an eyewitness as "a jaunty, man-of-the-world looking person, well-dressed and handsome, with a fine voice and taking appearance." But surely the military-looking gentleman in dark frock coat and stand-up collar, with flashing eyes and short dark beard, could not be the awkward country youth Garrison had at one time interviewed in the Whittier kitchen? It was he, and in the breast pocket of his frock coat reposed a poem, dedicated to his friend, which he expected to declaim the following day. The first stanza read:

> Champion of those who groan beneath
>   Oppression's iron hand:
> In view of penury, hate and death
>   I see thee fearless stand,
> Still bearing up thy lofty brow
>   In the steadfast strength of truth,
> In manhood sealing well the vow
>   And promise of thy youth.

A committee was appointed to draft a Declaration of Sentiments, and after a lengthy discussion decided to leave the composition of the document to Garrison. When at nine in the morning they knocked on the door of his room at the house of a colored Abolitionist and were told to enter, they found the lamp lit, the shutters closed, and Garrison before the writing table, at which he had spent the entire night, putting the last touches to the lengthy Declaration. The following paragraphs are significant:

> We fully and unanimously recognize the sovereignty of each State to legislate exclusively on the subject of the slavery which is tolerated within its limits; we concede that Congress, under the present national compact has no right to interfere with any of the slave States in relation to this momentous subject.
> Our principles forbid the doing of evil that good may come, and lead us to reject, and to entreat the oppressed to reject, the use of all carnal weapons for deliverance from bondage; relying solely upon those which are spiritual, and mighty through God to the pulling down of strongholds.

The Declaration failed to specify the nature of the "spiritual weapons" the society meant to employ. Garrison had purposely remained vague because serious differences existed about tactics. Many sincere opponents of slavery found this denunciatory method "unchristian" and doubted its efficacy. As we shall see, the American Anti-Slavery Society did not adopt his method, but neither did it put its faith in converting the slaveholders.

7

While the committee was deliberating, the convention listened to Whittier's poem and to a eulogy of Garrison pronounced by Lewis Tappan.

"Some men, Mr. President," said Tappan, "are frightened at a name. There is good evidence to believe that many professed friends of abolition would have been here, had they not been *afraid* that the name of William Lloyd Garrison would be inserted prominently into our proceedings. Sir, I am ashamed of such friends. We ought to place that honored name in the forefront of our ranks. The cause is under obligations to him which such an evidence of respect will but poorly repay. . . . He is said to be imprudent. . . . But if God had not endowed him as he has, and smiled propitiously on his *imprudences*, we should not now be engaged in the deliberation of this most interesting and important Convention. God has raised up just such a man as William Lloyd Garrison to be a pioneer in this cause . . . Let us not be afraid to go forward with him, even into the 'imminent breach,' although there may be professed friends who stand back because of him."

In his account of the convention in the *Liberator*, Garrison omitted Tappan's eulogy with the comment "the panegyric of our friends is incomparably more afflicting to us than the measureless defamation of our enemies."

The Declaration as written by Garrison underwent few changes, either in committee or in the convention. There was some debate concerning the statement "Every American citizen who retains a human being in involuntary bondage as his property is a man stealer." The convention amended this to read ". . . is, according to Scripture (Exodus, 21:16), a man stealer." Garrison acquiesced, but did not favor the amendment. "It matters not what the Bible may say, so far as these rights are concerned," was his comment. The delegates then solemnly signed the document, which had been copied on parchment. So novel was the participation of women in such a gathering that none of the female delegates thought it proper to sign, and no one suggested they should.

Arthur Tappan, who was not present, was elected President of the American Anti-Slavery Society. Garrison, who did not wish to hold any office, was chosen Secretary of Foreign Correspondence, but resigned a short time after.

8

The great majority of the nearly quarter of a million men and women who within the succeeding seven years joined the Anti-Slavery Society were plain, hard-working people, for the most part belonging to the farmer, artisan and lower middle class. The New England mill girls were often Abolitionists and quite a number of other wageworkers belonged, but, for reasons already given, workingmen did not usually predominate in the antislavery societies. In their enthusiasm and willingness to risk life, property and reputation for the cause of emancipation, the members of the society remind one of the early Christians. They would travel three hundred miles or more on horseback or by wagon to attend an Anti-Slavery meeting; would distribute Abolitionist literature among their neighbors, often at great personal risk; would conduct a station on the Underground Railroad, helping slaves to escape — indeed, were ready for almost any sacrifice.

A social crusade such as the Abolitionists were conducting was bound to attract many eccentrics. Some of these undoubtedly harmed the movement; others, however, did valuable work in spite of their peculiarities. Among the latter were the Come-Outers, whose special field of propaganda was the churches. If slavery was in conflict with the Declaration of Independence, how much more so with the Sermon on the Mount. Yet while many individual clergymen joined the antislavery movement, with the exception of the Quakers not a single religious denomination took a stand against slavery until public opinion made it impossible to remain neutral. Even the Quakers had ceased all propaganda against the South's "peculiar institution." "The gold of original Quakerism," wrote Whittier, "had become dim, and the fine gold changed. The spirit of the world prevailed among them, and had wrought an inward desolation."

The Come-Outers took it upon themselves to remind the churches of their duty. They thought nothing of interrupting a minister during the sermon to argue with him or to address his congregation. Once in New York when a proslavery minister said during a sermon "Slavery is a divine institution," a Come-Outer shouted: "So is hell!" In church, or when traveling, they insisted on occupying seats reserved for Negroes. Often they raised such a disturbance that they had to be forcibly removed. When they landed in jail, which happened not infrequently, they sang Abolitionist hymns at all hours of the day and night.

More extreme than the Come-Outers were the No-Organizationists, who believed in the superiority of individual to collective action and would have nothing to do with committees, chairmen, secretaries or anything else that smacked of organization. Nathaniel P. Rogers, a brilliant New Hampshire attorney, who "excommunicated" his church as unworthy of his presence, believed that to have a chairman at a meeting was high treason to liberty. "The church and the clergy even are allowed to rest in comparative quietness while he follows his crusade against chairmen, business committees, and societies," wrote Edmund Quincy.

Among those who affected singularity of appearance was Joseph Palmer. In a day when beards were considered disreputable he wore one of Old Testament proportions. When fellow townsmen conspired to deprive him of it, he put up such a valiant resistance that (with beard undamaged) he was locked up for "unprovoked assault" and remained in jail for more than a year, refusing to pay a fine. Charles C. Burleigh, a lawyer who disdained to practice law and was the most brilliant debater the movement boasted, wore a bushy blond beard and allowed his curly hair to cascade upon his shoulders. He was thin and tall and the singularity of his appearance was further enhanced by "high water pantaloons" dangling about his ankles. Once when he stood before an audience beside the bald-headed editor of the *Liberator*, a wag cried from the gallery: "Shave that tall Christ and make a wig for Garrison!" Another time when, covered with dust after a long foot journey, a bundle of antislavery pamphlets dangling from a stick on his shoulder, he knocked on the door of an Abolitionist in a small town in Massachusetts, the little girl who opened ran to her mother crying: "Oh, mother! the devil has come!" Hearing of this Garrison commented: "And no wonder — hair 'em, scare 'em."

There was Abigail Folsom, "that flea of conventions" as Emerson was wont to call her, whose notion of free speech was that she could talk at Abolitionist meetings as often and as long as she pleased, her subject invariably being the Bible. When the chairman would try to silence her, she would appeal to the spectators in the gallery. Once, in desperation, Wendell Phillips, Oliver Johnson and another Abolitionist carried her out in a chair. She offered no resistance, but cried: "I'm better off than my Master was: He had but one ass to ride — I have three to carry me."

A few there were who considered Garrison's denunciatory method as lacking real Old Testament flavor. Foremost among these was the Reverend Stephen S. Foster, who had resigned from the ministry and devoted all his time to Abolition. Complacency, Foster believed, was the real enemy. An infallible cure for complacency was to get people angry enough to fight. They might begin by fighting *you*, but never mind! They would be looking for arguments to answer you and eventually would become converts. Moreover, a riot could not help attracting attention and get others interested. So, the Reverend Foster went forth "not to bring peace, but a sword." James Russell Lowell, seeing him at an antislavery bazaar, immortalized him in the following lines:

> Hard by, as calm as summer even
> Smiles the reviled and pelted Stephen,
> Who studied mineralogy
> Not with soft book upon the knee,
> But learned the properties of stones
> By contact sharp of flesh and bones . . .
> A kind of maddened John the Baptist,
> To whom the harshest word comes aptest,
> Who struck by stone or brick ill-starred,
> Hurls back an epithet as hard,
> Which deadlier than stone or brick,
> Has a propensity to stick.

During a meeting at Syracuse, New York, at which Garrison was present, Foster let fly the remark that the Methodist Episcopal Church was "worse than any brothel in the city." Garrison described the riot that followed in a letter to his wife and added wistfully: "I could wish that bro. Foster would exercise more judgment and discretion in the presentation of his views; but it is useless to reason with him, with any hope of altering his course, as he is firmly persuaded that he is pursuing the very best course."

Ezekiel Rogers, an Abolitionist editor, who had a particular aversion for tobacco, wrote of this and other idiosyncrasies of Abolitionists: "Anti-slavery wants her mouths for other uses than for besotting tobacco-smoke. They may as well almost be rum-ducts as tobacco funnels. And we rejoice that so few mouths or noses in our ranks are thus profaned. Abolitionists are generally as *crazy* in regard to rum and tobacco as in regard to slavery. Some of them refrain from eating flesh and drinking tea and coffee. Some are so *bewildered* that they won't *fight* in the way of *Christian retaliation*, to the great disturbance of the churches they belong to and the annoyance of their pastors."

Yet notwithstanding all these peculiarities men like Ralph Waldo Emerson and Dr. William Ellery Channing, who at first criticized the movement, finished by acknowledging that its services to the cause of freedom had been invaluable. "We Abolitionists," said Samuel J. May, "are what we are, — babes, sucklings, obscure men, silly women, publicans, sinners, and we shall manage this matter just as might be expected of such persons as we are. It is unbecoming in abler men who stood by and would do nothing to complain of us because we do no better."

CHAPTER VI
Reign of Terror

WHEN on the eve of his departure for England, Garrison spoke at the African Church at Providence, Rhode Island, there was among the handful of white people in the audience "a plump and rosy creature, with blue eyes and fair brown hair" — Helen Eliza Benson. She was twenty-three, the youngest daughter of George Benson, a retired wool merchant from Brooklyn, Connecticut, where Samuel J. May was minister of the Unitarian Church. Benson and his two sons George and Henry were ardent Abolitionists. The elder, George, was in the wool business in Providence, and it was on a visit to him that Helen had the opportunity of hearing Garrison speak. She was impressed, but a greater thrill awaited her. When, the following morning, she entered her brother's office, she found him in conversation with the lecturer of the previous evening. George introduced her, and we have Garrison's word for it that her "sweet countenance and pleasant conversation" affected him agreeably.

After his return from England he paid a visit to Brooklyn and was a guest at "Friendship's Valley," as friends of the Bensons had named their hospitable country place. To Helen's elder brother he wrote: "I confess, in addition to the other delightful attractions which are there found, the soft blue eyes and pleasant countenance of Miss Ellen [sic] are by no means impotent and unattractive." They were sufficiently so to make him renew the visit repeatedly. As he observed the girl's dexterous ways and noticed her sunny, even disposition, he began seriously to consider abandoning bachelorhood. Once when they drove together to Canterbury, he was on the point of declaring himself, but courage failed him and the words remained unspoken. By this time, however, they were exchanging letters and in one of them he told her that he loved her and asked her to be his wife. He was accepted, and in the spring of 1834 again visited the Bensons, her acknowledged suitor. What especially impressed him on that occasion was that Helen received him with her customary simplicity, making no attempt to dazzle him by special attention to her dress. "Truly," he wrote, "not one young lady out of ten thousand, in a first interview with her lover, but would have endeavored falsely to heighten her charms and allure by outward attractions." She, fearing lest he had misunderstood, wrote him after his departure: "I have been considering how much the colored people think of dress, and how much of their profits are expended for useless ornaments that foolishly tend to make a show and parade. As much stress will of course be laid on Garrison's *wife* by that class, it behooves me to be very circumspect in all things, when called upon to fill so important a station."

They were married at her father's house on September 4, 1834. The officiating clergyman was Samuel J. May. They set up housekeeping at Roxbury, three miles from the center of Boston, in a modest little house it pleased them to call "Freedom's Cottage." Isaac Knapp came to board with them. They were poor, Garrison earning only about seven hundred dollars a year lecturing and writing, but their needs were few and it was not for nothing Helen had been nicknamed "Peace-and-Plenty." When Garrison would appear worried about the smallness of his income, she would say, smiling: "Never mind, bread and water agree with me perfectly." Although a firm believer in Abolition, she was retiring by nature and seldom appeared in public. This did not displease her husband. On the first anniversary of their marriage he wrote to George: "I did not marry her expecting that she would assume a prominent station in the anti-slavery cause, but for domestic quietude and happiness. . . . She is one of those who prefer to toil unseen — to give by stealth — and to sacrifice in seclusion."

Garrison was in the habit of often working in his office until midnight, and it was a source of constant anxiety to Helen that he might be waylaid on the lonely three-mile walk to the suburb and taken aboard a ship to be transported to Georgia. But the colored people of Boston were aware of the danger and unknown to him had taken the necessary precautions. When at midnight he would emerge from Merchants' Hall, two sturdy Negroes, armed with cudgels, would follow him at a distance and did not retrace their steps until the door of Freedom's Cottage had closed behind him. On several occasions he noticed that he was being followed, and, unaware that those shadowing him were doing so to protect him, he, too, could not help feeling uneasy. So, with the coming of spring, they abandoned Freedom's Cottage and moved to Boston — 23 Brighton Street.

2

Angelina Grimké, daughter of a prosperous South Carolina planter, has given a shocking description of the treatment of household slaves. They slept on the bare floor and were allowed but two meals a day, from which "they are often kept . . . by way of punishment." This may seem surprising to those who have read sentimental stories about cherished Negro "mammies," but when one stops to consider how hard the lot even of free white domestics was a generation or two ago, it requires no strain on the imagination to picture to oneself the condition of colored household help over whom master and mistress exercised absolute power. "Every master of slaves is born a petty tyrant," said Colonel George Mason of Virginia in the Federal Convention. Garrison's statement that it was "nothing uncommon" when walking along the street in Baltimore to hear "the distinct application of a whip and the shrieks of anguish" following every blow, applied to all Southern cities and towns. "The whole commerce between master and slave is a perpetual exercise of the most boisterous passions; the most unremitting despotism on the one part, and degrading submissions on the other," wrote Thomas Jefferson. He knew whereof he spoke. In 1811, Lilburn Lewis, a son of Jefferson's sister, who owned a plantation at Livingston, Kentucky, was guilty of an atrocity towards a household slave rare even in the annals of an institution which in South Carolina had made it necessary to pass a law forbidding slaveholders "willfully to cut out the tongue, put out the eye, castrate or cruelly scald, burn or deprive any slave of any limb or member." Lewis had given a seventeen-year-old household slave an "elegant" pitcher and ordered him to fetch water from a spring. The boy had the misfortune to break the pitcher. Jefferson's nephew had him tied to a broad bench, and with an ax cut off his feet, his legs at the knee-joints, his hands, his arms, and finally his head! He had assembled all the slaves on the plantation to witness the atrocity, but such was the authority of the master and the helplessness of the slave that no one dared interfere.

That household slaves often shirked work is understandable. As Harriet Martineau remarked after a journey through the South:

"Every man, woman and child would rather play for nothing than work for nothing."

3

If, as the result of the absolute power of the master over the slave, the treatment of household slaves left much to be desired, that of the field slaves, left to the mercy of drivers and overseers, was far worse. "The treatment of the slaves is in general as good as the circumstances and the *cruel necessity of the case* will permit," the Colonization Society conceded in its Second Annual Report.[1] Unfortunately the "cruel necessity of the case" called for harsh and even brutal treatment. How otherwise could a reasoning being be made to work for nothing in the hot sun fifteen hours a day and over? "Such services can only be expected from one who has no will of his own; who surrenders his will in implicit obedience to another. Such obedience is the consequence only of uncontrolled authority over the body. There is no remedy. This discipline belongs to the state of slavery. . . . It constitutes the curse of slavery to both the bond and the free portion of our population. But it is inherent in the relation of master and slave," said Judge Edmund Ruffin of North Carolina in a famous decision.

If one reads the advertisements for fugitive slaves (some 5400 were annually advertised in the Southern press as having run away) one finds them replete with statements such as these: "will no doubt show the marks of recent whipping if taken"; "stamped N.E. on the breast and having both small toes cut off"; "has some scars on his back that show above the skin, caused by the whip"; "has a scar on one cheek, and his left hand has been seriously injured by a pistol shot"; "from being whipped, has scars on his back, arms and thighs"; "has an iron band around his neck"; "has a ring of iron on his left foot"; "has on a large neck iron, with a huge pair of horns and a large bar or band of iron on his left leg"; "branded on the left cheek, thus 'R', and a piece is taken off her left ear on the same side; the same letter is branded on the inside of both legs." It is significant that in every case the advertisement gives the full name and address of the owner, making it evident that no odium attached in the South to the maiming or scarring of a slave. It was all part of "the cruel necessity of the case."

[1] Italics the author's.

4

Overwork and semistarvation were common. The preamble to a South Carolina law limiting the slave's working day to fifteen hours (a provision that was not and could not be enforced), read: "Whereas *many* [2] owners of slaves, do confine them so closely to hard labour that they have not sufficient time for natural rest, etc." Dr. William Ellery Channing, who at one time lived in Virginia, as conservative a critic as can be quoted, in a description of a "model" Virginia plantation, wrote: "A superficial observer would have called the slaves happy. Yet they were working under a severe, subduing discipline, and were overworked to a degree that shortened life." In Louisiana, Alabama and Mississippi it was common practice to "work-out" a slave in seven years. The Agricultural Society of Baton Rouge, Louisiana, issued a report in 1829, in which there was an estimate of the expenditures necessary to conduct a "well-regulated sugar estate." Among the expenditures listed was a two and a half per cent annual wastage of slave power, over and above the increase from births! But for the fact that large numbers of slaves were constantly imported from the slave-breeding States, and that Negroes continued to be smuggled in from Africa until the outbreak of the Civil War, there can be no doubt that overwork and ill treatment would have exterminated the Negro population in several Southern States.

That the slaves were undernourished we know from the testimony of Southerners. In 1833 Thomas Clay said in an address to the Presbytery of Georgia: "The quantity of food allowed by custom is a peck of corn a week. The present economy of the slave system is to get all you can from the slave, and give in return as little as will barely support him. . . . From various causes, the slave's allowance of food is not adequate to the support of a laboring man." In 1854, the Southerner J. D. B. De Bow, in his *The Industrial Resources, etc., of the Southern and Western States*, gave an estimate furnished by a large cotton planter of the cost of raising cotton. The cost of feeding one hundred slaves, including "hospital and overseer's table," is given as $750 per annum, or about two cents a day per slave! Other expenses, such as clothing, bedding, sacks for gathering cotton, etc., were estimated at an equal amount. The planter who

[2] Italics the author's.

furnished these estimates expressed his impatience at Northern ignorance of the heavy expenses to which the cotton planter was put, hence it may be taken for granted that he was more likely to have overestimated than underestimated the expense of feeding the slaves. The two cents a day for clothing, bedding and so on must have been ample, considering the kind of clothing and bedding the slaves received. The clothing was made of "Negro-cloth," a coarse mixture of cotton and hemp, so irritating to the skin that the slaves were constantly scratching, and so inadequate as protection against the cold that the Honorable T. T. Bouldin of Virginia charged in 1835 that "many Negroes die from exposure to bad weather. They are clad in flimsy fabric, that will neither turn wind or rain." The poet Julian Ursyn Niemcewicz, who accompanied the Polish patriot Kosciuszko on his journey to America after the Revolution, charged that the "huts" of the slaves were "far more miserable than the poorest cottages of our peasants." It should be remembered that Polish peasants were serfs, among the most wretched in Europe.

5

In countries living under an official or unofficial censorship it frequently happens that the outside world is better acquainted with what transpires within their borders than are their own citizens. Even so it was with the South. The Southerner De Bow, who superintended the United States census of 1850, estimated that there were in the South 160,974 slaveowners and 186,551 slave hirers. Only one Southerner in every six belonged therefore to a slaveowning or slave-hiring family. The nonslaveholders, unless employed as drivers or overseers, knew little or nothing of the life of the slave. This should not surprise us, for even a slaveholder's own family was often kept in ignorance. Angelina Grimké, who did not leave her father's plantation until she was a grown woman, prefaced her description of the life of household slaves by saying: "I have seen almost nothing of slavery on plantations. My testimony relates exclusively to house servants." John S. Wise, son of the famous Virginia Governor Henry A. Wise, wrote in his book *The End of an Era* that he had never even heard of a slave auction until he visited an uncle in Philadelphia, who took him to see a theatrical performance of *Uncle Tom's Cabin*. The Negro leader Frederick Douglass, who escaped from slavery in Maryland, informs us that when one talked to a slave and asked him concerning the treatment he was receiving he would invariably praise his master, even if his back was scarred by the lash and he had an ear cropped. White men who knew and whose conscience revolted dared not protest. Hinton Rowan Helper published his flaming indictment of slavery, *The Impending Crisis*, in the North, and its sale was forbidden in the South. James G. Birney and Cassius M. Clay, slaveholders whose eyes had been opened, attempted to inform their fellow Southerners. If they escaped with their lives it was due to the fact that they belonged to powerful Southern families. Clay had two loaded brass cannon commanding the door that gave access to the office of his paper, the *True American*, at Lexington, Kentucky, and a keg of powder with fuse attached, so he could blow up the building if a mob invaded the premises.

6

The Executive Committee of the American Anti-Slavery Society decided not to follow Garrison's denunciatory method in their propaganda. Lewis Tappan wrote to George Thompson: "The fact need not be concealed from you that several emancipationists so disapprove of the harsh and, as they think, the unchristian language of the *Liberator*, that they do not feel justified in upholding it." The method they decided to adopt had much to recommend it. Garrison, wishing to exert pressure upon the South, addressed himself principally to the North; the Society decided to address itself mainly to the South — not to slaveholders and slave hirers, but to the non-slaveholding five-sixths of the South's population. Lists of intelligent nonslaveholders were compiled and literature was sent to them by mail. The first week of every month the Society published a small folio paper called *Human Rights;* the second week, a small magazine illustrated with woodcuts, the *Anti-Slavery Record;* the third week, an enlarged sheet of the Society's official organ, the *Emancipator;* finally, a juvenile magazine, the *Slave's Friend*. All were printed in large quantities and by far the greater part was mailed to Southerners. Every possible care was taken not to offend Southern susceptibilities. Slavery was condemned on religious and moral grounds in language devoid of passion. Extracts from letters and documents of Southern origin called attention to the cruelty and injustice of the system. Washington, Jefferson, Patrick Henry and other Founding

Fathers who, although slaveholders themselves, had favored emancipation were profusely quoted. One fault could be found with the society's propaganda: the disastrous effect of slavery upon the economy of the South and the fortunes of nonslaveholders was given insufficient attention. No one, however, could claim that the publications lacked moderation. Indeed, the South itself furnished proof of the reasonableness of the appeal. In 1835, Governor John Gayle of Alabama demanded of the Governor of New York the extradition of Ransom G. Williams, publishing agent of the American Anti-Slavery Society. He had been indicted by the Grand Jury of Tuscaloosa for having sent into the State a copy of the society's official organ, the *Emancipator*, containing the following paragraph:

> God commands and all nature cries out, that men should not be held as property. The system of making men property has plunged 2,250,000 of our fellow-countrymen into the deepest physical and moral degradation, and they are every moment sinking deeper.

Tons of literature had been mailed by the society to citizens of Alabama, yet the above was the most incendiary statement the State's prosecutor had been able to unearth — the only one on which he considered it possible to base an indictment! Obviously the slaveholders wanted no interference of any kind. In the words of Lincoln, their contention was "That if any one man choose to enslave another, no third man shall be allowed to object." When Dr. Channing wrote a brochure against slavery so moderate that according to some it "put people to sleep," he was abused as roundly as Garrison. In 1854 the editor of the Richmond *Enquirer*, who knew his slaveholders, caustically remarked: "That man must be a veritable verigreen who dreams of pleasing slaveholders, either in church or state, by any method but that of letting slavery alone." They were determined that the people of the South should not learn the truth about slavery and were ready to resort to any method to accomplish their purpose.

7

Vigilance Committees were formed throughout the South. They were prosecutor, judge and jury. Said Senator William C. Preston of South Carolina: "Let an abolitionist come within the borders of

South Carolina, if we can catch him, we will try him, and notwith-standing all the influence of all the governments on earth, including the Federal Government, we will hang him."

Amos Dresser, a former student at Lane Theological Seminary, disregarded the warning. Wishing to earn some money to complete his education, he contracted with a publisher to sell the "Cottage Bible" in Tennessee. He had the imprudence to take with him a quantity of Abolitionist pamphlets, which he intended selling or giving to those who appeared interested. In Nashville he was arrested and tried by the Vigilance Committee. At midnight, by the light of torches, before a crowd that filled the public square, he was stripped to the waist, forced to kneel, and given twenty lashes across his bare back. His belongings were confiscated and he was given twenty-four hours to leave town. The Nashville *Banner* declared: "Dresser had not laid himself liable to any punishment known to our laws, the defect of which, in that respect, we trust will be remedied at the approaching session of the General Assembly."

In Mississippi several men "suspected" of being Abolitionists were hanged. The editor of the Columbia (S. C.) *Telescope* wrote: "Let us declare, through the public journals of our country, that the question of slavery is not and shall not be open to discussion — that the very moment any private individual attempts to lecture us upon its evils and immorality, in the same moment his tongue shall be cut out and cast upon the dunghill."

The New Orleans Vigilance Committee offered twenty thousand dollars for the delivery of Arthur Tappan, President of the American Anti-Slavery Society. Six Mississippi slaveholders subscribed an equal amount for the capture and delivery of Garrison. Search of boats and railway trains from the North was resumed and passengers were questioned. At Charleston, South Carolina, the Committee of Twenty-One, composed of leading citizens, led by a former governor, broke into the Federal Post Office during the night and confiscated thousands of copies of antislavery publications addressed to Southerners. The next evening a crowd of three thousand watched the papers go up in flame and Garrison and Tappan hanged in effigy. A storekeeper in Norfolk, Virginia, opened up a subscription for the heads of Garrison and Tappan, while another in Richmond displayed a bowie knife in his window marked "For Garrison." Assassination and kidnapping was openly advocated by the Southern press. The Richmond *Whig*, at one time noted for its liberalism,

declared: "Let the hell-hounds of the North beware . . . We have
feared that Southern exasperation would seize some of the prime
conspirators in their very beds, and drag them to meet the punishment of their offenses. We fear it no longer. We hope it may be so,
and our applause as one man shall follow the successful enterprise."

8

Public meetings were held in Richmond, Charleston, New Orleans
and many other Southern cities and towns calling upon Federal
officialdom and the business community of the North to put a stop
to the agitation. These calls were not unmixed with threats. If
Congress confirmed the right of the Abolitionists to flood the South
with their propaganda by transmission through the mails, then it
would be regarded as a "common enemy." It was not for *that* the
several States had conferred upon the General Government the
power to establish post offices and post roads. Bankers in New
York, Philadelphia and Boston were told that if they wanted to safe-
guard loans made to Southerners they had better bestir themselves.
Northern business in general was warned that if it wished to keep
the South as a customer it must silence the Abolitionists.

Federal officialdom responded with alacrity. President Andrew
Jackson in his message to Congress of December 7, 1835, said: "I
would . . . respectfully suggest the propriety of passing such a law
as will prohibit, under severe penalties, the circulation in the
Southern States, through the mail, of incendiary publications
intended to instigate the slaves to insurrection." When the Postmaster General, Amos Kendall, a native of Massachusetts, was informed by the postmaster of Charleston that he had given permission to the Committee of Twenty-One to board mail packets and
confiscate all Abolitionist literature before it reached his office, he
replied: "I cannot sanction and will not condemn the step you have
taken." When the postmaster of New York wrote to him that he
"took the responsibility" for refusing to forward papers mailed by
the American Anti-Slavery Society, he received the reply that
Kendall would do the same if he were in his place.

Business was equally accommodating. Banks and insurance companies undertook to reason with Arthur Tappan, but the stubborn
Puritan proudly replied: "You ask me to betray my principles, to be
false to God and humanity: I will be hanged first." Whether in jest

or in earnest, someone offered five thousand dollars on the New York Stock Exchange for Arthur Tappan's head. A mob appeared out of nowhere and made a furious assault upon his wholesale house, but was beaten back by the employees with little assistance from the authorities. The residence of Lewis Tappan was taken by storm, the costly furniture flung into the street and piled in a heap with the torch applied. Lydia Maria Child wrote from Brooklyn, New York: "I have not ventured into the city, nor does one of us dare to go to church to-day, so great is the excitement here. You can form no conception of it. 'Tis like the times of the French Revolution, when no man dared trust his neighbors. Private assassins from New Orleans are lurking at the corners of the streets to stab Arthur Tappan."

Benjamin Robbins Curtis, future Associate Justice of the Supreme Court of the United States, wrote to his friend George Ticknor, then traveling in Europe: "The topic which engrosses the public attention to the exclusion of almost every other, is the 'Anti-Slavery Society.' . . . Dreadful scenes have already occurred in Mississippi. The mob have hung numerous persons, *suspected* of being emissaries of the Society, without legal trial; and so great have been the commotions excited in many parts of the South, and so excited is the public mind there, that there are strong fears, felt here by the friends of the Union that, unless something is done here to check the abolitionists, and convince the South that the great body of the people of the Northern States are unfavorable to the Society, the Union will not continue for a single year."

There were riots in Washington, Baltimore, Philadelphia and New York, and numerous smaller communities, during which Abolitionists and Negroes were assaulted, Negro churches and schools demolished and other property damaged. In Philadelphia the mob set fire to an orphan asylum for colored children and for three days raged unchecked through the Negro district, looting and burning. In Haverhill, Massachusetts, the rioters rolled a cannon into place to batter down the doors of the Freewill Baptist Church, where May and Whittier spoke.

The business —

> Of letting rapine loose, and murder,
> To go *just so far*, and no further;
> And setting all the land on fire,
> To burn *just so high*, and no higher —

is, however, a venturesome business. The mobs were getting out of hand. In New York and Philadelphia the military finally had to be called to protect people who, if they had not instigated the riots, had looked on complacently as long as Abolitionists and Negroes were the only sufferers. At Charlestown, Massachusetts, the mob sacked and burned the Ursuline Convent, whereupon the Irish of Boston prepared to attack Harvard College, and students organized for defense.

So business took measures to curb the rioting, but only for a while. Whenever the slaveholders demanded renewed action, newspapers would open their campaign of incitement, pulpits would resound with sermons in defense of slavery and denunciations of the Abolitionists, orators would excite the populace with epithets such as "fanatics," "disorganizers," "amalgamationists," "traitors," "Jacobins," "incendiaries," "cutthroats," "infidels" and so on, and the rioting would be resumed. But the Abolitionists never wavered. They would not surrender the right to free speech, freedom of the press and of assembly at the behest of the slaveholders and their Northern allies. And, gradually, by their steadfastness, by their indomitable courage, they gained the respect of some of their severest critics. Dr. William Ellery Channing, whom May once thought it necessary to rebuke for his bitter criticism of the Society, in November, 1836, penned this tribute to the Abolitionists: "To them has been committed the most important bulwark of liberty, and they have acquitted themselves of the trust like men and Christians. Of such men I do not hesitate to say, that they have rendered to freedom a more essential service than any body of men among us . . . From my heart I thank them. I am myself their debtor. I am not sure that I should this moment write in safety, had they shrunk from the conflict, had they shut their lips, imposed silence on their presses, and hid themselves before their ferocious assailants. I thank the Abolitionists that in this evil day they were true to the rights which the multitude were ready to betray. Their purpose to suffer, to die, rather than surrender their dearest liberties, taught the lawless that they had a foe to contend with whom it was not safe to press."

9

It was during a lull in the rioting that George Thompson, Lecturing Agent of the London Anti-Slavery Society, of whom John

Bright and Lord Brougham have said that he, more than any other man, was responsible for emancipation in the British colonies, came to the United States on Garrison's invitation. The immixture of a foreigner in so controversial a domestic problem was bound to be resented. Garrison must have known this. Indeed, Buxton and others had warned him. But it was complacency, not resentment and excitement, he feared. In 1838 he addressed this criticism to David Paul Brown in Philadelphia: "Sir, slavery will not be overthrown without excitement, a most tremendous excitement. And let me say, there is too much quietude in this city. It shows that the upholders of this wicked system have not yet felt that their favorite sin has been much endangered. . . . Your cause will not prosper here — the philosophy of reform forbids you to expect it — until it excites popular tumult, and brings down upon it a shower of brickbats, and rotten eggs, and is threatened with a coat of tar-and-feathers."

When a few days later Pennsylvania Hall was burned by a mob, he wrote to his mother-in-law: "Awful as is this occurrence in Philadelphia, it will do incalculable good to our cause; for the wrath of man worketh not the righteousness of God. Our friends are all in excellent spirits, shouting, Alleluia! for the Lord God omnipotent reigneth! Let the earth rejoice!"

From this, one may infer that what has been called the "Reign of Terror," far from discouraging Garrison, was considered by him a salutary sign, a stirring of life and conscience. If, therefore, he foresaw the excitement George Thompson's coming was likely to create, he must have considered it an additional reason why the visit should take place. He evidently got more than he bargained for, for he was to write: "I supposed he would meet with a good deal of opposition, but I did not invite him to martyrdom. I did not imagine he would be subjected to such diabolical treatment as was afterward shown him."

When Thompson's arrival became known newspaper editors fairly foamed at the mouth. "Itinerant stirrer-up of strife," "Apostle of fanaticism," "Foreign fanatic," "Paid agent of the enemies of republican institutions," were some of the epithets hurled at the visitor. The Richmond *Enquirer* wrote: "It is outrageous enough for Tappan and Garrison to be throwing firebrands into the South — but for that impertinent intruder, Thompson, to mingle in our institutions; for that foreigner, who has nothing American about him, in name, interest or principle — the outrage exceeds all the bounds of patience."

How Thompson managed to hold out for an entire year, speaking night after night, amidst flying brickbats, the crash of shattered glass, jeers, hoots, catcalls and curses, is difficult to comprehend. Once a brick hurled through a window grazed his hair. Twice he was saved from the mob by heroic women, who notwithstanding his protest formed a protective ring around him. Several times he escaped only by being hurried out at a back door, while his friends held back his pursuers. He was quick-witted and sometimes managed to gain the favor of a hostile audience by an apt repartee. When a Southerner shouted: "We wish we had you at the South. We would cut your ears off, if not your head!" he shot back: "Would you? Then should I cry all the louder, 'He that *hath* ears let him hear!'"

Few men tasted sweeter triumph than did George Thompson. When during the Civil War relations between England and the United States became strained, Thompson, then a member of Parliament and the idol of the British working class, left nothing undone to marshal public opinion for the support of the North. He who in 1835 had to be smuggled at night on board a vessel in Boston Harbor to elude a mob, in 1864 was received with public honors and popular acclaim. The degree of Honorary Doctor of Laws was conferred upon him by Wesleyan University, the president and faculty of which had once vilified and denounced him. He addressed a joint meeting of Congress, the President and his Cabinet attending, and was invited to the White House, where Lincoln personally expressed his appreciation.

10

With the exception of New York, where the office of the American Anti-Slavery Society was located at 144 Nassau Street, no other city was as deeply involved in antislavery propaganda as Boston. It was there, in the office of the *Liberator*, that the heart of Abolition pulsated. Boston had better do something if it wished to keep the South's friendship. Fifteen hundred leading citizens signed a call for a mass meeting to be held in Faneuil Hall. Mayor Theodore Lyman Jr. was to preside. Richard Fletcher, a distinguished attorney, Peleg Sprague, former United States Senator, and Garrison's onetime idol Harrison Gray Otis were to be the speakers. Invitations were sent to prominent slaveholders to come and witness Boston's salaam to slavery. Benjamin Robbins Curtis wrote to George Ticknor: "Numerous Southern gentlemen came from all parts of the country to be present at the meeting."

The madman who tried to sweep back the ocean was engaged in no more hopeless task than were the sponsors of the meeting. Fletcher, after being elected to Congress, joined the opponents of slavery in that body. Seth Sprague, Peleg's venerable father, became an ardent Abolitionist and denounced slavery from the same platform on which his son now meant to defend it. Many of those who signed the call for the meeting later joined the antislavery forces. One, Charles F. Hovey, left a large bequest to the Abolitionist movement, naming Garrison and Phillips as two of the administrators. But in the meantime slavery was to have its day in Boston. Garrison wrote in the *Liberator:* "The old Cradle of Liberty, it seems, is to be desecrated by a meeting of the friends of slavery and slave-holders! Better that the lightning of heaven should smite and devour the building — better that the winds should scatter it in fragments over the whole earth — better that an earthquake should engulph it — than that it should be used for so unhallowed and detestable a purpose!"

The meeting should have satisfied the visitors from the South. Denunciations of Garrison and Thompson were so vehement that Garrison's friends implored him to leave the city. He reluctantly consented, since Helen, who was with child, refused to leave without him. After they had left, the city woke up one morning to find a double gallows erected in front of Garrison's house on Brighton Street with the inscription: "For Garrison and Thompson — By Order of Judge Lynch." Nothing less than a hanging party would have satisfied the planters. The Richmond *Whig* declared: "The people of the North must go to hanging these fanatical wretches if they would not lose the benefit of Southern trade; and they will do it."

11

Garrison and Helen returned to Boston after a month's absence, towards the end of September. Much as Garrison favored excitement, he restrained himself sufficiently to abstain from holding public meetings. But then the Boston Female Anti-Slavery Society announced an anniversary meeting at Congress Hall (formerly Julien

Hall) at which George Thompson was to be one of the speakers. There was a growl from the newspapers. What was the use of Faneuil Hall meetings if that "foreign vagrant Thompson and his associates in mischief" were allowed to resume their attacks upon slavery? The *Commercial Gazette* served notice on the Abolitionists that if they attempted to hold a meeting they would meet with determined opposition. "The resistance will not come from a *rabble*, but from men of property and standing, who have a large interest in the community." The proprietor of the hall was prevailed upon to withdraw his consent and the meeting was postponed.

But not for long. The women announced that they would hold their meeting on October 21, 1835, at three o'clock in the afternoon, at the hall adjoining the office of the Anti-Slavery Society at 46 Washington Street. In view of the tenseness of the situation admission would be restricted to members and their guests. No speakers were mentioned in the announcement, but Garrison and Burleigh had been invited to address the gathering. The newspapers took it for granted that Thompson, too, would speak, and indulged in a fresh outburst of vituperation.

About noon on the day of the meeting a handbill made its appearance in the business district calling upon "the friends of the Union to snake Thompson out. A purse of $100 has been raised by a number of patriotic citizens to reward the individual who shall first lay violent hands on Thompson, so that he may be brought to the tar-kettle before dark." If an anonymous letter received by Garrison from a "Well-wisher" is to be believed, there existed a plot to drag him and Thompson to the Common, strip them of their clothing and, by means of acid and indelible ink, dye their faces and hands "in a manner that would never change from a night negro color," after which they were to be tarred and feathered.

While the circular was being distributed, Garrison was dining at home with his wife and a colored friend.[3] He appeared unconcerned, and if Helen felt any anxiety she did not betray it. "Though she was conscious," Garrison wrote, "of the danger to which in all probability I should be exposed, yet she made no plea in advance as to the duty and expediency of my remaining at home, at least for her sake."

At the height of the riot Helen tried to reach the hall, but the

[3] It was then customary in Boston to dine at two o'clock.

crowd was so dense that she was unable to do so. When she learned that Garrison was in the hands of the mob, she quietly said: "I do not believe my husband will be untrue to his principles."

12

The hall in which the meeting was to take place was on the second floor and separated from the office of the Anti-Slavery Society by a wooden partition. A similar partition divided it from the corridor leading to the stairway. The threatening situation had discouraged all but a score of women, white and colored, from putting in an appearance. When Garrison arrived, a hundred or so men and youths were loitering before the building, the entrance to which was guarded by policemen. The officers of the law must have arrived late, for he had to elbow his way through a crowd of young men that filled the stairway and the corridor and overflowed into the hall. There were cries of "That's him! That's Garrison!" but he was not molested.

The President of the Boston Female Anti-Slavery Society, Miss Mary S. Parker, was reading a report, but the crowd in the corridor and around the doorway was so noisy that little could be heard. Moreover, some of the young men were scaling the partition, which threatened to collapse. So Garrison, who had seated himself, rose again, went to the door and said: "Gentlemen, perhaps you are not aware of the fact that this is a meeting of the Boston *Female* Anti-Slavery Society, called and intended exclusively for ladies, and those who have been invited to address them. Understanding this fact, you will not be so rude or indecorous as to thrust your presence upon this meeting. If, gentlemen, any of you are *ladies* in disguise, why, only apprise me of that fact, give me your names, and I will introduce you to the rest of your sex, and you can take seats among them accordingly."

Those who had penetrated into the hall withdrew into the corridor, but they would not permit the door to be shut and swung it back and forth until a hinge broke. The noise, which had somewhat subsided, increased in volume when Burleigh of the long hair and bushy beard put in an appearance. Outside the crowd had swelled and now filled the street from wall to wall. Cries of "Thompson! Thompson!" were hurled up at the windows. Garrison, realizing that his and Burleigh's presence endangered the women, held a consultation with Miss Parker, after which the two men withdrew through the connecting door to the Anti-Slavery office. Garrison sat down at a table, picked up a quill and began writing a letter, but hands now began fumbling at the door giving on the corridor. Soon heavy boots assailed the lower panel, which burst and splintered. Eyes peered and voices cried: "There's Garrison! That's him! Let's get him!"

Garrison put down the pen, turned to Burleigh and said: "Better let them in." His friend went to the door, but instead of unlocking it, took out the key and pocketed it.

In the street below Mayor Lyman had arrived with police reinforcements. He tried to appease the crowd by announcing that Thompson was not in the building. But if Thompson was not, Garrison was. The cries changed to "Garrison! Garrison! Out with him!" The police managed to clear the stairway and the corridor, and Lyman hastened upstairs. Miss Parker had just finished reading a letter from Francis Jackson, a Boston merchant who invited the women to meet at his house if meeting at the hall proved too hazardous.

"Go home, ladies! Go home!" the Mayor cried excitedly.

"What renders it necessary for us to go home?" Miss Parker asked unperturbed.

"I am the Mayor of the city, and I cannot now explain. Do you wish a scene of bloodshed and confusion? If you do not, go home."

Then up rose a tall, beautiful young woman with a casque of golden hair. It was Maria Weston Chapman, wife of Henry Chapman, a well-to-do shipping merchant. Her blue eyes flashed as she said:

"Mr. Lyman, your personal friends are the instigators of this mob; have you ever used your influence with them?"

"I have no personal friends. I am merely an official. Indeed, ladies," he almost pleaded, "you must retire. It is dangerous to remain. If you will go *now*, I shall protect you, but I cannot unless you do."

"If this is the last bulwark of freedom," cried Mrs. Chapman, "we may as well die here as elsewhere."

But not all were as intrepid as she. A motion to adjourn carried.

"Two and two, each with a colored friend, to Francis Jackson's on Hollis Street!" commanded Mrs. Chapman, as accompanied by the Mayor the women marched from the hall.

13

Several Abolitionists had managed to join Garrison, and one loudly declared that he was done with nonresistance. "When the civil arm is powerless, my own rights are trodden into the dust, and the lives of my friends are put in imminent peril by ruffians, I will henceforth defend myself and them at all hazards," he said. Garrison laid his hand on his shoulder and admonished: "Hold, my brother! This is the test of our endurance. Of what value or utility are the principles of peace and forgiveness, if we may repudiate them in the hour of peril and suffering? Do you wish to become like one of those violent and bloodthirsty men who are seeking my life? I will perish sooner than raise my hand against any man even in self-defense, and let none of my friends resort to violence for my protection."

Mayor Lyman, having assured himself that the women were in no danger, now came into the office, not so much to confer with Garrison, as because the mob howled for the wooden signboard reading ANTI-SLAVERY ROOMS.

There is some difference of opinion regarding the Mayor's intention. He has claimed that he gave orders to unhook the sign and take it into the office, lest it become a target for missiles. The fact, however, is that it landed in the street, where it was broken into fragments, which were carried off as souvenirs. Garrison refused to believe that this was due to an accident, and later criticized the Mayor severely for having humored the mob. "If he could have saved my life, or the whole city from destruction by that single act, still he ought not to have obeyed the mandate of the mob — no indeed!" He had no patience with the Mayor, who, he said, "shamefully truckled to wealth and respectability. If it had been a mob of workingmen assaulting a meeting of merchants, no doubt he would have acted with energy and decision, and they would have been routed by force. But broadcloth and money alter the case: they are above the law, and the imperious masters of the poor man."

14

The Mayor advised Garrison to flee. The mob was becoming unmanageable. If the stairway was stormed, the police would be unable to hold it. A window in the corridor gave upon Wilson's Lane. Below the window was the sloping roof of a carpenter's shed. Garrison could drop to the roof of the shed and leave the scene unobserved. He allowed himself to be persuaded. "He appeared," says Burleigh, "as he had done through the whole tumult, calm, collected and cheerful." John Reid Campbell insisted on accompanying him. They dropped to the roof, Garrison almost losing his footing. As they jumped to the ground they saw the mob tearing into the Lane.

The owner of the carpenter shop, Joseph K. Hayes, was one of Garrison's unknown sympathizers. Years later, when Captain of the Watch and Police, he resigned his office rather than aid in the rendition of a fugitive slave. He admitted the two men, locked the door, and told Garrison to run upstairs and hide in the storage loft. He and his workmen would try to hold back his pursuers. Garrison considered further flight useless and wished to surrender to the mob, which already was banging at the door, but finished by going upstairs with Campbell. His friend had him station himself in a corner and placed planks in front of him, hiding him completely from view. No sooner had this been accomplished than a dozen men bounded up the stairway, seized Campbell and demanded to know the whereabouts of Garrison. He replied that he had no intention of telling. They dragged him to the window, exhibited him to the mob and shouted: "This is not Garrison, but a friend of his. He knows where Garrison is, but won't tell."

"Throw him out of the window! We'll take care of him!"

But already Garrison had been found. Who now cared for Campbell? His captors hurried him to the window. A howl of mingled rage and exultation greeted him. He had removed his glasses, and being extremely nearsighted, saw only a blur of faces. "Throw him out! Throw him out!" the mob howled. He called back: "Be patient. I'm coming." A voice close to him said: "Don't let's kill him outright." A rope was looped about his chest. Outside a ladder was placed against the window sill. Garrison was lifted out of the window and, held by the rope, slid down the ladder into the hands of the mob. Before he reached the ground, someone tore off his trousers. His hat fell off and was trampled under. His coat was torn from his body, his shirt torn to tatters. Amidst hoots and shouts he was dragged by the rope down Wilson's Lane towards State Street.

15

Charles Sprague, the banker poet, witnessed three scenes from the window of his office that impressed themselves indelibly in his memory. He saw Garrison dragged by a rope down Wilson's Lane, by a mob hungry to lynch him. He saw Anthony Burns, a fugitive slave, escorted by hundreds of soldiers — infantry, cavalry and artillery — on his way to the steamer that was to take him back to slavery in Virginia, with all Boston trying to save him! He saw the youthful Colonel Robert Gould Shaw riding proudly at the head of the Fifty-fourth Massachusetts, a Negro regiment marching off to war to the tune of "John Brown's Body." Between the first scene and the last, more than a quarter of a century. He thus noted down the first scene: "I saw an exasperated mob dragging a man along without his hat and with a rope about him. The man walked with head erect, calm countenance, flashing eyes, like a martyr going to the stake, full of faith and hope. The crowd turned into State Street, and I saw him no more."

And now two men of gigantic stature, the brothers Daniel and Aaron Cooley, prosperous trucking contractors, seized the prisoner, cast aside the rope and hurried him along. The crowd cheered. What minion of the law could hope to wrest him from the hands of such stalwarts? But what were the Cooleys shouting? "Don't hurt him! He shan't be hurt! He is an American!" And why did they not take him down State Street towards the Common? Why were they rounding the City Hall?

Suddenly realizing that they were being cheated of their prey, the mob surged forward with a howl. But the Cooleys, like swimmers breasting a wave, swept aside the attackers. They gained the stone steps leading to the North entrance of the City Hall, disappeared inside, hurried Garrison up the stairway to the Mayor's office. Lyman, who had followed with several policemen, stationed himself on the stairway and told the pursuers that they would pass only over his dead body. His resolution was not put to the test. The mob, confused and baffled, hesitated to attack.

16

Dressed only in tattered undergarments, but unhurt, Garrison stood in the Mayor's office. It is significant that his grotesque appearance did not tempt any one, either then or later, to be facetious at his expense. On the contrary, Ebenezer Bailey, a proslavery member of the Common Council, when asked how Garrison had behaved, replied: "No man could have done better. He showed perfect courage and self-possession. He was only very absurd in one thing. He kept saying, 'Oh, if they would only hear me five minutes, I am sure I could bring them to reason.' Now, you know, that that was ridiculous, for they were all ready to tear him to pieces." What might well have provoked amusement was his solicitude about his hat. The remainder of his clothing he seemed to have given up for lost, ruefully remarking that it was a "bran'-new" suit he had been wearing, but he kept on asking if anybody had seen his hat. To his disappointment nobody had. A pair of trousers, a coat, a cap, a shirt and a stock were found for him, and his rescuers and the officials present now took counsel about how to proceed further.

The police had cleared the City Hall of intruders, enabling the Mayor to join the conclave in his office. But the crowd showed no disposition to disperse. Lyman climbed onto the ledge outside the window and spoke to the rioters, but without avail. He and Deputy Sheriff Parkman were of the opinion that the only safe place for Garrison was the county jail. Would he consent to be locked up for the night? He said he would "if it did not cost him anything." So the necessary papers were made out, but it was still a question how to transport him to the Leverett Street jail without having him again fall into the hands of the mob. A ruse was resorted to. A two-horse cab drew up before the south entrance and immediately policemen cleared a passage, drawing the crowd to that side of the building. In the meantime a second cab halted before the north entrance and Garrison, flanked by Lyman, Parkman, Bailey and several policemen, emerged from the City Hall. But the arrival of the second cab had not remained unnoticed and a number of rioters rushed forward. Parkman and the policemen grappled with them. Bailey belabored them with his umbrella. Garrison jumped into the cab. The driver swung his whip and the horses set off at a gallop.

The cab crossed Washington Street, plunged into Court Street. Here hands seized the heads of the horses, clung to the wheels. Cries of "Cut the traces! Cut the reins!". . . A rioter jerked open the door . . . A constable flung him aside, jumped in beside Garrison . . . A rope, probably the same that had done service before, dexterously lassoed the cab. Men pulled. For a moment the cab balanced on two wheels, then righted itself as the constable cut the rope. The driver, standing up in his seat, belabored the heads of the assailants and the backs of the horses impartially. Again the horses set off at a gallop. . . . At Bowdoin Square young men blocked the way into Green Street. The driver swung the vehicle into Cambridge Street, apparently racing towards the bridge, then veered into Lynde Street, towards Leverett Street and the county jail. Before the jail, another crowd; but Lyman was there with a force of police. A path was cleared. . . . The jail door opened, and amidst hoots and jeers Garrison entered the strange haven of refuge.

That evening several people called and found him in the best of spirits. The Alcotts came and Whittier, now a member of the Legislature. Garrison told the poet with mock seriousness he was sorry he could not accommodate him in his cell, but would put in a good word for him with the sheriff. Sheriff Sumner, who was Charles Sumner's father, came to pay his respects and Knapp came to tell his partner that Helen had yielded to the entreaties of friends and had left for Canton. When the visitors had departed, Garrison amused himself with decorating the walls of his cell with inscriptions in verse and prose, as once he had done in Baltimore.

He then acceded to the request of the authorities that he leave the city for a few days. Parkman drove him to Canton, where Helen fell into his arms. Together they took the train for Providence; there George Benson received them.

PART TWO

Brothers-in-Arms

CHAPTER I

The Patrician

WHEN the mob besieged the Anti-Slavery Rooms, a tall, fair-haired young lawyer with an office on Court Street, intrigued by the noise from the direction of the City Hall, went to investigate. When he reached the scene of the riot and saw Garrison, almost naked, dragged by a rope down Wilson's Lane, he felt shocked and indignant. Turning to a bystander he inquired: "Who is that man and where are they taking him?"

"That's Garrison," was the reply. "They're going to hang him. Serves him right, the damned Abolitionist!"

The young lawyer belonged to one of the city's most patrician families and was not particularly interested in Abolition, but the reply did not cool his wrath, and noticing John C. Park, colonel of the militia regiment of which he himself was a member, he went up to him and said: "This is a shameful business. Why does the Mayor stand there and argue? Why does he not call out the Regiment? Why does he not call for the guns?"

Pointing to the rioters, the Colonel replied: "The Regiment is in front of you."

Sure enough! Many of the store and office clerks surrounding Garrison and dragging him along were members of the Regiment, as were some of the younger men dressed in broadcloth and wearing tall hats who were brandishing canes and shouting: "Down with him! Lynch him! Hang him!" He saw men whom he was wont to meet in the salons of the city and whom he had heard pay lip-service to law and order encouraging the rioters. While he looked on bewildered, the Cooleys seized Garrison and hurried him towards the City Hall. Believing the riot to be over, the young man turned and walked thoughtfully back to his office.

Such was Wendell Phillips's first contact with the movement in the leadership of which he was ultimately to supplant Garrison.

2

He was born in Boston, on November 29, 1811, the eighth of nine children. His father, John Phillips, had been an important man in the political and social life of the city and State, having been Public Prosecutor, Member of the House of Representatives, State Senator and Judge of the Court of Common Pleas. At the time of his death in 1823 he was Mayor of Boston, the first elected to that office after the community acquired a city charter. Wendell's mother, Sally Walley, was the daughter of a prosperous Boston merchant. The family mansion on the corner of Beacon and Walnut Streets, overlooking the Common, was one of the most imposing in the city.

Behind John Phillips were five generations of American ancestors — ministers, merchants, statesmen, soldiers. The founder of the American branch of the family was the Reverend George Phillips, of Boxted, Essex County, England, a gentleman by birth and a graduate of Cambridge. He came to the New World in 1630 on the *Arbella*, in the company of Isaac Johnson, Richard Saltonstall and Governor Winthrop, founded a church at Watertown (now a part of Boston) and helped Winthrop govern the colony. He was a stern Puritan and has been quoted by Wendell as having said: "If you think me a minister by the calling they gave me in England, I will throw off my robe, for a corrupt church cannot make a true minister." George Phillips's son, the Reverend Samuel Phillips, was one of Harvard's earliest graduates and when past sixty suffered a short imprisonment for calling Randolph "a wicked man." One of his grandsons became Lieutenant Governor and together with a brother founded the Phillips Academies at Andover, Massachusetts, and Exeter, New Hampshire, besides endowing the Chair of Theology at Dartmouth College. Wendell's father, descended from a collateral branch, was reared at the house of his granduncle the Lieutenant Governor, his own father having died when he was two. He attended the Phillips Academy at Andover, and was graduated from Harvard. He had a reputation for eloquence and in 1794 delivered a Fourth of July oration part of which found its way into schoolbooks and was declaimed by several generations of Boston schoolboys. When a member of the convention for the revision of the State constitution, he remarked: "I hope our case may not be like that of a man whose epitaph may be read in an Italian church-yard: 'I was well; I wanted to be better; I took medicine and here I lie!' "

Wendell Phillips's mother was an orthodox Calvinist, but her husband appears to have rebelled against the authority of the Church, for in 1860 Wendell was to say: "I would never join one of those petty despotisms which usurp in our day the name of a Christian Church. I would never put my neck into that yoke of ignorance and superstition led by a Yankee Pope, and give my good name as a football for their spleen and bigotry. That lesson I learned of my father long before boyhood ceased." More than any doctrinal tenet his mother impressed this maxim upon him: "Be good and do good. Add other things if you may — these are central." His father bade him be faithful to the maxim: "Never ask another to do for you what you would not do for yourself, if you could." He taught him the use of carpenter's tools, with which Phillips became so expert that his mother used to say: "A good carpenter was lost when Wendell became a lawyer."

The boy showed an early inclination towards oratory. When he was five his favorite amusement was to arrange the dining room chairs to represent an audience, open the family Bible and proceed to address them. When his father asked: "Wendell, don't you get tired of this?" he replied: "No, Papa, I don't get tired, but it's rather hard on the chairs."

Edward Everett Hale assures us that his parents would as soon have sent him to jail as to a public school. The usual educational pilgrimage of the son of a Boston patrician was by way of the Boston Latin School to Harvard and Harvard Law School. A boy could not enter the Latin School until he was nine, was able to read and write and had some knowledge of English grammar. Phillips was sent to the private school of Mr. Farrar to acquire these rudiments and did not enter the Latin School until he was ten. His favorite playmates at that time were John Lothrop Motley, future historian of the Netherlands, and Thomas Gold Appleton, son of a pioneer manufacturer. They usually played in the Motley attic, where there were ancient chests filled with colonial finery — cloaks, doublets and plumed hats — which served for the enactment of "more or less impromptu melodramas." Fantastically arrayed, they would strut about the attic flinging high-flown phrases and scraps of verse at one another. Appleton informs us that even then Phillips's voice was "very pleasant to listen to and his gestures as graceful as could be."

Motley's imagination was so fired by this play acting that he set to work on a romantic novel of which he finished two chapters. "It opened," wrote Phillips, "not with 'one solitary horseman,' but with two, riding up to an inn, in the Valley of the Housatonic. Neither of us had ever seen the Housatonic, but it sounded grand and romantic."

3

The Boston Latin School, founded in 1635, which "dandled Harvard College on its knee," was located on the corner of Chapman Place and School Street. The headmaster was Benjamin Apthorp Gould. The boys were summoned to classes in summer at eight, in winter at nine by the bell in the little belfry. The institution lived up to its promise of a classical education. Only three or four of some two dozen textbooks were in English, the others in Greek or Latin. Not until 1821, the year Phillips became a pupil, was there an English department at the school. Athletics formed no part of the curriculum and the scholars were cautioned against playing on the Common, where they would be exposed to contact with the lower classes. Such plebeian amusements as swimming in the Charles in summer and skating or throwing snowballs in winter were likewise taboo. The result was that the rising generation of genteel Bostonians were a rather puny lot, no match for the "port chucks," as the pugnacious boys of that boisterous quarter were called. But to this Phillips was a conspicuous exception. He was tall for his age, well-formed, handsome and vigorous. If kicking a football about on the Common was considered vulgar, surely there could be no objection to his taking fencing and boxing lessons, and he insisted on doing so. He went rowing on the Charles, hunted and was often seen on horseback. One of his colleagues at the Latin School has said that he ranked high among the students on account of his "beauty, elegant manners and social position." Motley had been sent to the historian Bancroft's Round Hill school at Northampton, but Phillips acquired a new friend in Charles Sumner. He tried to interest him in athletics, but found him "a recluse and a studious boy."

Declamation received particular attention at the Boston Latin School. There were five public declamations a year, to which parents and friends of the pupils were invited. The boys who made the best showing took part in the annual prize declamations. The favorite orations were, in English, Patrick Henry's "Call to Arms" and Daniel Webster's "Appeal for Union"; in Latin, Cicero's "Arraignment of Catiline." Phillips took part in two prize declamations and both times received a prize, but not the first prize. Apparently some of the pupils had more discernment than the faculty. "What first led me to observe him and fixed him in my memory," wrote one of his fellow students, "was his elocution; and I came to look forward to declamation day with interest, mainly on his account, though there were many admirable speakers."

Theodore D. Weld has said that as a boy Phillips was subject to bursts of temper so extravagant that his schoolmates would sometimes provoke him to see him fly into a rage. When he was fourteen, however, he went to a revival at the Hanover Street Church, where Dr. Lyman Beecher's sulfurous exhortations so impressed him that back in his room he fell on his knees and begged God to accept him. "From that day to this," he said shortly before his death, "whenever I have known a thing to be wrong, it has held no temptation. Whenever I have known it to be right, it has taken no courage to do it."

4

Phillips was not yet sixteen when he entered Harvard College. His father had died and his mother decided that he should live in Cambridge. The College had few buildings. The library was in Harvard Hall, in the belfry of which hung the college bell. The students' rooms were bare and cheerless. A few had fireplaces, but the majority of the students had to be content in winter with a calorific radiant in which was placed a cannon ball heated an angry red. A favorite prank was to shatter the silence of the night by sending one of these balls bouncing down the stairway.

There were some two hundred students in the college proper — the "Seminary," as President Quincy called it. Three fourths boarded at Commons Hall, paying three dollars per week — "a large sum," George Ripley wrote to his mother. There was a perpetual feud between the students and the contractor who supplied the food, the inadequacy of which may have been responsible for a habit the students had of robbing gardens and hen roosts. "I can recall members of my class, afterwards grave dignitaries," wrote Thomas

Wentworth Higginson, "who used to go out in small parties on autumn evenings with large baskets, and bring them back laden with apples, pears, grapes and melons from the region now known as Belmont." Chickens were roasted by being suspended from a string before one of the rare fireplaces in a student's room. A favorite treat was a concoction of corn meal, nutmeg, ginger, eggs, water, molasses and butter, cooked in an iron pot. Harvard's Hasty Pudding Club was named in honor of this delicacy.

Phillips was spared most of the discomfort. His family could well afford to provide him with the best. Higginson, whose brother was at the college at the same time as Phillips, assures us that he "was the only student of that period for whom a family carriage was habitually sent out to Cambridge on Saturday morning to bring him into Boston for Sunday." He became a member of Phi Beta Kappa and belonged to the best student clubs — the Porcellian, the Gentlemen's Club, the Owl Club, the Hasty Pudding Club. The first two, which admitted only members of the *jeunesse dorée* and to which many sons of wealthy Southern planters belonged, elected him president. "I never asked him what he thought of Southern pride and assumption in those days," wrote his fellow student, the Reverend Edgar Buckingham, "but was it not singular that, from having been the most admired companion and most ardent champion of Southern men in his youth, he should have become in after years an opponent of Southern principles, than whom there has been none more powerful in the country?"

In his Journal Emerson expressed an unfavorable opinion of Harvard's Southern contingent. "The young Southerner," he wrote, "comes here a spoiled child . . . very good to be spoiled more, but good for nothing else, — a mere parader. He has conversed so much with rifles, horses and dogs that he has become himself a rifle, a horse and a dog, and in civil, educated company, where anything human is going forward, he is dumb and unhappy, like an Indian in a church. . . . Their question respecting any man is like a Seminole's — How can he fight? In this country, we ask, What can he do? His pugnacity is all they prize in a man, dog, or turkey." That a young man of Emerson's temperament, lacking (as he himself has ruefully confessed) all "animal spirits," could find little charm in such company is understandable. It was otherwise with Phillips. While one side of his nature found satisfaction in intercourse with brilliant young Motley, studious Charles Sumner and witty Edmund

Quincy, son of the President of the University, another side was charmed by the Southern *joie de vivre*. Like his Southern friends he enjoyed fencing and hunting, and he liked horses so well that he made a personal friend of a horse trainer named Rarey. Although later a temperance advocate, he enjoyed drinking as a student, and when a proposal was made to organize a temperance society at the College, he took the floor against it and managed to defeat it. As for slavery, Sumner tells us that he and Phillips discussed the subject sometimes, but that neither had the faintest notion to what extent it would later absorb them.

So, according to his friend Buckingham, Phillips became "the especial pet of the aristocracy. . . . Indeed, he had the credit of being their leader." This was resented by the Commons, and when he stood for captain of the Harvard military organization, the Washington Corps, he was defeated. Having taken him down a peg, the students relented and elected him adjutant and later first lieutenant. He cut a fine figure in a black coat with brass buttons, white trousers and feathered shako. On festive occasions the Corps would march proudly to Porter's Tavern, in what later became North Cambridge, to partake of an ample repast and of its famous potation, a frothy flip made of ale, rum and seasonings. The concoction was so much to their taste that (Higginson assures us) the return from the tavern was seldom "regular and decorous" and afforded much amusement to the community.

5

"The true teacher," said Bronson Alcott, "defends his pupils against his own influence. He inspires self-trust. He guides their eyes from himself to the spirit that quickens him. He will have no disciples. A noble artist, he has visions of excellence and revelations of beauty which he has neither impersonated in character nor embodied in words. His life and teachings are but studies for yet nobler ideals." Emerson, about whom it has been said that he was to Alcott what Plato was to Socrates, wrote in his Journal: "I have been writing and speaking what were once called novelties, for twenty-five or thirty years, and I have not now one disciple. Why? Not because what I said was not true; not that it has not found intelligent receivers; but because it did not go from any wish in me to bring men to me, but to themselves. I delight in driving them from me . . .

This is my boast that I have no school follower. I should account it a measure of the impurity of insight, if it did not create independence."

Such, however, was not the opinion of those in authority at Harvard. On a public occasion President Quincy illustrated his method of dealing with undergraduates with this quotation from Matt Prior:

> Be to their faults a little blind;
> Be to their virtues very kind;
> And clap your padlock on the mind!

Little wonder that Emerson exclaimed: "There is not the slightest possibility that the college will foster eminent talent in any youth. If he refuses prayers and recitations, they will torment and traduce and expel him, though he were a Newton or a Dante." Phillips was to say: "Would any young enthusiast on fire with a new reform be crazy enough to go to State Street, Beacon Street or Harvard College for countenance? If so, he must be *very* young, and will soon learn better."

The college authorities took particular care that the students did not "refuse prayer." Attendance at morning and evening chapel was obligatory. Morning chapel was at six, and President Quincy, who was in the habit of rising at four and as a consequence sometimes fell asleep on the most unexpected occasions, always attended. An instructor in a kind of elevated sentry box surveyed the auditorium and noted down the names of those who failed to show proper devotion. Phillips went to chapel willingly. The effect of his conversion had not yet worn off. In his room the Bible lay always open on the table, and Dr. Buckingham has testified: "I remember well his appearance of deep devoutness during morning and evening prayers in the chapel, which so many attended only to save their credit with the government." He and his friend Motley managed, however, to resist having a padlock clapped on their minds. Once when Phillips was in Motley's room, the latter's tutor entered and found the table littered with novels. He elevated his eyebrows and said: "How is this?"

Motley, not in the least disconcerted, replied: "Well, you see, I am pursuing a course of historical reading. I have now reached the novels of the nineteenth century. Take them in bulk, they are tough reading."

He was "rusticated" for a time, but remained unrepentant. "In his room," wrote Phillips, "he had a small writing table with a shallow drawer. I have often seen it half-full of sketches, unfinished poems, soliloquies, a scene or two of a play, prose portraits of pet characters, etc. These he would read to me, though he never volunteered to do so; and every now and then he burned the whole, and began to fill the drawer again."

Phillips had his own idea of preparing for his future career, which he envisaged as neither of an agitator nor of a successful lawyer. "His dream would have been a life in the United States Senate, as he himself told me," Higginson wrote in a letter. His classmate Dr. Morrison wrote: "He was always studying remarkable passages as an exercise in composition, and to secure the most expressive forms of language. In this he did not accept the aid of teachers. His method was his own." There were no elective studies in those days, but when Phillips did not feel like applying himself to a particular subject he usually managed to find a way to neglect it. He had no taste for Spanish and managed to avoid serious study of the language by getting the professor, a former Spanish revolutionary, to devote most of his time to relating his revolutionary adventures. He studied mathematics, history, natural and moral philosophy, composition, rhetoric and forensics. He neglected Greek, but devoted much time to Latin, learned to read and speak French fluently and acquired a working knowledge of German. He was a good student. He had graduated from Latin School fourth in a class of twenty-nine, and was to graduate from Harvard eighth in a class of sixty-five.

He devoted a year to the study of English history, especially at the time of the Civil War. It was not in his nature to delve into things profoundly. According to Higginson he himself said that he knew but one thing thoroughly — the history of the English Revolution. Speaking before his Alma Mater when an old man, he said: "When I was a student here, my favorite study was history. The world and affairs have shown me that one half of history is loose conjecture, and much of the rest is the writer's opinion. But most men see facts, not with their eyes, but with their prejudices. Any one familiar with courts will testify how rare it is for an honest man to give a perfectly correct account of a transaction. We are tempted to see facts as we think they ought to be, or wish they were. And yet journals are the favorite original sources of history."

His favorite authors were, in Latin, Tacitus and Juvenal; in French, Sully, Rochefoucauld, de Retz, Pascal, Fénelon, de Tocqueville, Guizot and Hugo; in English, Richardson, Scott, Swift, Johnson, Taylor, Messinger, Milton, Southey, Lamb, Elizabeth Barrett Browning, Disraeli and Walpole. He had a prodigious memory and his speeches and lectures are replete with quotations. As many as twenty-one have been counted in a single lecture. Yet he showed a curious contempt for "book-learning." In the address before his Alma Mater he was to say: "What is education? Of course it is not book-learning. Book-learning does not make five per cent of that mass of common sense that 'runs' the world, transacts its business, secures its progress, trebles its power over Nature, works out in the long run a rough average justice, wears away the world's restraints, and lifts up its burden. . . . Almost all the great truths relating to society were not the result of scholarly meditation, 'hiving up wisdom with each curious year,' but have been first heard in the solemn protests of martyred patriotism and the loud cries of crushed and starving labor. When common sense and the common people have stereotyped a principle into a statute, then book-men come to explain how it was discovered and on what ground it rests. The world makes history, and scholars write it, — one half truly, and the other half as their prejudices blur and distort it."

It does not appear that it was necessary to burn the midnight oil to keep up with studies at Harvard. George Ripley wrote to his mother: "I am not obliged to study at all hard to perform the exercises allotted me. At present our lessons can all be learnt in three, or at most four hours."

6

When someone asked Phillips how it happened there was so much learning at Cambridge, he replied: "Because nobody carries any away." Yet he did carry away something of great value — the teachings of Edward T. Channing, Boylston Professor of Rhetoric and Oratory, who stood almost alone in combating the spread-eagle style of public address fashionable at that time, and dared to express his dislike of the pompous oratory of Daniel Webster and Edward Everett.

> Channing, with his bland, superior look,
> Cold as a moonbeam on a frozen brook,
> While the pale student, shivering in his shoes,
> Sees from his theme the turgid rhetoric ooze . . .

sang Oliver Wendell Holmes. He insisted on directness and simplicity in the written and spoken word: "I believe that showy writing is always cold, and reaches but a very little way below the surfaces of men's minds." He agreed with Samuel Johnson that when an author has written a page which appears to him especially eloquent the best place for it is the wastepaper basket. When a student spoke in a composition about "Afric's sable sons," Channing drew a determined line through the words and substituted "negroes." He liked the blunt Anglo-Saxon word, the terse, pointed sentence, without adornment or circumlocution. He "hated a purple patch as he hated the devil." How greatly Phillips profited by this teaching is evident from his speeches. Simplicity is their hallmark. Ninety per cent of the words he uses are of two syllables or less. His average sentence is composed of twenty-three words and conveys the thought it was meant to convey as unmistakably as a rifleshot.

Still another lesson Channing tried to impress upon his pupils: sincerity and uncompromising devotion to principle. He found an apt pupil in Phillips, whose favorite motto became: "One with God is a majority." But in his student days Phillips was far from being a radical. In 1830 and again in 1831, he took part in "public exhibitions" at Harvard. On the second occasion, at the Commencement Exercises, he supported the negative of the question, "Will the Present Proposed Parliamentary Reform Endanger the Monarchical and Aristocratical Portions of the British Constitution?" His contention was that it would not, but that the admission of wealthy merchants and manufacturers to the ranks of the nobility would benefit that class, many of whose members had become impoverished: "Wealth, the evidence of personal industry and skill . . . entitles a man to admission to its [the nobility's] ranks."

In 1830, when he supported the negative of the question, "Whether Attachment to Ancient Usages Be a Greater Evil than Fondness of Innovation," he had this to say concerning the French Revolution:

"Insanity was listened to as wisdom. The vilest were exalted to power. Every mad suggestion was carried into practice . . . And what was the result? When the interests of millions had been sacrificed to the madness of rulers, when the resources of a great nation had been wasted in civil commotion, when the blood of the bravest and best had been shed in torrents, an exhausted people surrendered themselves to a despotism and a despot, compared with which the former government was freedom, their former ruler an angel of light. And this is innovation! Witness the wide wasting spirit of change."

He was not yet nineteen when he said that. More than half a century later, he again spoke at Harvard, at the Phi Beta Kappa Centennial Anniversary, attended by delegates from nearly every university in the country and by the foremost scholars and literary men of the land. Again he referred to the French Revolution, this time in these terms:

". . . The French Revolution, the greatest, the most unmixed, the most unstained and wholly perfect blessing Europe has had in modern times, unless we may possibly except the Reformation and the invention of printing . . . 'It is unfortunate,' says Jefferson, 'that the efforts of mankind to secure the freedom of which they have been deprived, should be accompanied with violence and even with crime. But while we weep over the means, we must pray for the end.' Pray fearlessly for such ends; there is no risk! 'Men are all tories by nature,' says Arnold, 'when tolerably well off; only monstrous injustice and atrocious cruelty can rouse them.' Some talk of the rashness of the uneducated classes. Alas! ignorance is far oftener obstinate than rash. Against one French Revolution — that scarecrow of the ages — weigh Asia, 'carved in stone,' and a thousand years of Europe, with her half-dozen nations meted out and trodden down to be the dull and contented footstools of priests and kings . . . Bentham's conclusion, from a survey of five hundred years of European history, was, 'Only by making the ruling few uneasy can the oppressed many obtain a particle of relief.' "

Clemenceau said that he did not think much of a man who at twenty was not a Socialist. Phillips was a conservative at twenty; but by the time he was sixty he was sufficiently radical to have been claimed as a convert by followers of Karl Marx.

7

Phillips was graduated from Harvard College on August 31, 1831, with the degree of Bachelor of Arts. That same year he entered Harvard Law School. He took up the study of law without great enthusiasm, one of a class of forty. "If I had followed my own bent, I should have given my time to mechanics or history," he was to say.

The guiding spirit of Harvard Law School was Judge Joseph Story, who had resigned from the Supreme Court of the United States to become a professor at Harvard at an annual salary of one thousand dollars. Later in his career Phillips took issue with Judge Story on several occasions. This should not surprise us, considering that when, after the attempt to lynch Garrison, Harriet Martineau asked the jurist "whether there was not a public prosecutor who might prosecute the assault, if the abolitionists did not, [he] replied that he had given his advice (which had been formally asked) against any notice whatever being taken of the outrage, — the feeling being so strong against the discussion of slavery, and the rioters being so respectable in the city." But in his student days Phillips was fond of Story. No stuffed shirt was the Judge, but a pleasant-faced, amiable talkative man, short, stocky, bald (except for a tuft of hair in front, which he was in the habit of raking with a pocketcomb), fond of a joke and brimful of youthful enthusiasm. When Fanny Kemble, the famous British actress, came to Boston and students pawned their belongings to be able to feast their eyes upon her, Judge Story was almost equally enthusiastic and lauded her in the classroom.

Phillips, inoculated with Dr. Beecher's horror of the theater, asked: "Judge Story, you come from Puritan ancestors. How do you reconcile all this theatergoing with their teachings?"

The great jurist replied ecstatically: "I do not try to reconcile it. I only thank God I am alive in the same era with such a woman."

One day John Quincy Adams, who was a member of the Board of Overseers of Harvard and as matutinal in his habits as Josiah Quincy, came in during a lecture accompanied by the president of the College. The two visitors were shown to chairs on the dais and Judge Story went on with his lecture. After a while he noticed that the students seemed strangely amused. Glancing at the two visitors he saw that both were peacefully slumbering. "Gentlemen, you see before you a melancholy example of the evil effects of early rising," said Story and resumed his discourse.

8

Phillips was twenty-three when he was graduated from Harvard Law School and admitted to the bar. A fine figure of a man — six feet tall, deep-chested, broad-shouldered and with a soldierly bearing.[1] His complexion was ruddy. His reddish-blond hair waved back from a high, domed forehead. His gray-blue eyes, small and piercing, had a kindly twinkle. His aquiline nose gave force and dignity to his countenance. His well-formed lips, which he was in the habit of compressing, and his firm rounded chin spoke of resolution. "To my mind," wrote his college friend Dr. Buckingham, "he was the most beautiful person I had ever seen, handsome, indeed, in form and feature . . . a young Apollo. I remember, in his room, measurements were made of him to see how near his proportions came to that example of Grecian ideas of manly beauty."

His clothing was in keeping with his personality. The Boston *Transcript* spoke of the "studied negligence" of his clothing and his partiality for "slouched hats and slouched coats." His friend James Redpath wrote, "Phillips is always well-dressed — not a speck on his clothing, and yet you can never remember what he wears"; his friend Carlos Martyn, "He had the enviable faculty, often commented upon, of never having his garments appear either shabby or new. . . . He was never seen in a 'loud' cravat or ultra coat."

All his life he retained the bearing and manner of the aristocrat. A titled Englishman visiting Boston said to George Ticknor, pointing towards two men walking together down Park Street: "They are the only two men I have seen in your country who look like gentlemen." The two were Wendell Phillips and his friend Edmund Quincy. Once when Phillips was told that the members of a certain club in the city had spoken disparagingly of a speech he had made, the champion of the slave and of labor replied haughtily: "They are men of no family." James Redpath remarked: "No one can say that he is condescending — for he isn't — nor haughty, for he is haughty only to the powerful and great; but somehow I have often heard workingmen say he seemed to them as if he were not of them, and they were puzzled to understand his advocacy of their cause."

But the cause of labor no more than that of the slave troubled Phillips when he was graduated from Law School. He spent nearly a year in Lowell working in Thomas Hopkinson's office, then returned to Boston, rented desk space in a law office on Court Street and hung

---

[1] Phillips's biographers give his height as five feet, ten inches. In a letter to Mr. and Mrs. Sargent, January 1, 1879, Phillips wrote: "Ask Ann to show you my description: — Six feet in my socks — sixty-eight years old — and with 'squirrel tails' for whiskers."

out his shingle. He did reasonably well, paying all his expenses during the two years he remained in practice. But his heart was not in the work. "Very much was office work, drawing up legal papers, wills, etc.," Ann Phillips has said. It was a public career that attracted him. That he could have been successful as a lawyer admits of no doubt. His carefully reasoned and elaborately documented argument before a legislative committee for the impeachment of Judge Loring proves his legal ability. Charles Sumner has said: "When Mr. Phillips became an Abolitionist he withdrew from the roll of Massachusetts lawyers the name of one who would have been among the greatest."

It was while he sat in his office in Court Street that the noise of the mob besieging the Anti-Slavery Rooms drew him towards the City Hall, where he witnessed the attack on Garrison, but it should not be supposed that this immediately turned him into an Abolitionist. "I did not understand anti-slavery then," he was to say twenty years later; "that is I did not understand the country in which I lived. My eyes were sealed, so that, although I knew the Adamses and Otises of 1776, and the Mary Dyers and Ann Hutchinsons of older times, I could not recognize the Adamses and Otises, the Dyers and Hutchinsons, whom I met in the street of '35." However, he as well as Sumner was now definitely interested. A couple of months after the riot, Sumner wrote to his friend Dr. Lieber, in Europe: "We are becoming abolitionists at the North fast; the riots, the attempts to abridge the freedom of discussion . . . and the conduct of the South generally have caused many to think favorably of immediate emancipation who never before inclined to it."

9

One day, in the early spring of 1836, Sumner was visiting Phillips in his office when their mutual friend Alford entered and told them of his engagement to Miss Mary Grew of Greenfield. Congratulations were offered, affording Alford an opportunity to state the real purpose of his visit. "I am going to Greenfield with my *fiancée* tomorrow," he said, "and a cousin of hers, a Miss Ann Terry Greene, is to accompany us. Now you know that in my condition 'two's company,' etc, and I wish you would go, both of you, and take care of the other lady. She will require the two of you, for she is the aurora borealis in human form — the cleverest, loveliest girl you ever

met. But I warn you that she is a rabid Abolitionist. Look out or she
will talk you both into that *ism* before you suspect what she is at."

Sumner turned to Phillips and said: "It's but fair to help him out.
Do as you'd be done by, eh, Wendell?"

Phillips was not averse to meeting a young woman described in
such glowing terms and promised to be on hand. Sumner also promised, but when early the following morning he looked out at the
window and saw flurries of rain and snow driven by an easterly
wind, he exclaimed ungallantly: "I won't go on a stage ride on such
a day as this for any woman!" and went back to bed. Perhaps he
thought that he would be a fifth wheel anyway, and as it turned out
he would have been, for no sooner had Phillips and Miss Greene
laid eyes upon each other than all the rest of the world receded into
the background. "When I first met Wendell," she was to say, "I
used to think, 'It can never come to pass; such a being as he could
never think of me.' I looked upon it as something as strange as a
fairy-tale." As Alford had predicted, she could not keep quiet about
Abolition: "I talked Abolition to him all the way up — all the time
there." She must have talked it exceedingly well, for Phillips was
too good a conversationalist to have enjoyed idle chatter. He learned
that she was an orphan, the daughter of a wealthy shipping merchant, and had been reared by Mrs. Chapman, her father's cousin by
marriage, whom she had accompanied to the Anti-Slavery Rooms
the day of the riot. "He came again and it sealed his fate," she wrote.
It sealed it in more ways than one: he fell in love and became an
Abolitionist. "My wife made an Abolitionist out of me; and she always preceded me in the adoption of the various causes I have advocated," he was to say later.

Carlos Martyn, who knew Ann, has written: "She had then and
ever retained a singular transparent beauty — blue eyes, magnificent
long hair, Hebe's complexion, and the form of a Juno." A school
friend of the young woman wrote that she had "a good color, a
strong voice and a hearty laugh." But this apparent good health was
deceptive. Since childhood she had been often confined to bed as a
result of a mysterious malady, which the Phillips family physician,
Dr. David Thayer, diagnosed somewhat inconclusively as "a defect
of nervous organization." This, however, did not discourage Phillips. His friend Thomas Appleton wrote: "He called upon her often
. . . but was not admitted, owing to her feeble health; but finally
he almost broke his way to her and offered her his hand. She said

that she would never marry a man unless he would swear eternal enmity to slavery." He replied: "My life shall attest the sincerity of my conversion." She must have had a foreboding of the lifelong care she would require, for she attempted to discourage him: "When we were engaged I used to say 'now are you sure you are not deceiving yourself? I am not what you think. Break it off if you want to.' "

It was at the Chapman house, in what was then Chauncy Place, that Phillips first met Garrison. A curious contrast between the two men! One tall, blond, a Harvard graduate and a man of the world — the other dark, bald, bespectacled, looking "more like the typical New England minister of the Gospel, than the relentless agitator that he was," the self-taught son of a drunken seaman. Yet according to Phillips's own testimony, Garrison's influence upon him was greater than that of any man. Ten years after the meeting he wrote to him: "I owe you, dear Garrison, more than you would let me express — my mother and my wife excepted, — more than to anyone."

10

Phillips joined the Massachusetts Anti-Slavery Society, and on March 28, 1837, at the society's quarterly meeting in Lynn, publicly identified himself with the Abolitionist movement — a momentous step that changed the entire course of his life. To the Boston Brahmins, Abolitionists were dangerous revolutionaries, Jacobins who assailed an important form of private property, to which other forms of such property were intimately related. That a scion of so old and honorable a family should so far forget himself as to join such a movement was considered a public scandal. People whom Phillips had known since childhood ignored him on the street. He ceased to be invited. His mother was deeply grieved. "My good, noble, dear mother, we differed utterly on the matter of slavery. She grieved a good deal over what she thought was a waste of my time and a sad disappointment to her," he wrote after her death in 1845. His brothers and sisters were not only grieved, but angry. Carlos Martyn has written that Phillips's later interest in lunacy reform was partly due to the fact that attempts were made to have him confined in a sanitarium as a lunatic, not a difficult matter at that time. He escaped that fate, but had written *Finis* to a promising legal career, and had to abandon all political ambition. "Born of six generations of Yankees, I knew the way to office and turned my back on it thirty years ago," he was to say. A few wealthy Bostonians realized the sacrifice he had made, and respected him for it. One later said to Higginson: "I am no Abolitionist, and yet, I never meet Wendell Phillips in the street without wanting to pull my hat off to him. For I remember what he might have been, had he sacrificed like the rest of us, his scruples to his ambition." The Boston *Daily Globe* wrote after his death: "He was the one man in a million who would cut loose from such surroundings, turn his back on such a brilliant outlook."

On October 12, 1837, Phillips and Ann Greene were quietly married. Soon after the wedding the incident occurred that made his name known to opponents of slavery throughout the land.

11

Elijah P. Lovejoy was a Presbyterian minister, a native of Maine and a graduate of Waterville College. As editor of the St. Louis *Observer*, a religious publication, he advocated gradual emancipation by action of the Slave States. Yet had Garrison himself come to wave his flaming sword in St. Louis, he could not have met with fiercer opposition. So menacing became the attitude of the proslavery element, that influential men who had pledged their support to the paper begged the editor to desist. He replied: "I deem it my duty to take my stand upon the Constitution. Here is firm ground; I feel it to be such; and I do most respectfully, but decidedly declare to you my fixed determination to maintain this ground. We have slaves it is true, but I am not one."

One day a St. Louis Negro killed a police officer while resisting arrest. A mob formed, broke into the prison, seized the prisoner, chained him to a tree and burned him to death. Several members of the mob were arrested, but were released when the judge, whose name not inappropriately was Lawless, thus instructed the Grand Jury: "When men are hurried by some mysterious, metaphysical, electric frenzy to commit a deed of violence, they are absolved from guilt. If you should find that such was the fact in this case, then act not at all. The case transcends your jurisdiction; it is beyond the reach of human law." Lovejoy condemned the lynching and the judge's instructions, whereupon a new mob formed, invaded his printing office during his absence and destroyed everything of value.

The rioters then marched to the suburb where the editor lived with his wife's mother. The heroism of his wife, who barred the way to the intruders while he made his escape, alone saved him from a coat of tar and feathers.

He now decided to move the paper to Alton, Illinois, some thirty miles up the Mississippi. With the help of friends he acquired a new press and shipped it by boat to Alton. But the arm of the Slave Power was long. The population of Alton being mostly of Southern origin, it was not difficult to prepare a warm reception for him. No sooner had the press been landed than a mob seized it and threw it into the Mississippi. A second and a third press met the same fate, while the house into which the editor moved with his family had to withstand a nightly shower of stones and filth.

When it became known that Lovejoy had managed to raise money to purchase still another press and that its arrival was momentarily expected, a mass meeting was called. Several speakers expressed their sympathy with the editor, who, they said, was an honorable man and had broken no law. Nevertheless they were of the opinion that he was a disturbing element in the community and a resolution was presented asking him to leave. Before it was put to a vote, he was given an opportunity to address the meeting. An eyewitness related that when he finished speaking many were in tears and that, but for a speech made by a ministerial colleague, who bade him remember that Paul had considered it no disgrace to flee from Damascus, the resolution would have been defeated.

Lovejoy said, in part:

"Think not that I would lightly go contrary to public sentiment around me. The good opinion of my fellowmen is dear to me, and I would sacrifice anything but principles to obtain their good wishes; but when they ask me to surrender this, they ask for more than I can, than I dare give.

"God in his providence has devolved upon me the responsibility of maintaining my ground here; and, Mr. Chairman, I am determined to do it. A voice comes to me from Maine, from Massachusetts, from Connecticut, from New York, from Pennsylvania — yea, from Kentucky, from Mississippi, from Missouri — calling upon me, in the name of all that is dear in heaven or earth, to stand fast; and, by the help of God, I will stand.

"Why should I flee from Alton? Is not this a free state? When

assailed by a mob at St. Louis I came hither, as to the home of freedom and of the laws. The mob has pursued me here, and why
should I retreat again? When can I be safe, if not here? Have not
I a right to claim the protection of the laws? What more can I have
in any other place? Sir, the very act of retreating will embolden
the mob to follow me wherever I go: No, sir, the contest has commenced here; and here it must be finished. Before God and you all,
I here pledge myself to continue it, if need be, till death. If I fall,
my grave shall be made in Alton."

On a bluff overlooking the town and the river there is a grave
marked by a simple monument with this inscription:

HIC JACET
LOVEJOY
Jam parce sepulto [2]

Lovejoy died, struck by five bullets, while with the aid of a handful of friends — a *posse comitatus* empowered by the Mayor — he
tried to defend his fourth press from destruction by a mob.

12

The news of the murder of Lovejoy reached Boston on November 19, 1837 — twelve days after the occurrence. The murder was
the culmination of a long series of lawless acts by the proslavery
element. They who incessantly reiterated that the Constitution conferred upon the planters the right to hold men in bondage, never
hesitated to disregard the constitutional right of their fellow citizens
to freedom of speech and of the press. Dr. William Ellery Channing
headed a petition signed by one hundred prominent citizens requesting the use of the municipally owned Faneuil Hall for a
meeting of protest. There were, however, many Bostonians who
subscribed to the opinion expressed by the Reverend Hubbard Winslow and endorsed by Judge Story that "Republican liberty is liberty
to say and do what the prevailing voice and will of the brotherhood
will allow and protect." So the petition was denied on the ground
that "the meeting might be regarded as the public voice of the city"
and result in "a scene of confusion which would be disreputable to
the city and injurious to the glory of that consecrated Hall."

----

[2] Here lies Lovejoy; now spare his grave.

Dr. Channing replied in an open letter: "Has it come to this? Has Boston fallen so low? May not its citizens be trusted to come together to express the great principles of liberty, for which their fathers died? Are our fellow citizens to be murdered in the act of defending their property and of asserting the right of free discussion; and is it unsafe in the metropolis, once the refuge of liberty, to express abhorrence of the deed?"

The municipality relented and gave permission for a meeting on December 8, with the proviso that it was to take place in the forenoon, so as to minimize the possibility of disorder.

The Anti-Slavery Society wisely abstained from official connection with the contemplated protest. The *Liberator* gave the story of the murder with lines of mourning framing its columns, but Garrison expressed his regret in an editorial that Lovejoy, a minister of the gospel, should have resorted to arms to defend his property. "In the name of Jesus of Nazareth," he wrote, "who suffered himself to be unresistingly nailed to the cross, we solemnly protest against any of his professed followers resorting to carnal weapons under any pretext or in any extremity whatever." Whether Phillips was invited to speak at the meeting — hence whether the speech that placed him in the forefront of antislavery orators was prepared or extemporaneous — has been the subject of controversy. The preponderance of evidence is to the effect that he had been invited. The circumstances under which the speech was delivered were, however, of such a nature that some improvisation was unavoidable, and it is precisely the improvised part that proved most effective. This is not surprising, since he was at his best in debate. One reason for the confusion regarding his having been invited to address the meeting is that he remained in the auditorium with Ann and several of her friends and did not ascend the platform until the incident occurred which made him decide not to wait until the chairman called upon him to speak, but to take the floor then and there.

13

Faneuil Hall was presented to the municipality in 1742 by Peter Faneuil, a wealthy merchant of Huguenot ancestry who had amassed a fortune in the West Indian slave trade. It was originally a two-story building, consisting of a market place in the basement, surmounted by a hall, which, as specified by the donor, the people were to use freely when wishing to discuss public affairs. It was destroyed by fire in 1761, rebuilt two years later and in 1805 greatly enlarged. In Revolutionary days protest meetings were held there against the Stamp Act and the tax on tea. Otis, Sam Adams and Hancock frequently addressed the people from its platform. Hence it became known as the "Cradle of Liberty." A gallery, decorated in the center with a gilded eagle, encompassed the hall, and on the walls were portraits of Washington, Warren, the two Adamses and Hancock. The absence of seats made it possible to accommodate as many as five thousand people.

Notwithstanding the unfavorable hour the hall was filled. The crowd has been estimated at from twenty-five hundred to five thousand, among whom were sixteen women. Mrs. Chapman wrote to Harriet Martineau: "By night it has been closer packed; but never, they tell me, by day. I went (for the Woman Question), with fifteen others. The indignation at us was great. People said it gave the meeting the air of an Abolition gathering to have women there; it hung out false colors." Of the men, about a third were in sympathy with the purpose of the meeting, a third agreed with the Reverend Winslow, while the remaining third were undecided. The chairman was Jonathan Phillips, a relative of Wendell. With him on the platform were Dr. Channing and several men prominent in the professional and business life of the city — Benjamin F. Hallett, George S. Hillard, William Sturgis, George Bond and others. Phillips had arrived with the women and stood with Ann close to the platform. Garrison was in another part of the hall.

The meeting opened with prayer by a local minister, after which the chairman introduced Dr. Channing, who made a brief address. Then Hallett read the resolutions, drawn by Channing. They made no mention of slavery, but referred entirely to the constitutional rights of freedom of speech and of the press. Having finished reading, Hallett moved that the resolutions be adopted and was seconded by Hillard. Jonathan Phillips was about to put the matter to a vote, when from that part of the gallery fronting the platform a stentorian voice cried: "Mr. Chairman!"

The crowd faced about towards the speaker.

Behind the gilded eagle stood the blowzy form of the Attorney General of Massachusetts, James Trecothick Austin. When prosecuting an Abolitionist he had said to the jury: "Can there be a safer mode of determining what is right or wrong than, Is it lawful?"

Now he had shifted his ground. Lovejoy, he boomed, might have been within the law, but he had been "presumptuous and imprudent." By throwing his press into the Mississippi, to prevent him from injuring the interests of the people of a neighboring State, the citizens of Alton had acted in the spirit of the heroes of the Revolution, who threw the tea overboard notwithstanding the legality of the tax imposed by the English Government. He would, he said, sink into insignificance were he to gainsay the principle of the resolutions just read, but what was the situation —

"We have a menagerie here with lions, tigers, a hyena, an elephant, a jackass or two, and monkeys in plenty. Suppose, now, some new cosmopolite, some man of philanthropic feelings, not only toward men, but animals, who believes that all are entitled to freedom as an inalienable right, should engage in the humane task of giving freedom to the wild beasts of the forest, some of whom are nobler than their keepers; or having discerned some new mode of reaching their understanding, should try to induce them to break their cages and be free. The people of Missouri had as much reason to be afraid of their slaves as we should have to be afraid of the wild beasts of the menagerie. They had the same dread of Lovejoy that we should have of the supposed instigator, if we really believed the bars would be broken and the caravan let loose to prowl about our streets. . . . He died as the fool dieth. His clerical character is no palliation of his conduct. I have as little sympathy for a minister of the gospel who is found, gun in hand, fighting in a broil with a mob, as I have for one who leaves his pulpit to mingle in the debates of a popular assembly in matters that do not concern his sacred office. In either situation he is marvellously out of place."

Having aimed this parting shot at Dr. Channing, of whose congregation he was a member, Austin turned on his heel and left the gallery amidst deafening cheering and applause. "I gave up all hope of a favorable termination of the meeting," wrote Mrs. Chapman.

Phillips had removed the long surtout with short cape he was wearing and handed it to an acquaintance. Ann, alarmed, seized his arm.

"What are you going to do, Wendell?"

"I'm going to speak, if I can make myself heard."

He mounted the platform and waited while the crowd faced

towards him. "In a public speaker physical advantages are half the
battle," he said once. Certain it is that no man of ordinary appearance could have silenced that boisterous crowd. There were shouts
of "Question! Question!" but also of "Hear him!" "No gagging!"
"Order!" He made no attempt to obtain silence, but his distinguished appearance, his youth, his beauty, his self-possession spoke
for him. The noise subsided, rippled out. Then, for the first time,
was heard in that hall that melodious voice which, in the opinion
of a contemporary, resembled "the penetrating mellowness of the
flute and the violin rather than the blast of a bugle."

   "I hope [he said] I shall be permitted to express my surprise at
the sentiments of the last speaker — surprise not only at such sentiments from such a man, but at the applause they have received within
these walls. A comparison has been drawn between the events of the
Revolution and the tragedy of Alton. We have heard it asserted
here, in Faneuil Hall, that Great Britain had a right to tax the Colonies, and we have heard the mob at Alton, the drunken murderers
of Lovejoy, compared to those patriot fathers who threw the tea
overboard! [*Great applause.*] Fellow citizens, is this Faneuil Hall
doctrine? [*"No! no!"*] The mob at Alton were met to wrest from
a citizen his just rights — met to resist the laws. We have been told
that our fathers did the same; and the glorious mantle of Revolutionary precedent has been thrown over the mobs of our day. . . .
To draw the conduct of our ancestors into a precedent for mobs,
for a right to resist laws we ourselves have enacted, is an insult to
their memory. . . . Sir, when I heard the gentleman lay down
principles which place the murderers of Alton side by side with
Otis and Hancock, with Quincy and Adams, I thought those pictured lips [*pointing to the portraits in the Hall*] would have broken
into voice to rebuke the recreant American, — the slanderer of the
dead. [*Great applause and counter applause.*] The gentleman said
that he should sink into insignificance if he dared to gainsay the principles of these resolutions. Sir, for the sentiments he has uttered, on
soil consecrated by the prayers of Puritans and the blood of patriots,
the earth should have yawned and swallowed him up." [*Pande-
monium! Deafening cheers combined with boos and hisses. Cries of
"Take that back!"*]

*   *   *

George Bond and William Sturgis rushed to Phillips's side. Phillips's supporters, thinking they meant to stop him, chorused: "Phillips or nobody! Phillips or nobody!" Others cried: "Make him take back 'recreant'! Make him take it back! He shan't go on till he takes it back!" All this while Phillips stood unperturbed, looking down at the crowd curiously. It was his baptism of fire. For more than a quarter of a century he was to face audiences like this and worse, far worse! He was to remain unperturbed when rocks and rotten eggs fell all around him and pistol shots were momentarily expected. Once when men climbed the platform with a rope with which they meant to hang him, he was to wave them aside with a haughty gesture, saying: "Wait till I tell this story." Now he merely waited for the noise to subside, while Sturgis, managing to make himself heard above the din, cried: "I do entreat you fellow-citizens, by everything you hold sacred, — I conjure you by every association connected with this Hall, consecrated by our fathers to freedom of discussion, — that you listen to every man who addresses you in a decorous manner."

Phillips resumed:

"Fellow-citizens, I cannot take back my words." He pointed out that Lovejoy and his friends had armed themselves with the approval of the Mayor.

"They were not merely citizens defending their property, they were in a sense the *posse comitatus*, adopted for the occasion into the police of the city, acting under the orders of the magistrate. It was civil authority resisting lawless violence. Where then was the imprudence? Is the doctrine to be sustained here that it is *imprudent* for men to aid magistrates in executing the laws? . . . If, Sir, I had adopted what are called Peace principles, I might lament the circumstances in this case. But all you who believe, as I do, in the right and duty of magistrates to execute the laws, join with me and brand as base hypocrisy the conduct of those who assemble year after year on the 4th of July, to fight over the battles of the Revolution, and yet 'damn with faint praise,' or load with obloquy, the memory of this man, who shed his blood in defence of life, liberty, property, and the freedom of the press!"

Referring to the Reverend Hubbard Winslow's definition of liberty, he said:

"If this be so, what are republican institutions worth? Welcome the despotism of the Sultan, where one knows what he may publish and what he may not, rather than the tyranny of this many-headed monster, the mob, where we know not what we may do or say, till some fellow-citizen has tried it, and paid for the lesson with his life. This clerical absurdity chooses as a check for the abuses of the press, not the law, but the dread of a mob. By doing so, it deprives not only the individual and the minority of their rights, but the majority also, since the expression of *their* opinion may sometimes provoke disturbance from the minority."

Having won over that part of the audience with no settled conviction and silenced the proslavery portion, he now hazarded an oratorical *tour de force:* he momentarily rebuffed his audience only to draw it to him again with a triumphant turn of rhetoric. "*Presumptuous* to assert the freedom of the press on American ground!" he said. "Who invents this libel on his country? It is this very thing which entitles Lovejoy to greater praise. The disputed right which provoked the Revolution — taxation without representation — is far beneath that for which he died. [*Strong and general expressions of dissent.*] One word, gentlemen. As much as *thought* is better than money, so much is the cause in which Lovejoy died nobler than a mere question of taxes. James Otis thundered in this Hall when the King did but touch his pocket. Imagine, if you can, his indignant eloquence had England offered to put a gag upon his lips."

An ear-splitting cheer burst forth from the crowd. Men waved their hats, some jumped up and down in their enthusiasm. It was an ovation. He waited for the noise to subside, then said:

"I am glad, Sir, to see this crowded house. It is good for us to be here. When Liberty is in danger, Faneuil Hall has the right, it is her duty, to strike the key-note for the United States. I am glad, for one reason, that remarks such as those to which I have alluded have been uttered here. The passage of these resolutions, in spite of this opposition, led by the Attorney-General of the Commonwealth, will show more clearly, more decisively, the deep indignation with which Boston regards this outrage."

Having said this he retired to the back of the platform.

When "the whirlwind applause had died away," there came from all sides of the hall demands that the resolutions be put to a vote. It was done. There was a roar of "Ayes!" When the negative was called for not a single voice was raised. Again the hall resounded with cheers.

George William Curtis has said that Phillips's speech of that day ranks with Patrick Henry's Williamsburg and Lincoln's Gettysburg address as one of the three greatest oratorical triumphs in America's history. From that day on, Phillips was recognized as the foremost orator in the Anti-Slavery Movement — one whom no speaker cared to follow.

CHAPTER II

The Schism

OPINIONS about Garrison's ability as a leader differ widely. Henry Ward Beecher has called him "one of the most unfortunate of all leaders for the best development of anti-slavery feeling." He conceded that he was "a man of no mean ability; of indefatigable industry; of the most unbounded enterprise and eagerness; of courage that amounts to recklessness," but added: "Had he possessed, as a balance to these, conciliation, good nature, benevolence, or even a certain popular mirthfulness . . . he had been the one man of our age. These all he lacked." Wendell Phillips, however, said at a meeting of the Massachusetts Society: "Such is my conviction of the soundness of his judgment and his rare insight into all the bearings of our cause, that I distrust my own deliberate judgment, when it leads me to a different conclusion from his."

It has already been remarked that in personal intercourse Garrison was amiable, patient, reasonable, courteous. This, however, was not always the case when he expressed himself at business meetings of the Society or indulged in polemics with fellow Abolitionists. "The moment any one, even a real friend," wrote the editor of the *Christian Mirror*, "has put his foot out of the traces, he has turned the butt of his whip and laid on his blows most unmercifully." Men who had proved their friendship found it necessary to rebuke him for his manner of dealing with his critics. Samuel J. May wrote to him: "I am not satisfied with the course you and your partizans have pursued. It appears to me not consistent with the non-resistant, patient long-suffering spirit of the Gospel." The Reverend George Bourne, whose *The Book and Slavery Irreconcilable* had been responsible for Garrison's conversion to "Immediatism," wrote: "To talk of non-resistance with the constant extraneous pugnacity which has been recently displayed upon disconnected topics, like old Billy's negro, chokes me!" Lewis Tappan, a member of the Executive Committee whose conduct Garrison was to characterize as "criminal," admonished: "We cannot afford to drive away, or 'knock on the head' friends who are substantially right. No, no. We must be patient, forbearing, forgiving, especially to those of our own household." The Reverend Daniel Wise reported Garrison to have spoken at a quarterly meeting of the Massachusetts Society, "as if he were whip-master-general and supreme judge of all abolitionists; as though he wore a triple crown, and wielded an irresponsible sceptre over all the embattled hosts of anti-slavery troops."

That Garrison possessed a generous streak of egotism is undeniable. "Take egotism out," Emerson wrote in his Journal, "and you would castrate the benefactors. Luther, Mirabeau, Napoleon, John Adams, Andrew Jackson; and our nearer servants — Greeley, Theodore Parker, Ward Beecher, Horace Mann, Garrison — would lose their vigour."

2

While Garrison's dictatorial manner aggravated the situation, differences between him and some of the other Abolitionist leaders were too fundamental not to have eventually resulted in a parting of the ways. His aggressive mode of propaganda and his assaults on the churches, the clergy and the Sabbath (he had become an anti-Sabbatarian) were resented, but the two principal bones of contention were Woman's Rights and nonresistance, the latter implying virtual repudiation of organized government.

Since the beginning of the century women had entered industry on a considerable scale — the great majority of cotton-mill workers were women — but they were debarred from all participation in government. Colleges and even high schools were closed to them. When a woman married she lost control of her property. The story is told of a Massachusetts man who married an heiress and willed her own property to her on condition that she did not remarry. A woman without a male escort could not obtain a room at a respectable hotel. A certain Mrs. Chickering, whose husband commuted to New York, came to the city to accompany him to the theater. In some way they failed to connect. It was too late to return to the country. After much pleading she obtained a room at a hotel, but only on condition that one of the hotel porters was to sleep outside her bedroom door. When the evangelist Charles Finney allowed women to pray at his revivals, Dr. Lyman Beecher wrote to a friend: "A greater evil, next to the loss of conscience and chastity, could not befall the female sex. No well educated female can put herself up, or be put up, to the point of public prayer, without the loss of some portion at least of that female delicacy, which is above all price."

Abolitionists were in advance of their time on the slavery question, but not necessarily on other matters. Clerical gentlemen among them had from the beginning looked askance at the infiltration of women into the movement. They had no objection to women belonging to an auxiliary society that confined its activities to raising money and circulating petitions, but that women should speak in public or help formulate the policies of the organization was not to be thought of. They became seriously alarmed when two female opponents of slavery, Sarah and Angelina Grimké, defied convention to the extent of lecturing in public.

Sarah and Angelina were the daughters of a prosperous South Carolina planter and had been reared on their father's plantation. As was usually the case with members of a prosperous planter's family, they were able to learn but little of the treatment of field slaves, but what they saw of the treatment of household slaves was sufficient to fill them with a horror of the institution. When their father died and left them the plantation, they freed their slaves, moved to Philadelphia, joined the Orthodox Quakers and began addressing small private gatherings of women, charging no fee and paying their own expenses. Soon meeting places had to be found to accommodate all who wanted to hear them, and before long they were speaking to mixed audiences. When they refused to confine themselves to the slavery problem and began advocating Woman's Rights, even Whittier became alarmed. Sarah wrote to a friend: "Brothers Whittier and Weld are anxious we should say nothing on the woman question; but I do not feel I could surrender my right to discuss any great moral subject." Soon another young Quakeress, Abby Kelley, began lecturing in public. She had been thrust into the work by Theodore D. Weld, who told her: "Abby, if you don't, God will smite you!" Abby did, with a vengeance. She later married the turbulent Stephen S. Foster and where the two appeared there usually was no lack of excitement.

As early as 1802, one Deborah Sampson Gannett had lectured in public, but she was not a "respectable" woman, having masqueraded as a man and served three years in Washington's army. Her lecture,

which had been written for her, was moreover from beginning to
end an apology for her unwomanly conduct. Frances Wright, who
began lecturing in 1828, was likewise not considered respectable,
being irreligious and having peculiar ideas about marriage. But here
were three young women, wearing Quaker dress, devout and of
irreproachable character, touring the country and preaching reform! Church people, men and women, flocked to hear them.
Something had to be done about it if the social fabric was not to
disintegrate. So thought the General Association of Massachusetts,
and issued a Pastoral Letter to the Orthodox Congregational
Churches, declaring:

> The power of woman is in her dependence, flowing from
> the consciousness of that weakness which God has given her
> for her protection. . . . But when she assumes the place and
> tone of man as a public reformer, our care and protection of
> her seem unnecessary; we put ourselves in self-defence against
> her; she yields the power which God has given her for protec-
> tion, and her character becomes unnatural. If the vine, whose
> strength and beauty is to lean upon the trellis-work and half
> conceal its clusters, thinks to assume the independence and the
> overshading nature of the elm, it will not only cease to bear
> fruit, but will fall in shame and dishonor in the dust.

Ministers were warned not to permit "females" to speak in their
churches, and one clergyman preached a sermon against Abby
Kelley from the text: "I have a few things against thee, because
thou sufferest that woman, Jezebel, which calleth herself a proph-
etess, to teach and to seduce my servants to commit fornication."
Abby finally retaliated by introducing a resolution at the tenth
annual meeting of the Massachusetts Anti-Slavery Society, "That
the sectarian organizations called churches are combinations of
thieves, robbers, adulterers, pirates and murderers, and as such form
the bulwark of American Slavery."

All this had repercussions in the American Anti-Slavery Society.
The Executive Committee, fearful of increased opposition and wishing to avoid dissension among the membership, promptly disclaimed
responsibility for the female lecturers, and its official organ, the
Emancipator, published the disclaimer. But the women found plenty
of champions, foremost among whom were Garrison and Phillips.
"The mightiest intellects of the race, from Plato down to the present
time; some of the rarest minds of Germany, France and England, —

have successively yielded their assent to the fact that woman is, not perhaps identically, but equally endowed with man in all intellectual capabilities. It is generally the second-rate men who doubt, — doubt perhaps, because they fear a fair field," Phillips was to say. As for Garrison, in January, 1838, he published this announcement in the *Liberator:* "As our object is Universal Emancipation — to redeem woman as well as man from a servile to an equal condition — we shall go for the Rights of Woman to their fullest extent." He was as good as his word. In May of that year, at the New England Anti-Slavery Convention, a resolution was passed inviting women not only to become members, but to participate in all proceedings. For the first time a woman — the spirited Abby Kelley — was appointed a member of an important committee. The resolution met bitter opposition from the clerical contingent which accused Garrison of upholding a change in the sphere of woman's action which was "a moral wrong — a thing forbidden alike by the word of God, the dictates of right reason, the voice of wisdom and the modesty of unperverted nature."

3

If the subject of Woman's Rights was a serious bone of contention, Garrison's nonresistance doctrine proved even more so. "Garrison did not so much insist on the right of Negroes to be free as he denied the right of any man whatever, or of any body of men, forcibly to coerce another man in any way," wrote Leo Tolstoy, who, like Garrison, drew his inspiration from the New Testament. Assuming that the New Testament enjoins nonresistance under all circumstances and that Christ's teachings on the subject were not motivated by the exigencies of the situation, Garrison's acceptance of the doctrine is still puzzling. When he had repudiated orthodoxy he had abandoned belief in the divine inspiration of the Bible, about which he wrote: "It is to be examined with the same freedom as any other book, and taken precisely for what it is worth. It must stand or fall on its own inherent qualities, like any other volume. . . . When the various books of the Bible were written, or by whom they were written, no man living can tell. This is purely a matter of conjecture; and as conjecture is not certainty, it ceases to be authoritative. . . . 'What is writ, is writ,' and must stand or fall by the test of just criticism, by its reasonableness and utility, by the probabilities of the case, by historical confirmation, by human experience and observation, by the facts of science, by the intuition of the spirit."

If this means anything it assuredly means that nonresistance, along with every other teaching in the Bible, should not be accepted on faith but should "stand or fall by the test of just criticism, etc." One is inclined to believe that Garrison trusted more to "the intuition of the spirit" than to any other test when in the Declaration of Sentiments of the Peace Convention, held in Boston in September, 1838, he wrote: "The history of mankind is crowded with evidences proving that physical coërcion is not adapted to moral regeneration; that the sinful dispositions of men can be subdued only by love; that evil can be exterminated from the earth only by goodness; . . . that there is great security in being gentle, harmless, long-suffering, and abundant in mercy; that it is only the meek who shall inherit the earth, for the violent who resort to the sword are destined to perish with the sword."

Frederick Douglass was more realistic when in 1865 he wrote to President Johnson: "Experience proves that those are most abused who can be abused with greatest impunity. Men are whipped oftenest who are whipped easiest." Nonresistance *invites* oppression, hence promotes not the regeneration, but the degeneration of oppressor and oppressed. "A man without force," wrote Douglass, "is without essential dignity of humanity. Human nature is so constituted that it can not honor a helpless man, though it can pity him, and even then can not do so long if signs of power do not arise."

Garrison's philosophy of nonresistance led to what, from want of a better term, might be called Christian Anarchism. In the Declaration of Sentiments of the Peace Convention he wrote: "As every human government is upheld by physical strength, and its laws are enforced virtually at the point of the bayonet, we cannot hold any office which imposes upon its incumbent the obligation to compel men to do right, on pain of imprisonment or death. We therefore exclude ourselves from every legislative and judicial body, and repudiate all human politics, worldly honors, and stations of authority. If we cannot occupy a seat in the legislature or on the bench, neither can we elect *others* to act as our substitutes in any such capacity."

Not only armies and navies but all police power was therefore to be abolished, and not only capital punishment, but punitive measures of any kind, since all involved the actual or potential use of force. Until that happy day believers in nonresistance were urged to abstain from all participation in government. It need not surprise us that Garrison found himself involved in numerous contradictions. He was already a believer in nonresistance when he wrote in the *Genius* that men like Francis Todd of Newburyport should be "sentenced to solitary confinement for life," and he was still a believer in the doctrine when he refused to sign a petition for Jefferson Davis's release from Fort Monroe. Moreover, since the tongue and the pen can inflict as cruel wounds as the sword, and since Garrison seldom hesitated to inflict such wounds, it may well be argued that he never was a nonresistant.

4

Garrison's infatuation with nonresistance was the result of his tendency towards mysticism, which made him a convert to Perfectionism and later aroused his interest in Spiritualism. Perfectionism, advocated by John Humphrey Noyes, founder of the Oneida Community, has been defined by one of Noyes's disciples in these words: "As the doctrine of temperance is total abstinence from alcoholic drinks, as the doctrine of anti-slavery is immediate abolition of human bondage, so the doctrine of Perfectionism is immediate and total cessation from sin." Perfectionists aimed to live in accordance with the law of Christ, which implied renouncing allegiance to a government permitting such iniquities as slavery, war, capital punishment, and so forth. If, like Garrison, they continued to pay taxes, they did so under protest, "as one gives up one's purse to a highway man."

It was all part of what John Morley called "A great wave of humanity, of benevolence, of desire for improvement — a great wave of social sentiment, in short — that poured itself among all who had the faculty of large and disinterested thinking." It brought with it such varied social and religious movements as Transcendentalism, Come-Outerism, Perfectionism, Millerism, Fourierism, Owenism, Fanny Wrightism, Abolitionism, Woman's Rights, the Labor Movement, agitation for the Abolition of Imprisonment for Debt and Capital Punishment, Prison Reform, Dress Reform, and others. The best and wisest spirits of the age fell under the spell of one or more of these movements. They saw three million human beings kept in bondage for the benefit of less than one tenth their number, saw labor crushed and plundered, woman treated as a minor, seventy-five thousand people (of whom half owed less than twenty dollars) imprisoned for debt, the churches giving their blessing to it all — and so they were ready to grasp at anything promising relief. Albert Brisbane, Horace Greeley, William E. Channing, George Ripley, Parke Godwin and others saw hope in Fourierism. Robert Owen experimented at New Harmony. Bronson Alcott embarked on the Fruitlands adventure. Emerson became a Transcendentalist tinged with Perfectionism. Thoreau indulged in a species of Come-Outerism. Scores of communistic colonies dotted the land. The Millerites expected the end of the world and the second coming of Christ. The Grahamites would not kill even a mosquito. Garrison espoused nonresistance and Perfectionism but remained above all an Abolitionist.

One cannot help thinking, however, that there might have been still another reason why nonresistance appealed to him. Abolitionists who did not believe in nonresistance must, he felt, favor a slave rebellion: "If those whose yokes they are endeavoring to break by the fire and hammer of God's word, would not in their opinion, be justified in appealing to physical force, how can they justify others of a different complexion in doing the same thing? And if they conscientiously believe that the slaves would be guiltless in shedding the blood of their merciless oppressors, let them say so unequivocally — for there is no neutral ground in this matter, and the time is near when they will be compelled to take sides." Most opponents of slavery preferred to remain noncommital. Richard H. Dana Jr. said that when he considered what the white race was and what the Negro race was, his sympathy in case of a slave rebellion would be with his own race. It does not appear unlikely that reluctance to declare himself as favoring a slave rebellion was a contributory factor to Garrison's conversion to nonresistance.

Among those who believed that Jefferson's motto "Rebellion to tyrants is obedience to God" applied to the Negro as well as to the white man was Wendell Phillips. Nor did he hesitate to declare himself. When told what Dana had said, he commented: "My sympathy would go with the right." At a public meeting in Boston he was to say: "No, I confess I am not a non-resistant. The reason why I advise the slave to be guided by a policy of peace is because he has no chance. If he had one, — if he had as good a chance as those who

went up to Lexington seventy-seven years ago, — I should call him
the basest recreant that ever deserted wife and child if he did not
vindicate his liberty by his own right hand. . . . I do not shrink from
the toast with which Dr. Johnson flavored his Oxford Port — 'Success to the first insurrection of the blacks in Jamaica!' I do not shrink
from the sentiment of Southey, in a letter to Duppa, — 'There are
scenes of tremendous horror which I could smile at by Mercy's
side. An insurrection which should make the negroes masters of
the West Indies is one.' "

5

Phillips had abandoned his law practice. "Sometime in 1838," he
wrote in 1855 to an acquaintance, "having come to the conviction
that I could not swear to support the United States Constitution,
as I could not conscientiously aid in executing its pro-slavery clauses,
I threw up my profession, feeling that I ought not any longer to act
under the oath to the constitution required of all attornies." According to Ann Phillips, however, the practice had abandoned him: "He
never thought of giving up his practice, until his clients left him after
the Faneuil Hall speech; and then, but not till then, he gave up his
office on Court Street, and gave himself, heart and soul, to the cause
of abolition." Whatever the reason, he now had plenty of time on
his hands. He did not have to worry about earning a livelihood. Being one of nine children, his portion of his father's estate was modest,
yet his and Ann's combined fortune has been estimated at from one
hundred to two hundred thousand dollars. Assuming that it was one
hundred and fifty thousand, their annual revenue from that source
alone could, with the high interest rate then prevailing, not have been
less than seven or eight thousand, equivalent to more than double that
amount today.

In 1839 Phillips was chosen General Agent of the Massachusetts
Anti-Slavery Society, of which Garrison was Corresponding Secretary. He devoted himself unstintingly to the work, refusing all
compensation. He and Ann were then living with Phillips's mother,
and although the young woman was often confined to bed, she insisted that he go "abolitionizing," which meant making frequent
speaking tours. Roads were bad, transportation facilities poor, hotel
accommodations left much to be desired. Often he stayed at the
house of a fellow Abolitionist, seldom a prosperous member of the

community. "In the early days of the cause we used to kiss each other like the early Christians," he wrote, which must have been embarrassing to the former president of the Porcellian and Gentlemen's Clubs. Farmers' wives usually took their babies with them to meeting, and the speaker had to contend with squalling infants as well as with interruptions by opponents of the cause. But he was a democrat by conviction, if not by nature, and managed to adapt himself. When the Negro Charles Remond was ordered out of the railway carriage in which he and Phillips were traveling, the scion of several generations of Boston Brahmins insisted on going with him into the second class coach, "a mere box with pine seats," saying: "If you cannot ride with me, I can ride with you." When on the boat between New York and Newport, Frederick Douglass had to spend the night on the forward deck, "with horses, sheep and swine," Phillips refused to take a stateroom and all night walked the deck with him. "I could not persuade him to leave me to bear the burden of insult and outrage alone," wrote Douglass.

Phillips had been "abolitionizing" for five months when the family doctor recommended that he take his wife to Europe for a change of climate and scene. The family supported the physician. Phillips realized that it was not so much Ann as him they hoped to cure. A prolonged absence in Europe might awaken his interest in other matters and "cure him of his fanaticism." But wishing to leave nothing undone that might contribute to Ann's recovery, he consented. So, in June, 1839, he and Ann took passage for London. They did not tarry long in the British capital but crossed the channel, and traveled by easy stages with the *diligence* to Paris, Lyons and finally to Rome, where they meant to spend the winter.

6

"We are (O sorrowful fact!) a divided house. That sweet fellowship which formerly prevailed in our ranks is gone, and, I fear, irrevocably," Garrison wrote in March, 1839, to his sister-in-law, Mary Benson. The ministerial contingent in the Massachusetts Society had declared war upon him. They objected to Woman's Rights, to nonresistance, to the no-government doctrine, to his views regarding corporal punishment of children, to his attacks on the Sabbath, the clergy and the churches. The Reverend Amos A. Phelps, former General Agent of the Massachusetts Society, said that under Garrison's leadership it had degenerated into "a woman's rights, no-government anti-slavery society," and expressed the opinion that the editor of the *Liberator* was "a wicked man, utterly unfit to be engaged in any moral enterprise." The Reverend John L. Bosquet wrote: "He [Garrison] wants to overthrow all government, even that of Jehovah . . . make himself the Universal Lord, and make all men slaves to him." The Reverend Orange Scott accused him of believing in "spiritual wives," which, he said, was part of the Perfectionist doctrine. Garrison, referring to one of his clerical opponents, declared: "There is no malignity like that of a corrupt priest when he finds that his mask of profession fails to conceal his moral deformity," and said of clerical gentlemen in general: "It is becoming more and more apparent that they are nothing better than hirelings, in the bad sense of that term — that they are blind leaders of the blind, dumb dogs that cannot bark, spiritual popes — that they are mighty hindrances to the march of human freedom, and to the enfranchisement of the souls of men."

For people so divided to remain in the same organization became impractical. The insurgents formed the Massachusetts Abolition Society, recognition of which by the Executive Committee in New York was resented by the Massachusetts Board of Managers and led to bickerings regarding the State's contribution to the national treasury. The new society launched the *Massachusetts Abolitionist*, at one dollar a year, to compete with the *Liberator* at two and a half dollars a year. The old organization promptly began publication of the *Cradle of Liberty*, at seventy-five cents a year. The new paper contained "the cream of the anti-slavery matter in the *Liberator*," or, as one critic put it, "the butter without the hairs." Garrison pronounced the new organization and their paper "the worst foe that liberty has to contend with — the most dangerous form of pro-slavery." Little wonder that old Seth Sprague was to write in a letter: "If the devil was ever chained, certainly he has been let loose on the old Massachusetts Anti-Slavery Society."

As if this were not enough, Isaac Knapp, now married, had become increasingly addicted to alcohol. This became so embarrassing that Garrison's friends decided to buy out his partner, offering him three hundred dollars for his interest in the publication. Since the paper had an annual deficit of from one to two thousand dollars and

the printing equipment was of little value, the offer was not ungenerous. Knapp, however, demanded that an appraisal be made by
a committee of printers. The committee awarded him one hundred
and seventy-five dollars. After the sale he went from bad to worse
and became a derelict. Garrison took pity on him, sheltered him and
his wife and collected some money for him. Then Garrison's opponents decided that the poor fellow might be a serviceable tool and
took him in hand. Soon a circular appeared in which Knapp accused
his former friend of having deprived him of his interest in the paper
by "treachery and duplicity" and announced the early publication
of *Knapp's Liberator*. One issue of the paper appeared, then Knapp
vanished from the scene.

7

The dissension in the Abolitionist ranks had taken still another
turn. James G. Birney, Myron Holly, Alvan Stewart, Henry B.
Stanton, Gerrit Smith, Elizur Wright and others were determined
to take the slavery problem into politics. Now, as a matter of fact,
the Abolitionists had been in politics for a long time. The Anti-
Slavery Society had nearly a quarter of a million members and hundreds of thousands of sympathizers. A candidate for political office
was sure to be waited on by a committee from the Society with the
request that he fill out a questionnaire. Was he in favor of the abolition of slavery and the slave trade in the District of Columbia? Did
he favor abolition of the internal slave trade? Before Garrison's conversion to Perfectionism he himself had been active in this work.
In 1834 he had voted for Amasa Walker for Congress and after the
election had rebuked the colored voters of Boston for having voted
for Walker's opponent. Even after his conversion he felt proud of the
political influence his organization was exercising. In November,
1837, he wrote to Elizabeth Pease: "In Massachusetts, where only two
years since, abolition was a mere football among all political parties
to show their contempt and dexterity in kicking it, these same parties are now 'bowing and scraping' to us, with cap in hand, at every
new election, knowing as they do that we hold the balance of power
in our hands, and can award victory or defeat according to their
espousal of the cause of liberty."

In 1839, Phillips, replying to an inquiry regarding the best way of advancing the Abolition cause, wrote: "Band yourselves together, agitate, discuss, read, petition, write your representatives and *vote*. By and by your ballots will settle every question and right every wrong."

Birney and other politically-minded Abolitionists were, however, not satisfied with questioning candidates and voting for opponents of slavery in the Whig and Democratic Parties, but wished to organize an antislavery party. Whether it was wise to launch a political party based primarily on a moral issue is questionable. Yet the Liberty Party, now about to be born, helped to prepare the way for its successors, the Free-Soil and Republican Parties.

Obviously political Abolitionists had little sympathy with Garrison's no-government doctrine. James G. Birney declared that the constitution of the American Anti-Slavery Society required members to use their suffrage in behalf of the slave. Those who had conscientious scruples against voting should, he said, withdraw from the organization. Garrison rejected Birney's interpretation of the constitution, saying that voting was optional. When at a meeting of the Massachusetts Society, Stanton put the question to him: "Mr. Garrison, do you or do you not believe it is a sin to go to the polls?" he replied: "Sin for *me*." He was, however, not far from agreeing with Thomas Paine that "the trade of governing has always been a monopoly of the most ignorant and the most vicious of mankind." He himself was to write: "Is there one man in the United States — in the whole world — who can honestly and truly affirm, before God, that by becoming a politician he has improved his manners or morals, his head or his heart, or has elevated the tone of his piety, or felt new emotions of spiritual life? If so, we have yet to see that man. Are there not thousands of good men who have a far different confession to make?"

But the political Abolitionists were quite willing to run the risk of contamination. So, on April 1, 1840, one hundred and twenty-one of them met at Albany, New York, to form an antislavery party. It was not a representative gathering. Only six States had sent delegates, all but seventeen of whom were from New York. Nevertheless those present organized the Liberty Party, nominating James G. Birney of Kentucky for President. The platform adopted at a convention in New York City the following month, made but vague mention of any other issue except slavery. On May 12, the seventh annual meeting of the American Anti-Slavery Society was to take place,

when the battle lines would be drawn between the supporters and
opponents of Woman's Rights and political and non-political Abolitionists.

8

"If you would not see our broad platform in any degree narrowed,
if you would preserve it from the spirit which is seeking to dash it to
fragments, if you would still rally under an anti-sectarian banner, and
unite with the wise and good of every name for the salvation of your
country and the deliverance of the oppressed, then you will throng
to the anniversary of the parent society on the 12th of May
next."

With this appeal the Board of Managers of the Massachusetts
Society hoped to rally the Abolitionists to Garrison's side in the impending struggle. But he and his friends had no intention of leaving
the outcome to chance. Garrison might eschew politics, but he was
an excellent politician. Special trains were chartered to carry the
New England delegates to Providence, Rhode Island, where the
steamboat *Massachusetts* (likewise chartered for the occasion) was
to take them to New York. Passage and entertainment were free.
"It was our anti-slavery boat-load that saved the Society from falling into the hands of the new organizers, or more correctly, disorganizers," Garrison wrote to Helen.

One thousand and eight delegates assembled in the auditorium of
the Fourth Free Church. The atmosphere was tense. President
Arthur Tappan had absented himself. Francis Jackson, one of the
vice presidents, took the chair. The chairman's first duty was to ap-
point a Business Committee. He named Garrison and ten others, including Abby Kelley. This brought the Woman's Rights question
squarely before the convention. Jackson declared Miss Kelley's appointment confirmed *viva voce*. Division was called for. Garrison
won by about a hundred votes. Lewis Tappan and Amos Phelps
rose and asked to be excused from serving on the committee: "To
put a woman on a committee with men is contrary to the constitution of the Society; it is throwing a firebrand into the anti-slavery
ranks; it is contrary to the usages of civilized society."

That same evening Garrison's opponents met at the home of Lewis
Tappan and founded a new organization — the American and Foreign Anti-Slavery Society. It lived thirteen years, but remained un-

important. There was little reason for its existence: the political Abolitionists had their party, the others the old organization.

In the convention Garrison now carried everything before him. "We have made clean work of everything — adopted the most thoroughgoing resolutions, and taken the strongest ground, with crashing unanimity," he wrote to Helen. A new Executive Committee, composed of his partisans, took the place of the old. A resolution concerning the Liberty Party regretted "the course pursued by the recent Convention of the friends of immediate emancipation at Albany . . . and highly as we respect the gentlemen whose names were brought before the public as nominees of that Convention, we cannot advise our friends to waste their energies in futile efforts to promote their election."

9

Following the schism the membership of the old organization declined from nearly a quarter of a million to sixty thousand. John Jay Chapman has written that Garrison's distinctive work was done before 1840. There can be no doubt that the truly significant battle against slavery was now to be waged on the political field, where Birney, Chase, Giddings, Hale, Sumner, Adams, Mann, Greeley, Frémont, Lincoln, were to be the leaders. It would be a mistake to think, however, that Garrison and Phillips, who for a quarter of a century remained joint leaders of the American Anti-Slavery Society, did not continue to play important roles. The society was still a formidable propaganda machine, indeed more formidable than it had been for some time, since now comparatively free from strife. Entirely free from dissension it would never be. Phillips at an annual meeting was to say: "If there is anybody here who does not like quarreling, I advise him to go and join the conservatives, for he will find reformers always in a tempest." The society continued to make converts by the thousands and tens of thousands, but it could not hold them. In April, 1844, Phillips wrote ruefully to Elizabeth Pease: "As fast as *we*, the Old Organization, make abolitionists, the new converts run right into Liberty Party, and become almost wholly hostile to us. This results from the strong leaning of our national character to politics." This peculiar relationship between the Abolitionists and the political antislavery movement continued after the formation of the Republican Party. Frederic Bancroft, in his *Life of William*

Henry Seward, calls the Abolitionists "the recruiting officers for the Republicans." So great was their influence that even when they made serious blunders, as for example in their disunion propaganda, few Republican newspapers or speakers dared to criticize them. "Lincoln, too, was silent, he attacked only the disunionists of the South," wrote Albert J. Beveridge.[1]

The Old Organization still had another function to perform. Political opponents of slavery wisely did not hesitate to run the risk of contamination by descending into the arena of politics, yet many became contaminated to the extent of voting for a constitutional amendment guaranteeing that the Federal Government would never interfere with slavery. It was well therefore that there were Garrison, Phillips and their purist host — the indestructible core of the Anti-Slavery Movement — "whose active hostility was yearly becoming more dangerous."[2]

[1] Albert J. Beveridge, *Abraham Lincoln, 1809-1858*. (Houghton Mifflin Company, Boston and New York, 1928.)
[2] Frederic Bancroft, *op. cit.*

CHAPTER III

The World's Anti-Slavery Convention

THIS man is such a perfect artist," wrote Emerson concerning Phillips, "he ought to be walking all the galleries of Europe and yet he is fighting these hard battles." In the spring of 1840, however, Phillips was walking "that little world of dazzling, bewildering beauty, the Vatican," [1] and could often be seen lost in admiration before the Laocoön and the Apollo. He visited the Colosseum by moonlight, looked up at Trajan's Pillar "by the very steps the old Roman feet once trod," mused in the Pantheon, "on which Paul's eyes might have rested," meditated "in the half-buried ruins of Nero's golden house where the frescoes are blooming and fresh after eighteen hundred years." He stood in St. Peter's and later wrote to Garrison: "There is much to admire in the democratic method of Catholic worship. No 'sit-thou-here' and 'stand-thou-there' spirit class out the audience; no hateful honeycomb of pews deforms the church." What pleased him even more was to see affixed to the door of the cathedral the bull of Pope Gregory XVI against slavery and the slave trade.

The hope of Phillips's family that a prolonged stay in Europe would wean him away from the Abolitionist movement was, however, doomed to disappointment. When he and Ann had been eight months in Europe, a letter arrived informing them that both had been appointed delegates to the World's Anti-Slavery Convention, which was to convene in London on June 12, 1840. So they traveled to London and discovered on their arrival that the woman question, mainly responsible for the schism in the American movement, was going to plague the international gathering. The old and new organizations into which the American movement had split had both sent delegates, the former several women — Ann Phillips, Lucretia Mott, Elizabeth Cady Stanton, Sarah Pugh and others. When the London Committee heard of the arrival of the women delegates it

[1] Letter from Rome to a relative, January 5, 1840.

was thrown into a panic. As one of the committee put it: "Such a thing had never been heard or thought of in any part of Europe." The World's Convention was held in Freemasons' Hall, and an eye-witness reported: "Entering the vestibule little groups might be seen gathered here and there, earnestly discussing the best disposition to make of those women delegates from America. The excitement and vehemence of protest and denunciation could not have been greater if the news had come that the French were about to invade England."

Garrison was not there to champion the women's cause. He had not wished to leave while the New York convention was in progress. So the women turned to Phillips, who promised to do his best and went into the fray with this admonition from Ann: "Wendell, don't shilly-shally." Having vainly argued the women's cause before the committee, he decided to appeal to the convention. When the venerable Thomas Clarkson had concluded his welcoming address, Phillips moved that a committee be appointed to prepare a correct list of the delegates "and to include in such a list all *persons* bearing credentials from any anti-slavery society."

The debate that followed may be said to have heralded the birth of the Woman's Rights Movement in America, for at its conclusion Lucretia Mott and Elizabeth Cady Stanton decided to launch such a movement immediately after their return. The right of the women to take part in the convention was not only disputed by the great majority of British delegates, but also by the delegates of the new organization. The Irish leader Daniel O'Connell, while not present at the debate, supported the women, and the famous temperance advocate Father Theobald Mathew was to express his regret at their exclusion.

Phillips was urged to withdraw his motion, because the convention was "not ready to meet the ridicule of the morning papers, and to stand up against the customs of England." He replied: "When we have submitted to brickbats and the tar-tub and feathers in America, rather than yield to the custom prevalent there of not admitting colored brethren into our friendship, shall we yield to parallel custom or prejudice against women in England? We cannot yield this question if we would, for it is a matter of conscience. But we would not yield it on the ground of expediency."

In 1838 John Quincy Adams, holding up a petition, said on the floor of Congress: "There is one from a man whom I take to be a profound humorist, and a keen and deep satirist. His petition is that

Congress would enter into negotiations with the Queen of Great
Britain to prevail on her to abdicate the throne of the nation. And
why? Because affairs of state do not belong to women." The delegates to the World's Convention could, however, not see the humor
of denying women, in a nation ruled by one of that sex, the right
to participate in a convention for the discussion of a problem to the
solution of which a woman, Elizabeth Heyrick, had made an out-
standing contribution.[2] Phillips's motion was overwhelmingly defeated. George Thompson, who had given him halfhearted support,
said: "I hope as the question is now decided, that Mr. Phillips will
give us the assurance that we shall proceed with one heart and one
mind." The Phillips of later years would have refused to participate
in a convention from which several of his colleagues were unjustly
excluded; now, to the women's surprise and disappointment, he
replied: "There is no unpleasant feeling in our minds. I have no
doubt the women will sit with as much interest behind the bar as
though the original proposition had been carried in the affirmative.
All we asked was an expression of an opinion; and having obtained
it, we shall now act with the utmost cordiality."

The general opinion among the women was that he had "shilly-
shallied."

2

Accompanied by N. P. Rogers, C. L. Remond (a colored delegate) and William Adams (a Quaker), Garrison sailed for England
on the twenty-second of May, with little hope of arriving in time
to take part in the World's Convention. Rogers was the New Hampshire attorney who later repudiated all forms of organization and
saw in every chairman or secretary a budding dictator. He was,
however, a delightful companion, and George Thompson had said
of him that he was the most cultured man he had met in America.
It was well that Garrison had brought company along, for without
it he would have been a lonely man indeed. He wrote to Helen:

"Our passengers (of whom I complained) have not improved
either in their manners or morals, and most cordially hate me for
the burning rebukes which I have faithfully administered to them.

---

[2] By her pamphlet, *Immediate and Gradual Abolition.* (London, 1824.)
British Abolitionists adopted her proposal for immediate emancipation in
the British colonies.

Unspeakably happy as I should be to enjoy your society at the present time, I have felt thankful that you did not accompany me; for no virtuous woman could tolerate, for one moment, the language and conduct of such immoral creatures. Not a good thought, not a sensible remark, has fallen from any of their lips since we started; but swearing, drinking and smoking have been the order of the day."

When the ship took on a load of fresh haddock and flounders off the coast of Ireland, one of Garrison's fellow passengers asserted that haddock "bore the marks of the fingers of Jesus, ever since Peter made his memorable draught of fishes." Garrison, not believing him to be serious, said it was an excellent fish story. The passenger became highly incensed, asserted the miracle was well authenticated and said he would not tolerate having his veracity impugned. Everything seemed to have conspired to make the journey a trying one. The Quaker William Adams was punched by the second mate with whom he remonstrated for mistreating a sailor. When the pilot boarded the ship he brought with him copies of the London *Chronicle* containing the account of an attempt made on Queen Victoria's life by a mulatto youth of seventeen. Nothing more was needed to prove to Garrison's fellow passengers the criminal tendencies of the Negro race and the unpardonable folly of those who stood up in its defense. Garrison's opinion that the youth might be mentally unbalanced (as proved to be the case) was scoffed at, and when he remarked that a crime did not become more reprehensible because the offender happened to be a Negro, "they yelled like so many fiends broke loose from the bottomless pit." It was with a sigh of relief that he and his friends disembarked at Liverpool and took the train for London.

3

When Garrison arrived in the British capital, the convention was still in session, but having learned of the exclusion of the women delegates he refused to participate and joined the women in the visitors' gallery. A World's Anti-Slavery Convention in which the acknowledged leader of the world's most powerful antislavery movement refused to take part was somewhat of an anomaly. Extraordinary efforts were made to get him to change his mind. Each time his name was mentioned the delegates rose, turned towards the gallery, where he sat with the scorned women delegates, and applauded, "as if they thought they could clap him down." There was a constant going back and forth of delegates who wished to shake his hand and plead with him to relent. A resolution was passed that it was "the unanimous desire" of the convention that he and those of his friends who had followed his example should join in the proceedings. The London Committee held a meeting and sent him a special invitation. All in vain. "They might as well have expected to remove the pillars on which the gallery stood," wrote Rogers.

The spectacle of the stern, uncompromising man, a self-constituted exile in the gallery, caught the public's fancy. The newspapers played up the story. Invitations from prominent Britishers poured in upon Garrison. Lady Byron came and sat down by his side. The Duchess of Sutherland, whom the Queen alone outranked and whose husband was the wealthiest man in the Kingdom, sent him an invitation and commissioned the Academician B. R. Haydon, whom the London Committee had engaged to immortalize the convention upon canvas, to make a copy of Garrison's likeness for her. The celebrated Mrs. Opie, the Quaker financier Samuel Gurney, felt honored to have him as their guest. He accepted an invitation to dine with Robert Owen, notwithstanding the misgivings of some of his British friends, who "quaked with fear lest it might give us a bad name." His conversation with Owen did not change his opinion that, except where slavery was concerned, "it is internal rather than outward reorganization that is needed to put away the evil that is in the world."

Garrison lectured his British hosts on the evils of alcohol and as often as he could manage had the colored delegate Remond accompany him. In this his conduct was exceptional, even among Abolitionists. When the artist Haydon asked the Reverend John Scoble, delegate of the new organization, if he had any objection to his placing Remond between him and George Thompson, "The emancipator shrank." He immediately suggested that "placing the negro in the distance . . . would have much greater effect." Thompson had no objection, but did not seem overenthusiastic. "Lloyd Garrison comes to-day," Haydon noted in his diary. "I'll try him and this shall be my method of ascertaining the real heart." He was not disappointed: "I asked him and he met me at once directly."

The World's Anti-Slavery Convention terminated with a great meeting at Exeter Hall. Neither Garrison nor Phillips was invited to speak, as it was feared they might take advantage of the opportunity to plead for Woman's Rights. Phillips wrote to Oliver Johnson: "You will hardly believe me when I say, that abolitionists could meet in Exeter Hall to hear of American slavery, and place on their list of speakers the names of Stanton and Birney, and forget that man, sitting silent beside them, to whom it was owing that Birney and Stanton, as abolitionists, had a being — indeed, that there was anything like American abolition at all."

4

Before embarking for England, Garrison had written to Helen: "I am writing in Wall Street, where the money-changers congregate, and where affluence and beggary are seen side by side . . . It is rightly named *Wall* Street — for those who habitually occupy it in quest of riches at the expense of mankind, are *walled* in from the sympathies of human nature, and their hearts are fleshless and hard as the paving-stones on which they tread or the granite and marble buildings which they have erected and dedicated to their idol Gain."

He felt sure, however, that "inner reform" would take care of this unfortunate situation, "for Jesus has not died in vain. He shall save his people from *sins* — and, being saved from these, they will be saved from all the consequences of sin; for they will thus love their neighbor as themselves, and love 'worketh no evil.' "

Why he had given up all hope for "inner reform" on the part of the slaveholders, but felt sure of its efficacy with men whose hearts were "fleshless and hard as the paving-stones on which they tread," he did not explain. In England he saw additional evidence that reform of some kind was long overdue. "I could not enjoy the beautiful landscape of England, because of the suffering and want staring me in the face on the one hand, and the opulence and splendor dazzling my vision on the other," he wrote to Samuel J. May.

In Glasgow he was billed to speak on American Slavery in Dr. Wardlaw's Chapel. As he entered the Chapel accompanied by George Thompson, a shabbily dressed man at the door held out a handbill to him. Garrison took it and read: HAVE WE NO WHITE SLAVES? The document was signed A WHITE SLAVE.

The Chapel was filled. George Thompson presided. Leading citizens occupied the platform. The audience was eager and enthusi-

astic. Towards the end of his lecture Garrison took the handbill
he had received at the door from his breast pocket and read it to
the audience. Then, in answer to the query "Have we no white
slaves?" he said:

"No — broad as is the empire, and extensive as are the possessions
of Great Britain, not a single white slave can be found in them all.
. . . Wretched as is the operative's lot, he is still a man, still a
freeman, as contrasted with those who are held and treated as chattels — still the owner of his own body — still an equal in the eye of
British law . . . still a husband, from whose embrace no ruffian
can tear his wife . . . But although it is not true that England has
any white slaves, either at home or abroad, it is true that there are
thousands of her population, both at home and abroad, who are
deprived of their just rights — who are grievously oppressed — who
are dying, even in the midst of abundance, of actual starvation?
Yes, and I precisely call upon British abolitionists to prove themselves the true friends of suffering humanity abroad, by showing
that they are the best friends of suffering humanity at home. Are
they not so?"

To his discomfiture, there rang from all parts of the hall a re-
sounding "No!" while the prosperous citizens on the platform
looked decidedly uncomfortable. Garrison appeared confused, but
quickly collected himself and said: "I am sorry to hear it — I hope
that it is not true of all of them — I am sure it is not true of the
abolitionists in the United States, for they sympathize with the oppressed, as well as the enslaved throughout the world."

5

When in August of that year Garrison returned to Boston, the
colored people of the city gave him a public reception in Marlboro'
Chapel. Many white people were present. Speeches of welcome
were made, to which Garrison replied, in part:

"In England I have seen dukes, marquises, and earls, and royalty
itself, in all the hereditary splendor of an ancient monarchy, surrounded with luxury and pomp, and the people impoverished and
oppressed to sustain it all; *but here, in New England, one looks for
such inequality in vain . . .*[3] And now I want the colored people
to sympathize with all who need their sympathy. I want them to

[3] Italics the author's.

call on British abolitionists to sympathize with the oppressed and suffering classes in their own land. I beseech them to put forth the finger of warning and entreaty to their British friends, in view of all the sufferings of those at hand, even at their doors."

In 1845 the Lowell millworkers, at Garrison's own door, thus petitioned the Massachusetts Legislature:

> We, the undersigned, peaceable, industrious, hard-working men and women of Lowell, in view of our condition — the evils already come upon us, by toiling from thirteen to fourteen hours per day, confined in unhealthy apartments, exposed to the poisonous contagion of air, vegetable, animal, and mineral properties, debarred from proper physical exercise, time for Mental discipline and Mastication cruelly limited; and thereby hastening us on through pain, disease, and privation, down to a premature grave . . .

A popular ballad in Lowell described the fate of a working girl, supposed to have died from overwork. One stanza read:

> That night a chariot passed her
> While on the ground she lay;
> The daughters of her master
> An evening visit pay —
> Their tender hearts were sighing
> As negroes' woes were told;
> While the white slave was dying
> Who gained their father's gold.

CHAPTER IV

"No Union with Slaveholders!"

FOLLOWING the World's Convention, Phillips remained in London a fortnight, sufficiently long to take part in several social affairs, to visit Daniel O'Connell in company with Garrison and to deliver a speech in Freemasons' Hall. O'Connell, who had begun agitation for the repeal of the union with England, was scheduled to deliver an important speech in Parliament, so the two friends were fearful they might be intruding. But as they were ushered into the library of the great man's house in Merrion Square, they found him reclining on a sofa reading a novel by Dickens. "I saw him," wrote Phillips, "at sixty-six years of age. He had a magnificent presence, impressive in bearing, massive like Jupiter. Webster himself hardly outdid him in the majesty of his proportions." Phillips enjoyed telling the story of a Bostonian who visited the Irish leader furnished with a letter of introduction. O'Connell, with his usual heartiness, took him by both hands and said: "I'm glad to see you. I'm always glad to see anybody from Massachusetts, a Free State."

"But," said the visitor, "this is slavery you allude to, Mr. O'Connell. I should like to say a word to you in justification of that institution."

"Very well, sir," replied O'Connell. "Free speech in this house. Say anything you please. But before you begin to defend a man's right to own his brother, allow me to step out and lock up my spoons."

The speech Phillips delivered was in support of the fantastic scheme of British Abolitionists to compete American slavery out of business by inducing the East India Company to raise cotton in India. "They can procure," wrote Thomas Clarkson, "not tens of thousands, but tens of millions of free laborers to work; what is of the greatest consequence in this case, the price of labor with these is only from a penny to three half-pence a day. What slavery can stand against these prices?"

In the sixteenth century Las Casas had wished to save American Indians from slavery by suggesting to the Spaniards that they should import Negroes; now Clarkson wished to free American Negroes by dooming East Indians to an existence no better than that of the slave. Phillips must have had his misgivings, since the last sentence of his speech reads: "Take care that in driving our cotton from your shores, you do not admit a single pound that be equally blood-stained with our own." The New York *Herald*, needlessly alarmed, berated "the villainous designs of the abolitionists to destroy the interests of the Southern planters."

In July Wendell and Ann crossed the North Sea to Belgium, whence they traveled up the Rhine to Cologne. Ann tried the baths in the Bavarian Alps, but found they did her more harm than good. They toured Switzerland, visited Milan, Florence and other cities of Northern Italy, then traveled to Naples, where they ascended Vesuvius and wandered musingly through the ruins of Herculaneum and Pompeii. Phillips wrote to Garrison: "Every reflecting mind at home must be struck with the many social evils which prevail; but the most careless eye cannot avoid seeing the painful contrasts which sadden one here at every step; wealth beyond that of fairy tales, and poverty all bare and starved at its side . . . The Apollo himself cannot dazzle one blind to the rags, want and misery which surround him . . . In our country the same contrast exists, but it is not so painfully prominent as here." He was beginning to feel dissatisfied with his idle existence and with the emptiness of mere sensual enjoyment. "None know what it is to live," he wrote to his friend, "till they redeem life from monotony by sacrifice. There is more happiness in one such hour than in dwelling forever with the beautiful and grand. . . . Nothing brings home so vividly to Ann as the sight of an occasional colored man in the street; and so you see we are ready to return to our posts in nothing changed."

2

There was rejoicing among Abolitionists in Boston. Phillips had returned, and Remond, who had been touring Ireland, had brought with him an appeal, headed by Daniel O'Connell and Father Theobald Mathew and signed by seventy thousand Irishmen, calling upon their compatriots in America to give all possible support to the Abolitionists. Irish immigrants were no friends of Abolition.

Garrison's indifference to the wageworker's lot and fear lest emancipation result in a great influx of Southern Negro labor were
mainly responsible. It was hoped that the Appeal would have a
salutary effect, and the Abolitionists resolved to make the most of it.

On the evening of January 28, 1842, Faneuil Hall was filled as it
had not been since the memorable Lovejoy meeting. It was cold in
the hall, so cold that reporters had to blow on their fingers while
taking notes, but this did not dampen the enthusiasm of the Irish
who had come to hear Phillips and others speak about O'Connell
and the Irish Address. That at this time Phillips still believed in the
efficacy of the ballot as a weapon against slavery may be judged
from the following paragraph:

"I trust in that love of liberty which every Irishman brings to
the country of his adoption, to make him true to her cause at the
ballot-box, and throw no vote without asking if the hand to which
he is about to trust political power will use it for the slave. When
an American was introduced to O'Connell in the lobby of the House
of Commons, he asked, without putting out his hand, 'Are you from
the South?' 'Yes, sir.' 'A slaveholder, I presume?' 'Yes, sir.' 'Then,'
said the great liberator, 'I have no hand for you!' and stalked away.
Shall his countrymen trust that hand with political power which
O'Connell deemed it a pollution to touch?"

Referring to the attitude of the Church of Rome towards slavery,
he said:

"I remember that a long line of popes, from Leo to Gregory, have
denounced the sin of making merchandise of men; that the voice of
Rome was the first to be heard against the slave-trade, and that the
bull of Gregory XVI, forbidding every true Catholic to touch the
accursed thing, is yet hardly a year old."

It was pleasing to the Irish, who had heard their religion assailed
by Lyman Beecher and others, to hear this tribute to Catholicism.
They cheered him to the echo. But the hope of the Abolitionists
that the Address would be heeded was disappointed. Bishop Hayes
of New York called the genuineness of the document into question,
at the same time saying that even if it were genuine it should not
be heeded, since Irish leaders had no business interfering in America's domestic affairs. This led to an incident which reveals a trait
of Phillips's character that should be kept in mind when we hear
him denounce Lincoln and others in terms that appear shocking.
He was extraordinarily impulsive. His enthusiasm made public men

appear to him either as heroes or as scoundrels, while his impulsiveness not infrequently transformed today's hero into a villain on the morrow, perhaps only to have him emerge as an even greater hero on some future occasion. When it became evident that the Irish intended to heed their bishop's advice, Phillips wrote to Richard Allen of Dublin, Ireland:

"What we want you and O'Connell to think it your duty to do is to send us a scorching, bitter, unsparing, pointed rebuke (and publish it in your own papers also as well as send it to us) telling the repealers here that you don't want the money or voices of slaveholders or their friends — that you repudiate all connection with a Repeal Society which holds its peace on Negro slavery in order to cozen favor with those whose hands are bloody with its guilt."

For one reason or another O'Connell thought it inadvisable to enter into controversy with the bishop, whereupon Phillips wrote to Richard D. Webb of Dublin: "We are all red hot against O'Connell. He won't shake hands with slaveholders, no — *but he will shake their gold. . . .* How contemptible O'Connell behaves."

In later years he was to call O'Connell "the greatest man the Irish race ever produced," and was to relate how when the Irish leader entered Parliament, the "West India interests" offered him the support of twenty-seven members if he would promise not to join the antislavery forces, but were indignantly repulsed. He was to relate how when the Louisiana planters, angry at the release by British authorities of Negro mutineers from the slave ship *Creole*, sent O'Connell a draft for one thousand pounds for the Repeal Society, the Irish leader held up the draft at a meeting in Constitution Hall in Dublin and said: "Old Ireland is very poor, but thank God she is not poor enough to take the unpaid wages of anybody." Then, handing the draft to the treasurer, he commanded: "Send it back!"

3

On January 12, 1842, "Old Man Eloquent," John Quincy Adams, rose in the House of Representatives and said: "I hold in my hand the petition of Benjamin Emerson and forty-five other citizens of Haverhill, Massachusetts, praying Congress to adopt immediate measures for the peaceful dissolution of the Union."

Several Southern representatives jumped to their feet. One demanded that the petition be burned in the presence of the House.

Resolutions censuring Adams for presenting it were introduced. The debate raged for days. When Adams pointed out that a few years before Robert B. Rhett of South Carolina had sought to present a similar petition of which Rhett himself was the author, he spiked the guns of his Southern critics. Would he withdraw the petition if the resolution of censure was withdrawn? He would not. How much more time then did he need to present his case? He replied that when Warren Hastings was on trial, a single speech by Burke had lasted several months. He believed he might be able "to close in ninety days." The South threw up the sponge. John M. Botts of Virginia moved that the resolution of censure be tabled. The motion carried.

The Haverhill petitioners were Democrats of the Locofoco variety. Their reason for wishing the Union dissolved was that "a vast proportion of the resources of one section of the Union is annually drained to sustain the views and course of another section without adequate return" and that "this Union, if persisted in, in the present course of things, will certainly overwhelm the whole nation in utter destruction."

The Haverhill petition was only a beginning. Fear that the annexation of Texas would enormously increase the power of the slaveholders over the Federal Government resulted in disunion sentiment throughout the North, especially in New England. The fear was not altogether groundless. The annexation resolution as finally drawn by John C. Calhoun (then Secretary of State) provided that "New States of convenient size, not exceeding four in number, in addition to said State of Texas . . . may hereafter . . . be formed out of the territory thereof." This eventually might mean ten additional proslavery senators. Petitions similar to the one from Haverhill came from Ohio and New York. William Slade of Vermont said in Congress that if Texas was annexed he would not give "a snap of his finger" for the Union. When he became Governor of his State, he declared in a message to the Legislature: "Upon the consummation of the threatened measure, I do not hesitate to say that it would be the duty of Vermont to declare her unalterable determination to have no connection with the new Union, thus formed without her consent and against her will." The Maine Legislature declared annexation "tantamount to disunion." Both Houses of the Massachusetts Legislature passed a resolution declaring that they would consider annexation "not binding," and that the State would "never by any act or deed give her consent to the further extension of slavery to any part of the world." Six members of the House, among whom were Adams and Giddings, issued an address to the Free States in which they said: "We hesitate not to say that annexation, effected by any act or proceeding of the Federal Government or any of its departments, would be identical to dissolution." Whittier wrote to Samuel E. Sewall: "Disunion before Texas!" and penned the lines:

> Make our Union-bond a chain,
> We will snap its links in twain,
> We will stand erect again.

Dr. William Ellery Channing wrote: "Better that we should part than be the police of the slaveholders, than fight his battles, than wage war to uphold an oppressive institution. . . . The free States declare that the very act of admitting Texas will be construed as a dissolution of the Union." Judge William Jay wrote to Edward A. Davis of Philadelphia: "Should the slaveholders succeed in their design of annexing Texas, then indeed would I not merely discuss, but with all my powers would I advocate an immediate dissolution. I love my children, my friends, my country too well to leave them a prey to the accursed government which would be sure to follow." The clank of arms reverberated in a speech John Quincy Adams delivered in North Bridgewater: "No! the people of the United States will never sanction the annexation of Texas to the United States. . . . I say to you my constituents, as I said to the young men of Boston: Burnish your armor — prepare for conflict — and, in the language of Galgacus to the ancient Britons, think of your forefathers — think of posterity!"

It was against this background that Garrison and Phillips launched their disunion propaganda and unfurled their slogan, "No Union with Slaveholders!"

4

Garrison had often raged at the proslavery clauses in the United States Constitution. In 1832 he had written, in the *Liberator*:

"There is much declamation about the sacredness of the compact which was formed between the free and slave States, on the adoption of the Constitution. A sacred compact, forsooth! We pronounce it the most bloody and heaven-daring arrangement ever made by men for the continuance and protection of a system of the most atrocious villainy ever exhibited on earth. Yes — we recognize the compact, but with feelings of shame and indignation; and it will be held in everlasting infamy by the friends of justice and humanity throughout the world."

When he became a Perfectionist and adopted the no-government doctrine he repudiated personal allegiance to the Constitution, hence to the Union. In 1842, encouraged by the disunion sentiment sweeping through the North, he came out openly for disunion. "DISSOLUTION NOW, Texas out of the question," he wrote. He declared the Constitution with its proslavery clauses to be "A Covenant with Death and an Agreement with Hell."

That Garrison should have arrived at the conclusion that the Union should be dissolved need not surprise us. He had succeeded magnificently in arousing Northern public opinion against slavery, but there was no sign whatever that the South was in the least affected. Indeed, slavery seemed more firmly entrenched than ever. At the beginning of his campaign there had been considerable sentiment for gradual emancipation in the Border States. That sentiment had now disappeared. Its disappearance was not due to resentment at Abolitionist propaganda, as claimed by Daniel Webster, but to economic causes. Owing to the exhaustion of the soil, slavery had ceased to be profitable in most of the Border States. Since then, however, those States had turned increasingly to slave breeding, with excellent financial results. The proposed annexation of Texas opened up new horizons for the slave-breeders. Garrison had come to realize that as far as influencing the South was concerned, his campaign of moral *pressure* had been no more successful than the moral *suasion* of the Quakers. More than that, he had become convinced that William Jay was right when he wrote to Henry I. Bowditch: "It is far more probable that a continuance of our present connection will enslave the North than that it will free the South."

Dissolution of the Union would accomplish two things: it would eliminate the danger of slavery expansion into Northern territory and its baneful influence on Northern institutions; it would end the complicity of the North in the maintenance of slavery. The slavery clauses of the Constitution obliged the North not only to return fugitive slaves, but to help maintain the slaves in subjection. "We have a right to call on you to give your blood to maintain the slaves of the South in bondage. Gentlemen, deceive not yourselves; you cannot deceive others. This is a pro-slavery government. Slavery is stamped on its heart — the Constitution," Robert Toombs of Georgia declared on the floor of Congress. Granting that dissolution would put an end to all this, one thing it would not do: *it would not free the slaves*. Indeed, it would make slavery more secure, by guaranteeing it against interference from the North. This obvious consequence of dissolution Garrison was loath to admit. He tried to make himself and others believe that dissolution would help the slave, by making it possible for him to free himself, as the South could then no longer count on the North to help suppress slave rebellion. Answering Theodore Parker, who wrote that he could not consent "to cut himself off from the slave population," he said: "What! is it to forsake the slave when I cease to be the aider and abettor of his master? What! when the North is pressing down upon four millions of slaves like an avalanche, and we say to her, 'Take off that pressure — stand aside — give the slave a chance to regain his feet and assert his freedom!' is that turning our backs upon him? Rely upon it, there is not an intelligent slaveholder at the South who is for a dissolution of the Union. . . . If it be otherwise, God grant that she may soon take the step, and see whether she will be able to hold a single slave one hour after the deed is done!"

That this reasoning was unrealistic, it is hardly necessary to point out. Garrison seldom made use of this argument. Usually he fell back on "obedience to the higher law." "This is with me a question of abstract morality — of obedience to the 'higher law,'" he declared. "My difficulty is a moral one. The Union was founded at the expense of the slave population of the land. I cannot swear to uphold it. As I understand it, they who ask me to do so, ask me to do an immoral act — to stain my conscience — to sin against God. How can I do this? I care not what consequences may be predicted."

Thus the country beheld the curious spectacle of Garrison advocating Northern secession so slavery might end, and Calhoun advocating Southern secession so it might endure! Both were wrong. Northern secession would not have ended slavery, but would have made it more secure; Southern secession did not preserve slavery, but destroyed it. Phillips was nearer right than he supposed when he wrote in the *Liberty Bell:* "It may yet come to pass that it will be given out as a subject for themes at Harvard: Which did the most, Garrison or Calhoun, for the downfall of American slavery."

5

In October, 1842, George Latimer, a fugitive slave and (according to John Quincy Adams) "the son of a very respectable gentleman from Norfolk, in Virginia, a member of one of the most distinguished and respectable families in that State" was arrested in Boston. When in 1830 Garrison had arrived in Boston from Baltimore, two fugitive slaves — husband and wife — were arrested and returned to their owner; the only protest was a letter Garrison wrote to the Boston *Transcript*. How different the situation now! Able lawyers hastened to the fugitive's defense. Protest meetings were held throughout the State. A special newspaper — *Latimer Journal and North Star*, edited by Dr. Henry I. Bowditch and William F. Channing — appeared every other day to keep the public informed. Four thousand people crowded into Faneuil Hall to listen to Phillips and other speakers.

It was on this occasion that Phillips for the first time publicly renounced allegiance to the Constitution: "Many of you, I doubt not, regret to have this man given up, but you cannot help it. There stands the bloody clause in the Constitution, — you cannot fret the seal off the bond. The fault is in allowing such a Constitution to live an hour. . . . When I look upon these crowded thousands, and see them trample upon their consciences and the rights of their fellow-men at the bidding of a piece of parchment, I say my *curse* be on the Constitution of the United States."

The Latimer case was settled by payment of four hundred dollars to the slaveholder, but this did not end the matter. Sixty-three thousand people signed a petition to the Legislature "to forbid all persons holding office under the laws of the State from aiding in the arrest or detention of persons claimed as fugitives from slavery; to forbid the use of jails or other public property for their detention; and to prepare amendments to the Federal Convention that should forever separate the people of the State from all connection with slavery." A Personal Liberty Law embodying most of these demands passed the following year.

After his public repudiation of the Constitution it did not take Phillips long to overtake Garrison in his disunion propaganda. In May, 1844, at the twelfth annual meeting of the Anti-Slavery Society, he introduced a resolution to the effect "that the abolitionists of this country should make it one of the primary objects of their agitation to dissolve the American Union." Until dissolution was an established fact they should renounce their citizenship: "*Resolved*, That secession from the present United States Government is the duty of every abolitionist; since no one can take office under the United States Constitution without violating the anti-slavery principles, and rendering himself an abetter of the slave-holder in his sin."

When asked to stand for Congress he declined with the words: "I cannot enter there without recognizing the Constitution, which recognizes slavery."

"But you would gain there a great help toward reforming the Constitution and abolishing slavery."

"God did not send me into the world to abolish slavery, but to do my duty," he replied.

Doing his duty meant satisfying his "Puritan conscience." In 1862, at a public meeting in Washington, he declared: "I have labored nineteen years to take nineteen States out of the Union, and if I have spent any nineteen years to the satisfaction of my Puritan conscience it was these nineteen years."

That duty to their consciences rather than duty towards the slave animated the two Abolitionist leaders was the opinion of Garrison's sons, who wrote: "All other considerations yielded to this religious purification of themselves before their Creator."

6

To do Garrison and Phillips justice it is necessary to consider the cultural atmosphere in which they moved. Theirs was an individual-istic age. The foremost New England thinkers of their time — Emerson, Thoreau, Alcott, Channing — taught that all social reform must begin with the individual. To set things right, begin by follow-ing the dictates of your conscience and leave the consequences to God. "Nothing is at last sacred but the integrity of your own mind," wrote Emerson. After Phillips had lectured in Concord on dis-union, Thoreau wrote to Garrison: "We would fain express our appreciation of the freedom and steady wisdom, so rare in a re-former, with which he declared that he was not born to abolish slavery, but to do right. . . . Here is one, who is at the same time an eloquent speaker and a righteous man." Thoreau and Alcott made a gesture at refusing to pay taxes, and Thoreau handed a document to the town clerk of Concord reading, "Know all men by these presents that I, Henry D. Thoreau, do not wish to be regarded as a member of any incorporated society which I have not joined."

It will always remain a moot question to what extent, if any, the end justifies the means. Nicolai Lenin has written: "Morality is that which serves the destruction of the old exploiters' society." When Lincoln undertook to return fugitive slaves, he was saying in effect: "Morality is that which serves to preserve the Union." Our age has set the precedent of punishing individuals for failing to practice civil disobedience or non-collaboration in matters the civilized world regards as crimes against humanity. Who will say that slavery was not such a crime? "Somehow the same historians," wrote Professor Richard Hofstadter, "who have been indulgent with men who exaggerated because they wanted to be elected have been extremely severe with men who exaggerated because they wanted to free the slaves." [1]

Neither Garrison nor Phillips followed Thoreau's and Alcott's example in refusing to pay taxes. Phillips wrote to a friend: "Taxes are not voluntary. Did Jesus support Nero when he paid a tax? I seek to be in this country like an alien, a traveller. Such can't avoid direct taxation; but are they responsible for the use government makes of the money? We are not responsible for what we can't prevent."

Garrison addressed an appeal to the "Friends of Freedom in the United States" in which he said: "The strongest political influence which Northern voters can wield for the overthrow of slavery, is to cease sustaining the existing compact, by withdrawing from the polls, and calmly waiting for the time when a righteous government shall supersede the institution of tyranny . . . Henceforth, therefore, until slavery be abolished, the watchword, the rallying-cry, the motto on the banner of the American Anti-Slavery Society shall be, NO UNION WITH SLAVEHOLDERS!"

A few Abolitionists who held office resigned. Francis Jackson sent his resignation as Justice of the Peace to the Governor of Massachusetts and renounced allegiance to the Constitution: "Henceforth it is dead to me and I to it. While I retain my liberty, I will be a party to no compact which helps to rob any other man of his."

[1] Richard Hofstadter, *The American Political Tradition: and the Men Who Made It.* (Alfred A. Knopf, New York, 1948.)

CHAPTER V
Essex Street

AT the dedication of Phillips's statue in Boston the remark was made: "The worldly side of Phillips's life may be summed up in these words: He was born in Beacon Street and he died on Common Street." In between was "little noisy, sunny, dusty, cosy, dirty Essex Street," [1] where he and Ann lived for over forty years.

They had returned to Boston in July, 1841. A half hour's journey from the city, at Nahant, a fashionable summer resort, Phillips's mother owned a roomy country house. Here the two young people spent the remainder of that summer and the early autumn. Although the house was a mile from the nearest dwelling they did not live in seclusion. Besides Phillips's mother, there was his sister and her five children, while other members of the family frequently came for a longer or shorter stay. Phillips's relations with his brothers and sisters lacked cordiality, which is hardly surprising considering that they had questioned his sanity and had wished to have him confined. Ann, whom they held principally responsible for his straying from respectability, was not a favorite with them. She wrote to Elizabeth Pease, the English Quakeress who had become her confidante: "We are considered heretics and almost infidels, but we pursue the even tenor of our way undisturbed. Sometimes Wendell goes off abolitionizing for two or three days, but I remain on the ground."

In October they moved to 26 Essex Street, into a house Ann had inherited from her father. The red-painted brick building — three stories and an attic — contained two dwelling units. The corner unit, with a shop on the ground floor, was occupied by a retail provision merchant; the other, which was to be Phillips's home for practically the remainder of his career, had a recessed front door, reached by half a dozen stone steps, and an ornamental iron balcony on the second floor. Nothing now remains of the house except the entrance door, a cherished possession of the Bostonian Society.

[1] Letter of Phillips to Mrs. Garrison, August 20, 1847.

The interior of the house after Wendell and Ann established themselves was little more prepossessing than its exterior. It was not the kind of home one would have associated with a man of culture whose annual income from Lyceum lectures and capital investments was, during the greater part of his career, between fifteen and twenty thousand dollars. Dining room and kitchen were on the first floor. The former had a sepulchral appearance and was seldom used, for Ann was usually confined to her room, where Phillips, when not on the road lecturing, kept her company at her meals. The stairway with its worn runner led to a double parlor on the second floor. The front parlor, about twenty feet square, painted a yellowish white and carpeted in maroon, was Phillips's study. The furniture was of mahogany and consisted of a horsehair sofa, a large table with side leaves in the center of the room, an armchair, a few chairs, and a small table beneath a pier glass between the two tall windows. Both tables were covered with a confusion of books, newspapers, magazines, letters and sheets of writing paper. A half-dozen paintings adorned the walls. The back parlor contained Phillips's library of some twenty-five hundred volumes and stacks of newspapers and magazines. Two bedrooms on the third floor and rooms in the attic for the two maids completed the establishment. "It was such a domicile," wrote James R. Gilmore, who visited Phillips in 1862, "as any reasonably prudent man could support on $1500 a year."

There was little space in the house for the entertainment of visitors, but Wendell and Ann did little entertaining. Ann's illness would have made social activity difficult in any event, besides which they were ostracized by that portion of Boston society to which by birth Phillips belonged. The new friends he had made found little time for social amenities and did not feel quite at home with him. "In all cases his democratic habit had the good-natured air of some kindly young prince; he never was quite the equal associate that he seemed," wrote Thomas Wentworth Higginson, who stated that Phillips was "almost a recluse."

There was, however, a certain amount of going back and forth between the Phillips house and the homes of other Abolitionists, several of whom lived in the immediate neighborhood. It was a walk of five minutes or less to the homes of Francis Jackson, Charles F. Hovey, the Garrisons, the Chapmans, the Lorings, the Weston sisters. In 1847 Theodore Parker moved into a house in Exeter Place, directly in the rear of the Phillips homestead, so that their gardens touched. A prodigious man was Parker, a glutton for knowledge, who read fifteen languages and spent sixteen hours a day in his study among his books and miniature bears — bears of ivory, of metal, of wood, of plaster, in every conceivable posture. Phillips, when ready to go to bed, would look across the intervening space at the lighted windows of Parker's study and murmur: "The trophies of Miltiades will not let me sleep."

2

Ann seldom left her room. Some of Phillips's friends never laid eyes on her. "I never saw his wife, though in his conversations and his correspondence with me he often spoke of her, and it was my privilege to exchange many communications with her," wrote Phillips's college friend Dr. Edgar Buckingham. He called her Egeria, after the goddess of ancient Rome whom Numa, second King of Rome, claimed to consult in a secret grotto. Others, less charitable, apparently considered her illness imaginary. "Since I have been ill," she wrote to Miss Pease, "the world has worn quite another aspect to me, for many I had thought friends have fallen off and many have misunderstood the nature of my state of health so much that there is no pleasure in communication with them." Whatever the nature of her illness, she could have found no more indulgent husband. Once when her condition was particularly serious, Phillips nursed her for sixty days without once leaving the house. That she was not always considerate may be inferred from the fact that she never hesitated to interrupt his nightly repose. When she called he would strike a match to light a candle, and he told Abby Kelley Foster that one morning he counted twenty-one burned-out matches. The family physician has stated that he himself once counted fifteen. Nor was she always good-humored. She confessed to Miss Pease that she was "cross very often," and Carlos Martyn, an intimate friend, has written that "there were times when she was fretful and exacting." He adds that Phillips "never lost his temper or his patience on such occasions." That she loved him, if not altogether unselfishly, admits of no doubt. She was wont to refer to him as "her better three quarters" and would say possessively: "We are one, you know."

To alleviate her suffering — which, imaginary or not, must have been acute — mesmerism, then much in vogue, was resorted to. As trustworthy practitioners of the art were rare, Phillips himself undertook to mesmerize her. She wrote to Miss Pease: "So poor, devoted Wendell is caught one hour of his busy day and seated down to hold my thumbs. . . . I grow sicker every year, Wendell lovelier; I more desponding, he always cheery, and telling me I shall live to be not only 'fat and forty, but fat and scolding eighty.' . . . For his sake I should love to live; for my own part I am tired, not of life but of a sick one." Fits of despondency were frequent. "I have had a dreadful winter," she wrote in February, 1845, "so sick that life is a burden to me. I do not know what to do. I am tired of suffering. I have no faith in anything."

To remain "cheery" under such circumstances must not have been easy. Apparently Phillips managed it. He is even reported by a former Mayor of Boston, Dr. Samuel A. Green, to have said: "There is more sun and fun in Essex Street than anywhere else in Boston." His letters to Miss Pease, however, were not always cheerful. Occasionally there crept in a note of impatience, as when he wrote in February, 1850: "Ann is as usual three-fourths of the time on the bed — prostrated — too many thoughts — too many tears — too many cares . . . Her last life was in England, perpetual sick chamber since." But at another time: "Ann is . . . so much my motive and prompter to everything good that I fear, should I lose her, there'd be nothing left of me worth your loving." When in 1863 a volume of his addresses appeared, he presented Ann with a copy inscribed: "Speeches and Lectures. By Ann Phillips."

Ann being fond of flowers, Phillips saw to it that the sickroom was always gay with their colors, fragrant with their perfume. "The sunny south chamber," wrote a relative of Ann's, "having an outlook down Harrison Avenue, was bright with flowers, of which the invalid was passionately fond. In midwinter she would have nasturtiums, smilax and costly exotics, later the brilliant tulips, and then the blossoms of spring, the May-flowers and anemones, until the garden rose and the sweetbrier appeared." She read little. "Your humble servant," she wrote to Miss Pease, "reads generally the *Standard*[2] and the *Liberator*, and that is pretty much all the literature her aching head will allow her to pursue." But she awaited eagerly the passage of the organ-grinder. "Wendell, don't forget the organ money," she would remind him. The organ man, knowing that he would be well rewarded, never failed to give his entire repertoire be-

[2] *National Anti-Slavery Standard.*

fore the Phillips house, and she would listen until the last notes had faded in the distance.

Nothing in her appearance denoted the invalid. "She had a good color, a strong voice, and a hearty laugh, so that it was difficult to think her ill," wrote her relation. Her appetite was excellent and Phillips did his best to satisfy it. When at home he himself did the marketing, buying two boxes of strawberries when one would have sufficed, so the most luscious from each box might be picked for Ann's portion, carefully feeling the pods of peas, to make sure they were soft and tender, "as Ann wanted them," selecting potatoes as nearly as possible of equal size because that always pleased her. They took their meals together at a small table in her room. "We dine in French," he used to say, meaning that they were in the habit of conversing in that language during their meals.

At home he was no great talker. "Silence would reign at 26 Essex Street unless I broke it," Ann remarked to a friend. What Phillips liked best — better perhaps than lecturing or reading — was to bring forth his kit of carpenter's tools and set to work repairing a door, a window, or anything else about the house. As formerly his mother, so now Ann used to say that a first-rate mechanic was lost when he became an intellectual.

Notwithstanding the lack of supervision, the house was kept in order and meals were served on time. He had solved the servant problem by paying the highest wages in Boston and being kind and considerate. After his mother's death he fell heir to his childhood nurse, who had been with the family for more than a generation, and installed her as cook. The woman adored him. When he was in the house she would leave the kitchen door open, so she might hear his step. "Bless him, there is more music in his footfall than in a cathedral organ," was her adoring comment. When she grew too old to work he installed her in a house of her own and visited her often, always with an armful of presents.

Phillips and Ann were fond of children and having none of their own sometimes borrowed those of their friends and acquaintances, giving them the run of the house and the garden. If the noise troubled Ann, Phillips would take them into his study and supervise their play. Among the children frequently at the Essex Street house was Phoebe Garnaut. Her widowed mother, Mrs. Eliza Garnaut, a Welshwoman who had married a Frenchman, was Matron of the "Home for the Shelter of Orphan and Destitute

Children" in Albany Street. Phillips wrote after her death that "she gave her nights to sick chambers where, save her unwearied love, none but the physician ever entered. . . . I am indebted to her for a new lesson of practical Christianity." When in 1849 she died, twelve-year-old Phoebe came to live at the Phillips house. She was never legally adopted, but was considered so much a member of the household that people referred to her as "Phoebe Phillips." Her presence had a wholesome effect on Ann. Phillips felt so encouraged that he thought of still further enlarging the household by getting Elizabeth Pease to come and live with them: "We should make a happy house, you and Ann, Phoebe Garnaut and I, for Phoebe is our little girl, now that her mother is gone, and Ann busies herself with lessons and French exercises, as when she herself went to school." In 1853 he wrote: "I teach her this winter. We think the confinement of school is bad for her. So she and I study French, Latin, Geography, Arithmetic, History and Grammar."

Phoebe remained with them eleven years, until her marriage, in 1860, to George W. Smalley, a journalist. She followed her husband to England when he became London correspondent of Greeley's New York *Tribune*.

3

For over thirty years Phillips was one of the most popular Lyceum lecturers in America. His annual revenue from that source has been estimated at from ten to fifteen thousand dollars. Yet he spent the last years of his life in straitened circumstances, and at his death there was barely enough money to pay his debts. He had suffered no financial reverses and it is doubtful if he and Ann ever spent for their own needs more than half the original income from their combined capital, but their generosity was quixotic. Among Phillips' papers was found a notebook in which he jotted down the incidental charity he dispensed from his pocket. In thirty years this alone amounted to nearly sixty-five thousand dollars. When he sent money by post he nearly always pretended he was acting as Ann' secretary: "Ann wishes to enclose a check for twenty dollars (which I do)" — "Ann was delighted to hear from you. She bids me no delay to reply. So I have mailed a check for $30." He aided scores of indigent Abolitionists, including the editor of the *Liberator*.

Organized charity's "cold statistical Christ" did not preside over is benevolence. He preferred to be deceived many times rather than run the risk of failing to aid someone truly in need. "Thus it was natural," wrote Edward Everett Hale, "that every outcast, of every color and nation, when he might find himself in need in Boston went first to Mr. Phillips's door. . . . He gave lavishly whenever he thought he ought to give, not only of his time, but of his money; exactly how much no one but himself knew. His house became a sort of bureau of charity, investigation and relief, so that whenever a man, woman, or child was not known at the overseers of the poor, at the 'Provident' or the 'Associated Charities,' it was the more certain he was known at Mr. Phillips's. He gave alms literally to all sorts of men." James Redpath wrote: "I have seen pictures . . . the surprised look of some Kansas boy whom I had introduced to him, for instance, when he found that Phillips had slipped a twenty dollar gold piece into his hand as he was shaking hands on parting. And no fugitive slave, or workingman, or working girl, or young student ever went away, that I ever heard of, empty-handed."

There was Mrs. Van Benthuyson, widow of a nephew of Jefferson Davis. Born and reared in the North, she moved with her children to Boston when her husband, a Confederate officer, died in action in 863. Forced to find some way to augment her small income, it occurred to her that she might lecture before literary clubs on "The Real Condition of the South." James R. Gilmore had given her a letter of introduction to Phillips, who helped her get started. Sometime later Gilmore happened to be in Boston and called on her. She told him of a meeting with Phillips and on returning to his hotel, he put down what she had said.

After the death of both principals Gilmore wrote an article about Phillips in which he gave the woman's story in her own words:

And now I must tell you something about him. A few nights ago I lectured at a place about ten miles from Gloucester, and nearly that far from the railroad. In the morning I had to ride that distance in a blinding snowstorm to catch the train to Boston, and when I got upon the car I met Mr. Phillips. He beckoned me to a vacant seat by his side, and when I had taken it he asked me where I had spoken the night before. I told him, and then he said:

"I wouldn't be impertinent, but tell me how much did they pay you?"

"Five dollars," I answered, "and my fare to and from Boston."

"Five dollars!" he exclaimed. "Why, I always get $100 or $200; and your lecture must be worth more than mine, for you can give facts, I only opinions."

"Small as it is, I'm very glad to get it, Mr. Phillips. I would talk at that rate every night during the winter."

We rode on for a little while in silence, then, drawing a roll of bank notes from his vest pocket, he said to me in a hesitating way. "I don't want to give offense, but you know I preach that a woman is entitled to the same pay as a man if she does the same work. Now, I was paid $100 for my talk at Gloucester, last night, and if you will kindly let me divide it with you I shall not have had any more than you, and the thing will be even."

I refused to accept the money; but he quickly took my reticule from my lap and opening it, put the roll of bank notes into it. When I got here to my lodgings I counted the roll and found it contained $100 — all that he had received for his lecture at Gloucester.

Phillips was once heard to remark that the sentence "Phocion always remained poor, though he might have been very rich," which he had been given to translate as a boy in Latin School, suited him as a motto. A few days before his death he told a friend that his idea of living had been "to walk with open heart and open hand from day to day."

CHAPTER VI

The Orator

J AMES BRYCE, author of *The American Commonwealth*, said
of Phillips that "He was in the opinion of competent critics one
of the first orators of the century, and not more remarkable for the
finish than for the transparent simplicity of his style, which at-
tained its highest effects by the most direct and natural methods."
John Bright declared that "there was no orator superior to him who
spoke the English language." In October, 1844, Emerson wrote in his
Journal: "I wish that Webster and Everett and also the young political aspirants of Massachusetts should hear Wendell Phillips speak,
were it only for the capital lesson in eloquence they might learn of
him. This namely, that the first and the second and the third part of
the art is, to keep your feet always firm on a fact." Chauncey Depew,
in an interview with Oswald Garrison Villard, declared Phillips to
have been "the greatest of American orators," and added that he felt
qualified to pronounce this judgment, since he had heard "all the
leading speakers from Clay and Webster through the administration
of Wilson." The poet Whittier expressed the opinion that Phillips
was "the greatest orator in the country, if not in the world." Susan B.
Anthony considered him "a matchless orator . . . the like of him
we shall never see again."

An orator's ability to charm and to convince does not necessarily
depend on the soundness of his reasoning. Indeed, the curse of oratory
is that it often persuades notwithstanding the fallacy of the argument.
The principal factors in an orator's success are the personality of the
speaker, the timeliness of his appeal, his delivery and manner of
presentation. Phillips's argument was not always sound and he was
usually a generation or more ahead of his listeners. The impression
he produced and the influence he wielded must therefore principally be ascribed to the potency of the remaining factors.

The testimony of his contemporaries leaves no doubt that his
personality seldom failed to impress. James L. Hughes, in an article

entitled *World Leaders I Have Known*, wrote of him: "He had the most remarkable head, face and bodily poise I ever saw." Richard Hinton, who competed with him for the favor of Lyceum audiences, said: "He was possessed and moulded of grace." John D. Long, editor of the Boston *Daily Globe*, spoke of his "noble carriage, fine, clear look and stamp of manliness." Others employ such expressions as "beautiful face," "fine figure," "fine bearing and classical features." We may therefore take it for granted that when Phillips stepped to the front of the platform, buttoned up his frock coat, put his right foot a little forward, and notwithstanding a slight feeling of nervousness that troubled him at the beginning of a speech, relaxed into an attitude of graceful ease, his audience could not help being favorably impressed.

He usually began in a low voice, which increased in volume until it reached what might be called a conversational pitch — "the conversational raised to its highest power," said Higginson. His voice had no great range and was thin in the higher register, but in the middle and lower it was resonant, well-modulated, mellifluous. It was uncommonly penetrating and has been compared with the sound of a violin. He never raised his voice. His most vitriolic and denunciatory utterances were delivered in a conversational tone. "It was as if he simply repeated, in a little louder tone, what he had just been saying to some familiar friend at his elbow," wrote Higginson. Theodore Parker has said that Phillips "seemed to suppress rather than to express all he felt," while Horace H. Hagan remarked that "he could sound the trumpet call of defiance and annihilate with the thunderbolt of indignant scorn, in a conversational tone." He dropped his g's, like an Englishman, and said "isn't" and "wasn't," but Higginson assures us that it "did not sound inelegant." He made more gestures than he was generally given credit for, but they were "so fit that they seemed as natural as breathing."

His language, like his delivery, was characterized by naturalness and simplicity. He shunned oratorical ornamentation and redundancy. This at first surprised by its novelty, then delighted by the intimacy it established between speaker and audience and was singularly persuasive. Charles Eliot Norton told about a Bostonian who once when Phillips was speaking heard a man behind him "applauding and stamping his feet with the utmost enthusiasm, exclaiming at the same time, 'The damned old liar! The damned old liar!'" The president of a college, who although a member of the

Anti-Slavery Society differed radically with Phillips, said that he always went to meetings of the society determined to vote against Phillips's proposals, yet invariably voted for them. Dr. George Edward Woodberry wrote: "He bound me with a spell. I cannot describe his oratory. I have heard many others make addresses; I never heard any other man speak." Horace Greeley, between whom and Phillips there was no love lost, paid this tribute to his oratory: "American oratory is so preponderantly boisterous and convulsive, so disfigured by contortions and volcanic fervor of manner . . . that he has done us good service by affording a striking example of eloquence without rant, earnest and devoid of vehemence, and fervor without ostentation. . . . This 'arch fanatic' has persisted in talking to audiences quietly and naturally. . . . We think the first impression of almost every boy who hears him is that oratory is a far easier and simpler achievement than he is led to suppose it."

Those who tried to imitate him quickly discovered that it was neither easy nor simple. In the words of Emerson, there had to be "a man behind the speech." That in Phillips's case this was not wanting was recognized by his severest critics, who seldom managed to withhold admiration. Rufus Choate said of one of his speeches that it was "outrageously magnificent." The editor of the Boston *Courier* wrote on one occasion: "Never were the splendid abilities of this most accomplished and able fanatic more amply displayed than on this occasion. Sentiments most repugnant to the feelings of every patriot were absolutely applauded when clothed in the graceful and magnificent diction of this anti-slavery Cicero." The Richmond *Enquirer* called him "an infernal machine set to music."

He was most effective when most bitter. The Boston *Traveller* claimed that admirers "who had not yet learned that it is lightning and not thunder that kills, would sometimes hiss or interject cutting remarks, so he would let himself out once to show what he could do." When he indulged in invective "It was not," said George William Curtis, "as invective is generally understood, a torrent of scathing words. He commonly beheaded his opponent with a single stroke of his blade." Frederick Douglass admired him most in debate. Phillips would listen to a long and involved argument without taking a single note, then reply point for point. He made ample use of metaphor, quoted aptly and abundantly, especially from de Tocqueville's *Democracy in America;* he let fly apothegms that would fasten themselves in the memory and he had Lincoln's love of a good story.

He could play the entire scale of human emotions save one — "He could not," said Frederick Douglass, "bring tears to mature eyes." He once asked Anna Dickinson, particularly successful in making audiences weep, why he could never succeed in doing so. "Because, Mr. Phillips, you never cry yourself," she replied.

2

In the course of his career he delivered some two thousand speeches and lectures, not one of which he read from manuscript. He considered reading fatal to the impression a speaker aimed to produce. "I once spent the night with a clergyman, an old friend, who had the habit of reading his sermons," he said once. "I asked him why he did so. He went on to give me the reasons, and became animated. 'Well,' said I, 'I am tired to-night, but I have been very much interested in what you said. Nevertheless, if you had *read* your remarks I should have gone to sleep.' "

He seldom put his speeches on paper. "Speaking and writing," he said once, "require such different habits of mind, that success in one arena makes failure quite sure in the other." He considered "being chained to an inkpot, a mild form of slavery." To Lydia Maria Child he wrote: "My individuality starves on paper." His usual method of preparation was to saturate himself with a subject, then lie down on the sofa in his study and ruminate. A few opening sentences and the peroration might be written down and committed to memory, for the rest he trusted to the inspiration of the moment. The method suggests indolence and according to his friend Frank P. Stearns was responsible for the inaccuracies and exaggerations of which he was sometimes guilty. When a speech he had delivered was to appear in print it was set up in type from the stenographic transcript and underwent endless revision. Concerning one of Phillips's speeches which appeared in the *Liberator*, Garrison wrote to Oliver Johnson: "Such revision, correction, alteration, and addition you never saw, in the way of emendation! I proposed to Phillips to send the altered 'slips' to Barnum as a remarkable curiosity."

It were a mistake to assume, however, that he was incapable of writing clearly and forcefully. He wrote several pamphlets and magazine articles that are not inferior to his best speeches. Several of the speeches and lectures (by no means those of least merit) he wrote

out in full. Copies of his Phi Beta Kappa centennial address, which
took three hours to deliver, were furnished to the press before its
delivery at Harvard College. Reporters present claimed that he
did not vary by so much as a word from the printed text.

3

In the minds of many the term "agitator" has a derogatory meaning. Phillips claimed the appellation with pride. He hoped to go down
in history as the leading agitator of his time. When asked to deliver
a Phi Beta Kappa oration at Yale, he said that he would do so on
condition that he might choose for his subject "The Scholar in a
Republic, of Necessity an Agitator." The condition was accepted
and the address made so favorable an impression that a week later he
was asked to repeat it at Brown University.

In his Phi Beta Kappa centennial address at Harvard he said:

"Agitation is an old word with a new meaning. Sir Robert Peel,
the first English leader who felt himself its tool, defined it to be
'marshalling the conscience of a nation to mould its laws' . . . Parties
and sects laden with the burden of securing their own success cannot afford to risk new ideas. 'Predominant opinions,' said Disraeli,
'are the opinions of a class that is vanishing.' The agitator must stand
outside of organizations, with no bread to earn, no candidate to
elect, no party to save, no object but truth, — to tear a question open
and riddle it with light."

It was the agitator's duty to spur the people to constant viligance,
so the ground already won might not be lost:

"Eternal vigilance is the price of liberty; power is ever stealing
from the many to the few. The manna of popular liberty must be
gathered each day or it is rotten. The living sap of to-day outgrows
the dead rind of yesterday. The hand entrusted with power becomes,
either from human depravity or *esprit de corps*, the necessary
enemy of the people. Only by continued oversight can the democrat
in office be prevented from hardening into a despot; only by un-
intermitted agitation can a people be sufficiently awake to principle
not to let liberty be smothered in material prosperity . . . Never
look, therefore, for an age when the people can be quiet and safe. At
such times Despotism, like a shrouding mist, steals over the mirror
of Freedom . . . As health lies in labor, and there is no royal road

to it but through toil, so there is no republican road to safety but in constant distrust." [1]

He had an unbounded faith in the common sense of the masses:

"The accumulated intellect of the masses is greater than the heaviest brain God ever gave to a single man . . . [2] '*Vox populi, vox Dei*.' I do not mean this of any single verdict which the people of to-day may record. In time the selfishness of one class neutralizes the selfishness of another. The people always mean right, and in the end will do right."

He agreed with John Bright that "the first five hundred men who passed in the Strand would make as good a Parliament as that which sits at St. Stephen," and favored the utmost freedom of discussion:

"Let us always remember that he does not really believe his own opinion who does not give free scope to his opponent. Persecution is really want of faith in our creed. . . . He who stifles free discussion, secretly doubts whether what he professes to believe is really true. . . . Men are educated and the State uplifted by allowing all — every one — to broach all their mistakes and advocate all their errors. The community that will not protect the most ignorant and unpopular member in the free utterance of his opinions, no matter how false and hateful, is only a gang of slaves!"

When called a fanatic he replied: "That convenient epithet 'fanatic,' has been flung at every reformer, whose arguments could not be answered, for eighteen hundred years." It was, he said, "a disingenuous artifice of the helpless conservative and the demagog."

4

Phillips, like Garrison, considered the use of harsh language indispensable to arouse public opinion:

"The scholar may sit in his study and take care that his language is not exaggerated, but the rude mass of men are not to be caught by balanced periods — they are caught by men whose words are half battles. From Luther down, the charge against every reformer has been that his language is too rough. Be it so. Rough instruments are

[1] Distrust is to liberty what jealousy is to love. — ROBESPIERRE.
[2] There is someone who is cleverer than Voltaire, cleverer than Bonaparte, cleverer than any of the Directors, than any Minister in the past or in the future; and that person is everybody [*tout le monde*]. — TALLEYRAND.

used for rough work. . . . The slaveholder is not appeased by delicate language. If he perceives in the individual an earnest purpose and a pledged determination against his system, he hates him just as much for that purpose wrapped up in honied phrase, as if it were expressed in rough old Saxon."

His most vehement assaults were not upon the slavery system but upon individuals, especially those who recognized slavery as a great wrong yet were willing to temporize — upon Clay, Webster, Choate, Seward, Greeley, Lincoln. "Men blame us for the bitterness of our language and the personality of our attacks," he said. "It results from our position. The great mass of people can never be made to stay and argue a long question. They must be made to feel it, through the hides of their idols. When you have launched your spear into the rhinoceros hide of a Webster or a Benton, every Whig and Democrat feels it."

He did not follow the custom of not speaking ill of the dead:

"We will gibbet the name of every apostate so black and high that his children's children will blush to hear it. Yet we bear no malice, — cherish no resentment. We thank God that the love of fame, 'that last infirmity of a noble mind,' is shared by the ignoble. In our necessity we seize this weapon in the slave's behalf, and teach caution to the living by meeting out relentless justice to the dead."

The death of Henry Clay drew from him the following comment:

"When we think of such a man as Henry Clay, his long life, his mighty influence cast always into the scale against the slave . . . when we think how the slave trembled at the sound of his voice, and that from a multitude of breaking hearts there went up nothing but gratitude to God when it pleased Him to call that great sinner from this world, — we cannot find it in our hearts, we could not shape our lips to ask men to do him honor."

Rufus Choate, who spoke with disdain of the "glittering and sounding generalities of natural right which make up the Declaration of Independence" and jeered at the "philanthropy" of the Abolitionists, received after his death no eulogy from Wendell Phillips. Phillips called upon the Genius of Rome, of England, of France to parade before his audience their great men of the law who at the risk of fortune and of life itself had fought against injustice, exclaiming in conclusion: "Then New England shouts, 'This is Choate, who made it safe to murder; and of whose health thieves asked before they began to steal!'"

5

In the early part of the nineteenth century it was not uncommon for people to listen to a Sunday evening sermon lasting two or three hours. There was little else by way of entertainment to be found in smaller communities. Occasionally an itinerant lecturer came and usually found an appreciative audience. In 1826, Josiah Holbrook, whose domain was the natural sciences, organized at Millbury, Massachusetts, the first American Lyceum with "the diffusion of useful knowledge" for its avowed object. Three years later there were Lyceum groups in every State of the Union, and until the end of the century the institution was, to all intents and purposes, a school for adult education. Ralph Waldo Emerson, Edward Everett, Rufus Choate, Horace Greeley, Henry Ward Beecher, Horace Mann, George William Curtis, John B. Gough were among the favorite Lyceum lecturers, but none retained public favor longer than Wendell Phillips. He made his debut in the Lyceum in 1836, and for nearly half a century — until his death in 1884 — appeared before Lyceum audiences. His fee quickly mounted from twenty-five dollars to two hundred dollars and over. So great was his drawing power that committees often journeyed to Boston to persuade him to come.

At first his lectures dealt with travel, science, invention, discovery and antislavery. Later, current topics, various kinds of reform, foreign affairs, biography, finance, religion and other subjects were added to his repertory. It was said that he could talk interestingly about a broom handle. He once declined to give a lecture on trees, saying that his knowledge of the subject was confined to the ability to distinguish an oak from an elm, but when during a music festival he was asked to speak about music, concerning which his knowledge was equally rudimentary, he talked for an hour about its harmonizing influence, having been inspired by the unchallenged presence of a colored man in the audience. He was none too well qualified to instruct in some of the other topics. While he fancied himself an authority on finance, his ideas on that subject were of the crackpot variety. Generally speaking he cared more for effect than for accuracy. In his lecture "The Lost Arts," which he prepared in 1838 and delivered more often than any other (though assuredly not two thousand times, as has been claimed), he made some serious mis-

statements, which he failed to correct when they were called to his
attention.

When lecturing on the Lyceum he seldom lost an opportunity for
antislavery propaganda. When asked to name his price for a lecture
he would say: "If you want a literary lecture the price will be so and
so [a high one], but if you will let me speak on slavery I will come
for nothing and pay my own expenses." When engaged to speak on
some other topic he usually managed to slip in a few allusions to
slavery, often with the result that he would be invited to speak on
that subject the following year.

The Lyceum season was from November until April and lecturing trips were usually of three weeks' duration, with short intervals
in between. When his wife's condition was worse than usual Phillips
only took engagements close to Boston, otherwise he might travel as
far as the Mississippi. "I know every locomotive, every conductor,
and the exact depth of mud in every road in the country," he used
to say. To a friend he wrote: "In eleven days I have slept on a
regular bed but four nights." Often he traveled by wagon over roads
that were rivers of mud: "Mud over the hubs of the wheels, literally,
one horse was smothered in it." He carried with him a container of
his favorite tea and a large gray woolen shawl which he spread be
tween the bedsheets at night. Before speaking he usually fortified
himself with three cups of tea and three raw eggs.

Audiences ranged from fifteen hundred to four thousand and
represented a crosscut of the community — business and professional
men, farmers, mechanics and their wives, sometimes a few ultra-
modern women in "Bloomer" costume. Inclement weather did not
discourage them. "Rain, clouds, damp, mud, and grim heavens. Still
the audiences are large," he wrote.

The following amusing incident which took place on one of his
Lyceum tours was told by himself:

In the old Anti-Slavery days I lectured in Cincinnati. At the
same time there was a convention of ministers in session. The
next morning I took the cars, seating myself quite near the
door. The car was full of white cravats, so that it looked like
an adjourned session of the convention. Presently, a sleek, well-
fed man bustled on to the platform, and addressing the brake-
man, asked:
"Is Mr. Phillips on board?"
"Yes," was the reply, "there he sits back of the door."

The man came into the car — he was evidently a clergyman. In a loud voice he cried, pointing his finger at me:

"Are you Mr. Phillips?"

"I am, sir."

"Are you trying to free the niggers?"

"Yes, sir, I am an Abolitionist."

"Well, why do you preach your doctrines up here? Why don't you go there?" pointing toward Kentucky, just across the Ohio river.

"Excuse me," said I, "are you a preacher?"

"I am, sir."

"Are you trying to save souls from hell?"

"Yes, sir, that is my business."

"Then why don't you go there?"

There was a roar, and my critic vanished in the next car.

6

When Lucy Stone came to Malden, Massachusetts, to speak on Woman's Rights, a Universalist minister in that fashionable Boston suburb announced the event from the pulpit in these terms: "This evening at the Town Hall, a hen will attempt to crow." This was considered a great witticism. Few things are harder to bear than ridicule, but Phillips espoused the women's cause undeterred by the fact that in doing so he was exciting the risibility even of such a man as Theodore Parker. "Wendell, why do you make a fool of yourself?" Parker asked him on his return from a Woman's Rights Convention. "Theodore, this is the greatest question of the age; you ought to understand it," Phillips replied. Parker became a convert less than a year later.

In Reconstruction days serious differences arose between Phillips and the Woman's Rights Movement. "Wendell Phillips proposed bluntly that the association forget for the time its main object and concentrate on the Negro," wrote the historian of the movement, Inez Haynes Irwin. In his opinion the "Negro's hour" had sounded, but not yet the "woman's hour." — "When we mow our grass in July, and dig potatoes in September, but put off gathering Baldwin apples till October, it is economy and good sense — but no injustice to the apples," he argued. "July is the 'grass's hour'; October is the 'apple's hour.'" The women did not heed him and refused to support the Fifteenth Amendment, granting suffrage to the Negro, unless woman suffrage were included.

CHAPTER VII

"The Prince of New England Infidelity"

IN 1860, at the twenty-seventh anniversary of the American Anti-Slavery Society, Elizabeth Cady Stanton said: "To Garrison we owe more than to any other man of our day, all that we have of religious freedom."

Garrison's service to religious liberalism was that of propagandist. He was no profound original thinker like Emerson, nor a diligent student of the sources of religion like Theodore Parker. He knew the Bible thoroughly and few men quoted it more aptly, but he had not dug deeply into exegesis, the higher criticism or comparative religion. His abandonment of religious orthodoxy began with a revolt against the forced observance of the Sabbath. With the exception of Louisiana, which was largely Catholic, every State in the Union had Blue Laws. Garrison had at one time wished to make these even more drastic, but by 1836 he wrote: "Certain we are that all attempts to coerce an observance of the Sabbath by legislation, has been, must be, and should be nugatory," and pointed out that the Puritans had never been more bent on enforcing observance than when banishing Baptists and hanging Quakers.

By 1838, he had progressed sufficiently to write to Helen from Philadelphia: "Prayer and worship are all embodied in that pure, meek, childlike state of heart which affectionately and reverently breathes but one petition — 'Thy will be done, on earth as it is in heaven.' Religion, dear Helen, is nothing but love — perfect love toward God and toward man — without formality, without hypocrisy, without partiality — depending on no outward form to preserve its vitality and prove its existence." In November, 1855, he wrote to Maria Weston Chapman: "'Blessed are,' not *shall be* 'the merciful. Blessed *are* they who are persecuted for righteousness' sake,' etc. etc. The reward is ever in the performance of the deed." That same month he wrote to Francis Jackson: "It was your good fortune to throw off, at a much earlier period in life than I did, the fetters of that terrible theology which has so long held mastery over the New England mind, making one universal blight of human existence here below, and filling a future state of existence with inconceivable dangers and unutterable horrors." When his religious evolution was completed he was not far from agreeing with John Adams that "every honest, well-disposed, moral man, even if he were an atheist, should be accounted a Christian."

Having espoused religious liberalism Garrison proceeded to advocate it with the same ardor he put into his antislavery propaganda, and (it must be admitted) not always without detriment to the antislavery cause. In a letter to Henry C. Wright he explained: "Some would say that it is very poor policy to be talking about such subjects, if I wished to secure aid for the anti-slavery cause. . . . Thank God! it is not policy, but principle, by which I mean to be governed in my intercourse with my fellow-men; and while I desire at all times to be governed by a sound judgment, and not to be guilty of rashness, I will not desist from declaring 'the whole counsel of God,' as opportunity may offer, whether men will hear or forbear. As Wendell Phillips once finely remarked — 'God has not sent me into the world to abolish slavery, but to do my duty.' " Lincoln would have remarked that "one war at a time" was enough, and Garrison himself had once written: "Every reflecting mind may easily perceive that to disregard the dictates of sound expediency may often be as injurious to our enterprise as to violate principle," but he had become convinced that "every truth strengthens and forms a part of every other truth," and that striking the shackles from man's mind was as important as striking them from the limbs of the slave.

With a sublime faith in human tolerance he threw open the columns of the *Liberator* to untrammeled discussion of religious problems. "Whoever holds to an opinion or sentiment," he wrote, "which he is not pleased to see dealt with boldly and searchingly, gives evidence that he has taken it upon trust, usage, parental, educational, traditional authority, and not upon his own clear-wrought, unbiased convictions." On the twentieth anniversary of the *Liberator* his proudest boast was: "If I have taught the American press anything, it is this — the duty of allowing both sides of every question to be impartially canvassed." It is hardly surprising that Wendell Phillips should have written to Elizabeth Pease: "You who know the *Liberator*, know that it requires a pretty *full*-grown *man* to relish its

Wm. Lloyd Garrison.

*From a Mezzotint Engraving by John Sartain (1836),
After a Painting by M. C. Torrey (1835)*

meat," and that Amasa Walker should have declared it to be the *Liberator's* fault and merit that "it is always a little ahead of public sentiment."

2

Not content with providing a forum for the discussion of religion in his paper, Garrison occasionally arranged a "convention" where people of every shade of religious opinion could come and air their views. The most famous of these took place in the Chardon Street Chapel in Boston, in November, 1840. It lasted three days and attracted world-wide attention. The call was issued by Bronson Alcott, on behalf of an organization characteristically named "The Friends of Universal Reform," but it is generally conceded that Garrison pulled the strings. The purpose of the gathering was "to examine the validity of the views which generally prevail in this country as to the appointment of the first day of the week as the Christian Sabbath, and to inquire into the origin, nature and authority of the institutions of the Ministry and the Church as now existing." Edmund Quincy, who presided, declared: "It was the most singular collection of strange specimens of humanity that was ever assembled." Emerson reported in the *Dial:* "Madmen, madwomen, men with beards, Dunkers, Muggletonians, Come-Outers, Groaners, Agrarians, Seventh-Day-Baptists, Quakers, Abolitionists, Calvinists, Unitarians and Philosophers, all came successively to the top and seized their moment, if not their hour, wherein to chide, or pray, or preach, or protest." But he conceded that "The assembly was characterized by the predominance of a certain plain, sylvan strength and earnestness, whilst many of the most intellectual and cultivated persons attended its counsels." Abigail Folsom was there quoting interminably from St. Paul. Father Taylor, the "sailor preacher," was there and in a voice like a foghorn "roared and ranted most outrageously." Joseph Palmer, possessor of the most formidable beard in the Republic, was there and spoke in defense of beards, which he said God in his infinite wisdom had conferred upon the human male and for which it behooved him to be grateful. But present also were Alcott, Emerson, Thoreau, Channing, Parker, Lowell, Quincy, Ripley and others to whom was due the cultural fame of Boston and its environs. Some half a hundred orthodox clergymen attended and made a valiant effort to stem the tide of heterodoxy. Debates were heated. Epithets such as "infidel," "atheist," "bigot," "witch-burner" flew thick and fast. Come-Outers and No-Organizationists repeatedly challenged the authority of the Chair, saying they wanted "neither chairman, nor secretary, nor committee, bishop or pope." But Emerson, probing below the surface, remarked that "if there was not a parliamentary order, there was life, and the assurance of that constitutional love for religion and religious liberty, which, in all periods, characterizes the inhabitants of this part of America."

When in 1848 Garrison issued a call for an Anti-Sabbath Convention to meet in Boston, he encountered opposition from his closest collaborators in the Abolitionist movement. Edmund Quincy complained to Richard D. Webb: "It really seems as if the Devil always would put his foot in it, whenever the anti-slavery cause has got into a tolerable position, so as to keep it in hot water." Phillips wrote to Elizabeth Pease: "I did not sign the Call, though agreeing with its principles; mainly because I feel no such necessity for a specific movement against the Sabbath. The popular mind seems to me clearing itself up fast enough for all practical purposes: these theological reforms have but a secondary interest for me."

"The Prince of New England Infidelity," as the orthodox press now referred to Garrison, did not keep his light under a bushel at the Anti-Sabbath Convention. The Boston *Recorder* reported: "The most influential speaker, whose dictates, whether opposed or not, swayed the whole course of things, was the redoubtable Garrison himself. At every turn in the business, his hand grasped the steering-oar; and, let his galley-slaves row with what intent they would, he guided all things at his will."

In 1853 Garrison arranged a Bible Convention, whose purpose it was to inquire into the divine inspiration of the Scriptures. Yale's Trinity College being a hotbed of orthodoxy, he decided that Hartford, the seat of the College, was the proper place to hold the convention. He got more than he bargained for, reporting in the *Liberator* that the divinity students "attempted to break up the meeting by stamping, shouting, yelling, groaning, grunting, hissing, mocking, cursing, whistling, making indecent and insulting expressions, on one occasion turning off the gas and extinguishing the lights, so that the meeting was for some time compelled to suspend its proceedings, and behaving throughout like a troop of demons let loose from the pit."

3

Phillips, while not altogether agreeing with his friend's religious views, confessed that "On the great central question of inspiration, I am myself an inquirer," and wrote to Miss Pease: "The best prayer I could offer for any whose fate I was to influence, would be that they might be worthy to sit with Garrison in another world." Whether he willed it or not he sometimes found himself obliged to join Garrison in his assault on organized Christianity, for they found the Church athwart their path on numerous occasions. When they began their campaign against capital punishment they encountered such determined opposition from the clergy that Garrison did not think it unreasonable to suggest that the office of public executioner should be reserved for members of the cloth. Even in the temperance movement they had to deal with the hostility of the Church, since they considered it advisable to invite the active collaboration of women, which the clergy bitterly opposed. In 1853, at the World's Temperance Convention in New York, Miss Antoinette L. Brown, who a short time later became the first ordained female minister of the gospel in the Christian world, attempted to address the convention, but was howled down by the churchmen in the audience. "I have seen many tumultuous meetings in my day," wrote Garrison, "but I think on no occasion have I seen anything more disgraceful to our common humanity . . . Venerable men, claiming to be holy men, the ambassadors of Jesus Christ, losing all self-respect and transforming themselves into the most unmannerly and violent spirits, merely on account of the sex of the individual who wished to address the assembly."

Garrison came to grips with organized Christianity not only in the United States, but with the Free Church of Scotland, whose emissaries visited America to solicit funds. They traveled through the South as well as the North and obtained large contributions from congregations whose leading members were slaveholders. "Her representatives are blameworthy," Garrison wrote, "not because they got money in the Southern States, but because they got it most foully by keeping silence on the subject of slavery." He felt so strongly about this that he again crossed the Atlantic and joined Frederick Douglass, Henry C. Wright and other Americans already there in an indignant protest. They found plenty of sympathizers.

Enthusiasts smeared the steps of the churches with red paint, symbolical of the blood of the Negro. "SEND BACK THE MONEY! in large capitals stared from every street corner," wrote Frederick Douglass; "SEND BACK THE MONEY! adorned the broad flags of the pavement; SEND BACK THE MONEY! was the chorus of the popular street song; SEND BACK THE MONEY! was the heading of leading editorials in the daily newspapers."

In spite of all this, the Free Church did not imitate Daniel O'Connell in refusing Southern gold. "The laity, I believe, would send it back, but the divinity prevents it," Garrison wrote.

In Orthodox religious circles the editor of the *Liberator* and his friend Theodore Parker (who filled Music Hall every Sunday to overflowing and whose pulpit Garrison was sometimes asked to occupy) were said to be the two "best hated men in America." How bitter that hatred was may be judged from the fact that a revivalist in Park Street Church once prayed to the Almighty to "put a hook in his [Parker's] jaws, paralyze his tongue, or in some way break him down, empty Music Hall and scatter his congregation."

CHAPTER VIII

Family Portrait

GARRISON was an excellent husband and father, but an indifferent provider. His family did not suffer want, but was constantly on the verge of doing so. "I am never so far in funds as to have a spare dollar by me, using what economy I can," he wrote to a friend. He had an abiding faith that God would provide, and, according to Oliver Johnson, "help always did come, — sometimes in unexpected and surprising ways." It was not merely a question of providing for his family: "My house is a semi-hotel, with the numerous anti-slavery friends and visitors whom I am called to entertain and whose presence is welcome." Cranks and bores came in droves and were received with patience and courtesy. Many came to seek charity and such were never turned away empty-handed. Once Garrison gave away his only change of trousers, his good pair, by mistake. "Well, *he* has a good pair anyway," he consoled himself.

Although opposed to the use of alcohol and tobacco he was remarkably tolerant about it. His best friend, George Thompson, was addicted to snuff. He put up for years with Isaac Knapp, who was frequently drunk, and when their partnership was dissolved sheltered him and his wife gratuitously for weeks. His brother James, who appeared in Boston broken in health and spirit and unable to control his craving for alcohol, lived with him until his death, contributing nothing. Garrison's patience with him was such that it amazed the poor fellow, who wrote to him during a short absence: "My only wonder is how you can put up with such treatment even from a brother."

Until 1853, when the Garrisons went to live in Dix Place, near Holly Street, they were constantly moving. One of Garrison's sons has written that his father liked to move, especially if the house they were going to occupy was newly built. It gave him satisfaction to be the first occupant. If he remained in Dix Place eleven years it was due to the fact that his admirers bought the house and presented it to him.

Without the aid of generous friends the family could not have survived, for the *Liberator* never paid expenses. Fortunately Francis Jackson, Wendell Phillips, Charles Hovey and other Abolitionists of ample means kept an eye on the household and were ever ready to come to the rescue with money or provisions. "I see you have a houseful of people. . . . Your husband's position brings him many guests and expenses which do not belong to him," read a note accompanying a barrel of flour presented by Hovey. Nevertheless there were times when things grew pretty desperate, as may be judged from the following letter, which Edmund Quincy wrote to Richard D. Webb in January, 1843:

"His [Garrison's] family has been in much trouble the past year. His brother James, a poor drunken sailor, was upon his hands for a long time, and died last summer. Garrison's behavior to this poor fellow was very beautiful. Then his wife's sister, Mary Benson, was ill for a long time and also died in his house. Then all his children had the scarlet fever, and some of them, I believe, the lung or brain fever, and his wife the rheumatic fever; and in addition to all his troubles, the funds of the *Liberator* fell short towards the end of the year, and he was without money, for his necessary expenses, though I suppose he had credit. All of which circumstances made the last a very trying year for him."

The Garrisons had seven children, five boys and two girls. One of the girls died at the age of two; a boy, at the age of seven, was the victim of an accident: he was fatally scalded in a defective steam bath.

2

Richard D. Webb, a Dublin Quaker whose acquaintance Garrison had made on his first journey to Europe, was the owner of a printing shop and once published a pamphlet explaining Garrison's nonresistance doctrine, "just to raise a little bit of a row." He was, however, no blind worshiper and once wrote about his friend: "He is the most delightful man I have ever known — magnanimous, generous, considerate, and, as far as I can see, every way morally excellent. I can perceive that he has large faith, is very credulous, is not deeply read, and has little of the curiosity or thirst for knowledge which educated people are prone to."

Credulous Garrison undeniably was. Boston newspapers of that time advertised a bewildering variety of patent nostrums — Schenck's Pulmonic Syrup, Buchan's Hungarian Balsam of Life, Dr. Warren's Sarsaparilla, Tomato and Wild Cherry, Dr. Church's Celebrated Cough Drops, his equally renowned Pectoral Pills, and others. Garrison, who believed himself to be a prey to a variety of bodily ills and frequently informed his friends that he had "not long to live," accepted the claims of the patent medicine manufacturers at their face value. His son Wendell wrote that he bought their concoctions "rather against a rainy day than for present need, for they remained unopened in the closet. Or, if not unopened, their contents were frequently very slightly diminished, for my father carried his *immediatism* into medicine: it was instant relief he sought, and he was impatient of gradual recovery." He dosed his friends, too, if given half a chance. When Nathaniel P. Rogers, who accompanied him to the World's Convention in London, took ill while they were together in New York, Garrison wrote to Helen: "I have luckily been able to buy some balsam of liverwort for him, and have administered a few doses, to good effect." His brother James was made to swallow Thomsonian remedies, and Garrison reported to his brother-in-law George W. Benson: "Bro. James is slowly improving in health, but his case is a bad one. He has already taken three courses of Thomsonian medicine, and will continue to take them until he is cured." Unfortunately James died before the cure was completed.

In the *Liberator* he often gratuitously recommended this or that patent nostrum from which he believed he had benefited. Edmund Quincy had his own idea about this and in 1853 wrote to Webb: "He is quite ignorant of physiology, and has no belief in hygiene, or in anything pertaining to the body except *quack medicines*. That he has survived all he has taken is proof of an excellent constitution. You remember his puff of Dr. Church's Anti-Scrofulous Panacea, in which he said that he felt it 'permeating the whole system in the most delightful manner.' 'Permeating the system!' said Hervey Weston, with the malice of a regular practitioner; 'why, it was the first time he had taken a glass of grog, and he didn't know how good it was!' — some sort of spirits being the basis of all these sort of quackeries."

If there was a quack doctor within reasonable distance, Garrison was sure to seek him out. From Providence, Rhode Island, he wrote to Helen that he intended to consult a "Botanical doctor." "It may do me good; it certainly will not if I do not try it." He sweated in a Thomsonian infirmary, took the water cure in a hydropathic establishment, consulted "healing mediums," who, according to Edmund Quincy, "examined his internals with the back of their heads." In 1843 Quincy wrote to Webb: "He has some sort of swelling in his breast, about the region of the heart, which he believes will soon destroy him. He always speaks of it as an animal or devil (I don't mean that he thinks it is either) busy about his heart, which will soon put an end to him. However, Dr. Warren, our most eminent surgeon, and one of the first in the world, does not regard it as anything serious."

Unlike most hypochondriacs Garrison was of a cheerful disposition. "His was the happiest life I ever saw . . . I never saw him unhappy," testified Wendell Phillips. Oliver Johnson wrote: "Never in a single instance did I see him in a discouraged mood." Garrison's son Wendell: "I cannot recall his ever coming home in other than a bright and joyous mood." When Helen would look anxious, wondering how to make ends meet, he would put his arm about her and march her up and down the room, singing:

> In the days when we were gypsying,
> A long time ago . . .

Alfred Webb, son of Richard, wrote to one of Garrison's sons that once when Garrison was in Dublin he accompanied him to a photographer. "While we waited at the artist's we looked out of the window. It was a stormy day. The wind blew off a man's hat, and he had a stiff race after it, and I remember the shock to my feelings that such a great and good man as your father should remark, that he always enjoyed seeing a man running after his hat!" When the sun was shining he frustrated all of Helen's efforts to protect the carpets and the upholstery, by pulling up the blinds and looping up the curtains. The Crystal Palace in London was, he said, his idea of an ideal place to live in.

Though a believer in "Immediatism" he had a tendency to procrastinate. He seldom did today what he could put off till tomorrow. When he had to catch a train he invariably managed to leave the house sufficiently late to make it necessary for him to sprint.

3

The Garrisons had a maid-of-all-work, but he was ever ready to help with the housework, not excepting such menial tasks as shining the shoes of his guests. As for helping with the children — "If there is anything I am fitted for it is to tend babies," he told Helen. When away from home he wrote affectionate letters: "Dear Helen, I can truly affirm, that I never absented myself one hour from you as a matter of choice. . . . The strength of my love you will probably never fully know; for I am not accustomed to the use of fond terms, and feel a thousandfold more than I can express." "My dear one, how are you and the little ones and all the household? Do send me a letter to Utica, and give me all the domestic particulars that you can think of." He had retained his fondness for cats and from his correspondence the family cat emerges a cherished member of the household: "Remember me to Mary Ann [the maid]. My goodwill to the cat," or "I need not ask George to look after the cat in my absence, for he is my natural successor in that line — only he must not give her too much at a meal."

Once when the Garrisons were visiting the Bensons in Brooklyn, the editor took his wife, mother-in-law and small son out for a ride. Eager to display his skill as a driver he made a sharp turn at full speed, with the result that the buggy overturned. Helen's arm was dislocated at the elbow. It was incompetently treated and remained almost useless the rest of her life. The fact that she never reproached him and minimized the discomfort endeared her to him even more.

In a day when few parents spared the rod, Garrison, in accordance with his principles of nonresistance, abstained from corporal punishment. His clerical critics considered this further proof of infidelity. One of them wrote: "I had as soon my son should be taught that the Bible is not true, as that I have not the right, under God, to chastise him; for he now understands that if done it is done by the direct sanction of the Almighty." Garrison's grandson, Oswald Garrison Villard, has, however, testified that he remembers "the nonresistant grandfather leading a terrified, and therefore decidedly nonresistant imp of a grandson into durance vile in a cupboard prison . . . for having wickedly and malevolently assailed other urchins with what the Abolitionists would, in their Biblical language, have called 'carnal weapons.'"

He refrained from imposing his ideas upon his offspring. "God forbid," he wrote to Elizabeth Pease, "that I should ever take such a responsibility upon myself — that I should ever bring my children up in this one-sided manner! The one distinct and emphatic lesson which I shall teach them is, to take nothing upon authority — to dare to differ in opinion from their father, and from all the world — to understand, as clearly as possible, what can be said against or in favor of any doctrine or practice, and then to accept or reject it according to their own conviction of duty."

One day his little daughter Fanny was asked by some of her schoolmates if she had been baptized. She replied that she did not know, but would ask her father. "No, my darling," he told her, "but you have had a good bath every morning, and that is a great deal better." When she told her playmates what her father had said, one of them sneered: "Oh, yes; you are the daughter of an infidel."

In a memoir of her father Fanny related that once, when she was a little girl, she heard Garrison say: "I met a man this morning who thought I had horns." As far as she could see, her father's bald head was innocent of the adornment. However, the next time he lifted her to his shoulder, she carefully felt his skull to make sure no horns were about to sprout. Her favorite way of warming her hands was to place them on her father's shiny bald pate. Once when she did so he said: "You come to my incendiary head, my darling, to warm your cold hands."

Garrison had the satisfaction of having many children named after him. In some cases, however, the parents were given the choice of bestowing a different name on their offspring or forgoing the baptismal ceremony.

4

Helen was the balance wheel of the establishment and sometimes restrained her husband's extravagant generosity, but she had ways of her own to be helpful to others. Once she went from house to house selling a pamphlet written by a French political refugee, stopping only when she had disposed of four hundred copies and was able to turn over one hundred dollars to her protégé. While she fully agreed with her husband on Abolition, she did not blindly follow when he went seeking the truth in the bypaths of Perfectionism and Spiritualism. The Fox sisters and other mediums had cre-

ated a vogue for Spiritualism comparable with that of psychoanaly-
sis in our day. In all the salons of the country the spirit world was
being discussed. "Society" sat around little tables not to play bridge
but to watch the tables move. Mediums and spirit photographers
reaped a golden harvest. Lydia Maria Child had a spirit photograph
made and described the result in a letter to Mrs. Samuel E. Sewall:
"There were two heads behind my own; one of them a vulgar-
looking man, the other a fat-faced girl with fluffy hair; neither of
them faces I had ever seen before, or ever desired to see again. The
whole proceeding indicated trickery."

It is hardly surprising that so impressionable a man as Garrison
should have taken an interest in Spiritualism. He attended several
séances at one of which Jesse Hutchinson, one of the famous Hutchinson singers who had died, appeared for his benefit and indulged in
various antics. Garrison remained somewhat skeptical, and wrote:
"As yet, we must confess that we have never read anything, pur-
porting to come from any distinguished person in the spirit world,
that seemed to be equal to his genius and ability while here in the
flesh; and this is what makes us doubt, more than anything else (notwithstanding so many inexplicable phenomena), whether the communication actually comes from the source supposed."

PART THREE
The Crisis

CHAPTER I

The Compromise

TEXAS had been annexed with a constitution specifying that slavery should never be abolished. Provision had been made that the new State could ultimately be divided into five separate States. The war with Mexico was going well and an immense territory was expected to be added to the Union. By extending the Missouri Compromise line to the Pacific, the slaveholders hoped to bring most of that territory under their sway.[1] The secessionist propaganda in the North had subsided. "Manifest Destiny" had swept many opponents of slavery and even Abolitionists like Cassius M. Clay off their feet. Southern policy was triumphing all along the line.

On August 8, 1846, President Polk, in a special message to Congress, asked for an appropriation of two million dollars "for the purpose of settling our differences with Mexico." A bill was introduced covering the amount. David Wilmot of Pennsylvania, a Northern Democrat well-liked by his Southern colleagues, proposed an amendment, known as the Wilmot Proviso, specifying that neither slavery, nor any other form of involuntary servitude should be allowed in territory the United States might acquire from Mexico. The amendment carried in the House, was defeated in the Senate, but henceforth the political issue overshadowing all other issues was: *Shall slavery be permitted to expand further?*

The importance of the issue cannot be overestimated. Politically and economically slavery's future depended upon expansion. If no new Slave States were added to the Union, the South would soon find itself in the minority in the House as well as in the Senate. Politically slavery would be no longer safe. "If this policy should be carried out, woe, woe I say to the Union!" said the "Napoleon

[1] The Missouri Compromise of 1820 was an agreement that all territory acquired through the Louisiana Purchase below 36 degrees 30 minutes parallel of latitude should be slave territory; all territory above that line should be free. An exception was made for Missouri, admitted as a Slave State although wholly north of the line.

of Slavery," John C. Calhoun. Since slave labor exhausted the soil, the policy doomed slavery economically. Denied access to new territory, it would become unprofitable and die.

The movement to oppose slavery expansion gained momentum. In 1840 the Liberty Party had polled less than seven thousand votes. Four years later it polled nearly ten times that number and held the balance of power in New York and Michigan. Now a new political party, the Free-Soil Party, was born. The Whigs divided into "Cotton" and "Conscience" Whigs. The latter joined with radical New York Democrats (Barnburners), Liberty Party and Wilmot Proviso men in nominating Martin Van Buren for President and Charles Francis Adams for Vice President, at a convention in Buffalo. "We inscribe on our banner Free Soil, Free Speech, Free Labor and Free Men; and under it will fight on and fight ever, until triumphant victory shall reward our exertions," was the battle cry of the Free-Soilers, who polled nearly three hundred thousand votes in 1848. Many of Garrison's stanchest followers, such as Samuel J. May, joined the new party. Garrison and Phillips were not displeased, although Phillips complained that as fast as the Abolitionists made converts they deserted to the political movement. Garrison wrote to May: "As for the 'Free Soil' movement, I am for hailing it as a cheering sign of the times, and an unmistakable proof of the progress we have made, under God, in changing public sentiment. Those who have left the Whig and Democratic parties, for conscience's sake, and joined that movement, deserve our commendation and sympathy."

2

So again the Union was endangered, more seriously perhaps than on any previous occasion. "We are hardly able to keep the government alive. All is confusion," said Webster. This condition, Calhoun was to explain, had been brought about by a "fanatical party" which "has become an object of courtship to both the great parties." As a consequence the Union had sustained "five gaping wounds": the threat of the passage of the Wilmot Proviso; the proposed admission of California as a Free State with territory below the Missouri Compromise line; the insistent demand for the abolition of slavery in the District of Columbia; the demand for the abolition of the interstate slave trade; Northern opposition to the passage of a truly effective Fugitive Slave Law. A call was issued for a Southern Convention to be held on June 3, 1850, at Nashville, Tennessee, and no secret was made of the fact that unless the "wounds" were healed, secession would be the order of the day.

A spectator watching from the gallery proceedings of the thirty-first Congress would have received the impression that dissolution of the Union was imminent. "Never had any Congress convened under so much excitement," wrote Alexander H. Stephens. Southern representatives were determined to prevent the passage of bills abolishing slavery in the National Capital and the interstate slave trade. Representative Meade of Virginia shouted: "If these outrages are to be committed upon my people, I trust in God, sir, that my eyes have rested upon the last Speaker of the House of Representatives!" He was called a "disunionist" and a "liar" by Duer of New York and only the intervention of the sergeant-at-arms with the mace prevented a riot. Toombs of Georgia cried: "I am for disunion!" and Colcock of South Carolina, impressively calm, pledged himself, if the measures passed, to introduce a resolution declaring "that this Union ought to be dissolved."

But Garrison and Phillips had done their work well. Many in the North no longer took alarm at the threats of secession. While Southern senators and representatives were threatening disunion, petitions by the score circulated in almost every Northern State asking for the same thing. John P. Hale of New Hampshire presented in the Senate a petition from Pennsylvania and Delaware "praying for the immediate and peaceful dissolution of the Union." Phillips reiterated that he was a disunionist and proud of it, while an Abolitionist poet sang in the *Liberator:*

> Man is more than Constitution — better rot beneath the sod
> Than be true to Church and State while we are doubly false
> to God.

3

How could the Union be saved? The eyes of the country turned towards a man of seventy-three, Garrison's onetime idol Henry Clay. Although a slaveholder, he was known to favor gradual emancipation and to be opposed to slavery extension. "Coming from a Slave State," he was to say during the debate, "I owe it to myself, I owe it to truth, I owe it to the subject, to say that no earthly power could induce me to vote for a specific measure for the introduction of slavery where it had not before existed, either south or north of that line [the Missouri Compromise line]." Hollow-cheeked, dressed in black, a huge shirt collar emerging from his black satin stock, long gray hair fringing his bald head and falling upon his shoulders, he rose in the Senate and proposed this compromise:

California to be admitted as a Free State. The remainder of the territory acquired from Mexico to have Territorial government — the settlers themselves to decide if they wished to permit slavery. (Clay expressed the opinion that the soil was unsuited for slave labor anyway, so that the question was purely academic.) The Southern boundary of Texas to be extended to the Rio Grande. The slave trade to be abolished in the District of Columbia. Noninterference with the interstate slave trade. Congress to pass an effective Fugitive Slave Law.

Clay's proposal did not evoke enthusiasm from either side. Jefferson Davis, tall, soldierly graduate of West Point, declared: "I here assert that never will I take less than the Missouri Compromise line extended to the ocean, with the specific recognition of the right to hold slaves below that line; and that before such Territories are admitted as States, slaves may be taken there from any of the United States, at the option of their owners."

But the "Napoleon of Slavery" was still to be heard from. John C. Calhoun, death stamped upon his haggard features, appeared in the Senate supported by two colleagues and followed by a Negro servant. He had written out his speech and had given it to Senator Mason of Virginia, who read it in a clear voice, while the brooding eyes of the old leader scanned the faces of his colleagues.

"I have, Senators, believed from the first that the agitation of the subject of slavery would, if not prevented by some timely and effective measure, end in disunion," was the opening sentence. Disunion, he said, had already begun. With the exception of the Episcopal Church, all the Protestant denominations had divided on the slavery issue. The process had now communicated itself to both political parties, which were dividing along sectional lines. "How can the Union be saved? . . . The North has only to do justice by conceding to the South an equal right in the acquired territory; and to do her duty by causing the stipulations relative to fugitive slaves to be faithfully fulfilled." But this was not enough. Equilibrium between the North and the South must be guaranteed for all time by a constitutional amendment specifying that the Union was to be composed of an equal number of Free and Slave States.

Calhoun's speech created consternation among Southern opponents of secession. Foote of Mississippi accused him of having failed to consult his colleagues. The constitutional amendment the old leader demanded would, he said, cause so much delay as to "make disunion almost inevitable." Stephen A. Douglas was to say that to guarantee the slaveholders an equilibrium for all time was "a moral and physical impossibility." Who could reconcile these conflicting opinions? The nation's hopes revived when on March 7, 1850, Daniel Webster took the floor.

4

"I speak to-day for the preservation of the Union, 'Hear me for my cause.' "

Webster was sixty-eight when he uttered these words. He had grown pouchy and his raven hair was profusely streaked with gray, but his lofty forehead, his cavernous eyes, his firm mouth, his lordly gestures, his full, clear, sonorous voice, had lost little of their impressiveness. He was still·

> New England's stateliest type of man,
> In port and speech Olympian;
> Whom no one met, at first, but took
> A second awed and wondering look.[2]

As he rose to speak, not only the Senate but the entire nation waited breathlessly for what he was going to say.

Webster spoke for over three hours. It was probably true, as claimed by the Washington *Republic*, that while he spoke "fears for the Union melted," but that feeling was soon to be succeeded by one of profound discouragement, as crisis after crisis arose proving that Webster and Clay not only had settled nothing, but had aggravated the situation. Some of Webster's admirers had hoped that he would unfold a comprehensive plan for a permanent settlement of the problem. Seventeen years had now passed since England had emancipated eight hundred thousand slaves in the West Indies without damage to colonial economy or serious loss to the slaveholders. In 1850 the South was not ready for secession. Feel-

[2] Whittier: *The Lost Occasion.*

ing between Southern Secessionists and Southern Unionists was so bitter in Washington that blows were struck. If South Carolina had attempted rebellion, she would have received but little encouragement. A far-sighted statesman would have realized the danger and futility of further compromise and, taking advantage of the lack of unity in the South, would have proposed gradual emancipation with compensation. Phillips and others have charged that Webster's purpose was not so much to serve his country as to gain the support of the Southern Whigs for the Presidential nomination. This may or may not have been true, but if such was not his purpose then he displayed a remarkable lack of insight for one who in 1837 had said of the antislavery movement: "He is a rash man, indeed, little conversant with human nature, and especially has he a very erroneous estimate of the character of the people of this country, who supposes that a feeling of this kind is to be trifled with or despised. It will assuredly cause itself to be respected."

5

Webster's only allusion to a permanent settlement of the slavery problem was the following:

"In my observations upon slavery, as it has existed in the country, or as it now exists, I have expressed no opinion of the mode of its extinction or amelioration. I will say, however, — though I have nothing to propose on that subject, because I do not feel myself so competent as gentlemen who are themselves more intimately connected with slavery — that if any gentleman from the South shall propose a scheme of colonization, to be carried on by this government upon a large scale, for the transportation of the free colored people to any colony, or to any place in the world, I should be quite disposed to incur almost any degree of expense to accomplish that object."

Little wonder the nation was drifting into war, when its leading statesman confessed that he had "no opinion" to express concerning the "extinction or amelioration" of an evil that was tearing it asunder! As for his proposal to colonize the free Negroes, in 1822 he had left a colonization meeting at the Marlboro' Hotel in Boston in a dudgeon, exclaiming: "It is a scheme of the slaveholders to get rid of the free Negroes, I will have nothing to do with it."

He gave his unqualified support to Clay's compromise measures, agreeing with the Kentuckian that the conquered territory was unsuited for slave labor and that passage of the Wilmot Proviso would be a gratuitous insult to the South. "The law of nature — of physical geography — the law of the formation of the earth" forever excluded slavery from that territory. "What is there in New Mexico that could by possibility induce anybody to go there with a slave?" He would not take pains to reaffirm an ordnance of nature or re-enact the law of God. "I would put no Wilmot Proviso for the purpose of a taunt and reproach . . . to wound the pride of gentlemen and people of the Southern States."

Apparently he considered this argument conclusive. "This is the foundation of all," he said. Yet in the Appendix to the *Congressional Globe*[3] of February 23, 1849, there had appeared this statement by Senator Foote of Mississippi:

"No one, acquainted with the vast mineral resources of California and New Mexico, and who is aware of the peculiar adaptness of slave-labor to the development of mineral treasures, can doubt for a moment, that were slaves introduced into California and New Mexico, for the purpose of being employed in the mining operations there in progress, and hereafter, perhaps to be carried on to an extent conjectured by few, their labor would result in the acquisition of pecuniary profits not heretofore realized by the most successful cotton and sugar planters of the country."

William Jay wrote concerning Webster's famous "law of physical geography": "This law must have been enacted by the Creator since 1824, or its operation must have been previously suspended in deference to the Spanish government; for under that government, negro slavery did exist in New Mexico and California, and it ceased in 1824, not by the law of 'physical geography,' but by a Mexican edict. Thousands of slaves are employed in the mines of Brazil, and Mr. Webster does not explain how his law forbids their employment in the mines of California."

The persistence with which the slaveholders kept insisting on their right to take slaves into the conquered territory alone should have warned Webster that more than a mere formality was involved.

Webster's most serious blunder was his advocacy of the Fugitive Slave Bill, which his ardent admirer Senator Albert J. Beveridge has called "the most stringent act ever passed by Congress on slavery

[3] The *Congressional Globe* was the predecessor of the *Congressional Record*.

and one of the most inapt and impolitic laws ever enacted." What
Webster said of the Wilmot Proviso was precisely true of the Fugitive Slave Law, introduced by Mason of Virginia and included by
Clay in his "Omnibus Bill": it had no practical value and only
served to exasperate. It created consternation among the colored
people of the North and made Abolitionists by the thousand, but
the number of slaves returned was negligible.

After Webster's death the *New England Farmer*, published in
Boston, declared: "We learn on reliable authority that Mr. Webster confessed to a warm political friend, a short time before his
death, that the great mistake of his life was the famous Seventh
of March Speech, in which, it will be remembered, he defended
the Fugitive Slave Law, and fully committed himself to the compromise measures."

The irony of the matter was that a truly effective Fugitive Slave
Law (if, considering the sentiment in the North, an effective law
were humanly possible) would have been detrimental to the slaveholders. When slavery existed in the West Indies, those determined
to escape from bondage fled into the mountains. There were thousands of such fugitives, called Maroons, in San Domingo and other
West Indian Islands. The West Indian historian Bryan Edwards has
described their proud bearing and reckless courage. They organized
into bands, made the roads unsafe, sacked plantations, liberated
slaves, carried on so effective a guerilla warfare that the French and
Spanish governments were forced to make treaties with them guaranteeing their liberty. The reason Maroons were practically unknown in the United States was that the North provided a haven
of refuge. The Negro historian George W. Williams was even of
the opinion that the Underground Railroad was a godsend to the
slaveholders. "As soon as leaders arose among the slaves refusing
to endure the yoke," he wrote, "they came North. Had they remained, the direful scenes of San Domingo would have been enacted, and the hot vengeful breath of massacre would have swept
the South as a tornado and blanched the cheek of the civilized
world."

6

Garrison called Webster's speech "indescribably base and
wicked," but published it in full in the *Liberator*, later reprinting

the most objectionable parts under the heading: "The Late Satanic Speech of Daniel Webster." Phillips proceeded to tear Webster's argument to tatters in a pamphlet published a fortnight after the delivery of the speech. When one reads the pamphlet one cannot help wondering if he really was the disunionist he claimed to be. "The true friend of the Union," he wrote, "would seize this moment, when the slave-host sways to and fro with anxiety; when, thanks to the slandered abolitionists only, all of virtue the North has is aroused to the importance of the issue, and needs but a MAN as leader to dare and do all for Liberty — the true friend of the Union would seize such a moment, by some grand and comprehensive plan of abolition, to insure the future, instead of shutting his eyes like the ostrich, and imagining, that to be hoodwinked is to be safe. If, in some future struggle, Slavery, gathering its hosts from the Atlantic to the Pacific, 'fleshed with conquests,' shall do equal battle with the Union, and destroy it, its epitaph will be — 'Died, because its friends dared not, or were too selfish, to look danger in the face, and scotched the snake, not killed it.'"

His indignation knew no bounds when he reached that part of the speech dealing with the Fugitive Slave Law. The law of 1850 took enforcement out of the hands of State authorities and entrusted it to the Federal Government. The accused was denied a jury trial and could not testify in his own behalf — a provision not found in the law of 1793. Any one hindering a fugitive's arrest by offering resistance, hiding him or helping him to escape was to be fined one thousand dollars, serve six months in jail, and might have to pay another thousand to the owner. Commissioners before whom fugitives were to be tried were to receive ten dollars in case of conviction, five dollars in case of acquittal, which was responsible for the popular saying that the law "fixed the price of a South Carolina Negro at one thousand dollars and the price of a Yankee's soul at five dollars." Phillips wrote:

"Villain, gentle reader, is none too harsh a name for a man who professes his readiness to return fugitive slaves. . . . If God permits him to live, he will have ample time to appreciate, as the world advances, the foul blot he has ineffaceably made on the sun of his fame. It will be but a poor excuse for his biographer to urge that he squared his morality by the statute book of his time! . . . Full half of the villainy is volunteered, utterly gratuitous. There is nothing in the Constitutional provision which forbids the regulating of the whole process of slave surrender by all the jealous forms of *habeas corpus, jury trial*, etc., which the experience of ages shows to be indispensable for the protection of freemen who may be mistaken for slaves; on the contrary, the Constitution, fairly interpreted, requires the observance of a trial by jury . . . Without the slightest pretext of legal or constitutional obligation, therefore, without any reason in common sense, Mr. Webster volunteers his support of all these thoughtless and cruel and dangerous regulations."

Webster had expressed the conviction that "conscientious men," mindful of their constitutional obligations, would deliver fugitive slaves "with alacrity." This was too much for Phillips, who exclaimed: "If in the lowest deep, there be a lower deep for profligate statesmen, let all former apostates stand aside and leave it vacant."

Whittier, who had loved and admired Webster, read his Seventh of March speech and the poem that flowed from his pen was bitter with the bitterness of disillusion. Four of the stanzas read:

> So fallen! so lost! the light withdrawn
>   Which once he wore!
> The glory from his gray hairs gone
>   Forevermore!
>
> Of all we loved and honored, naught
>   Save power remains;
> A fallen angel's pride of thought,
>   Still strong in chains.
>
> All else is gone; from those great eyes
>   The soul has fled:
> When faith is lost, when honor dies,
>   The man is dead!
>
> Then pay the reverence of old days
>   To his dead fame;
> Walk backward, with averted gaze,
>   And hide the shame!

7

When President Millard Fillmore signed the Fugitive Slave Bill, Charles Sumner declared at a public meeting in Boston: "Other

Presidents may be forgotten; but the name signed to the Fugitive Slave Bill will never be forgotten. There are depths of infamy as there are heights of fame. I regret to say what I must; but truth compels me. Better for him had he never been born! Better for his memory, and for the good name of his children, had he never been President!"

The friends of the Compromise did their best to rally the North to the support of the measure. Nine hundred and eighty-seven prominent citizens of Massachusetts — including Francis Todd of Newburyport, whom Garrison had denounced for transporting slaves from Baltimore to a Southern slave mart — had addressed an open letter to Webster thanking him for "recalling us to our duties under the Constitution." They were now instrumental in having the signing of the Fugitive Slave Bill hailed in Boston with a salute of one hundred guns. In New York ten thousand people packed Castle Garden to hear General Winfield Scott and other luminaries sing the praises of the Compromise and the patriotism and wisdom of Daniel Webster. At Hartford, Connecticut, Dr. Nathaniel Taylor, head of the theological department of Yale University, addressed the citizens at a mass meeting and gave them the comforting assurance that surrendering fugitive slaves was "not contrary to the law of nature, to the law of nations or to the will of God." Dr. Orville Dewey, a Unitarian minister famous for his eloquence, vowed he would rather send "his own brother and child into slavery" than see the Union dissolved. (Whether to save the Union he was prepared to go into slavery himself he did not disclose.) Notwithstanding all this the Washington Correspondent of the New Orleans *Picayune* reported to his paper that the Fugitive Slave Law "ran counter to the whole current of public feeling in Webster's own region of country, to the expressed opinion of the State which he represents, and the all but unanimous sentiment of his party friends." That he was not mistaken was proved at the November election when the Webster Whigs suffered a crushing defeat. There were protest meetings throughout the North. At Syracuse, New York, Judge James W. Nye, future United States senator, said at a mass meeting presided over by the mayor: "I will tell my constituency that I will trample that law in the dust, and they must find another man, if there be one, who will degrade himself to do this dirty work." At Lowell, Massachusetts, a resolution was passed at a mass meeting calling upon colored people who had fled to Canada to return and pledging them protection. In Salem, Ohio, citizens passed a resolution threatening slave catchers with death. In Boston the aged Josiah Quincy headed a call for a protest meeting in Faneuil Hall. Charles Francis Adams presided. Richard H. Dana, Jr., Theodore Parker, Frederick Douglass and Wendell Phillips were the speakers. Dana advised the Negroes not to flee, promising to defend them without cost. Phillips said: "In this law the bulwarks of liberty are all broken, and it is a base libel to call it a constitutional law. We must trample it under our feet. It expects and provides for disobedience; God forbid that it should be disappointed. By peaceful resistance we must interrupt the slaveholders and say that the fugitive who has breathed Massachusetts air shall never go back. Many have been here from twelve to twenty years, and we are not going to people Southern plantations with men born in Massachusetts.[4] Disobey this law until the courts rule it unconstitutional."

8

"Men are as bad as God made them, and sometimes a great deal worse," Cervantes had Sancho Panza say. "Men are not as bad as the laws they make, and sometimes a great deal better," is equally true. Few of the people of the South were as cruel and unjust as their slave laws would indicate them to be, and few of the people of the North, including those who approved the passage of the Fugitive Slave Law, were capable of obeying it. A United States Marshal in Boston, coming to a house to arrest a fugitive slave, told the amazed householder: "If the man is not in, it does not matter; I'll be back tomorrow and take him." George S. Hillard of Boston, a prominent lawyer and enthusiastic Webster Whig, far from surrendering fugitive slaves "with alacrity," was rumored to be conducting a station on the Underground Railroad! (The rumor was substantiated a quarter of a century ago, when the house he had built at 62 Pinckney Street was remodeled. A secret chamber ventilated by an opening under a skylight and sufficiently large to hold several persons was discovered. On the floor were two tin plates and two iron spoons.) Wendell Phillips, speaking before the New

[4] The children of female slaves, even if born in a Free State of a free father, could be claimed by the slaveholders. Congress at one time allowed a claim of $141,000 made by the slaveholders of Georgia "for the loss of the offspring which the exiles [fugitives] would have borne to their masters had they remained in bondage."

York Anti-Slavery Society, told about a clergyman who preached a sermon in support of the Fugitive Slave Law. "It was printed in your *Journal of Commerce*. Daniel Webster praised it. Three weeks afterwards that very man was on the doorstep of a clerical friend of his and mine, with a fugitive slave behind him, who had got to his door. He could not practice his own doctrine. He came to his anti-slavery brother clergyman and said, 'Where do you put these folks? I don't know what to do, but she ought to be out of sight in an hour — you have some way — tell me of it.' It is base to incite others to deeds at which, whenever we are hidden from public notice, our hearts recoil."

Webster made speeches and carried on a voluminous correspond-ence in support of the law. "Any man," he argued, "can perform an agreeable duty — it is not every man who can perform a dis-agreeable duty. . . . No man is at liberty to set up or effect to set up his own conscience as above the law." Seward dryly re-marked: "The moral sense, the conscience of the age, has outgrown Mr. Webster." The scholarly Emerson wrote in cold fury in his Journal: "The word *liberty* in the mouth of a Webster sounds like the word *love* in the mouth of a courtezan."

In January, 1851, Webster's bitter enemy Charles Sumner was elected to the place in the United States Senate the former had vacated when becoming Secretary of State in Fillmore's Cabinet. The poet Longfellow rejoiced: "The papers are ringing with Sum-ner! Sumner! and the guns are thundering in triumph." Emerson wrote: "Could Mr. Webster obtain now a vote in Massachusetts for the poorest municipal office? Well, is not this a loss inevitable to a bad law? — a law no man can countenance or abet the execution of, without loss of all self-respect, and forfeiting forever the name of gentleman? . . . Union is a delectable thing, and so is wealth, and so is life, but they may all cost too much if they cost honor." In Europe Alexander Von Humboldt said: "I always liked Mr. Webster. He was a great man. I knew him and I liked him. But, after that, I hated him. He was the man who made the Fugitive Slave Law. If he had wanted to prevent it, he could have done it. That is the reason why I call it the Webster law. And ever after I hated him." Phillips said scornfully: "The time has been when you asked a Whig if he would return fugitive slaves, he would have answered, 'Is thine servant a dog that he should do this thing?' Now, in 1850, you answer, 'Not a dog, only a Webster.'"

Under these circumstances enforcement of the law was virtually impossible. In April, 1852, twenty months after the law went into effect, Phillips said: "Twenty-six have been sent back from Pennsylvania; only one from Boston; only a dozen from New York." Considering that there were some twenty thousand fugitive slaves in the North, some six hundred in Boston alone, this was indeed a sorry showing. It appears even more so when one considers that it cost the Government $6000, and the slaveholder $3000, to get back the single fugitive slave from Boston. In 1854 a second fugitive slave was returned from the same city at a cost of $65,000!

Yet the law created untold misery among the colored people of the North. Some ten thousand fled to Canada, whose Governor had in 1835 said to a colored delegation from Ohio: "Tell the republicans on your side of the line, that we royalists do not know *men* by their color. Should you come to us, you will be entitled to all the privileges of the rest of her Majesty's subjects." Hundreds of fugitives abandoned their families. Others sacrificed their property to obtain ready cash. Since the law deprived the suspect of the most elementary safeguards, a couple of free Negroes were seized, whereupon many free Negroes, considering themselves no longer safe, likewise fled to Canada. "The law," said Phillips, "has executed itself. The dread that they might be seized has broken up hundreds of happy families."

9

At the protest meeting in Faneuil Hall a Vigilance Committee of fifty had been appointed "to secure the fugitives and colored inhabitants of Boston and vicinity from any invasion of their rights by persons acting under the law." Phillips was a member of the Executive Committee, on which served Theodore Parker, Charles M. Ellis, Dr. Samuel G. Howe, Lewis Hayden (a colored attorney) and others. Howe, who was chairman, had fought by the side of Byron for Greek independence and managed to give a Byronic touch to the proceedings.

Phillips wrote to Miss Pease:

"The long evening sessions — debates about secret escapes — plans to evade where we can't resist — the doors watched that no spy may enter — the whispering consultations of the morning — some putting property out of their hands, planning to incur penalties, and planning also that, in case of conviction, the Government may get nothing from them — intimates forbearing to ask the knowledge which it may be dangerous to have — all remind one of the foreign scenes which have hitherto been known to us, transatlantic republicans, only in books. Yet we enjoy ourselves richly, and I doubt whether more laughing is done anywhere than in anti-slavery parlors."

Phillips was now regarded as the leader of the Abolitionists. "From the passage of the Fugitive Slave Law," said Archibald H. Grimké, "Garrison was thrown into the background by his great coadjutor. Forcible resistance to the black bill was now obedience to God. It was the dictate of the highest justice. The passage of the bill was the actual opening of hostilities between the two sections." Since Garrison maintained he was still a nonresistant it had been thought inadvisable to place him on the Vigilance Committee. It should be noted, however, that when he addressed the colored people at the Belknap Street Church on the Fugitive Slave Law, he did not recommend that they practice nonresistance, but that they "be consistent with their own principles."

The Vigilance Committee's first opportunity to intervene was when two slave catchers appeared in Boston to secure the return of William and Ellen Craft. William was a full-blooded Negro, Ellen, his wife, as white as most white persons. They had been household slaves and had at times obtained small gifts of money. When they had enough to take them out of slave territory by ordinary means of travel, they bought two railway tickets, boarded the train and departed. It was as simple as that. Ellen had put on man's clothing and had impersonated a young planter in delicate health who, accompanied by his servant, was traveling North to seek medical advice. The whole country laughed at their exploit. They had settled in Boston and were getting along well enough when the slave catchers appeared and obtained a warrant for William on the charge of having stolen the clothes he was wearing at the time of his escape — the clothes as well as his person being the property of his master. The charge of theft was made merely to simplify the proceedings, but the Vigilance Committee retaliated by obtaining warrants for malicious slander. Friends of the Compromise were obliged to furnish bail to the amount of ten thousand dollars to keep the would-be captors out of jail. William was furnished with a dirk, a revolver and a pistol and was taken to the house of Lewis

Hayden at 66 Southac (now Phillips) Street. Hayden, whose house was a station on the Underground Railroad, was not a man to be trifled with. Once, when he was sheltering several fugitives, he was informed that a raid was about to take place; whereupon he placed two kegs of gunpower in his cellar, attached a fuse and had everything ready to blow up the premises as soon as the raiders were inside. It is possible that the police got wind of the matter, for the raid never materialized. Ellen was taken to Ellis Gray Loring's place in Brookline, but, this being considered insufficiently safe, was moved to Theodore Parker's house at No. 1 Exeter Place. "For two weeks," said Parker, "I wrote my sermons with a sword in the open drawer under my inkstand, and a pistol in the flap of the desk, loaded and ready, with a cap on the nipple."

Finally the Committee decided the best way to defend was to attack. Parker and Loring, at the head of sixty Vigilantes, marched to the United States Hotel, where they confronted the slave catchers. "I told them," Parker related, "that they were not safe another night. I had stood between them and violence once, I would not promise to do it again. They were considerably frightened."

They must have been, for they left town that same day.

In February, 1851, Frederick Jenkins Shadrach, a colored waiter at the Cornhill Coffee House in Boston, was arrested as a fugitive. A formidable array of legal counsel appeared in his defense and secured a postponement. When all but the prisoner, his guards and two of his white supporters had left the courtroom, the door suddenly opened and in rushed Lewis Hayden at the head of a score of Negroes. They seized the prisoner and hurried him to a waiting carriage that drove at breakneck speed across the bridge to Cambridge. The fugitive remained secreted in West Cambridge until dark, when a wagon took him to Sudbury and eventually to freedom in Canada.

The bold rescue created a sensation in Washington. Webster pronounced it "treason." Henry Clay introduced a resolution calling upon the President to explain, declared himself "inexpressibly distressed" and proposed severer penalties for those who interfered with the law. President Fillmore sent a special message to Congress promising prosecution of the guilty parties. Garrison commented: "Henry Clay — with one foot in the grave, and just ready to have both body and soul cast into hell — as if eager to make his damnation doubly sure, rises in the U. S. Senate and proposes an inquiry into the expediency of passing yet another law, by which every one who shall dare peep or mutter against the execution of the Fugitive Slave Bill shall have his life crushed out!"

Three Negroes and two white men were brought to trial. Richard H. Dana Jr., John P. Hale and George Farley appeared for the defense. Prospective jurors were asked if they held views regarding the Fugitive Slave Law that would prevent them from bringing in a verdict according to the facts. The facts being well established, the defense and the prosecution were equally puzzled when the jury pronounced itself unable to reach a verdict. One of the jurors had held out stubbornly for acquittal. The case was dropped.

Several years later Dana met Francis E. Bigelow of Concord, who told him that he was the juror responsible for the mistrial.

"What were your reasons?" Dana asked.

"Well, you remember witnesses testified that they saw the accused help Shadrach into the carriage."

"I remember."

"The carriage was traced to West Cambridge, where the prisoner was put in a wagon at night and driven to Sudbury."

"I remember that too."

"Well, I drove that wagon to Sudbury."

10

When in 1776 a female slave belonging to George Washington had escaped to Portsmouth, the Father of his Country asked that she be returned to him, but added: "I do not mean, however, by this request, that such violent measures should be used as would excite a mob or a riot." If such were likely to be the result, or even if her arrest were to provoke "uneasy sensations in the minds of well disposed citizens," then Washington preferred to "forego her services altogether; and the example also, which is of infinite more importance." President Fillmore and his Secretary of State were, however, determined that neither riot nor "uneasy sensations in the minds of well disposed citizens" should stay the hand of the Federal Government on a future occasion. Their opportunity came in April, 1851, when Thomas Sims, a youth of seventeen, was arrested on complaint of a Georgia slaveholder. A strong guard was thrown around the courthouse, where Sims was confined in a room in that part of the building leased by the Federal Government. For further security a heavy chain was hung across the entrance and the judges of the Supreme Court of Massachusetts had their dignity somewhat ruffled by having to pass underneath.

Sims, a boy of spirit, said to his lawyers, Samuel E. Sewall and Robert Rantoul Jr., who volunteered their services: "Give me a knife and when the commissioner declares me a slave, I will stab myself through the heart before his eyes." The request was not heeded, but the defense availed itself of every technicality. Phillips addressed an immense crowd on the Common and spoke at protest meetings at Tremont Temple and Washington Hall. At Sims's request prayers were offered in his behalf in many Boston churches. All in vain. The commissioner ruled that the young Negro must be returned to his master. "And this is Massachusetts liberty!" cried the spirited youth as he was led from the courtroom.

"COME BY THE THOUSAND! Come to witness the sad scene of the State's disgrace!" read a handbill distributed by order of the Vigilance Committee. At five in the morning four hundred policemen and armed deputies assembled before the courthouse. In nearby Faneuil Hall a militia regiment was kept in readiness. Notwithstanding the early hour a large crowd had gathered. There were cries of, "Where is liberty?" "Is this Boston?" "Shame! Shame!" Sims, surrounded by marshal's deputies and policemen, was marched to Long Wharf, where the brig *Acorn*, belonging to a Boston merchant, was waiting to take him to Savannah. As he stepped on board a voice cried: "Sims, preach liberty to the slaves!" The sails were unfurled. The crowd intoned a hymn. A church bell tolled mournfully, then another and another. "Some," wrote Garrison, "were choked with cotton."

11

Garrison and Phillips had confidently expected that public opinion in Boston would not tolerate the rendition of a single fugitive slave. Both felt bitterly disappointed. On the first anniversary of the rendition of Sims, April 12, 1852, Phillips made a speech at the Melodeon in Boston in which he advised fugitives to defend their lives by force if necessary:

"I think we are bound, in common kindness and honesty, to tell them that there are but two ways that promise any refuge from the horrors of a return to bondage: one is to fly — to place themselves under the protection of that government, which with all its faults, has won the proud distinction that slaves cannot breathe her air.[5] AND THIS IS THE COURSE I WOULD ADVISE EVERY MAN ADOPT. THIS, UNLESS THERE ARE, IN HIS PARTICULAR CASE, IMPERATIVE REASONS TO THE CONTRARY, IS HIS DUTY. If this course be impossible, then the other way is to arm himself, and by resistance secure in the Free States a trial for homicide, — trusting that no jury will be able so far to crush the instincts of humanity as not to hold him justified. It is just possible that the fugitive slave, taking his defense in his own right hand, and appealing to the first principle of natural law, may so excite the sympathy of some and the fears of others, as to gain the attention of all, and force them to grapple with this problem of slavery and the Fugitive Slave Bill."

Sims had begged for a knife with which to stab himself to the heart in the courtroom; Phillips, however, believed that to shoot the commissioner would have a far better effect: "If a Morton or a Curtis could be shot on the commissioner's bench by the hand of him they sought to sacrifice, I have no doubt that it would have a wholesome effect."

He wished, however, to confine armed resistance only to the Fugitive Slave Law. As to slavery in general — "On that point, I am willing to wait. I can be patient, no matter how often that is defeated by treacherous statesmen. The cause of three millions of slaves, the destruction of a great national institution, must proceed slowly; and like every other change in public sentiment, we must wait patiently for it, and there the best policy is, beyond all question, the policy of submission; for that gains, in time, public sympathy."

One might have expected that Garrison, advocate of nonresistance, would have uttered a protest. Far from it! He offered a resolution in which, by inference, he declared that there was no reason for confining armed resistance to the Fugitive Slave Law, but that the slaves would be fully justified in rising in bloody insurrection:

"*Resolved,* That if 'resistance to tyrants,' by bloody weapons, 'is obedience to God,' and if our Revolutionary fathers were justified in wading through blood to freedom and independence, then every fugitive slave is justified in arming himself for protection and defence, — in taking the life of every marshal, commissioner, or other person who attempts to reduce him to bondage; and the millions

[5] The British and Canadian Governments.

who are clanking their chains on our soil find ample warrant in rising *en masse*, and asserting their right to liberty, at whatever sacrifice of the life of their oppressors." [6]

12

Sims regained his freedom in 1860, through the efforts of Lydia Maria Child. Having learned his whereabouts she wrote to his master asking how much he would take for the slave. Since Sims was a skilled mechanic, the master demanded eighteen hundred dollars. She then appealed by letter to a number of prominent men having no connection with the antislavery movement. "I resolved," she wrote to a friend, "that it should be done with pro-slavery money." The entire purchase price was furnished by Major General Devers, United States Marshal at the time of the rendition of Sims. He sent an additional one hundred dollars to be given to Sims when he entered free territory. "I suppose," wrote Mrs. Child, "that his idea of the necessity of sustaining law, and his great admiration for Daniel Webster, led him to do what pained his heart at the time and troubled his conscience afterward."

13

On October 24, 1852, Daniel Webster died. He had been in poor health for several years. Since the delivery of his Seventh of March Speech he had been troubled with insomnia. "I have had little sleep, not four hours a night, on an average for the whole six months," he wrote on September 10, 1850, to Peter Harvey. The attacks of the Abolitionists, his failure to obtain the Presidential nomination, the disintegration of the Whig Party, had affected him profoundly. Whatever his faults, there had been something Titanic about him. His passing was like the disappearance of a mountain peak dominating a landscape. Whigs, Democrats and Free-Soilers united to do

[6] In 1840, John Quincy Adams delivered a speech to the colored people of Pittsburgh during which he said: "We know that the day of your redemption must come. The time and manner of its coming we know not. It may come in peace, or it may come in blood; but whether in peace or in blood, let it come." Representative Dillett of Alabama quoted these words on the floor of Congress. Adams, unabashed, said with emphasis: "I say now, let it come." Dillett cried: "Yes, the gentleman now says let it come, though it costs the blood of thousands of white men!" Adams replied: "Though it costs the blood of *millions* of white men, let it come!"

him honor. The Abolitionists remained unmoved. Phillips wrote in the *Liberty Bell:*

"Daniel Webster is dead. If the Fugitive Slave Law could have died with him, he would indeed have slept in blessings. But the evil that men do lives after them: when it does not, we will speak nothing but praise of the dead. The abolitionists are sometimes blamed for their severe judgments of men whose general characters are good. The examples of bad men are of little importance. It is the faults of good men, of popular idols, that are dangerous; and precedents set by such need special protest. The curses of the poor have blighted his laurels. He is mourned in ceiled houses and the marts of trade. But the dwellers in slave huts and the fugitives along the highways thank God they have one enemy the less."

In Faneuil Hall George S. Hillard, leading orator of the Webster Whigs in Massachusetts, eulogized the dead leader: "His voice of wisdom and power, which was at home among us, has penetrated wherever there was an oppressor to be rebuked, or a victim to be cheered. Everywhere it has brought hope to the struggling and the down-trodden, and confusion to the wrong-doer."

The words have an ironic ring when one considers that they were uttered by the same George S. Hillard whose house at 62 Pinckney Street was a station on the Underground Railroad.

CHAPTER II

Gathering Storm

IN March, 1852, appeared Harriet Beecher Stowe's *Uncle Tom's Cabin*. As a serial in the *National Era*, of Washington, D. C., the novel had attracted little attention; in book form its success was phenomenal for that time. Twenty thousand copies were sold in three weeks, three hundred thousand in a year. It did even better in England, where nearly half a million copies were disposed of in six months. Two theaters in London presenting a stage version turned away crowds nightly. Eventually the book was translated into almost every language.

George Thompson wrote to Garrison: "Behold the fruit of your labors and rejoice." Phillips, too, was of the opinion that a large part of the book's success was due to the Abolitionist movement. In a speech before the Massachusetts Anti-Slavery Society he said: "If the old antislavery movement had not roused the sympathies of Mrs. Stowe, the book had never been written; if that movement had not raised up hundreds of thousands of hearts to sympathize with the slave, the book had never been read." He pointed out that when Richard Hildreth's *Archy Moore* (later renamed *The White Slave*) had appeared in 1835, it had fallen on deaf ears, although not unworthy of comparison with Mrs. Stowe's novel. "To the cause which changed 1835 to 1852 is due somewhat of the influence of *Uncle Tom's Cabin*."

Garrison was not altogether pleased with the book. He could not help wondering if the qualities with which Mrs. Stowe had endowed Uncle Tom would have made the same appeal to her and to her readers had her hero been white. He had serious doubts about this, having noticed that white men who practiced humility were accorded neither respect nor admiration. "Talk not to them of peacefully submitting to chains and stripes — it is base servility! Talk not of servants being obedient to their masters — let the blood of the tyrants flow! How is this to be explained or reconciled? Is there one law of submission and nonresistance for the black man and another law of rebellion and conflict for the white man? When it is the whites who are trodden in the dust, does Christ justify them in taking up arms to vindicate their rights? And when it is the blacks who are thus treated, does Christ require them to be patient, harmless, long-suffering, and forgiving? And are there two Christs?"

The South's rage at Mrs. Stowe's novel rose to the point of frenzy. The editor of the *Southern Literary Messenger* ordered a review in accordance with the following formula: "I would have the review as hot as hell-fire, blasting and searing the reputation of the vile wretch in petticoats who could write such a volume." A bookseller in Mobile, Alabama, having ordered a few copies at the request of customers, was forced to flee.

2

Uncle Tom's Cabin created sympathy for the Negro, especially for the fugitive slave, and made enforcement of the Fugitive Slave Law increasingly difficult, but it furnished further proof that a purely moral issue cannot move the masses politically. At the Presidential election that year the only political party hostile to slavery — the Free-Soil Party — suffered a crushing defeat. It was a "Wilmot Proviso Party," having come into existence as a result of the fear that slavery would spread to territory conquered from Mexico. When as a result of the Compromise of 1850 the Wilmot Proviso lost its significance, the party began to disintegrate. In 1848 the Free-Soil candidate for President, Martin Van Buren, had polled 290,000 votes, in 1852 John P. Hale polled 156,000, out of a total of three million.

The Whig Party likewise showed signs of disintegration. Its platform differed so little from that of the Democrats that there did not appear to be much reason for the party's existence. Webster perceived this shortly before his death, remarking that after the November election the Whig Party would be known "only in history." His prophecy came nearly being fulfilled. The Whig candidate, General Winfield Scott, carried only four States. Franklin Pierce of New Hampshire, a "Northern man with Southern principles," was elected President.

Political antislavery men felt profoundly discouraged. They saw the Slave Power more firmly intrenched than ever, with nothing to oppose it except the Abolitionist movement, which lacked political and economic footing. Henry Wilson was to write: "No darker day, not even during the most critical period of the Rebellion, has ever marked the history of the Republic." As for old-time Whigs, they saw the ruin of their party and hardly knew where to turn. Abraham Lincoln of Illinois declared that he "was beginning to lose interest in politics."

Emboldened by their success, the slaveholders now made a move that proved fatal to their cause.

3

Senator Stephen A. Douglas of Illinois was a dumpy little man of forty, slightly more than five feet tall, with a large head, bushy dark brown hair, short thick neck and barrel-like chest. He had a pugnacious jaw, penetrating deep blue eyes and was by far the ablest Democrat in Congress. Among his constituents he was often referred to as the "Little Giant." He had married the daughter of a prosperous North Carolina planter, who a year after her marriage inherited from her father a Mississippi plantation with one hundred and fifty slaves.

The antislavery cause owes much to Douglas. The Kansas-Nebraska Bill he piloted through Congress, in 1854, took antislavery out of the realm of religion and ethics and planted it solidly in that of politics and economics. The bill proposed the organization into two vast Territories of all the land situated between the Missouri and the Rocky Mountains, bounded by Canada on the North, by the Indian Territory on the South and about equal in size to the combined area of all the Free States. It declared the Missouri Compromise of 1820 "null and void" and left the question of whether slavery should be permitted in a Territory to the decision of the settlers themselves. This was the famous doctrine of "popular sovereignty," derisively called "squatter sovereignty" by its opponents. It was Douglas's contention that the Compromise of 1850, which provided that method of decision for the Territory of New Mexico, had "superseded" the Missouri Compromise. There can be no doubt that neither Clay nor Webster had intended this, but both were dead and could not speak for themselves. Their fatal compromise was now used as a pretext to make an area equal to the combined area of France, Italy and Spain potential slave territory.

The interest of slaveholders in the new Territories was, for the present at least, mainly political. They wished to people them with proslavery settlers so the political balance between Slave and Free States could be maintained. It would not be necessary, they believed, to transport many slaves to the new Territories to accomplish their purpose. In Delaware there were only two thousand slaves against ninety thousand freemen, yet that State was safely counted in the slavery column.

The Kansas-Nebraska Bill created consternation among anti-slavery men in Congress and throughout the North. William Henry Seward saw "slavery not only luxuriating in all new Territories, but stealthily creeping into the free States themselves." Lincoln, whose interest in politics revived, gave the same warning. Horace Greeley wrote in the New York *Tribune* that "it would be better to blow up the Capitol than to permit the diabolical measure to become law." A group of senators and representatives sent an impassioned appeal to the country. Over three thousand New England clergymen signed a petition of protest. Garrison and Phillips suddenly found themselves popular and were vigorously applauded by audiences hitherto hostile. The New York *Times* printed one of Garrison's speeches in full. Douglas was burned in effigy on Boston Common and in sundry other places. Protest meetings were held throughout the North. Emerson declared at Cooper Union, New York: "I respect the Anti-Slavery Society. It is the Cassandra that has fore-told all that has befallen, fact for fact, years ago; foretold all and no man laid it to heart. It seemed, as the Turks say, 'Fate makes a man should not believe his own eyes.' But the Fugitive Slave Law did much to unglue the eyes of men, and now the Nebraska Bill leaves us staring. The Anti-Slavery Society will add many members this year."

Notwithstanding all this, the bill passed both Houses of Congress. Phillips wrote to Elizabeth Pease: "The *Government* has fallen into the hands of the Slave Power *completely*. So far as national politics are concerned, we are beaten — there's no hope. We shall have Cuba in a year or two, Mexico in five; and I should not wonder if efforts were made to revive the slave trade, though perhaps unsuccessfully, as the Northern slave States, which live by the export of slaves, would help us in opposing that. Events hurry forward with amazing rapidity: we live fast here. The future seems to unfold a vast slave empire united with Brazil, and darkening the whole west. I hope I may be a false prophet, but the sky was never so dark."

4

Since the rendition of Sims no fugitive slave had been arrested in Boston. The Vigilance Committee had perfected its organization. Hotels and rooming houses were watched. A stranger suspected of being a slave catcher was placed under surveillance and his every move reported to the Committee. If the authorities were notified to be on the alert for a fugitive slave known or suspected to be aboard a ship expected to arrive in Boston on a given date, the information was known to the committee before it reached the interested official. In such a case Captain Austin Bearse was asked to keep himself in readiness. He was a native of Barnstable, had been a mate on a coasting vessel plying to Southern ports and had conceived an undying hatred of the South's cherished institution. He now owned a small schooner in which he took fishing parties down the harbor, but which was at the committee's disposal. On the appointed day agents of the committee would board the schooner and go to meet the ship. While officers of the law waited at the wharf to arrest the fugitive, the committee's agents would board the vessel far out in the harbor, and with a show of authority transfer the fugitive to the schooner. He would then be conveyed to a secret landing place where a closed carriage stood waiting that hurried him to safety. This maneuver was executed so often and with such unfailing success that one is led to suspect the officers of the law were not particularly anxious to have it miscarry. The committee was in existence from October, 1850, to April, 1861. Its records, in possession of the Bostonian Society, show that over three hundred fugitives were aided.

Three years after the rendition of Sims, the committee was finally outwitted.

5

It was "Anniversary Week" in Boston. The Abolitionists, the Woman Suffragists and various other organizations were holding their annual conventions. Hotels and rooming houses were crowded. The arrival of two Virginians, Colonel Charles F. Suttle of Alexandria and his agent William Brent, registered at the Revere House, remained unnoticed. Shortly after their arrival, on Wednesday, May 24, 1854, one Anthony Burns, a colored man employed in a Brattle Street clothing store belonging to one of his race, was stopped by an officer on his way home in the evening and told that he was under arrest for having robbed a jewelry store. Knowing that he could easily prove his innocence he offered no resistance. It would have been futile anyway, for at that moment six men emerged from a nearby tavern, surrounded him, picked him up bodily, and carried him down the middle of the street towards the courthouse, at the door of which stood United States Marshal Watson Freeman. Burns was taken to that part of the building leased to the Federal Government and placed under guard in a jury room.

The reason given the Negro for his arrest was only a ruse. He had been arrested on a fugitive slave warrant issued by United States Commissioner Edward G. Loring, Judge of Probate and Lecturer at Harvard Law School. That same evening Colonel Suttle and William Brent went to see the prisoner and identified him as the former's fugitive slave.

Though all possible precautions had been taken, news of the arrest leaked out. When in the morning Burns was brought into court three lawyers were on hand to defend him — Richard H. Dana Jr., famous author of *Two Years Before the Mast*, Charles M. Ellis and Boston's ablest colored lawyer, Robert Morris. Two members of the executive board of the Vigilance Committee, Wendell Phillips and Theodore Parker, arrived soon after.

"The prisoner sat in the dock," Parker wrote, "ironed, between two of the Marshal's guards," and looked "terrified, stupefied, intimidated." The clergyman received permission to speak to him. "I told him I was a minister and had been appointed at a meeting of citizens, minister at large in behalf of fugitive slaves, and asked him if he did not want counsel. He said, 'I shall have to go back. Mr. Suttle knows me — Brent knows me. If I must go back, I want to go back as easy as I can.'"

The previous night he had made damaging admissions concerning his identity. He was about to confirm these when Dana, addressing the court as *amicus curae*, obtained a postponement until Saturday.

6

The Vigilance Committee met on Friday. It had already voted to hold a protest meeting in Faneuil Hall Friday evening. Phillips now proposed that when an attempt was made to remove the prisoner, a solid wall of humanity should bar the way. During the resulting confusion Burns was to be seized, thrust into a waiting carriage and hurried to safety. Phillips had no doubt concerning the nature of the Commissioner's decision. He had called on him to ask for an order enabling him to see the prisoner. Loring had written out the order and had handed it to him with the words: "Mr. Phillips, the case is so clear, that I do not think you will be justified in placing any obstacles in the way of the man's going back, and he probably will."

The meeting adjourned without formulating any definite plan.

The youthful Reverend Thomas Wentworth Higginson, who had come from Worcester for the occasion, and his fellow towns-man Martin Stowell, now concocted a plan of their own, which Higginson described in these words: "The man must be taken from the Court-House. It could not be done in cold blood, but the effort must have behind it the momentum of a public meeting, such as was to be held in Faneuil Hall that night. An attack at the end of the meeting would be hopeless, for the United States marshal would undoubtedly be looking for just that attempt, and would be re-enforced accordingly; this being, as we afterwards found, pre-cisely what that official was planning. Could there not be an attack at the very height of the meeting? Let all be in readiness; let a picked body be distributed near the Court-House and Square; then send some loud-voiced speaker, who should appear in the gallery of Faneuil Hall and announce that there was a mob of negroes already attacking the Court-House; let a speaker, previously warned, — Phillips, if possible, — accept the opportunity promptly and send the whole meeting pell-mell to Court Square, ready to fall behind the leaders and bring out the slave."[1]

Higginson was firmly resolved to carry out this plan and managed to induce a score of men, white and colored, to serve as a spearhead for the drive of the expected multitude from Faneuil Hall.

[1] This and other quotations from Thomas Wentworth Higginson concern-ing the attack on the courthouse are from that author's volume *Cheerful Yes-terdays*. (Houghton Mifflin Company, Boston and New York, 1899.)

7

The change that had come over Boston, and for that matter over the entire North, as a result of the passage of the Kansas-Nebraska Act is illustrated by nothing so much as by the Burns case. At the time of the arrest of Sims five hundred of the city's business and professional men had enrolled as special constables to aid the Marshal in removing the prisoner. Now Marshal Freeman had to recruit his posse from among the dregs of the city. Dana was to say during the trial that since the Marshal had recruited his force "people have not felt it necessary to lock their doors at night, the brothels are tenanted only by women, fighting dogs and racing horses have been unemployed, and Ann Street and its cellars show sign of a coming millennium." Indeed, a check-up showed that nearly a third of the posse had a prison record.

On Friday evening Faneuil Hall was filled to suffocation. Curiously the success of the meeting contributed to the failure of Higginson's plan. "It was," he wrote, "the largest gathering I ever saw in that hall. The platform was covered with men; the galleries, the floor, even the outer stairways, were absolutely filled with a solid audience. . . . We could no more communicate with the platform than if the Atlantic Ocean rolled between. There was no private entrance to it, such as now exists, and in this seemingly slight architectural difference lay the failure of the whole enterprise."

George R. Russell, former Mayor of Roxbury, presided. Dr. Samuel G. Howe introduced a defiant resolution that passed with a roar: "That which is not just is not law, and that which is not law ought not to be obeyed. . . . No man's freedom is safe unless all men are free." John L. Swift, a young attorney, advised in the course of a fiery speech: "When we go from this Cradle of Liberty, let us go to the tomb of Liberty — the courthouse." Phillips was greeted with thunderous applause and the waving of hats. "There is no law in Massachusetts," he said, "and when law ceases, the people may act in their own sovereignty. I am against squatter sovereignty in Nebraska, and against kidnappers' sovereignty in Boston." Theodore Parker addressed the crowd as, "Fellow subjects of Virginia," which was greeted with howls and groans. Towards the end of his speech he declared: "Gentlemen, I am a clergyman and a man of peace; I love peace. But there is a means, and there is an end; liberty is the end, and sometimes peace is not the means towards it." He proposed that the crowd assemble in Court Square at nine o'clock the following morning, when Burns was to appear in court. There were cries of, "Let's go tonight! Let's pay a visit to the slave catchers at the Revere House!" . . . "Do you propose to go to the Revere House tonight?" asked Parker. "Then show your hands." . . . Many hands went up. Parker hesitated, then declared: "It's not a vote. We shall meet at Court Square at nine o'clock tomorrow morning."

There was confusion, conflicting cries of, "To the Revere House! To the courthouse!" Parker appeared bewildered. An eyewitness wrote: "Amid the uproar Wendell Phillips again ascended the platform. The different quality of the two men then appeared. Ere half a dozen sentences had fallen from his lips, the assembly had subsided into profound stillness."

It would be useless, Phillips said, to go to the Revere House to groan at the slave catchers. It was impossible to insult men of that stripe. If he believed anything could be accomplished that evening, he would be the first to go. ". . . But wait until daytime. The vaults of the banks in State Street sympathize with us. The Whigs who have been kicked once too often, sympathize with us. It is in your power to block up every avenue, that the man cannot be carried off. Do not, then, balk the effort of tomorrow by foolish conduct tonight, giving the enemy alarm. You that are ready to do the real work, be not carried away by indiscretion which may make shipwreck of our hopes. The zeal that won't keep till tomorrow will never free a slave."

Order had been restored. The meeting was about to adjourn without incident when a voice near the entrance cried: "Mr. Chairman, I am just informed that a mob of Negroes is in Court Square attempting to rescue Burns. I move that we adjourn to Court Square."

There was a rush for the doors.

8

It was about nine o'clock. The weather was balmy. In the massive courthouse many windows were lighted. The Supreme Court of Massachusetts was holding an evening session. A jury was deliberat-

ing. Marshal Freeman, anxious about the outcome of the Faneuil
Hall meeting, had assembled some fifty of his special deputies and
had armed them with cutlasses.

Higginson and his men, armed with axes and meat cleavers disguised in wrapping paper, had come singly, so as not to attract attention. He himself had brought only an umbrella, which he hung
on the railing of the courthouse steps and promptly forgot. The
conspirators had wrenched the heavy banister from the museum
steps to use as battering ram, and as the crowd from Faneuil Hall
surged into Court Square were battering away at the west door of
the building. A hinge broke, the door gaped open. Higginson and a
Negro forced their way in, only to be assailed with cutlasses by the
defenders. Higginson was wounded on the chin and he and his companion were forced to retreat. The deputies hurled themselves against
the door, shutting it. One fell back with a cry. A long knife thrust
through the shattered door panel had pierced his vitals. He was carried to a jury room and expired.

Higginson, blood dripping from his chin, seeing his followers
hesitating, cried: "You cowards, will you desert us now!" The men
rallied and again the banister crashed against the badly shattered door
forcing it wide open. The deputies retreated across the brightly
lighted vestibule, but the crowd in the Square showed no inclination
to second the attackers. "Then," wrote Higginson, "followed one of
the most picturesque incidents of the whole affair. In the silent pause
that ensued there came quietly forth from the crowd the well-known
form of Mr. Amos Bronson Alcott, the Transcendental philosopher.
Ascending the lighted steps alone, he said tranquilly, turning to me
and pointing forward, 'Why are we not within?' 'Because,' was the
rather impatient answer, 'these people will not stand by us.' He said
not a word, but calmly walked up the steps, — he and his familiar
cane. He paused again at the top, the centre of all eyes, within and
without; a revolver sounded from within, but hit nobody; and finding himself wholly unsupported, he turned and retreated, but without hastening a step."

Reinforcements of police were arriving, and the attackers scattered. As Higginson was about to leave, a street gamin pointed to his
umbrella, and said, "Mister, I guess you've left your rumberrill." He
picked up his umbrella and went away meditating that it was "one of
the very best plots that ever — failed."

9

Examination of Burns was postponed until Monday morning, Saturday being devoted to negotiations to obtain his release by purchase. The proposal that Burns be purchased came from Colonel Suttle's legal counsel. Feeling against giving up the fugitive ran so high that the attorneys were loath to make a plea for his surrender. Colonel Suttle did not feel happy either. When he looked out of the window of his room at the Revere House at any hour of day or night, he saw a group of colored men standing on the sidewalk opposite in silent vigil. This war of nerves, organized by the Committee, told upon him. He moved to a room in the attic and hired four guards. The proposal made by his attorneys appeared to him a welcome solution. As for Commissioner Loring he was so pleased that he wrote out a bill of sale with his own hand. The twelve hundred dollars demanded by Suttle were quickly subscribed by Boston businessmen. The case appeared settled when United States District Attorney Benjamin F. Hallett intervened. He insisted that the slain deputy must be avenged, spoke to Suttle about his duty to his fellow slaveholders and managed to persuade him to allow the law to take its course.

When Burns was led into court on Monday morning the courthouse was like a beleaguered fortress. A vast crowd surged about the building. All entrances were guarded by police and military. Federal soldiers and militia were at every window. A triple line of soldiers guarded the stairway leading to the courtroom. "So strictly was the guard maintained," wrote Charles Emery Stevens, an eyewitness, "that those who had passed the first sentries, were in some instances, arrested and detained upon the stairway by the last." In his closing plea Dana appealed to the Commissioner in these words: "The eyes of many millions are upon you, Sir. You are to do an act which will hold its place in the history of America, in the history of the progress of the human race. May your judgment be for liberty and not for slavery; for hope and not for despair: and may the blessing of him that is ready to perish come upon you."

Commissioner Loring postponed his decision until Friday morning. There were a number of technicalities which, had he felt so inclined, would have enabled him to decide in favor of Burns and yet remain true to his oath of office, but before Friday dawned he noti-

fied Suttle and Brent that he meant to pronounce in their favor. He
undoubtedly did this so they might escape the wrath of the populace, but it proved one of the reasons which later enabled Phillips to
demand his dismissal as Judge of Probate. On Friday morning,
June 2, before a hushed courtroom, with thousands waiting in Court
Square to hear the decision, Commissioner Loring, whose "countenance wore a haggard and jaded aspect," pronounced the verdict.

10

Phillips had said in Faneuil Hall: "The Nebraska Act I call knock-
ing a man down, the arrest of Burns is spitting in his face after he is
down." The Act became law three days before Commissioner Loring
rendered his decision. During those three days every train pulling
into Boston disgorged crowds of men who eagerly seized this opportunity to demonstrate their displeasure to the authorities in Washington. Six hundred came from Worcester alone. But if the people
were aroused, the Administration was determined. President Pierce
personally wired District Attorney Hallett: "Incur any expense
deemed necessary by the Marshal or yourself for city military or
otherwise, to insure execution of the law." Pressure was brought to
bear upon the Mayor, with the result that on the morning on which
Judge Loring gave his decision there were assembled on the Common:
the First Battalion of Light Dragoons, the Fifth Regiment of Artillery, the Fifth Regiment of Light Infantry, the Third Battalion of
Light Infantry and the Corps de Cadets. Most of the famous companies of citizen soldiery were there — the New England Guards,
the Pulaski Guards, the Independent Fusiliers, the Washington Light
Infantry, the Columbian Artillery, the American Artillery, the Bay
State Artillery and others.

The militia commanders and the captains of the municipal police
had been instructed to preserve order, but not to assist in the execution of the Fugitive Slave Law — a distinction without a difference.
Joseph K. Hayes, Captain of the South Station, in whose cabinetmaker's shop Garrison had at one time sought refuge from a mob,
promptly resigned. Special editions of the papers featured his resignation and he became a local hero. To the police and the militia was
assigned the task of clearing the streets leading from the courthouse
to Long Wharf, where a revenue cutter was waiting to take the
prisoner to Alexandria. He was to be escorted to the wharf by the

Marshal's posse of one hundred and twenty-five men, by five companies of Marines totaling one hundred and forty men, and by a cannon with its complement of artillery men from the Navy Yard at Charlestown. Altogether, in addition to the municipal police, fifteen hundred men were to be employed to deliver one fugitive slave to the South. Garrison's *Liberator*, sold in the streets and eagerly bought, contrasted the Government's action in the Burns case with its inaction when a representative of the Governor of Massachusetts, who had gone to Charleston to contest in the Federal Court the constitutionality of a South Carolina law affecting colored seamen, had been driven from that city by a mob.

The soldiers had been furnished eleven rounds of powder and ball. At eleven o'clock they loaded and marched off to clear Court Square. This accomplished, the cannon was placed at the courthouse entrance and pointed towards solidly packed Court Street. Besides the cannon a Federal officer stood like a statue, gazing stolidly before him. Towards one o'clock Major General Benjamin F. Edwards (in private life a State Street druggist) galloped up and informed the Marshal that to clear the streets completely was an impossibility. Some fifty thousand people were crowded in the one third of a mile between the courthouse and the wharf. The best he could do was to clear the driveway.

Phillips, Parker and Burns's attorneys bade farewell to the prisoner, assuring him that negotiations for his freedom would be continued. A deputy then wished to manacle Burns, who said that if this were done he would struggle every inch of the way. Marshal Freeman intervened and manacles were dispensed with. A cortège formed: an artillery battalion, a platoon of Marines, the Marshal's posse with Burns in their midst, two platoons of Marines, the cannon and its attendants, another platoon of Marines. At some distance in front rode mounted Dragoons, at some distance behind, Lancers. At strategic points along the line of march reinforcements were stationed. Police with arms interlocked contained the spectators to the sidewalks. Windows and roofs swarmed with onlookers. "There was lots of folks to see a colored man walk down the street," Burns remarked.

Groans and cries of "Shame! Shame!" greeted the soldiers. The façade of the office of John C. Park, distinguished attorney and Commander of the Ancient and Honorable Artillery, was draped with black. The Commonwealth Building displayed six flags, draped in mourning and at half mast. Opposite the old State House hung a coffin with the inscription: "The Funeral of Liberty." From the warehouse of Samuel May, octogenarian State Street merchant and relative of Garrison's friend of that name, a rope stretched to the building opposite supporting a huge American flag, *Union down.* Earlier in the day a citizen had tried to remove it, saying: "I'm an American. I'm not going to see the flag of my country disgraced." May had stopped him and had replied: "I, too, am an American and a native of this city and I declare that my country is eternally disgraced by today's proceedings."

On Commercial Street the crowd suddenly surged forward, broke through the line of police. Reserves stationed nearby went into action. Lancers galloped up. Infantry advanced on the double-quick. Swords flashed, horses reared, the foot soldiers charged with the bayonet. Shouts, screams, curses. Several were wounded, one seriously. Flushed with their victory and with the ample rations of rum they had received, the militiamen intoned, "Carry me back to old Virginny . . ." The multitude booed and groaned.

Finally the wharf was reached. Burns was placed aboard a small steamer which immediately cast off and conveyed him to the revenue cutter *Morris.* The bell of Brattle Street church tolled, other bells responded. The Reverend Daniel Foster, standing in the crowd near the wharf, lifted up his arms and cried: "Friends, let us pray!"

The Richmond *Enquirer* declared: "We rejoice at the recapture of Burns, but a few more such victories and the South is undone."

11

A Federal Grand Jury indicted Phillips, Parker, Higginson and several others. "Well, Wendell," Sumner wrote to Phillips, "your Faneuil Hall speech anent poor Burns and your treasonable efforts to humanize those whom the United States chattelizes, have at last, it should be seen, overtaxed the mercy of a long-suffering Government . . . You are indicted! What a small mouse for so big a mountain to bring forth — and after such prolonged travail, too. All right. 'Everything helps us.' "

Phillips was not worried about the indictment, which was dismissed after some legal skirmishing. It was Burns, pawn in the game between great political and economic forces, who troubled him. He wrote to Miss Pease: "Men talked of the good we might expect for the cause, but I could not think then of the general cause, so mournful and sad rose ever before me the pleading eyes of the poor victim, when he sat and cast his case on our consciences, and placed his fate in our hands. I could not forget the man in the idea."

Burns was sold by Suttle to a slave trader and it was fully a year before his whereabouts was discovered. The thirteen hundred dollars demanded by his new owner were quickly subscribed and he was freed. Barnum offered him one hundred dollars a week to tell his story in Barnum's Museum in New York. He declined with the remark: "He wants to show me like a monkey." As a slave he had often preached the gospel to his people. Offered a scholarship at Oberlin College, he accepted and prepared for the ministry.

Judge Loring did not fare so well. The women of Woburn sent him thirty pieces of silver. Bridgeport hanged him in effigy. Students deserted his classes at Harvard and the Board of Overseers of the University refused to confirm his reappointment as a lecturer. Twelve thousand people signed a petition to the Legislature that he be removed as Judge of Probate. Phillips appeared before the legislative committee and delivered the plea which Rufus Choate characterized as "outrageously magnificent." The Judge's removal was voted by both Houses of the Legislature, but the Governor refused to comply. Loring was not removed until 1858, and was then given a Federal post by the Buchanan administration.

The Burns case resulted in the passage of an exceedingly rigorous Personal Liberty Law, making enforcement of the Fugitive Slave Law in Massachusetts a complicated proceeding. But even this did not satisfy Bostonians. Business and professional men, few of whom had ever been identified with the antislavery movement, formed a secret society known as the Anti-Man-Hunting League, with branches throughout the State. Its purpose was to kidnap any slaveholder or slaveholder's agent who obtained a fugitive slave warrant and to hold him as a hostage. In Boston the League had over a hundred members, among whom was John A. Andrew, future Governor. Members were armed with billies and attended classes during which they learned punishing holds and practiced teamwork. They were given, however, no opportunity to exercise their prowess, for there were no further attempts to extradite fugitive slaves from Massachusetts.

12

About a month after Burns's arrest, on Independence Day, the Massachusetts Anti-Slavery Society held its annual outdoor celebration in a picnic grove at Framingham. Some three thousand people attended. Henry Ward Beecher has called the Anti-Slavery Society an "uncanonical Church . . . a Church without ordination." Garrison assuredly was its high priest. He now appeared on the platform to address his followers. He was in his forty-eighth year. His black frock coat, if a little shiny, was carefully brushed. He had abandoned the soft-collared shirt and loose tie he had been in the habit of wearing and his neck was encased in a stiff collar and stock. His face was pale and ascetic. Towards the end of his speech he said he would "now proceed to perform an action which would be testimony of his own soul, to all present, of the estimation in which he held the proslavery laws and deeds of the nation." He lit a candle standing on the table beside him, picked up a document and said: "This is a copy of the Fugitive Slave Law. Behold!" He touched the paper to the flame and as it blazed up said solemnly: "And let all the people say, Amen!" — "Amen!" echoed the crowd. He held up another document and said: "This is a copy of Judge Loring's decision in the Burns case." That, too, blazed up to the accompaniment of the same ritual. Next came a copy of the charge of Judge Benjamin R. Curtis to the Federal Grand Jury regarding the attack on the courthouse. Finally he held up a copy of the United States Constitution, "source and parent of all other atrocities — a covenant with death and an agreement with hell." He touched it to the flame, held it between finger and thumb until it had been completely consumed, then let the charred remains flutter to the ground, saying: "So perish all compromises with tyranny! And let all the people say, Amen!" . . . "Amen!" echoed the crowd.

CHAPTER III

The "Irrepressible Conflict"

FEAR lest slavery spread into territory taken from Mexico had been responsible for the birth of the Free-Soil Party. Fear that the Slave Power had engineered the repeal of the Missouri Compromise, so that slavery might expand into all the Territories, was responsible for the birth of the Republican Party. Self-interest, not sympathy for the slave, brought about the awakening. Workingmen, farmers, small businessmen — all who looked longingly towards the West as a land of promise — did not want to live in a slave economy. If the Abolitionists had not succeeded in awakening in them sympathy for the Negro, they had succeeded in convincing them that slavery had a blighting effect upon the fortunes of non-slaveholders in slave territory. The Abolitionists, moreover, had consistently pointed out that if slavery continued to exist in any part of the country, it was bound to become a menace to freedom throughout the land. In 1837, more than a score of years before Lincoln made his famous "House Divided" and Seward his "Irrepressible Conflict" speech,[1] Wendell Phillips had said at Lynn, Massachusetts:

"Pinckney's words have become true. 'The stream of liberty cannot flow unpolluted through the mire of partial bondage.' And this is the reason we render to those who ask why we are contending against Southern slavery, — *that it may not result in Northern slavery;* because time has shown that it sends its poisonous branches over all our fair land, and corrupts the very air we breathe. Our fate is bound up with that of the South, so they cannot be corrupt and we sound; they cannot fall and we stand. Disunion is coming unless we discuss this subject; for the spirit of freedom and the spirit of slavery are contending here for mastery. They cannot live together: as well, like the robber of the classic fable, chain the living and the dead together, as bind up such discordant materials and think it will last."

[1] See Appendix for extracts from Lincoln's and Seward's addresses.

In 1840 Garrison declared: "Freedom and Slavery are natural and irreconcilable enemies; it is morally impossible for them to exist together in the same nation; and the existence of one can only be secured by the destruction of the other."

The North, while not yet ready to lay the ax at the root of the evil, was determined that slavery should not be permitted to expand further. Democrats opposed to slavery expansion joined with Whigs, Free-Soilers, Liberty Party men and antislavery Know-Nothings to found the new party, which from a modest beginning in Wisconsin and Michigan quickly spread to all the Free States. Yet the Republican Party, like the Free-Soil Party, might have disintegrated had not the Slave Power by its assault upon Kansas proved that fear of its determination to expand into the Territories was not unfounded — proved it even to the satisfaction of so prudent a man as Abraham Lincoln, who declared that the intention of the slaveholders was "the planting of slavery wherever in the wide world local and unorganized opposition cannot prevent it."

2

Convinced that without expansion slavery was doomed politically and economically, Southern leaders were determined that Kansas should become a Slave State and should serve as a springboard for further conquests. On November 6, 1854, Senator David R. Atchison, former Speaker of the House, declared in a public address at Weston, Missouri: "If we cannot do this [take Kansas], it is an omen that the institution of Slavery is to fail in this and the other Southern States." As late as July, 1856, the editor of the Charleston (S. C.) *Courier* wrote: "Now, upon the proposition that the safety of the institution of Slavery in South Carolina is dependent upon its establishment in Kansas, there can be no rational doubt." Long before the first election took place in Kansas there sprang up in Western Missouri organizations whose purpose it was to see to it that slavery should prevail at the Kansas polls. At the first election, on November 29, 1854, armed bands of Missourians crossed the State line and elected the proslavery General J. W. Whitfield delegate to Congress. When on March 30, 1855, the Territorial Legislature was to be elected, invasion from Missouri assumed a military aspect. The Howard Committee, appointed by Congress, reported: "They came in wagons, — of which there were over one hundred — and on horseback. . . .

They were armed with guns, rifles, pistols and bowie-knives, and had tents, music and flags with them. They brought with them two pieces of artillery, loaded with musket balls." Contingents methodically invaded every voting district and, according to the Committee's report, cast 4908 illegal votes out of a total of 6320.

Of thirty-nine representatives elected to the Territorial Legislature all but one were proslavery men. The Howard Committee declared that "Every officer in the Territory, from constables to legislators, except those appointed by the President, owe their position to nonresident voters. None have been elected by the settlers, and your Committee have been unable to find that any political power whatever, however unimportant, has been exercised by the people of the Territory." Nevertheless, President Franklin Pierce, replying to a memorial of the Kansas settlers imploring protection, informed the petitioners that he meant to uphold the authority of the elected officials, "if necessary by the whole force of the government."

3

Assured of Federal support, the usurpers proceeded to rule with an iron hand. Those opposed to their rule were imprisoned or driven from the Territory. Property was confiscated or destroyed without legal process. The town of Lawrence, a Free State stronghold, effectively resisted the terror. Missourians seized the United States Arsenal at Liberty, Missouri, took cannon, muskets, rifles, gunpowder and anything else they might need, and marched upon Lawrence. They bombarded and burned to the ground a hotel the Emigrant Aid Society had erected and one other dwelling; destroyed two printing presses and, in the language of the Howard Committee, "proceeded to sack, pillage and rob houses, stores, trunks, etc., even to the clothing of women and children." Governor John W. Geary appointed by the President and far from friendly towards Abolitionists, wrote to a friend on December 22, 1856: "The persecutions of the Free State men here are not exceeded by those of the early Christians. . . . I am satisfied that there was a settled determination in *high quarters*, to make this a Slave State *at all hazards*. . . . This virulent spirit of dogged determination, to *force* slavery into this Territory, has overshot its mark and raised a storm."

The Free State settlers were confronted with the alternative of abandoning the Territory or taking up arms. Garrison's disciple

Charles Stearns, now a resident of Lawrence, who in Connecticut had preferred prison to serving in the militia, renounced nonresistance and joined the Free State settlers in an appeal to opponents of slavery everywhere to send arms and reinforcements. Shipments of Sharp's rifles labeled "Crockery," "Books," "Bibles," "Revised Statutes," "Hardware," etc., were soon on their way. Reinforcements, too, arrived and the supporters of slavery, finding themselves hard-pressed, sent forth a call for help. Atchison wrote: "We must have the support of the South. We are fighting the battles of the South. We want men, armed men. We must have money. Let your young men come in squads, as fast as they can be raised and armed." They came. Major Jefferson Buford came at the head of four hundred adventurers from Alabama, Georgia and South Carolina. "Kansas the Outpost," and "The Supremacy of the White Race," read inscriptions on their banners. The "Red Shirts" came from Virginia, with a flag inscribed "Southern Rights." A contingent from South Carolina flaunted a black flag adorned with a serpent and the inscription, "South Carolina Minute Men."

A veritable civil war followed. As in all wars — especially between fellow citizens — atrocities were committed by both sides. Men were killed in cold blood, towns laid waste, shops and houses looted and burned, horses and cattle driven off. The question whether the South would or would not secede was decided in Kansas. When the slaveholders failed to capture Kansas, slavery had to resign itself to gradual extinction or seek *Lebensraum* beyond the borders of the United States. Since Southern leaders knew the North would not embark on such an adventure for the purpose of increasing the number of Slave States, secession became inevitable.

4

In the autumn of 1855 the Free State settlers in Kansas organized a government of their own and adopted a constitution forbidding slavery in the Territory. To Garrison's and Phillips's disgust they decided to exclude all Negroes, bond or free. When submitted to a referendum the exclusion clause carried by a vote of three to one. Charles Stearns wrote to Garrison: "The common cry is, 'We want no slavery and no niggers.' . . . I am much disappointed in the character of the New England emigrants. They come here, as men go to California, mainly after money." Garrison wrote in the

Liberator: "While to propitiate the pro-slavery spirit, they have banished from their presence all free colored emigrants, at the very time they are complaining of having their own rights wrested from them, — with what face can they ask for the sympathy and co-operation of those who are battling for the cause of freedom on a world-wide basis? 'Let the dead bury their dead.'" He took issue with the Reverend Henry Ward Beecher, who had become so active in supplying Sharp's rifles to the embattled Kansans that Plymouth Church was facetiously referred to as "the Church of the Holy Rifles," and the weapons themselves as "Beecher's Bibles." "Convince us that it is right to shoot anybody," Garrison wrote, "and our perplexity would be where to begin — whom first to despatch, as opportunity might offer. We should have to make clean work of the President and his Cabinet." If anybody should be furnished arms, why not the slaves? "Why not first of all take measures to furnish *them* with Sharp's rifles? Their wrongs are beyond description; in comparison with which, those of the people of Kansas are wholly insignificant. Why strain at a gnat and swallow a camel? . . . Who will go for arming our slave population?"

Phillips was so incensed at the exclusion of free Negroes as to speak with disdain of the struggle in Kansas. "Yankees have gone into the half-barbarous West," he said, "to dispute their way inch by inch with the bowie-knives and revolvers of vagabonds. What are the squabbles around the ballot-boxes of Kansas?" Most Abolitionists, however, agreed with Horace Greeley, who wrote in the New York *Tribune:* "Why free blacks should be excluded it is difficult to understand; but if Slavery can be kept out by a compromise of that sort we shall not complain. An error of this character may be corrected; but let Slavery obtain a foothold there and it is not easily removed."

5

The struggle in Kansas was a boon for the Republican Party. By midsummer, 1855, eleven Republican senators had been elected and there were majorities against the Kansas-Nebraska Act in fifteen States. Early in 1856, Nathaniel P. Banks of Massachusetts, an outspoken opponent of slavery, was elected Speaker of the House after a parliamentary struggle lasting two months. Garrison termed his triumph "the first gun at Lexington of the new Revolution."

Southern senators and representatives, never noted for their self-restraint, became increasingly irritable. Threats of violence against their Northern colleagues were common. "Members of Congress went armed in the streets, and sat with loaded revolvers in their desks," wrote Senator Henry Wilson of Massachusetts.

On May 19 and 20, 1856, Charles Sumner delivered his famous address "The Crime Against Kansas." He assailed Senator Douglas of Illinois and Senator Pierce Butler of South Carolina. Butler having remarked in a speech that "in an issue made in Boston" it was "Southern arms and treasure" that had won independence for America, Sumner countered by pointing out that a representative of South Carolina had found it necessary to apologize in the Continental Congress for the little aid, financial and military, South Carolina had been able to render in the Revolutionary War.

Two days later, Congress having adjourned in deference to a deceased member, Sumner was seated at his desk in the Senate Chamber busy with correspondence when two representatives from South Carolina entered. One was Preston S. Brooks, a distant relative of Senator Butler, the other, Lawrence M. Keitt. Both carried heavy gutta-percha canes, and the former was armed with a deadly weapon, which might have been a bowie knife or a revolver. Brooks, a heavy-set man of thirty-six, approached the Massachusetts senator, and saying: "You have published a libel on my State, and uttered a slander upon a relative who is aged and absent," proceeded to belabor him with his cane.

Under ordinary circumstances Sumner, tall and muscular, would have found it easy to wrest the cane from his assailant and give him a dose of his own medicine. Brooks knew this, for speaking in his own defense in the House he was to say: "Knowing that the Senator was my superior in strength, it occurred to me that he might wrest it [the cane] from my hand, and then (for I never attempt anything I do not perform) I might have been compelled to do that which I would have regretted the balance of my natural life." This could have had no other meaning than that he had been prepared to resort to murder if Sumner happened to get the best of him. Sumner, however, was at a great disadvantage. Not only was he seated, but his long legs were wedged tightly under the small desk which was fastened to the floor. In attempting to rise he seriously wrenched his back and fell, while Brooks continued to rain blows upon him until the cane broke. Several men came running up, but Keitt kept them at a distance by menacing them with his cane. The head wounds sustained by Sumner were not serious, but his wrenched back was to trouble him for years.

Brooks was hailed as a hero by his Southern colleagues in Congress, who gave a dinner in his honor, and by the South generally. Loving cups and a variety of canes rained in upon him, a particularly handsome cane being presented to him by the faculty and students of the University of Virginia. Having been censored by the House, he resigned, was triumphantly re-elected and congratulated by the Secretary of War, none other than Jefferson Davis. The South's most influential newspaper, the Richmond *Enquirer*, declared: "In the main the press of the South applaud the conduct of Mr. Brooks, without condition or limitation. Our approbation, at least, is entire and unreserved . . . It was a proper act, done at the proper time and in the proper place."

With the exception of Seward, Sumner was the most important man in the Republican Party. Hardly a city or town in the North but held a protest meeting, at which speakers denounced Brooks and the South that approved and sustained him. In scores of communities "bully" Brooks was hanged or burned in effigy. Phillips declared: "We have dropped down to the level of a ruffian civilization. Aged, venerable men, conservative by wealth and position, say: 'We must send men to Congress who can fight; no matter what their principles, if they can fight.' What a satire on the freeëst government in the world!"

6

The Republican Party, having nominated John C. Frémont for President and launched a campaign the like of which had not been seen since the log cabin and hard cider days of 1840, was particularly anxious to make it clear that it was not an Abolitionist party and had no intention of interfering with slavery in the Slave States. Phillips said at Worcester, Massachusetts: "One of the keenest members of the Frémont Party asked me to urge Mr. Garrison to write an article against Frémont as bitter as he could make it." Garrison, however, did not give the Republicans the satisfaction of disavowing their candidate. "As against Buchanan and Fillmore," he wrote, "it seems to us, the sympathies and best wishes of every enlightened friend of freedom must be on the side of Frémont; so that if there were no moral barrier to our voting, and we had a million votes to bestow, we should cast them all for the Republican candidate."

Abolitionists took the hint and few of them being concerned about a "moral barrier" to their voting became enthusiastic workers for Frémont.

The South, however, was not deceived by the Republican strategy. She knew that to confine slavery meant to strangle it. Governor Andrew B. Moore of Alabama, in a message to the Legislature, denounced the Republican scheme of "confining it [slavery] within the limits of the States where it now exists, so as ultimately to render slaves valueless to their owners, and thus effect their emancipation." Howell Cobb of Georgia, addressing a Democratic meeting at Portland, Maine, said to the Republicans in his audience: "The only difference between you and Garrison is — he goes at the question boldly, like a man, and you are sneaking around it. Garrison says your Constitution protects slavery, and he is against the Constitution. Well, I admit that he is foolish, but at the same time, you are obliged to admit that he is bolder and honester than you are."

Phillips's attitude was contradictory. When the Republican Party was organized he had said: "There is merit in the Republican Party. It is this: It is the first sectional party ever organized in this country. It does not know its own face, and calls itself national, but it is not national; it is the North against the South." During the campaign, however, he was to say: "Republicanism! What is it? I will tell you. Its cardinal principle is this: Resist the last enormity of slavery, and endorse all that went before. . . . I want no man for President of the United States — I will acknowledge no man as an anti-slavery candidate for any office — who has not got his hand half-clenched, and means to close it on the jugular vein of the slave system the moment he reaches it."

The Democrats elected their candidate, James Buchanan, but Frémont polled over one million three hundred and forty-one thousand votes and carried all but four of the Free States.

7

In 1834, Dr. John Emerson, a surgeon in the United States Army, had been transferred from St. Louis, Missouri, to the frontier post of Rock Island, Illinois. He took with him a young Negro slave named Dred Scott. When subsequently transferred to Fort Snelling, in what was then the Wisconsin Territory, he took the Negro with him, and when in 1838 he returned to St. Louis, Dred Scott again accompanied him. In 1844 Dr. Emerson died and two years later Scott sued the widow for his freedom, claiming that having been taken to live in a Territory situated North of the Missouri Compromise line, he had become a freeman. The trial court of the State of Missouri decided in his favor, but in 1852 the Missouri Supreme Court reversed the decision on the ground that Scott had returned to Missouri voluntarily with his master.

When in 1820 the Missouri Compromise was agreed upon some Southern leaders had claimed that it was unconstitutional — that under the Constitution slaves could be taken anywhere in the United States, just as any other property. If their contention was correct then slaves could not be excluded from *any* Territory, and it was by no means certain they could be excluded from the Free States. The only authority competent to decide was the Supreme Court of the United States. The slaveholders, who appear to have had little doubt what the Court's decision would be, were anxious to test the matter, while in antislavery circles it was believed that whatever the nature of the decision it was bound to redound to the benefit of the antislavery cause. To bring the case into the Federal courts owner and slave had to live in separate States. Proslavery and antislavery interests now arranged to have ownership of Dred Scott temporarily transferred to a citizen of New York. The Negro was to remain in Missouri and was told that he would be given his freedom no matter what the outcome of the case. Thus, eventually, the case reached the Supreme Court of the United States, and on March 6, 1857, in a room on the ground floor of the northern wing of the Capitol, Chief Justice Roger Brooke Taney, then in his eighty-first year, read the historic decision.

The majority opinion of the Court was:

That the Missouri Compromise was unconstitutional, since the Constitution made no distinction between slaves and other kinds of property, but expressly conferred the right to hold property in slaves;

That "At the time of the Declaration of Independence . . . and for more than a century before, they [Negroes] had been regarded as being . . . so far inferior that they had no rights which the white man was bound to respect" — *ergo*, a Negro could not be a citizen of the United States.

* * *

There were differences of opinion regarding the meaning of the decision. Associate Justice John McLean, dissenting, was of the opinion that "the principle laid down will enable the people of a slave State to introduce slavery into a free State" — that, in other words, the entire United States was now open to slavery. Thomas Hart Benton said that it "made slavery the organic law of the land and freedom the exception." Lincoln was of the opinion that the Territories were now thrown open to slavery, but not the Free States. He expected, however, the Dred Scott decision to be soon followed by still another decision making slavery lawful throughout the United States. "Such a decision," he said, "is all that slavery now lacks of being alike lawful in all the States. Welcome or unwelcome, such decision *is* probably coming, and will soon be upon us, unless the power of the present political dynasty shall be met and overthrown."

The decision that Negroes were not citizens was, according to Associate Justice Benjamin Robbins Curtis (likewise dissenting), a menace to every citizen of the United States. He pointed out that at the time of the adoption of the Constitution, free native-born Negroes were not only regarded as citizens in five States, but if possessing other necessary qualifications, had the right to vote. If the Supreme Court could now deprive them of the rights of citizenship then it could likewise deprive other social classes of such rights. That such may well have been the intention of Southern leaders does not appear improbable. *De Bow's Review*, the most influential publication in the South, declared: "All government begins by usurpation, and is continued by force. Nature puts the ruling elements uppermost, and the masses below and subject to those elements. Less than this is no government. The right to govern resides in a very small minority; the duty to obey is inherent in the mass of mankind."

8

Reaction against the majority opinion of the Court was immediate and profound. Associate Justice John McLean, in his dissenting opinion, practically advised ignoring the decision: "Nothing that has been said by them [the majority of the Court], which has no direct bearing on the jurisdiction of the court against which they decided, can be considered as authority. I shall certainly not regard it as such." Lincoln was to say he did not believe the decision "was a political rule binding the voters, Congress or the President," and proposed "so resisting it as to have it reversed if possible, and a new judicial rule established on the subject." Horace Greeley declared editorially in the New York *Tribune* that the majority decision "deserved no more respect than if made by a majority of those congregated in a Washington bar-room."

Garrison and Phillips welcomed the decision. In their opinion it furnished conclusive proof that they had been right in labeling the Constitution a proslavery document. It should, they thought, now be obvious to everyone that as long as slavery continued to exist anywhere in the United States, its expansion could not be stopped except by war or by dissolution of the Union. Phillips wrote to Theodore Parker: "Well, on all legal points involved, the Supreme Court sustains my claims for a dozen years. It is infamous. But it is the law of the United States. How now about the Pro-slavery character of the Union? Am I not right in seeking to withdraw?"

Opponents of slavery now divided into three principal camps:

Republicans led by Seward, Sumner, Chase, Lincoln and others were for disregarding the Dred Scott decision and preventing any further slavery expansion. It was tacitly understood that if elected they meant, by constitutional means, to strangle slavery, which, they now conceded, must otherwise infect the entire country.[2] With the Presidency, Congress and the Supreme Court in antislavery hands there can be no doubt that the strangulation could have succeeded. Barred from the Territories, banned from the National Capital, deprived of the interstate slave trade, slavery could not long have survived.

In the second camp were the two principal Abolitionist leaders (Garrison and Phillips) and a portion of the membership of the Anti-Slavery Society. Their contention was that to disregard the Dred Scott decision was as unconstitutional as any direct measure taken against slavery. They believed the Republicans to be political innocents in imagining that the South did not see through their artful strategy and would permit slavery to be slowly strangled. Republican policy, in their opinion, would inevitably lead to Southern secession and civil war. They could see only one peaceful solution of the problem — to convince the North that the Union should be dissolved.

In the third camp were many members and former members of

[2] See Lincoln's and Seward's declarations in Appendix.

the Anti-Slavery Society who felt that to dissolve the Union was to abandon the slave, arguments of Garrison and Phillips notwithstanding. More realistic than the Republicans, they said the South would forcibly resist *any* interference with slavery whether the measures taken were constitutional or unconstitutional, timid or bold. They believed war to be inevitable. "There was a time," declared Gerrit Smith, "when slavery could have been ended by political action. But that time has gone by — and, as I apprehend, forever. There was not virtue enough in the American people to bring slavery to a bloodless termination; and all that now remains for them is to bring it to a bloody one." At the annual convention of the New England Anti-Slavery Society in 1858, Theodore Parker said: "The time has passed when the great American question of the nineteenth century could have been settled without bloodshed." Against this acceptance of war as the only possible solution, Garrison uttered this protest: "We are growing more and more warlike, more and more disposed to repudiate the principles of peace . . . Just in proportion as this spirit prevails, I feel that our moral power is departing and will depart . . . I do not believe that the weapons of liberty ever have been, or ever can be, the weapons of despotism. . . . Do not get impatient; do not become exasperated; do not make yourselves familiar with the idea that blood must flow. Perhaps blood will flow — God knows, I do not; but it shall not flow through any counsel of mine."

9

In January, 1857, John Brown of Osawatomie, Kansas, had come East to solicit aid for the Kansas settlers. He was a hard-bitten fanatic who fancied himself a soldier of the Lord — the Old Testament Lord of Hosts who used his servants to smite evildoers. His principal biographer, Oswald Garrison Villard, has declared that Brown's massacre of five proslavery men at Pottawatomie, Kansas, "cannot be successfully palliated or excused." It may, however, have been provoked by Brooks's attack on Sumner. Salmon Brown, a member of his father's guerrilla band, testified that on their way to Pottawatomie, word reached them of Brooks's exploit, together with the erroneous information that Sumner was not expected to live. "At that blow," he said, "the men went crazy — *crazy*. It seemed the finishing decisive touch."

Garrison met Brown at a reception given by Theodore Parker. "He saw in the famous Kansas chieftain," Garrison's sons have written, "a tall, spare, farmer-like man, with head disproportionately small, and that inflexible mouth which as yet no beard concealed. They discussed peace and non-resistance together, Brown quoting the Old Testament against Garrison's citations from the New, and Parker from time to time injecting a bit of Lexington into the controversy, which attracted a small group of interested listeners."

In the spring of 1859, Brown again came East to make final arrangements for his long-cherished project of invading Virginia and organizing armed resistance among the slaves. He attended the New England Anti-Slavery Convention in Boston, listened to the speeches and departed saying: "These men are all talk; what is needed is action — action!" He took neither Garrison nor Phillips into his confidence, the first being a believer in nonresistance, the second having shown himself lukewarm during the Kansas struggle. Mrs. Buffum Chace Wyman has quoted Phillips as saying: "I did not know he intended to attack Harpers Ferry; but I knew he was working in such ways. I had seen him. I knew he was down in that vicinity doing something about slavery. I did not know exactly what." The Eastern men whom Brown took into his confidence, and without whose financial assistance the raid could not have taken place, were Thomas Wentworth Higginson, Theodore Parker, Frank B. Sanborn, George L. Stearns, Dr. Samuel G. Howe and Gerrit Smith. Compromising letters written by them were turned over to Phillips by Brown's widow and eventually returned to the senders.

10

Had Brown died during the raid he would not be remembered. But as he lay with bandaged head on a pallet answering questions put to him by Governor Wise and Senator Mason of Virginia and by Representative Vallandigham of Ohio, and throughout his imprisonment and trial, he exhibited such an elevation of soul, such an unshakable conviction of having fulfilled a God-given mission, that a feeling of awe and impending doom entered into the hearts of millions as they read these words he scribbled on a piece of paper before leaving for the gallows: "I John Brown am now quite *certain* that the crimes of this *guilty land:* will never be purged away; but with Blood. I had *as I now think: vainly* flattered myself that without *very much* bloodshed; it might be done." Garrison wrote in the *Liberator:* "In recording the expressions of sympathy and admiration which are so widely felt for Brown, whose doom is so swiftly approaching, we desire to say — once for all — that, judging him by the code of Bunker Hill, we think he is as deserving of high-wrought eulogy as any who ever wielded sword or battle-axe in the cause of liberty; but we do not and cannot approve any indulgence in the war spirit."

On November 1, 1859, the day before sentence was pronounced, Phillips was to lecture at Beecher's Plymouth Church in Brooklyn, New York. The lecture was part of a Lyceum Course under the auspices of the young men of the church and an admission fee of twenty-five cents was charged. Phillips's subject was to have been literary, but he asked to be allowed to change it to "The Lesson of the Hour," by which, it was understood, he meant the Harpers Ferry raid. The church was packed. Theodore Tilton presided and several notables, including Senator Thomas Corwin of Ohio, were seated on the platform. In introducing the speaker, Tilton read this sentence from the Brooklyn *Eagle:* "If Old Brown and his accomplices are deranged, what are we to think of Wendell Phillips." The lecturer joined in the laughter that swept the church.

Phillips's lecture was a devastating philippic. "No civil society," he said, "no government can exist except on the basis of the willing submission of all its citizens, and by the performance of the duty of rendering equal justice between man and man. Whatever calls itself a government, and refuses that duty, or has not that assent, is no government. It is only a pirate ship. Virginia, the Commonwealth of Virginia! It is a chronic insurrection. . . . It is a pirate ship, and John Brown sails the sea a Lord High Admiral of the Almighty, with his commission to sink every pirate he meets on God's ocean of the nineteenth century . . . Virginia is only another Algiers. The barbarous horde who gag each other, imprison women for teaching children to read, prohibit the Bible, sell men on the auction-block, abolish marriage, condemn half their women to prostitution, and devote themselves to the breeding of human beings for sale, is only a larger and a blacker Algiers . . . John Brown has twice as much right to hang Governor Wise, as Governor Wise has to hang him."

What had happened at Harpers Ferry was, he said, the direct result of the Slave Power's assault on Kansas. If Stringfellow could take possession of the government arsenal at Liberty, Missouri, and invade Kansas on behalf of slavery without a protest worth mentioning from the Federal Government, then John Brown had a far better right to take possession of the arsenal at Harpers Ferry and invade Virginia in the name of freedom. "The South planted the seeds of violence in Kansas, and taught peaceful Northern men familiarity with the bowie-knife and revolver. They planted nine hundred and ninety-nine seeds, and this one is the first that has flowered; this is the first drop in the coming shower. . . . Virginia did not tremble at an old grey-headed man at Harpers Ferry; they trembled at a John Brown in every man's conscience."

Harpers Ferry, he said, was "the Lexington of to-day." The bravest men of the American Revolution were not those who triumphed at Saratoga and Yorktown, but "those who flung themselves at Lexington, few and feeble, against the embattled ranks of an empire, till then thought irresistible. Elderly men, in powdered wigs and red velvet, smoothed their ruffles, and cried, 'Madmen!' Full-fed custom-house clerks said, 'A pistol-shot against Gibraltar!' But Captain Ingraham, under the stars and stripes, dictating terms to the fleet of the Caesars, was only the echo of that Lexington."

To the accusation that Brown had violated the law, he replied: "Huss and Wickliffe violated laws; why honor them? George Washington had he been caught before 1783, would have died on the gibbet, for breaking the laws of his sovereign . . . Who say, then, that slave laws are not ten thousand times worse than any those men resisted? Whatever argument excuses them, makes John Brown a saint."

The speech received nation-wide attention. The New York *Herald* considered it "The most extraordinary address that was ever delivered by a man professing to be sane." That it should have been not only "tolerated, but applauded to the echo in the most popular church in the 'City of Churches,'" proclaimed "more forcibly than volumes of words the danger which is looming up in such formidable proportions." The Richmond *Enquirer* declared: "Upon such men as Wendell Phillips is the blood of John Brown." A correspondent in the New York *Times* suggested that Brown be freed on condition that Phillips surrender to the Virginia authorities. The editor of the Petersburg (Virginia) *Intelligencer* endorsed the suggestion. Phillips wrote to the New York *Times*: "You are authorized to say that Wendell Phillips stands ready to deliver himself up to Governor Wise to be legally tried for any offense he has committed, on condition that the Governor will pardon and free John Brown."

11

It was a strange and ominous coincidence that the Federal officer in command of the military who captured John Brown should have been Robert E. Lee; that behind the gallows during the execution stood another Federal officer who was to become known to fame as "Stonewall" Jackson, and that in the ranks of the Richmond militia that helped to guard the scaffold, rifle on shoulder, stood — J. Wilkes Booth!

Governor Henry A. Wise of Virginia, who after the outbreak of the rebellion told the citizens of Richmond "to take a lesson from John Brown," and who characterized the raider as "a man of clear head, of courage, fortitude and simple ingenuousness," showed his respect by having the coffin containing Brown's remains placed aboard a special train at Charles Town, under guard of fifteen civilians, and delivered to Brown's widow and friends waiting at Harpers Ferry. Phillips joined the funeral party in New York and accompanied it to North Elba. Wherever a stop was made — at Troy, Rutland, Vergennes and Westport — church bells tolled and citizens came to express their sympathy to Brown's widow. At Elizabethtown, where the funeral party remained overnight, citizens placed the coffin in the courthouse, where a guard of honor watched over it throughout the night. North Elba, where Brown's family lived, was twenty-five miles distant. To reach it over well-nigh impassable roads took the whole of the following day. Phillips delivered the funeral oration, during which he made a prediction that was not to be fulfilled: "I do not believe slavery will go down in blood. Ours is the age of thought. Hearts are stronger than swords." In New York, Philadelphia, Boston, Cleveland and scores of other places memorial meetings were held, and in countless towns and villages church bells tolled and prayers were said for the repose of the dead man's soul.

12

On the evening of December 2, 1859, the day of Brown's execution, a mass meeting was held at Tremont Temple, Boston, under the auspices of the American Anti-Slavery Society. Among the placards decorating the hall was one inscribed with these words of Lafayette: "I never would have drawn my sword in the cause of America, if I could have conceived that thereby I was helping to found a nation of slaves." Phillips having left Boston to speak at Brown's funeral, Garrison was the principal speaker. He read Brown's noble address to the court, then said: "Rather than see men wearing chains in a cowardly and servile spirit, I would, as an advocate of peace, much rather see them breaking the head of the tyrant with their chains. Give me as a non-resistant, Bunker Hill, and Lexington, and Concord, rather than the cowardice and servility of a Southern slave-plantation."

If Garrison thus qualified his nonresistance, his followers had abandoned it altogether. In the course of the speech he asked: "How many non-resistants are there here to-night?" In a hall so packed with people that some on entering had been lifted off their feet, a single voice cried, "I!"

In January, 1860, at the annual meeting of the Massachusetts Anti-Slavery Society, Garrison referred to Brown in these words: "Whereas, ten years since, there were thousands who could not endure my lightest word of rebuke of the South, they can now swallow John Brown whole, and his rifle into the bargain. In firing his gun, he has merely told us what time of day it is. *It is high noon, thank God!*"

CHAPTER IV

Secession

THE year 1860 was as truly a year of decision for the United States as can be found in the history of any nation. Armed with the Supreme Court's pronouncement in the Dred Scott case, which made the keeping of slaves in the Territories a constitutional right, the South imperiously demanded that Congress pass a territorial slave code for the protection of slaveholders wishing to keep slaves in the Territories. In anticipation of the dominion it expected to exercise over vast stretches of virgin country, the Slave Power had begun a campaign for the reopening of the African slave trade. Although some fifteen thousand African Negroes were yearly smuggled into the United States, this was not enough. The gates must be thrown wide open to permit the slaveholders to take full advantage of their increased opportunity. "We have not the population, and might as well abandon the race with our brethren of the North in the colonization of the Territories. It is useless to wage war about abstract rights, or to quarrel and accuse each other of unsoundness, unless we get more Africans," said the future Vice President of the Confederacy, Alexander H. Stephens. The future President, Jefferson Davis, wanted it understood that he had no sympathy with those "who prate of the inhumanity and sinfulness of the trade." Talk not to him of the horrors of the middle passage: "The interest of Mississippi, not of the African, dictates my conclusion." Former Governor J. J. McRae of Mississippi declared that the people of his State favored the reopening of the trade and that "should the South unite in so just a demand," the North would be forced to yield. In 1857 Governor Adams of South Carolina said that the laws against the African slave trade were "a fraud upon us," and John Forsyth, former Minister to Mexico, in an enumeration of the victories of the Slave Power, exclaimed: "But one stronghold remains to be carried to complete its triumph, and that is the abrogation of the existing prohibition of the African slave trade." *De Bow's*

Review printed article after article favoring the reopening of the trade, while the Southern Commercial Convention, meeting at Vicksburg in 1859, demanded the unconditional repeal of the law making the African slave trade equivalent to piracy. Had the South elected its Presidential candidate in 1860, the pressure for the reopening of the trade would have become irresistible. Shipping interests in the North would have helped. The pulpit would have been brought into line. Thus the Presidential election of 1860 decided whether the North American continent was to be inhabited mainly by Africans. With the Territories thrown open to slave labor and with thousands of Negroes pouring in from Africa, immigration from Europe would have stopped.

2

The North's answer to the menace was the growth of the Republican Party. It had been the hope of the slaveholders that the Dred Scott decision would cut the ground from under the feet of that party. If keeping slaves in the Territories was a constitutional right, what room was there for a political party whose principal reason for existence was to keep slavery out of the Territories? The Republicans met the situation by declaring the Court's decision not binding.[1] At a meeting in Cincinnati in 1859 Lincoln declared: "I say that we must not interfere with the institution of slavery in the States where it exists, because the Constitution forbids it, and the general welfare does not require us to do so. We must not withhold an efficient fugitive slave law, because the Constitution requires us, as I understand it, not to withhold such a law. But we must prevent the outspreading of the institution, because neither the Constitution nor general welfare requires us to extend it. We must prevent the revival of the African slave trade, and the enacting by Congress of a territorial slave code. We must prevent each of these things being done by either congresses or courts. The people of these United States are the rightful masters of both congresses and courts, not to overthrow the Constitution, but to overthrow the men who pervert the Constitution."

Add to this the recognition that slavery was a moral evil, and we have a fairly complete summing up of the Republican position, be-

[1] In 1861, however, Republicans in Congress voted to admit certain Territories without prohibition of slavery.

tween which and the position of Southern leaders was the stand taken by Stephen A. Douglas, leader of the Northern Democrats. Douglas did not regard slavery as an evil. He did not care, he said, if it was "voted up or voted down." Undoubtedly his sympathies were with the South, but to have adopted the Southern program would have meant suicide for the Democracy of the North — "tantamount to absolute ruin," said a Connecticut delegate to the Democratic National Convention. Douglas's formula was, in Lincoln's phrase, "the great patent everlasting principle of 'Popular Sovereignty,'" which left it to the settlers themselves to decide, when organizing their Territorial governments, if they wished to permit or exclude slavery. Since settlers from the Free States were certain to be in the majority, this should have satisfied the North, but for the fact that the Dred Scott decision plainly implied that neither Congress nor a Territorial Legislature could exclude slavery from a Territory. In his debate with Douglas at Freeport, Illinois, Lincoln had asked his opponent how he meant to overcome the constitutional impediment if, as he averred, the Supreme Court's decision should be respected. Douglas had replied that while a man might have the right to keep slaves in a Territory, he could not really do so unless sustained by majority opinion, "for the reason that slavery cannot exist a day or an hour anywhere, unless it is supported by local police regulations." By refusing to enact such regulations a Territorial Legislature could make the keeping of slaves virtually impossible. This gained the approval of many Republicans (including Horace Greeley) to such an extent that for a while it jeopardized the existence of the Republican Party. The wily Douglas had still another card up his sleeve with which he hoped to conciliate the South, whom his reply to Lincoln had thoroughly alarmed. He promised to abide by a decision of the Supreme Court whether or not the Federal Government was obliged to intervene when the absence of local police regulations made the keeping of slaves in a Territory difficult or impossible. Since the Supreme Court to which the matter was to be referred was the same that had decided the Dred Scott case, there could be little doubt concerning the nature of its arbitrament.

Thus, from a Southern viewpoint, there was little wrong with Douglas's proposal. Indeed, if the Democratic Party did not wish to alienate its Northern supporters, Douglas's legerdemain of Popular Sovereignty plus a Supreme Court decision was about the only way the matter could be handled. Then why did the South not sustain him? Why did she insist upon a policy which she knew perfectly well was doomed to defeat at the polls? One reason was that Douglas, dictatorial by nature, had made the mistake of quarreling with President Buchanan, thus incurring the enmity of the powerful Federal machine. The issue was, however, of too great importance to the South to permit us to believe that this was the principal reason. The real reason was that Southern leaders had finally reached the conclusion that Union with the North was a hindrance rather than an advantage to the South's future development along lines chosen by them. By dividing the Democratic Party and thus insuring the election of the Republican candidate they could create a situation which, they felt, would justify secession in the eyes of their constituents. Said Senator Alfred Iverson of Georgia: "In a confederate government of their own, the Southern States would enjoy sources of wealth, property and power unsurpassed by any nation on earth. Our expanding policy would stretch far beyond present limits. Central America would join her destiny to ours; and so would Cuba, now withheld from us by the voice and votes of Abolition enemies." Alexander H. Stephens wrote: "The truth is our leaders and public men . . . do not desire to continue it [the Union] on any terms. They do not wish any redress of wrongs, they are disunionists *per se* and avail themselves of present circumstances to press their object." Robert Rhett of South Carolina declared that secession was not "anything produced by Mr. Lincoln's election, or by the non-execution of the Fugitive Slave Law. It is a matter which has been gathering head for thirty years." Henry J. Raymond, National Chairman of the Republican Party and editor of the New York *Times,* was of the same opinion.

3

Thus it happened that when on April 23, 1860, the Democratic Party met in National Convention at Charleston, South Carolina, it found itself hopelessly divided. The party whose boast it had been that it was the only remaining great political party not sectional, but national, saw the Southern delegates to its National Convention walk out in a body. Adjournment was taken to Baltimore, in June, in the hope that in the interval the breach might be healed. The expectation proved vain, and when at the Baltimore Convention Douglas was nominated for President, he was as much a sectional candidate as Lincoln, whom the Republicans had nominated in Chicago in the meantime. Phillips commented: "The Democratic Party, agitating fiercely to put down agitation, break at last into a general quarrel in their effort to keep the peace." Garrison, addressing the annual meeting of the American Anti-Slavery Society, said: "Only think of it! The party which has, for so many years, cried out, 'There must be no agitation on this subject,' is now the most agitated of all the parties in the country! The party which declares that there ought not to be any sectionalism as against slavery, has now been sundered geographically, and on this very question! The party which has said 'Let discussion cease for ever,' is busily engaged in the discussion, so that, possibly, the American Anti-Slavery Society might adjourn *sine die*, after we get through with our present meetings, and leave its work to be carried on in the other direction!"

Garrison and Phillips had reason for self-congratulation. They, the nonpolitical Abolitionists, had been the principal instrument of Fate in accomplishing all this. It was their persistent, uncompromising propaganda, carried into every nook and cranny of the Free States by their devoted followers, that had leavened the North and had made and unmade political parties. If they had failed in having their Northern compatriots abandon race prejudice, if the native common sense of those compatriots rejected Northern secession which they proposed as a remedy, they had nevertheless succeeded in making them hate and fear slavery to such an extent that they were now willing to run almost any risk rather than see it extend its domain.

On May 16 the Republican National Convention had met in Chicago and had nominated Abraham Lincoln for President. Southern Democrats nominated John C. Breckinridge, then Vice President of the United States. The remnants of the Whig and American (Know-Nothing) Parties united under the name of Constitutional Union Party and nominated John Bell of Tennessee on a platform that ignored the issue agitating the country. The election of Abraham Lincoln seemed a foregone conclusion.

4

When the Republican National Convention met in Chicago the general opinion was that William Henry Seward would be its Presidential nominee. Lincoln received the nomination partly because many delegates, intimidated by the South's threats of secession, believed he would be less objectionable to the slaveholders, partly because he had not, like Seward, incurred the enmity of the Know-Nothings whose support was considered essential to victory in Pennsylvania, Indiana and Illinois. Seward, who had so often led the assault on slavery in the Senate, who had expressed his belief in a "higher law" before which even the Constitution must yield, who had proclaimed the awe-inspiring doctrine of an "Irrepressible Conflict" between liberty and slavery, in which one or the other must perish, could hardly have been an acceptable candidate to the South. True that Lincoln, if no believer in the "higher law," had in his "House Divided" speech anticipated Seward's "Irrepressible Conflict," but he had had the advantage of comparative obscurity and his speech was little known. A letter he wrote to his friend Joshua Speed, in August, 1855, shows him to have been no more friendly to the Know-Nothings than Seward, but he had never made such a compromising statement as, "I do not hesitate to recommend the establishment of schools in which they [the children of the foreign born] may be instructed by teachers speaking the same language and professing the same faith."

So Lincoln received the nomination and therewith chance, or Fate, or Providence, gave an ironical turn to events — for Seward, who lost the nomination because he was believed to be too uncompromising, would surely have compromised; while Lincoln, who won it because it was believed that if the worst came to the worst he might meet the South halfway (Had he not said: "Much as I hate slavery, I would consent to any extension of it rather than see the Union dissolved, just as I would consent to any great evil to avoid a greater one"?), insisted on keeping faith with the electorate.

Lincoln's nomination was received by Garrison without enthusiasm, but also without hostility. The fiery editor of the *Liberator* had mellowed. At fifty-five he no longer used the scourge with the same reckless abandon as in the past. Opprobrious epithets against slaveholders had become a rarity in his paper. He was even willing to concede that "Southern men are behaving very much according to human nature in its ordinary manifestations. . . . They are not unnecessarily brutal; they do the best they can under the circumstances." Once he had held that those who recognized slavery to be a moral evil and yet contented themselves with half-measures were more culpable than the slaveholders, many of whom sincerely believed it to be right; now, however, he was willing to await developments and to give the Republican candidate the full benefit of the doubt.

But if Garrison had mellowed, Phillips had not. He tolerated less than ever any deviation from the rigid program Garrison and he had formulated nearly a score of years before. "No Union with Slaveholders!" was still the policy of both, but now it was Phillips who wielded the scourge on backsliders and unbelievers. He assailed Lincoln with extraordinary vehemence. While from the vantage point of time Phillips's criticism appears extravagant, yet it is difficult to see how a friend of the Negro could have viewed Lincoln's nomination with anything but misgiving.

5

In his debate with Douglas at Charleston, Illinois, September 18, 1858, Lincoln had declared:

"I am not, nor ever have been in favor of bringing about in any way the social and political equality of the white and black races; I am not nor ever have been in favor of making voters of the free negroes, or jurors, or qualifying them to hold office, or having them marry with white people. I will say in addition that there is a physical difference between the white and black races which, I suppose, will forever forbid the two races living together upon terms of social and political equality; and in as much as they cannot so live, that while they do remain together, there must be the position of the superiors and the inferiors; and that I, as much as any other man, am in favor of the superior being assigned to the white man."

It was a complete reversal of his position of only two months earlier (July 10, 1858), when he declared in Chicago:

"Let us discard this quibbling about this man and the other man, this race and that race and the other race being inferior, and therefore they must be placed in an inferior position. Let us discard all these things, and unite as one people throughout the land, until we shall once more stand up declaring that all men are created equal."

Which did Lincoln really believe? When challenged by Douglas at Galesburg with the words: "I would despise myself if I thought that I was procuring your votes by concealing my opinions, and by avowing one set of principles in one part of the state, and a dif-

ferent set in another," he had replied: "I have not supposed and
do not now suppose, that there is any conflict whatever between
them." The fact that Abolitionists were numerous in Chicago and
rare in Charleston appears a more logical explanation. However, in
the course of the debate, he again stated: "I am not in favor of
negro citizenship." [2] We may therefore take it for granted that
Lincoln agreed with that part of the Dred Scott decision denying
citizenship to Negroes. In this he was many decades behind enlightened public opinion. In 1787, when the Constitution was ratified, free native-born Negroes, possessing other necessary qualifications, voted in New Hampshire, Massachusetts, New York, New
Jersey and North Carolina! In the Sixteenth Congress, Robert R.
Reid of Georgia had said: "For my own part, surrounded by slavery from my cradle to the present moment, I yet . . . would hail
that day as the most glorious . . . which should behold . . . the
black population of the United States placed upon the high emi-
nence of equal rights." In 1838, in the case of *The State* vs. *Manuel*,
the eminent Southern jurist Justice Gaston, speaking for the Supreme Court of North Carolina of which he was a member, made
the following pronouncement: "Slaves manumitted here become
free men, and therefore if born in North Carolina, are citizens of
North Carolina . . . The Constitution extended the elective franchise to every free man who had arrived at the age of twenty-one,
and paid a public tax: and it is a matter of universal notoriety that
under it free persons, without regard to color, claimed and exercised the franchise until it was taken from free men of color a few
years since by our amended Constitution."

In the matter of Negro citizenship, therefore, the Republican
candidate was far behind liberal opinion in the South as well as in
the North. He was, in fact, in accord with the Southern reaction
against that liberalism which for a time manifested itself among
upper-class Southerners.

That a friend of the Negro could hardly have regarded Lincoln
as an ideal candidate is further apparent from his letter to Elihu B.
Washburne of Illinois, January 29, 1859, in which, commenting on a
speech delivered in Congress by Washburne's brother, C. C. Wash-
burn, he wrote: "His objection to the Oregon constitution because
it excludes free negroes, is the only thing I wish he had omitted."
In conjunction with Lincoln's well-known view that free Negroes

[2] E. E. Sparks, ed. *The Lincoln Douglas Debates of 1858*, p. 303.

could not be integrated into the American economy this has a sinister ring. "What in the name of God will you do with these men, these eight hundred thousand free native-born of our common country? . . . I deny this pretended State right to exile any of its native-born freemen," John A. Bingham of Ohio had exclaimed during the debate in Congress on the Oregon Constitution. James M. Mason of Virginia predicted that Free State after Free State would adopt the same measure and free Negroes would be forced to go South and ask to be made slaves. It would be absurd to impute such an intention to Lincoln, but it does not appear unlikely that he would have welcomed a situation which would have forced the free Negroes to emigrate. In 1847 the Illinois Constitutional Convention adopted and submitted to a referendum a provision to forbid the immigration of colored persons. It was adopted by a vote of more than two to one. At no time did Lincoln utter a protest. On August 14, 1862, he had an interview at the White House with a committee composed of leading colored men, during which he said: "You and we are different races. We have between us a broader difference than exists between almost any other two races. Whether it is right or wrong I need not discuss; but this physical difference is a great disadvantage to us both, I think. Your race suffer very greatly, many of them, by living among us, while ours suffer from your presence. In a word we suffer on each side. If this is admitted, it affords a reason at least, why we should be separated."

Lincoln tried to induce the committee to aid him in colonizing American Negroes in Central America, and obtained an initial appropriation of $600,000 from Congress for that purpose. He sent some hundreds of Negroes to Cow Island, near Haiti, where many died from tropical disease before the remainder were repatriated. "Like all Southern men," wrote Benjamin F. Butler, "Mr. Lincoln did not understand negro character. He doubted very much whether the negro and the white man could possibly live together in any other condition than that of slavery." Lincoln later asked Butler, who had successfully organized the transport of a large body of troops, to report to him concerning the possibility of transporting the entire Negro population of the South to Liberia or South America at the conclusion of hostilities. Butler reported that with the transportation facilities then existing the plan was not feasible: "Negro children will be born faster than your whole naval and merchant vessels, if substantially all of them were devoted to that use, can carry them; especially as I believe that the increase will be much greater in a state of freedom than of slavery."

Lincoln had apparently accepted the inevitable, for in his reconstruction plan for Louisiana he favored the enfranchisement of educated Negroes and Negro soldiers, but not sufficiently so to insist upon the adoption of the measure.

The question arises: Was a President who believed that the only hope for the colored people of the South lay in emigration, qualified to provide for their future in the United States? Obviously not. Lincoln's reconstruction program, which Johnson inherited and tried to make a reality, was charitable to the former slaveholders, cruelly unjust to the freedmen. Only a man who truly believed in Lincoln's Chicago declaration of July 10, 1858, could have planned intelligently.

6

All this should be taken into consideration when one judges Phillips's criticism of Lincoln. It should likewise be remarked that one who had battled against slavery for a quarter of a century could hardly be blamed for looking with some suspicion upon a man who while claiming to have been opposed to human bondage all his life,[3] had remained virtually silent on the question until through the efforts and sacrifices of others it had become a promising political issue. Prior to October, 1854, when Lincoln for the first time spoke out resolutely against slavery, he had been more critical of the Abolitionists than of the South's "peculiar institution." Lincoln's English biographer, Lord Charnwood, wrote: "We feel with a great American historian that the North would have been depraved if it had not bred Abolitionists, and it requires an effort to sympathize with Lincoln's rigidly correct feeling — sometimes harshly expressed and sometimes apparently cold." [4]

While admitting the coldness, a friend of the Negro would have

---

[3] "I am naturally anti-slavery. If slavery is not wrong, nothing is wrong. I cannot remember when I did not so think and feel." Letter to A. G. Hodges of Frankfort, Kentucky, April 4, 1864.

[4] In a speech at Worcester, Massachusetts, September, 1848, Lincoln deeply offended many people in the audience by this reference to the martyred Elijah Lovejoy: "I have heard you have abolitionists here. We have a few in Illinois and we shot one the other day."

denied that Lincoln's attitude was "rigidly correct." He would have charged him with Southern bias, a charge frankly admitted by his scholarly biographer, Professor J. G. Randall. On October 15, 1858, in his debate with Douglas, we find Lincoln saying that he was bound by the Constitution to let slavery alone in States where it already existed and would do so anyway "even if there were no such Constitutional obligation." A friend of the Negro could not have helped considering this last assurance gratuitous and unworthy of a man who loved liberty and justice, not to speak of the fact that it was manifestly out of harmony with the famous "House Divided" speech. Indeed, the man who had at one time condemned the notion that "if any one man choose to enslave another, no third man shall be allowed to object," after his election was willing to agree to a constitutional amendment guaranteeing noninterference with slavery for all time![5] Nor can Lincoln's defense of the Fugitive Slave Law and his opposition to efforts to have it repealed be explained on constitutional grounds. There were many excellent lawyers in his day who considered the law unconstitutional and a menace to the free Negro no less than to the fugitive slave. Lord Charnwood has written that it "was the sort of Act which the President should have vetoed as a fraud on the Constitution."[6] To us whom the passage of time affords a comprehensive view of Lincoln's character, it seems well-nigh incredible that any one could have accused him of hardness of heart, but to Phillips, whose attention was focused on Lincoln's attitude towards the Negro — and in particular towards the fugitive slave — the charge did not appear unfounded. "I confess I hate to see the poor creatures hunted down and caught and carried back to their stripes and unrequited toil; but I bite my lips and keep quiet," Lincoln wrote in August, 1855, to his friend Joshua Speed. It would have been more in keeping with the popular ideal of Lincoln had he not kept quiet at such a time. Richard Henry Dana Jr. believed, like Lincoln, that the South had a constitutional right to demand the return of fugitive slaves, but this did not deter

[5] "I understand a proposed amendment to the Constitution . . . has passed Congress to the effect that the Federal Government shall never interfere with the domestic institutions of the States, including that of persons held for service. . . . I have no objection to its being made express and irrevocable." (First Inaugural Address, March 4, 1861.)

[6] Quotations from Lord Charnwood's *Abraham Lincoln* (Henry Holt and Company, New York, and Constable and Company, London) are made by special permission of the present Lord Charnwood.

him from condemning provisions of the Fugitive Slave Law whose constitutionality was highly questionable and offering his services free to any fugitive slave threatened with extradition.

What Phillips did not know was that in 1847 Lincoln's legalism and Southern bias so far overcame his compassion and benevolence as to make it possible for him to appear in court as counsel for one Robert Matson, a Kentucky slaveholder, in an action involving the surrender of a fugitive slave woman and her six children, in danger of being sold in the deep South. It has been claimed that Lincoln's speech in court was "fatal to his client." This, however, could hardly have been his intention and must have been due to a feeling of guilt. An eyewitness has testified that Lincoln "winced" perceptibly as the attorney for the defense quoted from John Philpot Curran's famous speech in an English court on behalf of a fugitive slave. Lincoln lost the case and was cheated of his fee, for which he had assiduously bargained.[7]

The Negro leader Frederick Douglass, who knew and respected Lincoln — and whom Mrs. Lincoln after the President's assassination presented with her husband's favorite walking stick, saying, "I know of no one who would appreciate this more than Fred Douglass" — yet felt constrained to say in 1876, at the unveiling of the Freedmen's Monument at Washington, D. C.:

"To protect, defend and perpetuate slavery in the United States where it existed Abraham Lincoln was not less ready than any other President to draw the sword of the nation. He was ready to execute all the supposed constitutional guaranties of the United States Constitution in favor of the slave system anywhere inside the slave States. He was willing to pursue, recapture, and send back the fugitive slave to his master, and to suppress a slave rising for liberty, though his guilty master were already in arms against the Government. The race to which we belong were not the special objects of his consideration. Knowing this, I concede to you, my white fellow citizens, a pre-eminence in his worship at once full and supreme. First, midst, and last, you and yours were the objects of his deepest affection and his most earnest solicitude. You are the children of Abraham Lincoln. We are at best only his step-children; children by adoption, children by force of circumstances and necessity."

[7] For details of the case, see Albert J. Beveridge, *Abraham Lincoln*, Vol. II, pp. 95–100.

7

Addressing the New England Anti-Slavery Convention on May 30, 1860, Phillips declared:

"Here is Mr. Lincoln . . . he says in regard to such a point, for instance, as the abolition of slavery in the District of Columbia, that he has never studied the subject; that he has no distinctive ideas about it . . . But so far as he has considered it, he should be, perhaps, in favor of gradual abolition, when the slave-holders of the district asked for it! Of course he would. I doubt if there is a man throughout the whole South who would not go as far as that. When South Carolina wants to free her slaves, he is ready to grant that she may. Then he goes into another question — that of the inter-State slave trade — which the South herself has, on frequent occasions, taken the opportunity to protest against. In regard to that, he is not at all in favor of stopping it. And in regard to the Fugitive Slave Bill, he has no objections to it, and he would have objections to introducing the question of repealing it, as an element of agitation. That is the amount of his anti-slavery, if you choose to call it such, which according to the Chicago thermometer, the Northern States are capable of bearing. The ice is so thin that Mr. Lincoln, standing six feet and four inches, cannot afford to carry any principles with him onto it! . . .

"Who is this huckster in politics? Who is this county court advocate? Who is this who does not know whether he has got any opinions? Why, he is like the tutor at Cambridge, of whom the students said that 'his mind was full of all manner of emptiness.' What is his recommendation? It is that nobody knows good or bad of him. His recommendation is, that out of the unknown things in his past life, journals may make for him what character they please. His recommendation is that his past is a blank and the statesman of New York, who has done (for so it may be said to the honor of William H. Seward) as much as any man in politics has done, to marshal the North on the political anti-slavery platform, is unavailable because of those efforts — nothing else."

On June 22 Phillips sent an article to the *Liberator*, which Garrison published with reluctance and only after Phillips had agreed to sign it as a personal expression of opinion. The article read, in part:

ABRAHAM LINCOLN, THE SLAVE-HOUND OF ILLINOIS

We gibbet a Northern hound today, side by side with the infamous Mason of Virginia. Mason's Slave Bill is based on that clause of the United States Constitution, which provides for the surrender of slaves escaping from one *State* into another *State* of the Union.

The Supreme Court of the United States has decided that the District of Columbia is not a *State* within the meaning of the Constitution. The District of Columbia is not, therefore, included in the terms of the Fugitive Slave clause. Whoever tries to extend the dominion of that clause over the District of Columbia, exhibits only his own voluntary baseness, can have no pretense of constitutional obligation, out-Mason's Mason, and stamps himself a hound of special "alacrity."

This deed ABRAHAM LINCOLN, Republican candidate for President has done!

Phillips offered as evidence an extract from a bill introduced by Lincoln in Congress on January 10, 1849, reading: "That the municipal authorities of Washington and Georgetown, within their respective jurisdictional limits, are hereby empowered and required to provide active and efficient means to arrest and deliver up to their owners, all fugitive slaves escaping into said district." The extract tended to prove that Lincoln attempted to extend the Fugitive Slave Law to the District of Columbia, where it was inoperative.

This last attack was unworthy of Phillips, being based on partial suppression of the evidence. What Lincoln had done was to introduce a bill for the gradual abolition of slavery in the District of Columbia. He hoped that by extending the operation of the Fugitive Slave Law to the District, the bill might be made to pass. Needless to say the representatives of the slaveholders and their allies would have nothing to do with it. When challenged by Giddings and others Phillips acknowledged the true nature of Lincoln's proposal, but renewed the attack, writing in answer to Giddings: "I lack words to utter my loathing for the man who, in this century, consents, for any reason, to ask the American people to institute slave-hunting, and legalize it where it does not legally exist. Yet this, Mr. Lincoln's friends confess he did; and their defense is, that he did it in order to purchase certain advantages. Had he offered to sell his wife or daughter for the same purpose, he would have been no more infamous or dishonored in my view."

Phillips then embarked upon a discussion of the Republican candidate's attitude towards the Fugitive Slave Bill. He conceded that men "who support the Constitution and accept office under it," were "bound to allow an 'efficient' [Fugitive] Slave Law, and in that Mr. Lincoln is consistent," but "they must not go whining about the country begging us not to think them base men, although they do base things, considering — seeing — because — the Constitution required it. . . . If his friends prefer, I will try always to call him a Constitutional Hound. But he who in person, or by deputy, hunts slaves, is a hound; no matter what his motive be, whether to save the party, get an office, or preserve the Union."

The contention that men who accepted office under the Constitution were bound to allow an efficient Fugitive Slave Law was repudiated by Seward, Sumner and other political antislavery men. Basing himself on the "Divine Law," which he claimed the slavery clauses in the Constitution violated, Seward said: "Extend a cordial welcome to the fugitive who lays his weary limbs at your door, and defend him as you would your paternal gods." Sumner claimed the right to believe with Andrew Jackson that "Each public officer, who takes an oath to support the Constitution, swears that he will support it as he understands it, and not as it is understood by others." He said defiantly in the Senate that he would not obey the Fugitive Slave Law and would tell others to do likewise. Phillips agreed with Lincoln's interpretation of the Constitution, but considered Seward's and Sumner's attitude more honorable. He wished, he said, he could say of Lincoln when he saw him swear allegiance to the Constitution as he could say of Giddings and of Sumner: "I respect him so much, that I do not believe he will do what he promises."

8

"Babylon is fallen, is fallen!" Garrison rejoiced in the *Liberator* when news of Lincoln's election reached him. Phillips, notwithstanding his previous attitude, did not hide his satisfaction. Speaking at Tremont Temple on November 7, he said: "If the telegraph speaks truth, for the first time in our history the *slave* has chosen a President of the United States. . . . Not an Abolitionist, hardly an antislavery man, Mr. Lincoln consents to represent the antislavery idea. . . . This position he owes to no merit of his own, but to lives that have roused the nation's conscience, and deeds that have ploughed deep into its heart. . . . The Republican party have undertaken a problem, the solution of which will force them to our position . . . Lincoln is in *place*, Garrison in power."

It was fortunate for the country that Garrison was *not* in power. After the October elections when Republican majorities in Pennsylvania, Ohio and Indiana presaged Lincoln's triumph the following month, Garrison had written: "Will the South be so obliging as to secede from the Union?" The South was willing to oblige. A special session of the South Carolina Legislature made arrangements for a Disunion Convention in Charleston on December 17. The city was decorated with palmetto flags, except for a lonely Stars and Stripes over Fort Moultrie. Delegates to the convention looked at it and smiled grimly. It would not remain there long, of that they felt sure. The North would not fight — it could not. Had not former President Pierce written to Jefferson Davis that "those who defy the law and scout constitutional obligations, will, if we ever reach the arbitrament of arms, find occupation enough at home"? Had he not said that "the fighting will not be along Mason and Dixon's line merely," but within the borders of Northern States and "in our own streets"? Of course he was right! Had not Douglas polled 1,376,957 votes, only half a million less than Lincoln and *nearly all of them in the North?* Had not just previous to the Presidential election 115,000 muskets been removed from Northern armories and sent to Southern arsenals by order of the Secretary of War? Had not the South for months stored up arms and munitions purchased in the North? Were not most of the officers of the small Federal army Southerners and was not that army scattered over Western outposts? Was not the fleet dispersed in foreign ports? Was not one Southern man equal to half a dozen Yankees? Had not the Attorney General of the United States, the Honorable John S. Black, in reply to an inquiry from President Buchanan, given his official opinion that Congress had no right to war against any State? Had not the President made it clear that he meant to abide by that opinion? Before that Black Republican, who had had "a gorilla imported from Mozambique for a father," would take office, all the Southern States would have joined South Carolina and a formidable army would be ready to teach the North a lesson if it chose to act foolishly. Civil war? They would have civil war a-plenty in the North, if they dared to attack, but not in the

South. In the South discipline prevailed. The lower classes knew their place and would fight unto death if it were explained to them that it was the intention of the Black Republicans to have Negroes marry their daughters.

And what a glorious prospect unfolded before the South! Cuba, Mexico, Central America would soon be theirs — an enormous slave empire extending all the way to Brazil, perhaps even further. The African slave trade would be reopened. Hundreds of thousands of slaves would come pouring in from Africa in a ceaseless stream. Northern shipowners would be only too glad to obtain a part of that traffic, as they had once. A race of lordly supermen would flourish in the South such as the world had never seen. Too long had the South worn the trammels of the Union, of the Declaration of Independence, of the old Constitution. Soon Alexander H. Stephens was to proclaim the foundation principle of the new slave empire in these words: "The new constitution has put at rest forever all agitating questions relating to our peculiar institutions — African slavery as it exists among us — the proper status of the negro in our form of civilization. . . . Our new Government is founded upon . . . the great truth that the negro is not equal to the white man; that slavery, subordination to the superior race, is his natural and moral condition."

9

The North was somewhat startled by its own temerity. It had given in so often, had compromised so much, that its own decisive "No!" spoken in defiance of the South's threats, sounded ominous in its own ears. It devoutly hoped that the South would be reasonable and would abide by the decision of the electorate. It was fully prepared to be more than reasonable itself. Republican leaders were willing to go a long way to appease the South, much further it developed than the President-elect was willing to go. The common people were opposed to secession. They agreed with Lincoln that "no State can in any way lawfully get out of the Union without the consent of the others," with Jackson that "the first line of separation would not last a single generation; new fragments would be torn off; new leaders would spring up; and this great and glorious republic would soon be broken into a multitude of petty States."

Many who had voted for one of Lincoln's opponents were even

more resolutely opposed to secession than the Republicans. Their wrath, however, was directed against the Abolitionists, whom they blamed for having forced the issue. Among them were businessmen and financiers to whom secession meant huge financial losses, and brokerage clerks in New York, Philadelphia and Boston whom the very threat of secession had thrown out of work. All such were in favor of compromise at any price and determined to prevent any further agitation that might endanger a compromise. When a group of young men, not affiliated with any organization, called a meeting at Tremont Temple, Boston, for the forenoon of December 3, to commemorate the execution of John Brown, and asked Phillips and others to address them on the subject, "How can American Slavery Be Abolished?" a mob composed mainly of businessmen and office clerks took riotous possession of the hall. "The gossip of the street says they were excusable on account of pecuniary losses, — they were men out of employ. The ringleader said he came there to save his property," Phillips commented after the riot. It was estimated that the South owed the North two hundred million dollars, a staggering sum in those days.

The invasion of Tremont Temple by a "broadcloth mob" was the beginning of an epidemic of rioting such as Boston had seldom witnessed. Whenever the Abolitionists attempted to hold a meeting, raging mobs filled the streets and the entire police and detective force of the city had to be called into action to prevent bloodshed and arson. But for a group of young men who constituted themselves a bodyguard for Phillips, the principal object of the mob's hatred, it is doubtful if he would have survived. George W. Smalley, the young journalist who married Phillips's foster daughter Phoebe Garnaut, was one of these. They armed themselves with revolvers and guarded the approaches to the platform at meetings where he spoke. When he would be leaving the hall they locked arms and formed an impenetrable ring around him. They mounted guard before his house and were with him night and day.

During this entire period Garrison appeared seldom in public, contenting himself with writing in the *Liberator*. This was partly due to reasons of health, partly to his greater faith in Lincoln, whom he believed capable of resolving the crisis. The leadership of the nonpolitical Abolitionists thus devolved upon Phillips. While one may disagree with the solution he proposed — as who to-day does not? — there is no denying his fearlessness and sincerity. He made

no attempt to conciliate his opponents. Far from it! When he spoke
at Music Hall on January 20, 1861, on "Mobs and Education," he
lashed the "broadcloth mob" that had invaded Tremont Temple a
fortnight earlier with such vitriolic invective that people sat with
bated breath, momentarily expecting a revolver shot to ring out
and lay him low. Only the determined appearance of his self-constituted bodyguard, stationed in the aisles and lined up before the
platform, prevented a riot. When he left the hall it required the
combined efforts of two hundred uniformed policemen, a large
force of detectives and his bodyguard to keep him from being
lynched by the mob. He must have remembered that day, more
than a quarter of a century ago, when he had stood in State Street
and saw Garrison dragged by a rope. The prospect that the same
thing now might happen to him did not seem to trouble him in the
least. "Always aristocratic in aspect," wrote Higginson, "he was
never more so than when walking through the streets of Boston
with a howling mob about him. . . . He would have gone to the
scaffold if necessary, I firmly believe, like the typical French
marquis in the Reign of Terror, who took a pinch of snuff from his
snuffbox while looking on the crowd."

Lydia Maria Child, in a letter to her friend, Mrs. S. B. Shaw, told
of an incident at a riotous meeting in Tremont Temple, on January 24, illustrative of Phillips's oratorical resourcefulness: "Mr.
Phillips tried to speak, but his voice was again drowned. Then by
a clever stroke of management he stooped forward and addressed
his speech to the reporters stationed directly below him. This tan-
talized the mob, and they began to call out, 'Speak louder! We want
to hear what you're saying.' Whereupon he raised his voice, and for
half an hour he seemed to hold them within the hollow of his hand."

Those were days full of excitement and danger, and Phillips
gloried in them. He went about Boston with his hand gripping a
revolver in his pocket. When a friend expressed concern that he
might be assailed from behind, he said nonchalantly: "Don't trouble
about that. I can see over my shoulder and before a man can touch
me, I will shoot." One day as he passed two well-dressed men conversing on a street corner, one remarked to the other, with a movement of the head towards Phillips: "I should like to put a bullet
through that man's heart." When relating the incident Phillips
remarked: "Benevolent, wasn't it?"

His friends had tried to persuade him to abandon the house in

Essex Street until the crisis had passed, but Ann no less than he vetoed the proposal. He had not objected, however, to putting the house in a state of defense, for an attack might be expected at any moment. Already the mob had invaded the Negro quarter, had broken into houses, smashed furniture, maltreated men and women. "Would you shoot any of those fellows if they were to break in?" a woman friend asked Phillips. "Yes, just as I would shoot a mad dog or a wild bull," he quietly replied. Higginson wrote: "I spent one night on guard at Phillips's house with his young henchmen, and was struck, then as before, with his high-bred bearing. . . . It was hard to make him adopt ordinary precautions; he did not care to have the police protect his house."

10

During the crisis Garrison's and Phillips's propaganda fell under two heads. They opposed any abandonment of the ground gained, any postponement of the Republican platform, any weakening of the North's determination not to permit slavery in the Territories. In this they were in agreement with Lincoln; but while the President-elect wished to combat secession with all the means at his disposal, they encouraged and welcomed it, considering it the realization of their program, "No Union with Slaveholders!"

In January, 1861, the Gulf States had followed South Carolina out of the Union. On February 8 the Confederate States of America was born at Montgomery, Alabama, and Jefferson Davis was chosen President. "The time for compromise has passed, and those who oppose us will smell powder and feel Southern steel," said Mr. Davis. But compromise — compromise at any price — was what the man slated for Secretary of State in Lincoln's Cabinet wanted. "Who's afraid?" Mr. Seward had said in September of the previous year at St. Paul, Minnesota. "They complain that, if we will not surrender our principles, and our system, and our right — being a majority — to rule, and if we will not accept their system and such rules as they will give us, they will go out of the Union. Who's afraid? Nobody's afraid, nobody can be bought."

Brave words! But now the "wily old scarecrow" spoke an entirely different language. Forgotten was the Irrepressible Conflict. The secession of seven Southern States and the formation of a Confederate Government was merely the result "of a simple and harmless disappointment in a Presidential election." John Morley has said that the Civil War was "the only war in modern times . . . that no skill or patience of diplomacy would have avoided"; Lincoln was to call it ". . . this mighty convulsion, which no mortal could make, and no mortal could stay," but Seward considered himself the supreme diplomat capable of resolving the crisis. His diplomacy consisted mainly of the proposal that the clause in the Republican platform opposing slavery extension be ignored. On January 12, 1861, he made a speech in the Senate in which he advocated a Constitutional amendment guaranteeing noninterference with slavery in the Slave States for all time and proposed that the remaining national domain be divided into two parts, one of which, New Mexico (which then included Arizona), should become slave territory. "Three thousand square miles of God's earth is a high price for the questionable advantage of Union with the slave States," Mrs. Seward wrote to him. He, however, was prepared to pay a much higher price. Eventually he was to propose to Lincoln that, on one pretext or another, war be declared on Spain and France and if necessary also on England and Russia! This, he believed, would unite the country against the foreign enemy. It was a policy marvelously calculated to furnish the rebels with powerful allies and insure the success of the rebellion.

Fortunately Lincoln meant to keep faith with the electorate and wrote to Seward: "I say now, as I have all the while said that on the territorial question — that is, the question of extending slavery under national auspices, — I am inflexible. I am for no compromise which assists or permits the extension of the institution on soil owned by the nation. And any trick by which it is to acquire territory, and then allow some local authority to spread slavery over it, is as obnoxious as any other, I take it that to effect some such result as this, and to put us again in the high road to slave empire, is the object of all these proposed compromises. I am against it."

11

Lincoln's law partner William H. Herndon was an Abolitionist. "I was in correspondence with Sumner, Greeley, Phillips and Garrison," he wrote in his *Life of Lincoln*. On February 1, Samuel E. Sewall received a letter from him which reassured the Abolitionists regarding Lincoln's intentions. Herndon wrote: "Mr. Lincoln yet remains firm as a rock. He is true game, and is strong in the faith of Justice, Right, Liberty, Man and God. He has told me not only once, but often and often, that rather than back down — rather than concede to traitors, his soul might go back to God from the wings of the Capitol. I believe it. He and I have been partners in law for thirteen years and I know him."

So Garrison was pleased with the President-elect. "It is much to the credit of Mr. Lincoln," he wrote, "that he has maintained his dignity and self-respect intact, and gives no countenance to any of the compromises that have yet been proposed." Phillips was not unfriendly. Lincoln, he said, belonged to those Republicans "who consider their honor pledged to fulfil in office the promises made in the canvas. Their motto is: 'The Chicago platform, every inch of it; not a hair's-breadth of the Territories shall be surrendered to slavery.'" Phillips's principal reason for opposing compromise would undoubtedly have received Lincoln's endorsement. He was opposed to it, he said, "Because it is suicidal. Secession appeased by compromise, is only emboldened to secede again tomorrow, and thus get larger concessions. The cowardice that yields to threats invites them."

Both Abolitionist leaders trained their guns on the future Secretary of State. Garrison wrote concerning Seward's policy: "The tiger is to be propitiated by crying 'pussy-cat!' and leviathan drawn out with a hook! . . . It is a penny-whistle used to hush up a thunderstorm of the first magnitude — capping Vesuvius with a sheet of straw paper! And this is all the statesmanship of Mr. Seward, in a crisis unparalleled in our national history!" Phillips was fearful that Lincoln might finally yield and urged him to dismiss Seward: "He [Seward] offers to postpone the whole Chicago platform, in order to save the Union, — though last October, at Chicago, he told us postponement never settles anything, whether it is a lawsuit or a national question. . . . This speech of Mr. Seward I regard as a declaration of war against the avowed policy of the President. If Lincoln were an Andrew Jackson, as his friends aver, he would dismiss Mr. Seward from his Cabinet. The incoming administration, if honest and firm, has two enemies to fight — Mr. Seward and the South."

12

Had the two Abolitionist leaders confined themselves to criticism of the compromisers they would have earned Lincoln's gratitude. But faithful to their motto — "No Union with Slaveholders!" — they argued that the Southern States should be allowed to depart in peace, and the sooner the better. "Sacrifice anything to keep the slaveholding States in the Union?" Phillips declared. "God forbid! We will rather build a bridge of gold, and pay their toll over it, — accompany them out with glad noise of trumpets, and 'speed the parting guest.' Let them not 'stand on the order of going, but go at once!' Let them take the forts, empty our arsenals and sub-treasuries, and we will lend them, beside, jewels of gold and jewels of silver, and Egypt be glad when they are departed."

Garrison wrote: "What, then, ought to be done? The people of the North should recognize the fact that the Union is dissolved, and act accordingly. . . . Now then, let there be a Convention of the Free States called to organize an independent government on free and just principles; and let them say to the slave States — 'Though you are without excuse for your treasonable conduct, depart in peace! Though you have laid piratical hands upon property not your own, we surrender it all in the spirit of magnanimity! And if nothing but the possession of the Capital will appease you, take even that, without a struggle! Let the line be drawn between us where free institutions end and the slave institutions begin! Organize your own confederacy, if you will, based upon violence, tyranny, and blood, and relieve us from all responsibility for your evil course!' " [8]

One may well ask: Had the two Abolitionist leaders agitated for over a quarter of a century, suffered innumerable hardships, risked their own lives and those of others, merely to be relieved "from all responsibility" for the evil of slavery, or had they done so to free

[8] Horace Greeley, in issue after issue of the New York *Tribune*, took a similar stand. General Winfield Scott declared: "Wayward sisters; let them go in peace." Earlier in his career Lincoln himself had made the following pronouncement: "Any people anywhere being inclined and having the power have the right to rise up and shake off the existing government, and form a new one that suits them better . . . *Any portion of such people that can may revolutionize and make their own of so much territory as they inhabit.* More than this, a majority of any portion of such people may revolutionize, putting down a minority, intermingled with or near about them, who may oppose this movement."

the slaves? Apparently both had managed to convince themselves that secession meant the end of slavery. "We rejoice in their departure," Phillips declared, "because we know their declaration of independence is the jubilee of slavery." Garrison made a similar statement. Neither furnished a single plausible argument to substantiate their theses. It was wishful thinking, nothing more. Yet, on the eve of the fall of Fort Sumter, Phillips was to say at New Bedford, Massachusetts: "There is another fearful element in the problem: we can no longer extend to the black race at the South our best sympathy and our best aid." During January and February of that year, at Boston Music Hall, he made even more significant admissions, saying that secession meant the reopening of the African slave trade and the acquisition of Central America by the South. ("Cuba she cannot have, France, England and ourselves forbid.") In other words he admitted that secession meant a vast increase in the number of slaves and great extension of slave territory.

In what way, then, was secession "the jubilee of slavery"? There had been some excuse for advocating disunion when the South controlled the President, Congress and the Supreme Court, and the danger appeared imminent that the Irrepressible Conflict would be resolved in favor of slavery; but to do so now, when the very act of secession proved that the South had given up all hope of extending slavery within the Union, was a grievous blunder. Indeed, the proposal really meant that he favored giving the South all Seward proposed to yield, and independence to boot; for if secession were agreed upon, the South assuredly would have claimed a share of the territory it had helped to wrest from Mexico.

PART FOUR

War and Reconstruction

Emancipation

GENTLEMEN, unless you sprinkle blood in the face of the people of Alabama, they will be back in the Union in less than ten days," said a member of the Alabama Legislature to the Confederate Cabinet at Montgomery. "I will tell you gentlemen what will put Virginia into the Southern Confederacy in less than an hour by Shrewsbury clock — strike a blow," declared Roger A. Pryor of Virginia in a speech delivered at Charleston and telegraphed to Montgomery. Hence the attack on Fort Sumter, to which Major Anderson had transferred his garrison of less than a hundred men from the more vulnerable Fort Moultrie. Besieged by seven thousand men with one hundred and twenty cannon, and short of food and munitions, the Fort surrendered on April 13, 1861, after a thirty-four-hour bombardment. The attack on the Fort accomplished what it was meant to accomplish: it rallied the South and forced the Border States to take position. But its effect upon the North was quite other than such prophets as former President Pierce had led the South to expect. There was no uprising of Northern Democrats. Their leader, Stephen A. Douglas, hastened to offer his services to Lincoln. The Breckinridge candidate for Governor of Massachusetts, Benjamin F. Butler, rallied with enthusiasm to the defense of the Union. As for the Northern disunionists — the Abolitionists — with few exceptions they did the same. "There was," wrote Garrison, "such an uprising in every city, town and hamlet of the North, without distinction of sect or party, as to seem like a general resurrection from the dead."

Having preached disunion for nearly a score of years, it must have been somewhat awkward for Garrison to challenge the South's right to secede. His problem was further complicated by the fact that he still claimed to believe in nonresistance. He had, however, no difficulty in rationalizing his stand to his own and his followers' satisfaction.

"Governments long established are not to be changed for light and transient causes," said the Declaration of Independence, from which followed that if one advocated so revolutionary a change as disunion, one's reasons must be unassailable. Garrison felt that he and his fellow-Abolitionists had had such reasons. They had tried by every conceivable means to get the South to abolish slavery. When all hope of emancipation, gradual or immediate, had vanished — when as a matter of fact it became apparent that the Slave Power meant vastly to extend its territory, they had advocated disunion so freedom might be preserved in the North and because they were unwilling to continue to share responsibility for the institution. The South had no reasons of comparable validity. The North had not interfered with slavery in the Slave States. Lincoln and the Republican Party had repeatedly stated that they had no intention of doing so. They were even willing to grant the South a constitutional amendment guaranteeing noninterference for all time. They were willing to enforce the Fugitive Slave Law as much as enforcement of a law against which the moral sentiment of the community revolted was possible. They merely demanded that slavery make no attempt to invade free territory. In view of all this, Garrison felt the South's action to be without legal or moral justification.

As for nonresistance, Garrison found a formula enabling him to eat his cake and have it. That the people of the North had rejected nonresistance he considered regrettable, but unavoidable: "We wish all the North were able to adopt these principles, understandingly, heartily and without delay; but according to the structure of the human mind, in the whirlwind of the present deadly conflict, this is impracticable." Since the people believed that wrong and injustice should be resisted by force, it was incumbent upon them to be true to their principles: "The worst thing they can do is to be recreant to their own convictions in such a crisis as this." Nor was it inconsistent with one's belief in nonresistance "to wish success to the innocent and defeat to the guilty party."

He was anxious that his followers should abstain from doing anything that might embarrass the Government, and wrote to Oliver Johnson: "It is no time for minute criticism of Lincoln, Republicanism, or even the other parties, now that they are fusing for a death grapple with the Southern slave oligarchy; for they are instruments in the hands of God to carry forward and help achieve the great object of emancipation for which we have so long been striving."

As President of the American Anti-Slavery Society he issued an
order postponing "until further notice" the annual meeting in New
York: "Let nothing be done at this solemn crisis, needlessly to check
or divert the mighty current of popular feeling."

2

Postponement of the annual meeting of the American Anti-Slavery
Society was a wise move, but when the New England Society held
its Fourth of July gathering, at Framingham, Massachusetts, the
extremists had their say. Stephen S. Foster expressed the opinion that
the outlook for the slave had never been more depressing and introduced a resolution to the effect that unless the Government declared
for emancipation "we can give it no support or countenance in its
effort to maintain its authority over the seceding States, but must
continue to heap upon it that obloquy which naturally attaches to all
who are guilty of the crime of enslaving their fellow men."

It was at Framingham, exactly seven years before, that Garrison
had dramatically held up a copy of the United States Constitution,
had called it "a covenant with death and an agreement with hell,"
and had consigned it to the flame crying: "So perish all compromises
with tyranny! And let all the people say, Amen!" Now he said: "I
cannot say that I do not sympathize with the Government, as against
Jefferson Davis and his piratical associates. There is not a drop of
blood in my veins, both as an Abolitionist and a peace man, that does
not flow with the Northern tide of sentiment. . . . Blessed be God,
that 'covenant with death' has been annulled, and that 'agreement
with hell' no longer stands. I joyfully accept the fact, and leave all
verbal criticism until a more suitable opportunity."

3

Garrison did not abstain from all "verbal criticism" during the
war. Indeed, considering the Administration's policy, especially during the first two years of the conflict, he would have been untrue to
his principles had he failed to protest. But he proved himself extraordinarily patient, understanding, considerate, keenly aware of the
difficulties with which the Government had to cope. He repeatedly
defended the President against attacks by Abolitionists at home and
abroad. No other private citizen in the United States was as helpful

to the Administration in creating good will for the Union cause in Great Britain. The aristocracy and the commercial classes of England wished the rebellion to succeed and applauded their Government's hostile attitude. It was vitally important to counteract their influence, and who but the British Abolitionists could be relied upon to do this? To arouse them to action was, however, no easy matter. On his visit to the United States in 1864 George Thompson said to Lydia Maria Child: "You should remember how your cause was made to appear in the eyes of the world. First your President's inaugural was largely taken up with assurances that fugitive slaves would be returned to their masters, and that those who attempted to interfere would be punished; secondly two of your generals volunteered offers to put down insurrection of the slaves, should they try to obtain their freedom; thirdly, slaves who escaped into your lines were sent back and cruelly scourged by the tyrants from whose power they had sought your protection; fourthly, Mr. Seward charged Mr. Adams not to speak of slavery, and, through him, gave assurance that 'the status of no class of people in America would be changed by the war'; fifthly, President Lincoln, after the war had continued more than a year, offered the slaveholders a hundred days to consider whether they would come back with their chattels, or still fight for their independence at the risk of the abolition of slavery. Was there anything in this to excite the enthusiasm of the English people about your war?"[1]

Yet it was precisely to his old friend George Thompson, now an influential member of Parliament, that Garrison appealed, begging him to rally the British antislavery forces to the support of the North. Thompson replied: "You know how impossible it is at this moment to vindicate, as one would wish, the course of Mr. Lincoln. In no one of his utterances is there an assertion of a great principle — no appeal to right or justice. In everything he does and says, affecting the slave, there is the alloy of expediency. The slave may be free — if it should be 'necessary,' or 'convenient,' or 'agreeable to his master.' What we want to see him do is, to take his stand upon the doctrine of human equality, and man's inalienable right to life, liberty and the pursuit of happiness. All else is paltering with conscience and with truth."

[1] The London *Spectator* defined the policy of the American Government towards slavery in these words: "The principle is not that a human being cannot justly own another, but that he cannot own him unless he is loyal to the United States."

Nevertheless he heeded his friend's appeal. Assisted by his son-in-law, Frederick W. Chesson, he organized the London Emancipation Society, which soon had branches in the principal cities of the United Kingdom. The London Emancipation Committee was especially active. It was composed of such luminaries as John Bright, John Stuart Mill, Richard Cobden, Lord Haughton, Herbert Spencer, Francis W. Newman, Newman Hall, Baptist Noel and others equally famous. Meetings were held throughout England and Scotland. John Bright did such valuable work that when Thompson paid a visit to Lincoln in 1864 he was surprised to see that "the only picture in the apartment" was a portrait of his illustrious colleague. In Glasgow Garrison's friends Andrew Paton and William Smeal were responsible for preventing a Confederate raider more formidable than the *Alabama* from leaving the Clyde till diplomacy had had time to catch up with the situation. In Manchester the Emancipation Society distributed six hundred thousand pamphlets and held over three hundred meetings. Indeed, such was the activity the editor of the *Liberator* managed to arouse among the British antislavery forces that one may well ask if diplomacy could have succeeded without him. John Jay, later Ambassador to Austria, was so impressed that he wrote in 1863: "The Anti-Slavery Movement in the United States, with few exceptions that more plainly show the rule, has been marked by statesmanlike characteristics, now crowned with success, and by a love of country that no delay, injustice and disappointment could impair or disturb."

As President of the American Anti-Slavery Society Garrison managed to put the weight of the organization's support behind the President. "Do you notice," wrote Samuel Bowles, editor of the Springfield *Republican*, to a friend, "that the '*Anti-Slavery Standard*' and the '*Liberator*,' the representatives of the old abolitionists, are both earnest for Lincoln? Yet a new crop of Radicals has sprung up, who are resisting the President and making mischief."

4

On April 9, 1861, Phillips spoke at New Bedford, Massachusetts. "The telegraph," said he, "is said to report to-night that the guns are firing, either out of Fort Sumter, or into it; that to-morrow's breeze, when it sweeps the North, will bring us the echo of the first Lexington battle of the new Revolution. Well, what shall we say of such an hour?"

Edward Everett Hale and others have charged Phillips with being careless in the preparation of his speeches and with often relying on the inspiration of the moment. Certain it is that what he now proceeded to say was not the result of mature reflection: "I am very sorry that a gun should be fired at Fort Sumter or that a gun should be fired from it. . . . A large body of people, sufficient to make a nation, have come to the conclusion, that they will have a government of a certain form. Who denies them the right? Standing with the principles of '76 behind us, who can deny them the right? What is a matter of a few millions of dollars, or a few forts? It is a mere drop in the bucket of the great national question. It is theirs just as much as ours. I maintain on the principles of '76, that Abraham Lincoln has no right to a soldier in Fort Sumter."

He felt convinced that the people of Massachusetts would refuse to have anything to do with the war: "You cannot go through Massachusetts and recruit men to bombard Charleston and New Orleans. The Northern mind will not bear it: you can never make such a war popular. The first onset may be borne; the telegraph may bring in news that Anderson has bombarded Charleston, and you may rejoice: but the sober second thought of Massachusetts will be, 'wasteful, unchristian, guilty.' The North never will endorse such a war."

The sober second thought of Wendell Phillips must have made him regret these words less than a week later. On April 15, the President issued his call for seventy-five thousand volunteers. The following day every train that pulled into Boston disgorged a crowd of young men who came to enlist, and the Sixth Massachusetts, fully equipped, entrained for the National Capital.

5

On Sunday morning, April 21, Phillips was to speak at Boston Music Hall. The announcement added to the prevailing excitement. Would he maintain that no attempt should be made to coerce the South? Four thousand people crowded into the hall; many were unable to enter. That there would have been a riot of formidable proportions had he made a speech similar to the one at New Bedford there can be no doubt, as it is likewise certain that this would not have deterred him. A local newspaper claimed, however, to have received information from a reliable source that he had reconsidered.

The fact that the pulpit from which he was to speak was decorated with the national colors and surmounted by an arch of bunting, laurel and evergreen was likewise considered a favorable omen.

Applause greeted him when he appeared in the rostrum. There was an expectant hush. Four thousand pairs of eyes were trained upon him. The young men of his bodyguard, not knowing what to expect, looked tense. Then, in that melodious, violinlike voice — not loud, yet penetrating into every nook of the hall — he pronounced these lines from Jeremiah which Garrison had suggested to him:

"Therefore thus saith the Lord: You have not hearkened unto me in proclaiming liberty every one to his brother, and every man to his neighbor; behold I proclaim a liberty for you, saith the Lord, to the sword, to the pestilence and to famine."

Then, after a pause —

"Many times this winter, here and elsewhere, I have counselled peace, — urged, as well as I knew how, the expediency of acknowledging the Southern Confederacy, and the peaceful separation of these thirty-four States. One of the journals announces to you that I come here this morning to retract those opinions. No, not one of them! I need them all, — every word I have spoken this winter, every act of twenty-five years of my life, to make the welcome I give this war hearty and hot. Civil war is a momentous evil. It needs the soundest, most solemn justification. I rejoice before God to-day for every word that I have spoken counselling peace; but I rejoice also with an especially profound gratitude, that now, the first time in my anti-slavery life, I speak under the stars and stripes, and welcome the tread of Massachusetts men marshalled for war."

At this point the shorthand writer bracketed [*Enthusiastic cheering*], and from then on, after every two or three sentences, we read [*Loud applause*], [*Prolonged cheering*], [*Enthusiastic and continued cheers*] and so on. But an unemotional listener who had heard Phillips speak in that same hall in February of that year must have marveled. "We do not want the Border States. Let them go, be welcome to the forts, take the Capital with them," he had said then; now he was saying: "Rather than surrender the Capital, cover every square foot of it with a living body; crowd it with a million men, and empty every bank vault at the North to pay the cost."

He no longer maintained that the South had the right to secede. "No government," he said, "provides for its own death; therefore there can be no Constitutional right to secede. . . . The South says, 'If you don't allow me the Constitutional right, I claim the revolutionary right.' The North responds, 'When you have torn the Constitution into fragments, I recognize the right of THE PEOPLE of South Carolina to model their government. Yes, I recognize the right of the three hundred and eighty-four thousand white men, and four hundred and eighty-four thousand black men, to model their Constitution. Show me one that they have adopted, and I will recognize the revolution.' "

The speech rolled on towards a sonorous peroration that brought the audience to its feet: "I believe in the possibility of justice, in the certainty of union. Years hence, when the smoke of this conflict clears away, the world will see under our banner all tongues, all creeds, all races, — one brotherhood, — and on the banks of the Potomac, the Genius of Liberty, robed in light, four and thirty stars for her diadem, broken chains under feet, and an olive branch in her right hand."

That day his bodyguard was needed to save him from the admiring multitude that wished to hoist him on their shoulders and carry him home in triumph. Sixteen thousand copies of the *Liberator* containing the speech were sold on the streets of Boston. George Thompson read it, and wrote to Garrison that he looked forward with joyful anticipations to the day "when I shall gaze upon that vision beheld by the eye of your prophet and unequalled orator — the great and (better still) the good and gracious Phillips."

6

Garrison and Phillips hated slavery more than they loved the Union. Lincoln loved the Union more than he hated slavery. They had at one time been willing to sacrifice the Union in the mistaken belief that this would free the slave. Now Lincoln was willing to sacrifice the slave in the mistaken belief that this would save the Union. Shortly after Lincoln's inauguration Secretary Seward wrote to Ambassador Dayton in Paris: "The condition of slavery in the several States will remain just the same whether it [the rebellion] succeeds or fails . . . It is hardly necessary to add to this incontrovertible statement the further fact that the new President has always repudiated all designs, whenever and wherever imputed to him, of disturbing the system of slavery as it has existed under the constitution and laws."

In a lecture delivered in New York and Boston in December, 1861, Phillips pointed out the fallacy of reconstructing the Union without "disturbing the system of slavery":

"I do not believe such reconstruction possible. . . . If the reason of the war is because we are two nations, then the cure must be to make us one nation, to remove that cause which divides us, to make our institutions homogeneous. If it were possible to subjugate the South, and leave slavery just as it is, where is the security that we should not have another war in ten years? Indeed, such a course invites another war, whenever demagogues please."

He warned Lincoln that unless he made haste to emancipate the slaves before Northern armies won an important victory, Jefferson Davis might forestall him and abolish slavery to gain the support of England and France:

"Unless England flings her fleets along the coast, the South can never spring into separate existence. . . . No one doubts now, that, should the South emancipate, England would make haste to recognize and help her. . . . The moment these States begin to appear victorious, the moment our armies do anything that evinces final success, the wily statesmanship and unconquerable hate of the South will write 'Emancipation' on her banner, and welcome the protectorate of a European power. . . . Indeed, the only way, the only sure way, to break this Union, is to try to save it by protecting slavery. . . . Unless we emancipate the slave, we shall never conquer the South without her trying emancipation. Every Southerner, from Toombs up to Frémont, has acknowledged it. Do you suppose that Davis and Beauregard, and the rest, mean to be exiles, wandering contemned in every great city of Europe, in order that they may maintain slavery and the Constitution of '89? They, like ourselves, will throw everything overboard before they will submit to defeat, – defeat from Yankees."

Was Phillips's argument sound? Did the danger really exist that the South might sacrifice slavery to gain independence? In July, 1862, Lincoln appealed to the representatives of the loyal Border Slave States to "commend . . . to the consideration of your States and people," the plan for compensated gradual emancipation with Federal aid he had proposed in March of that year. This, he felt, would eliminate all hope the Confederacy might still cherish that the Border States would join their fate to hers. The majority of the representatives proved obdurate, the minority, however, gave this written reply: "We will, so far as may be in our power, ask the people of the Border States, calmly, deliberately, and fairly to consider your recommendation. We are the more emboldened to assume this position from the fact now become history, that the leaders of the Southern rebellion have offered to abolish slavery amongst them as a condition to foreign intervention in favor of their independence as a nation.

"If they can give up slavery to destroy the Union, we can surely ask our people to consider the question of emancipation to save the Union."

In 1864, during the informal peace negotiations at Richmond between Colonel Jaques of Illinois, J. R. Gilmore of New York and Jefferson Davis, the Confederate President said: "We are not fighting for slavery. We are fighting for independence."

That slavery could be nominally "abolished," yet in practice remain as real as ever, was demonstrated when Presidential reconstruction was put to the test.

7

The President's emancipation proposal of March 6, 1862, offered pecuniary aid to any State "which may adopt gradual abolition of slavery . . . to compensate it for the inconvenience, public and private, produced by such change of system." Phillips, who had often privately stated that he demanded the whole loaf with the expectation of getting half, was not displeased. In a lecture before the Emancipation League of Boston he said: "If the President has not entered Canaan, he has turned his face Zionward." He interpreted Lincoln's offer to mean: "Gentlemen of the Border States, now is your time. If you want your money, take it, and if hereafter I should take your slaves without paying, don't say I did not offer to do it."

Garrison was more critical. He wrote to Oliver Johnson: "I am afraid the President's message will prove 'a decoy duck' or a 'red herring,' so as to postpone that decisive action by Congress which we are so desirous of seeing. Let us advocate no postponement of duty." Congress, where Thaddeus Stevens characterized Lincoln's proposal as "the most diluted, milk-and-water-gruel proposition that was ever given to the American nation," was, indeed, in advance of the President. In March, 1862, it forbade army officers to return fugitive slaves. In April (disregarding Lincoln's preference for gradual emancipation) it decreed immediate abolition of slavery in the District of Columbia. In June it snubbed the Supreme Court's decision in the Dred Scott case by forbidding slavery in all the Territories. In July it passed the famous Confiscation Act, freeing the slaves of Southerners who participated in the rebellion, confiscating their property and empowering the President to employ Negroes as soldiers.

Shortly after the President's gradual emancipation proposal Phillips journeyed to Washington, where he had been invited to speak. He was now a personage of national importance. Horace Greeley wrote that during the winter of 1861–1862 at least fifty thousand people heard him speak, while five million read his speeches, which many Republican papers printed in full. When he arrived in Washington and visited the Senate chamber, the Vice President of the United States left the chair to welcome him. The Speaker of the House invited him to dinner and discussed pending measures with him. Official Washington packed the Smithsonian to hear him speak and applauded enthusiastically. He paid a visit to Lincoln and gave this somewhat one-sided account of the interview: "I told him that if he started the experiment of emancipation, and honestly devoted his energies to making it a fact, he would deserve to hold the helm until the experiment was finished — that the people would not allow him to quit while it was trying."

From Washington he traveled Westward on a six weeks' lecture tour, drawing immense audiences. He was the unofficial leader of all who believed the war would have been fought in vain if it did not abolish slavery. But if his following had grown, so had the rage of his opponents. In Cincinnati his enemies were ready for him. The Cincinnati *Commercial* claimed that "five thousand tickets were given away in places and to persons of the worst repute, for the express purpose of raising a mob." The meeting was one of the most riotous he had ever attempted to address. The Cincinnati *Enquirer* reported that at one time, "a heavy boulder was thrown from the third tier of boxes. It struck a few feet from the speaker. It came crashing among the footlights like a cannon-shot." Phillips, as usual,

remained unperturbed and wrote philosophically to Sumner: "You
see Cincinnati mobbed and pelted with eggs me whom Washington
cheered. So it goes."

8

In January of that year, 1862, Major General David Hunter had
begged Secretary Stanton for an independent command, with the
avowed intention of forcing the President's hand on emancipation:
"Please let me have my own way on the subject of slavery. The
administration will not be responsible. I alone will bear the blame;
you can censure me, arrest me, dismiss me, hang me if you will, but
permit me to make my mark in such a way as to be remembered by
friend and foe." Stanton, whose father had been a friend of Benjamin
Lundy, was a political opportunist, but agreed with the Radicals in
Congress that the most formidable blow that could be struck at
the rebels was emancipation, and that it was long overdue. So
Hunter got his wish. He was appointed Commander of the Department of the South, comprising South Carolina, Georgia and Florida.
The high-sounding title was based on the fact that the Federals
occupied a few coastal points in those States. Hunter placed the
Department under martial law, and on May 9, 1862, made a bid for
immortality by issuing an order to the effect that "slavery and
martial law in a free country are altogether incompatible. The persons in these States . . . heretofore held as slaves, are therefore
declared forever free."

The previous year General Frémont, in command of the Department of the West, had declared the property of all inhabitants
of Missouri who had taken up arms against the Government confiscated, "and their slaves if any they have, free men." Lincoln had
revoked the order. This time he did not even wait until he received
official notification from Hunter, but, basing himself on reports in
the press, issued a proclamation declaring the General's order
"altogether void." But Hunter *did* force his hand. During the succeeding two months the pressure upon the President became well-
nigh irresistible. The Radical Republican and Abolitionist press
praised Hunter extravagantly. Petitions rained in upon Lincoln and
there was an endless procession of delegations coming to plead the
cause of emancipation. The "Jacobins" in and out of Congress (as
John Hay called the President's Republican opponents) were more

critical than ever. Governor Andrew of Massachusetts wrote that the people of his State "feel it a heavy draft on their patriotism" that they should be asked "to help fight rebels," without being permitted "to fire on the enemy's magazine." Harriet Tubman, who had led so many slaves out of bondage as to have acquired the nickname of Moses, declared at a public meeting: "God's ahead of Massa Linkum. God won't let Massa Linkum beat de Souf till he do de right ting. Massa Linkum he great man, and I'se poor nigger; but dis nigger can tell Massa Linkum how to save de money and de young men. He do it by setting de niggers free." Phillips, speaking at a Republican rally in Boston, was applauded when he declared: "President Lincoln with a senile lick-spittle haste runs before he is bidden to remove the Hunter proclamation. The President and the Cabinet are treasonable. The President and the Secretary of War should be impeached." Congressman George W. Julian wrote: "The popular hostility to the President at this time cannot be described, and was wholly without precedent, and the opposition to him in Congress was still more intense." [2]

Sumner pleaded with Lincoln to issue an Emancipation Proclamation on the Fourth of July to "make the day more sacred and historic than ever." The President replied that if he were to do so "half of the officers would fling down their arms." On July 12, however, he sent a Message to Congress again proposing "compensated gradual emancipation." "The change it contemplates would come gently as the dews of Heaven, not rending or wrecking anything," he wrote. That same day he summoned the representatives of the loyal Border States and urged them to use their influence with the people of their States so they would accept the measure. He made it clear that he would be unable to resist the pressure much longer: "He [Hunter] proclaimed all men free within certain States, and I repudiated the proclamation . . . Yet, in repudiating it, I gave dissatisfaction, if not offense, to many whose support the country cannot afford to lose. And this is not the end of it. The pressure in this direction is still

[2] In October of that year Congressman J. K. Moorhead, representing the Pittsburgh district, said to Lincoln in the presence of several colleagues: "Mr. President, I came as far as Harrisburg yesterday, and passed the evening with a number of the best and most influential men of our State, including some of those who have been your most earnest supporters, and they charged me to tell you that when one of them said, 'he would be glad to hear some morning that you had been found hanging from the post of a lamp at the door of the White House,' others approved the expression."

upon me, and is increasing. By conceding what I now ask you can relieve me, and, much more, can relieve the country on this important point." He promised that every effort would be made to colonize the freedmen outside the borders of the United States. "Room in South America for colonization can be obtained cheaply, and in abundance, and when numbers shall be large enough to be company and encouragement for one another, the freed people will not be reluctant to go."

The representatives of the Border States were not impressed. They considered compensated gradual emancipation combined with colonization an unstatesmanlike proceeding. "Stated in this form," they said in their written reply, "the proposition is nothing less than deportation from the country of sixteen hundred million dollars' worth of producing labor, and the substitution in its place of an interest-bearing debt of the same amount."

9

While these negotiations were going on, Lincoln had already decided to yield. His interview with the representatives of the Border States took place on July 12. On July 13 he attended the funeral of an infant child of Secretary Stanton. With him in the carriage were William H. Seward, Secretary of State, Gideon Welles, Secretary of the Navy, and Mrs. Frederick Seward, the former's daughter-in-law. Welles wrote in his *Diary:* "It was on this occasion and on this ride that he [Lincoln] first mentioned to Mr. Seward and myself the subject of emancipating the slaves by proclamation in case the rebels did not cease to persist in their war on the government and the Union, of which he saw no evidence. He dwelt earnestly on the gravity, importance, and delicacy of the movement, said he had given it much thought and had about come to the conclusion that it was a military necessity absolutely essential for the salvation of the Union, that we must free the slaves or be ourselves subdued."

"Father Neptune," as Lincoln was wont to call Welles, could hardly believe his ears, for what the President was saying was almost the exact opposite of what he had always claimed: "It was a new departure for the President, for until this time, in all our previous interviews whenever the question of the emancipation or mitigation of slavery had been in any way alluded to, he had been prompt and emphatic in denouncing any interference by the general government with the subject."

To the artist Carpenter the President later explained: "It had got to be midsummer, 1862. Things had gone on from bad to worse, until I had felt that we had reached the end of our rope on the plan of operations we had been pursuing; that we had played our last card, and must change our tactics or lose the game. I now determined upon the adoption of the emancipation policy; and, without consultation with, or knowledge of the cabinet, I prepared the original draft, and, after much anxious thought, called a cabinet meeting on the subject."

Salmon P. Chase, Secretary of the Treasury, quoted Lincoln as saying at the Cabinet meeting: "I have got you together to hear what I have written down. I do not wish your advice about the main matter — for that I have determined for myself. This I say without intending anything but respect for any of you. But I already know the views of each upon the question. They have been heretofore expressed and I have considered them as thoroughly as I can. What I have written is that which my reflections have determined me to say. If there is anything in the expressions I use, or in any other minor matter, which any one of you think had best be changed, I shall be glad to receive the suggestions . . . I am here. I must do the best I can, and bear the responsibility of taking the course which I feel I ought to take."

Secretary Seward suggested that the Proclamation be postponed until the North had gained a victory: "The depression of the public mind consequent upon our repeated reverses, is so great that I fear the effect of so important a step. It may be viewed as the last measure of an exhausted government, a cry for help; the government stretching forth its hands to Ethiopia, instead of Ethiopia stretching forth her hands to the government." Seward was opposed to the Proclamation and it appears probable that he meant to gain time, hoping the President would change his mind, or that he, Seward, would succeed in changing it for him. Joseph Medill of the Chicago *Tribune* was to write: "He is Lincoln's evil genius. He has been President *de facto*, and has kept a sponge saturated with chloroform to Uncle Abe's nose all the while."

Whether or not Seward was responsible, the President *did* change his mind. Early in September of that same year Cassius M. Clay returned from Russia, where he had been serving as Ambassador. He gave the following account of an interview with the President:

"I went to Lincoln and gave my reasons for a change of policy — that European Governments would go against us if we fought simply for the Union, but that England and France, especially, dared not interfere if we fought for the liberation of the slaves. . . . What was the use of fighting for the old Union with the cancer of slavery left? Better make peace on any terms. Let us nail our banner of universal liberty to the mast, and if fall we must, we would at least fall with honor, leaving a legacy of inestimable value to an immortal cause."

Clay quoted the President as replying: "There is much in what you say which has had my serious thought, but we have as much as we can now carry, and I fear if the proclamation of freedom should be issued Kentucky would go out to the South."

"No," answered Clay, "I have discussed the liberal issue all these years in my own State; those who would favor the rebellion are already in arms, those remaining are for the Union with or without slavery; ten men would not be changed."

It is difficult to understand why the President should have feared Border State defection in September when he did not fear it in July. While things were going badly in Virginia, Grant's victories in Kentucky and on the Tennessee and Cumberland Rivers had welded Kentucky solidly to the Union. When immediately after the interview Clay journeyed to Kentucky and made an address to a joint meeting of the Legislature during which he expressed the views he had previously expressed to Lincoln, he was "not only heard with patience, but often cheered." Missouri was now firmly in the hands of the Federals and Lincoln himself had reported in a message to Congress that three times as many Missourians had joined the Union as the Confederate armies. As for Maryland, when that same month Lee invaded that State and called upon Marylanders to join his army and throw off the yoke of the "oppressor," less than a hundred joined.

However, when on September 6 the rebel army reached Frederick, Maryland, the President is said to have "registered a vow in heaven" that he would issue an Emancipation Proclamation as soon as the Confederates should be driven out of Maryland. By September 13, however, he had again changed his mind. On that day a delegation of one hundred clergymen from Chicago called and begged him to issue the Proclamation and to employ Negroes as soldiers. He rejected the second proposal in language uncomplimentary to the Negro: "If we were to arm them, I fear that in a few weeks the arms would be in the hands of the rebels." [3] As for the Proclamation — "I do not want to issue a document that the whole world will see must necessarily be inoperative, like the Pope's bull against the comet! And what reason is there to think it would have any greater effect upon the slaves than the late law of Congress, which I approved, and which offers protection and freedom to the slaves of rebel masters who come within our lines? Yet I cannot learn that the law has caused a single slave to come over to us."

To any one acquainted with the facts, the President's reply must appear disingenuous. It has been estimated that since the beginning of the war some twenty thousand slaves who sought refuge with the Union army had been returned to their owners. After Congress passed the law to which the President was referring, slave catching by proslavery generals continued. Phillips wrote to Charles Sumner: "Do you mean to let your servants defy you in that way? foil your wish in that triumphant manner? If you do — excuse me — you're a caitiff Senate and that's a milk-livered Administration." The Committee on the Conduct of the War made an investigation, and on April 10 learned to its amazement and indignation from General Daniel Sickles that the President had never officially communicated the new order to the army! Senators Grimes and Sumner made an attack upon the army clique, and by implication upon the President, for ignoring a law of Congress, and Greeley in the New York *Tribune* joined in the attack. On July 28, 1862, in a letter to Cuthbert Bullitt of New Orleans, the President admitted that fugitive slaves who came to the Union lines had been driven back. In view of all this, what is one to think of Lincoln's statement that he could not learn "the law has caused a single slave to come over to us"?

The President went on to say: "There are some fifty thousand bayonets in the Union from the Border Slave States. It would be a serious matter if, in consequence of a proclamation such as you desire, they should go over to the rebels." Yet on July 13, when the situation in the Border States had been far worse, he had expressed no such fear, but had told Gideon Welles that emancipation was "a

[3] Eventually 178,975 Negro soldiers served in the Union army. Of these 29,298 died in the war — one in six, against one in ten among white troops. As will be seen later in this chapter, in 1864 Lincoln declared that without the aid of the Negroes the war would have been lost.

military necessity absolutely essential for the salvation of the Union, that we must free the slaves or be ourselves subdued."

10

On August 1, 1862, in the Grove at Abington, Massachusetts, Phillips delivered an attack on the Administration that reverberated throughout the world. A synopsis from the pen of Karl Marx appeared in the Vienna *Presse*.[4] The London *Times* declared: "Anything more violent is scarcely possible to imagine, and anything more daring in time of Civil War was never perpetrated in any country by any sane man who valued his life and liberty. In reading the speech . . . it is scarcely possible to avoid the conclusion that the speaker's object was to force the government to prosecute him."

The following are a few of the most striking paragraphs from Phillips's attack:

"I do not think that anything which we can call a *government* has any *purpose* to get rid of slavery. On the contrary, I think the present purpose of the government, so far as it has now a purpose, is to end the war and save slavery. I believe Mr. Lincoln is conducting this war, at present, with the purpose of saving slavery. . . . He knows as well as we do at this moment, as well as every man this side of a lunatic hospital knows, that, if he wants to save lives and money, the way to end this war is to strike at slavery.

"In the service of which political idea shall the war be waged, — in the service of saving the Union as it was, or the Union as it ought to be? Mr. Lincoln dare not choose between these two phrases. He is waging a war which he dare not describe, in the service of a political idea that he dare not shape into words. He is not fighting vigorously and heartily enough even to get good terms in case of a treaty, — not to talk of victory.

"I do not say McClellan is a traitor, but I say this, that if he had been a traitor from the crown of his head to the sole of his foot, he

---

[4] In a letter to Frederick Engels, August 7, 1862, Marx wrote: "The North itself has turned the slaves into a military force on the side of the Southerners, instead of turning it against them. The South leaves productive labor to the slaves and could therefore put its whole fighting strength in the field without disturbance. . . . The long and short of the business seems to me to be that a war of this kind must be conducted on revolutionary lines, while the Yankees have so far been trying to conduct it constitutionally."

could not have served the South better than he has done since he was commander-in-chief; he could not have carried on the war in more exact deference to the politics of that side of the Union.[5] And almost the same thing may be said of Mr. Lincoln, — that if he had been a traitor, he could not have worked better to strengthen one side, and hazard the success of the other. There is more danger to-day that Washington will be taken than Richmond.

"The war can only be ended by annihilating that oligarchy which formed and rules the South and makes the war, — by annihilating a state of society. No social state is really annihilated, except when it is replaced by another. Our present policy neither aims to annihilate that state of things we call 'the South' . . . nor replace it with a substitute. Such an aimless war I call wasteful and murderous. Better that that South should go to-day, than that we should prolong such a war. Until this nation announces, in some form or other, that this is a war, not against Jefferson Davis, but against a system . . . until we do that, we shall have no prospect of peace.

"I do not believe in the government. I do not believe this government has got either vigor or a purpose. It drifts with events. The President has not uttered a word which gives even a twilight glimpse of any antislavery purpose. He may be honest, — nobody cares whether the tortoise is honest or not; he has neither insight, nor prevision, nor decision. It is said in Washington Streets that he long ago wrote a proclamation abolishing slavery in the State of Virginia, but McClellan bullied him out of it. It is said, too, — what is extremely probable, — that he had more than once made up his mind to remove McClellan, and Kentucky bullied him out of it.

"The North, by an overwhelming majority, is ready to have him act, will indorse and support anything he does, yes, hopes he will go forward. True, it is not yet ripe enough to demand; but it is fully willing, indeed waits, for action. With chronic Whig distrust and ignorance of the people, Lincoln halts and fears. . . . I will tell you what he is. He is a first-rate *second-rate* man.[6] He is one of the best

---

[5] Attorney-General Edward Bates noted in his Diary a statement made by McClellan that "the South was right and he would never fight against it, that the southern Democracy had always governed the country and ought to govern it."

[6] "What little we know of the methods by which he now [in 1860] helped his own promotion suggests that the people who then and long after set him down as a second-rate person may have had a good deal to go upon." Lord Charnwood, *op. cit.*

specimens of a second-rate man, and he is honestly waiting, like any other servant, for the people to come and send him on any errand they wish. In ordinary times, when the seas are calm, you can sail without a pilot . . . to-day the nation's bark scuds, under the tempest, lee-shore and maelstrom on each side, needing no holiday captain, but a pilot, to weather the storm."

11

Garrison had an unshakable conviction that emancipation would be the outcome of the war notwithstanding the President's reluctance to make use of his war powers for that purpose. He believed Phillips's vehemence excessive, and some of the warmth went out of their friendship. To Oliver Johnson he wrote: "I have always believed that the anti-slavery cause has had aroused against it a great deal of uncalled-for hostility, in consequence of extravagance of speech, and want of tact and good judgment, on the part of some most desirous to promote its advancement. . . . Our work, as abolitionists, is still to impeach, censure and condemn where we must, and approve when we can; but in such an inflammable state of the country, the injunction: 'Be ye wise as serpents and harmless as doves,' deserves to be carefully heeded."

Horace Greeley, editor of the powerful New York *Tribune*, accused Phillips of discouraging enlistments. Phillips repudiated the charge in an open letter, saying: "Whether the administration will ever pilot us through our troubles, I have serious doubts: that it never will, unless it changes its present policy, I am quite certain. Where, then, is my place under a republican government which only reflects and executes public opinion? . . . Where, then, is my post, especially under an administration that avowedly sits waiting, begging to be told what to do? I must educate, arouse, and mature a public opinion which shall compel the administration to adopt and support it in pursuing the policy I can aid . . . That duty I try to do in my measure. My criticism is not, like that of the traitor presses, meant to paralyze the administration, but to goad it to more activity and vigor, or to change the Cabinet."

When many years later Phillips spoke at the Centennial Anniversary of Phi Beta Kappa of Harvard College, these words, which to some may appear like a criticism of his own attitude towards Lincoln, dropped from his lips: "Mark the critic out of office: how reckless of assertion, how careless of consequence; and then the caution, forethought and fair play of the same man charged with administration."

12

On September 22, 1862, nine days after his discouraging reception of the clerical delegation from Chicago, President Lincoln issued the preliminary Emancipation Proclamation. "All persons held as slaves within any State, or designated part of a State" whose people were in rebellion against the United States on the first of the new year "shall be then, thenceforward and forever free." The President promised that "efforts to colonize persons of African descent, with their consent, upon this continent or elsewhere," would be continued.

What had finally decided the President to act? It will be remembered that Seward had advised postponement of the Emancipation Proclamation until a victory had been won. On September 17 Lee was forced to retreat at Antietam. Yet, as we have seen, Lincoln was usually favorable to emancipation when things looked particularly desperate; when they improved he was inclined to draw back. There is reliable evidence to the effect that it was not McClellan's inconclusive victory but a threat by Congress to refuse to vote further credits for the army that put an end to Presidential vacillation.

James C. Welling was editor of the *National Intelligencer*, an influential periodical published in Washington. Allen Thorndike Rice, editor of the *North American Review*, assures us that Welling's relations with Lincoln were "intimate and often confidential." After the war he became Professor of Belles Lettres at Princeton and later President of Columbian College, Washington, D. C. (now George Washington University), and Regent of the Smithsonian Institution. In 1886 Welling wrote in his reminiscences of Lincoln:

"The most active and energetic wing of the Republican Party had become, as the war waxed hotter, more and more hostile to this 'Border State theory of war,' until, in the end, its fiery and impetuous leaders did not hesitate to threaten him [Lincoln] with repudiation as a political chief, and even began in some cases to hint the expediency of withholding supplies for the prosecution of the war. Thus placed between two stools, and liable between them to fall to the ground, he determined at last to plant himself firmly on the stool which promised the surest and safest support. . . . The President had been brought to believe that if he did not keep the Radical portion of his party at his back he could not long be sure of keeping an army at the front."

When the preliminary Emancipation Proclamation appeared, Edward Stanly, former South Carolina congressman whom the President had appointed Military Governor of North Carolina and who had taken the post with the understanding that slavery would not be disturbed, hastened to Washington to demand an explanation. He had several interviews with the President and finally called at the office of the *Intelligencer*. Welling wrote in his diary:

> *September 27th, 1862.* — Had a call at the Intelligencer office from the Honorable Edward Stanly, Military Governor of North Carolina. In a long and interesting conversation Mr. Stanly related to me the substance of several interviews which he had had with the President respecting the Proclamation of Freedom. Mr. Stanly said that the President had stated to him that the proclamation had become a civil necessity to prevent the Radicals from openly embarrassing the government in the conduct of the war. The President expressed the belief that, without the proclamation for which they had been clamoring, the Radicals would take the extreme step in Congress of withholding supplies for carrying on the war — leaving the whole land in anarchy. Mr. Lincoln said that he had prayed the Almighty to save him from this necessity, adopting the very language of our Saviour, 'If it be possible, let this cup pass from me,' but the prayer had not been answered.[7]

Welling's testimony received corroboration from Lincoln himself. On July 28, 1862, the President wrote to Cuthbert Bullitt of New Orleans: "The truth is, that what is done and omitted about slaves is done and omitted on the same military necessity. It is a military necessity to have men and money; and we cannot get either, in sufficient numbers or amounts, if we keep from or drive from our lines slaves coming to them." Besides corroborating Welling's testimony, this is an admission of the well-known fact that fugitive slaves who came to the Union lines were driven back.

* * *

[7] *Reminiscences of Abraham Lincoln by Distinguished Men of His Time.* Collected and edited by Allen Thorndike Rice, Editor of *North American Review* (New York, 1886), p. 582.

Garrison was not altogether satisfied with the preliminary Proclamation. "The President can do nothing for *freedom* in a direct
manner," he wrote to his daughter, "but only by circumlocution
and delay. How prompt was his action against Frémont and
Hunter." He considered, however, that the President had taken
"an important step in the right direction." Phillips was more enthusiastic. "A step!" he exclaimed. "It's a stride!"

13

The President's reluctance to issue the Proclamation may have
been partly due to his Southern bias — which, as Professor J. G.
Randall has pointed out, was by no means negligible — but was
mainly the result of a sincere conviction that gradual rather than
immediate emancipation was better for both Negroes and whites.
In his Message to Congress of March 6, 1862, he said: "In my judgment, gradual and not sudden emancipation is better for all." Moreover, he wished to combine gradual emancipation with progressive
colonization of the colored people outside the United States.

How gradually did the President expect emancipation to take
place? In 1854 he had said: "I do not suppose that in the most peaceful way ultimate extinction would occur in less than one hundred
years at least." Since things were now far from peaceful, the President, in his Message to Congress of December 1, 1862, made the
following proposal to the slaveholders, above whose head hung the
threat of the final Emancipation Proclamation:

Any State that abolished slavery before January 1, 1900, was to
receive pecuniary aid from the Federal Government in the form
of interest-bearing bonds. "Said bonds to be delivered by installments, or in one parcel, at the completion of the abolishment,
accordingly as the same shall have been gradual, or at one time
within such State." He made it clear that he much preferred emancipation to be gradual: "The time spares both races from the evils
of sudden derangement; while most of those whose habitual course
of thought will be disturbed by the measure will have passed away
before its consummation. They will never see it." This, as he had
said on a previous occasion, would make emancipation descend upon
the slaveholders "gently as the dews of Heaven." But how about
the slaves? Assuredly they would not have minded having their
"habitual course of thought" disturbed by the prospect of freedom.

According to Frederick Douglass many thought of little else, and slaveholders often had to resort to the expedient of making their slaves drunk during their leisure time to keep them from running away. The President's assurance that as far as freedom was concerned "they would never see it," could not have been especially heartening to them. But, said the President, they would have "the inspiring assurance that their posterity shall be free forever." However inspiring that assurance might have been, it was somewhat uncertain, since the President's plan contained the following startling provision: "Any State having received bonds as aforesaid, and afterwards reintroducing or tolerating slavery therein, shall refund to the United States the bonds so received, or the value thereof, and all interest paid thereon."

The President made it clear that he did not expect emancipation to be completed before the year 1900: "The aggregate sum necessary for compensated emancipation of course would be large. But it would require no ready cash, not the bonds even, any faster than the emancipation progresses. This might not, and probably would not, close before the end of the thirty-seven years."

He then spoke of "the future of the freed people," saying: "I cannot make it better known than it already is that I strongly favor colonization." He said nothing about the practical aspect of the problem, merely informing Congress that "Liberia and Hayti are, as yet, the only countries to which colonists of African descent from here could go with certainty of being received and adopted as citizens." White workingmen need not fear that the freedmen would overrun the North: "Their old masters will give them wages . . . till new homes can be found for them in congenial climes and with people of their own blood and race. . . . And in any event, cannot the North decide for itself whether to receive them?" This may have been a hint to the North that laws forbidding the immigration of Southern Negroes would be welcomed as part of the Administration's reconstruction plan.

Considering all this, one can hardly blame Frederick Douglass for saying at the unveiling of the Freedmen's Monument: "It must be admitted, truth compels me to admit, even here in the presence of the monument we have erected to his memory, Abraham Lincoln was not, in the fullest sense of the word, either our man or our model. In his interests, in his associations, in his habits of thought, and in his prejudices, he was a white man."

14

Garrison had already expressed his opinion of the President's "compensated emancipation" and colonization plan when Lincoln had presented it to Congress on July 12 of that year in a more succinct form. He had called it "puerile, absurd, illogical and untimely." As for Phillips, he wanted to know who would cultivate the Southern plantations if the Union were to be restored on the basis of the land's remaining in the hands of the planters and the slaves' being progressively freed and deported. Assuredly there was little hope of inducing white labor to go South and work by the side of slaves. The slaveholders would undoubtedly exert pressure upon the Government to allow them to import hordes of coolies from China. "The nation that should shovel down the Alleghenies, and then build them up again, would be a wise nation compared with the one that should deport four million of blacks, and then import four million Chinese to take their places. To dig a hole and then fill it up again, to build a wall for the purpose of beating out your brains against it, would be Shakespearian wisdom compared with such an undertaking."

Lincoln never relinquished the hope of colonizing the Negroes outside the United States. His interview with Butler concerning colonization took place shortly before his death. In June 1863, when thousands of Negroes were already serving in the army and many had died for the Union, he sent Postmaster General Montgomery Blair to Concord, New Hampshire, to deliver a speech on colonization. On July 4, 1863, at Framingham, Massachusetts, Phillips, after presenting various proofs that Blair's speech was an Administration document, declared: "It is an attempt to foist the Dred Scott Decision upon the Proclamation of January 1st. The tone of the speech is this: The Negro is inferior to us. But we cannot conquer without him and after that, the country needs his labor. He must fight for us; he must work for us. When he has done it there is no place for him in the country. He must fight to make the nation safe; he must work to make it rich. When he has done so, we kick him out of the States. After using his blood and toil, we must colonize the whole race, and we whites will enjoy in solitary dignity the wealth and the peace that the Negro's strength has helped us to win. What an unutterably mean way to acquire title to a country! I know nothing like it but the claim of the New Zealand chief, who said, 'I have a clear title to this land, for I ate the former proprietor.'"

The colonization Lincoln advocated was to have been voluntary, but there can be no doubt that had his proposal been taken seriously compulsion would have been used. At the time of the colonization craze of 1831, the matter came up for discussion in the Virginia Legislature. During the debate Mr. Brodnax said: "How easy it is for a party to visit a Negro one night, take him from his bed and family, and apply to him the general admonition of a severe flagellation, to induce him to go away. . . . I have certainly heard . . . that all the large cargo of emigrants, lately transplanted to Liberia, all of whom professed to be willing to go, were rendered so by some such ministration as I have described. Indeed, sir, all of us look to force of some kind or other, direct or indirect, moral or physical, legal or illegal."[8]

15

There were those in Congress who believed that the President would find some pretext not to issue the final Emancipation Proclamation. Congressman Charles Sedgwick wrote to John M. Forbes: "Some doubt his intention to issue the proclamation of 1st January; I do not. Many assert, more fear, that it will be essentially modified from what is promised. I do not fear this; but what I do fear is, that he will stop with the proclamation and take no active and vigorous measures to insure its efficacy." Professor T. Harry Williams has written: "The pressure of the Jacobins upon Lincoln during the last week of December was terrific. The radical machine threatened to defeat all appropriations for war supplies if the president did not publish his edict. Lincoln was quoted as saying that he would have been superseded by a dictator had he refused to proclaim emanci-

[8] L. E. Chittenden, Registrar of the Treasury under Lincoln, relates, in his *Recollections of President Lincoln,* that the President at one time conceived the idea of moving all Negroes in the United States to Texas. He asked Chittenden if he "knew any energetic contractor" who would undertake their removal. Chittenden replied that he knew New England contractors who, "if there was a fair prospect of profit, would not hesitate to contract to suppress the Rebellion in ninety days," and recommended the Vermonter John Bradley. Bradley was summoned to the White House and had a two-hour interview with Lincoln, whom he assured that he would "undertake to remove them all within a year." This tends to indicate that Lincoln sometimes played with the idea of compulsory colonization.

pation." [9] The President again yielded and on January 1, 1863, the famous edict appeared.

A President who had prayed to the Almighty to save him from the necessity of issuing the Proclamation could hardly have been expected to be enthusiastic about it. No more uninspired document ever flowed from Lincoln's able pen. Professor J. G. Randall has written: "Limitations in the famous proclamation itself, with its definite lack of kingdom-come quality, produce a sense of amazement. . . . One could almost say that he did not like his most famous act." [10] Professor Richard Hofstadter: "The Proclamation of January 1, 1863, had all the moral grandeur of a bill of lading." [11]

There is reason to believe that Lincoln hoped and expected to be able to recall the document. The Proclamation was so worded that it did not actually free a single slave. Not only were the Border States exempted, but all such parts of Virginia and Louisiana as were occupied by Union troops. In the words of Lord Russell: "It does not more than profess to emancipate slaves where the United States authorities cannot make emancipation a reality, and emancipates no one where the decree can be carried into effect." Months after the President had issued the final Proclamation he continued to oppose immediate emancipation in the Border States by action of those States themselves. Missouri slaveholders were now willing to adopt compensated gradual emancipation, but what proved to be the majority of the people of that State wanted emancipation to be immediate. Lincoln threw all his influence on the side of the slaveholders. James Taussig of St. Louis, sent to reason with the President, had an interview with him on May 10, 1863, and reported as follows:

"The President said that the Union men in Missouri who are in favor of *gradual emancipation* represented his views better than those who are in favor of *immediate emancipation*. In explanation of his views on this subject, the President said that in his speeches he had frequently used as an illustration, the case of a man who had an excrescence on the back of his neck, the removal of which, *in one operation*, would result in the death of the patient, while 'tinkering off by degrees' would preserve life. . . . *The President an-*

[9] T. Harry Williams, *Lincoln and the Radicals*. (The University of Wisconsin Press, 1941.)

[10] J. G. Randall, *Lincoln and the South*. (Louisiana State University, Baton Rouge, 1946.)

[11] *Op. cit.*

nounced clearly that, as far as he was at present advised, the Radicals in Missouri had no right to consider themselves the exponents of his views on the subject of emancipation in that State." [12]

What reason could the President have had for opposing immediate emancipation in the Border States, by action of those States themselves, more than four months after he had supposedly freed the slaves in the rebel States? Only one reason suggests itself. In his interview with the Border State representatives, July 12, 1862, he said that had the loyal Border States adopted his March proposal for compensated gradual emancipation, "the war would now be substantially ended" — by which he meant that the rebel States would then have been willing to adopt that same form of emancipation and to make peace. He evidently still cherished that hope even though its fulfillment now involved the recall of the Emancipation Proclamation.

In his Message to Congress of December 7, 1863, the President was to say: "I may add, at this point, that while I remain in my present position, I shall not attempt to retract or modify the Emancipation Proclamation, nor shall I return to slavery any person who is free by the terms of that proclamation, or by any of the acts of Congress." The assurance was given because of a persistent rumor that he meant to do just that, and it was given only after it had become evident that the people of the Border States were in advance of their President and wanted immediate not gradual emancipation. Lincoln's opposition to immediate emancipation in those States, long after he had issued the Emancipation Proclamation, makes it difficult not to arrive at the conclusion that during a considerable part of 1863 he still hoped to trade retraction or modification of the Proclamation for cessation of the rebellion — hence meant to "return to slavery" those whom he had freed *de jure*, but not *de facto*. Be it noted that he did not propose the adoption of a Constitutional Amendment abolishing slavery until it had become evident that his "tinkering off" policy would be rejected by the people of the Border States. "I now perceive its importance and embrace it," he was to say of the Amendment to the Committee that came to notify him of his renomination. He had perceived its importance long ago and had even warned that the Supreme Court might declare emancipation by Presidential Proclamation unconstitutional, but it was

[12] Italics, Taussig's. The President's friend, Henry J. Raymond, Chairman of the Republican Party, declared Taussig's account to be "substantially correct."

obviously impossible for him to advocate continuation of slavery in the Border States and adoption of a Constitutional Amendment abolishing slavery at the same time.

Time came when the President was to acknowledge that the Emancipation Proclamation, which he issued with such extreme reluctance, and the employment of Negroes as soldiers, which he had opposed even more stubbornly, were of inestimable value to the war effort and, in fact, saved the North from defeat. On August 26, 1864, he wrote to James C. Conkling: "I know as fully as one can know the opinions of others that some of the commanders of our armies in the field, who have given us our most important victories, believe the Emancipation policy and the use of colored troops constitute the heaviest blows yet dealt to the Rebellion, and that at least one of those important successes could not have been achieved when it was but for the aid of black soldiers.

"Among the commanders who hold these views are some who have never had any affinity with what is called 'Abolitionism,' or with 'Republican party politics,' but who hold them purely as military opinions."

Henry J. Raymond, Chairman of the Republican Party, whom Lincoln was wont to call "my Lieutenant-General in politics," has given an account of an interview the President had in 1864 with "some prominent Western gentlemen." He quoted the President as saying: "You cannot conciliate the South if you guarantee them ultimate success, and the experience of the present war proves their success is inevitable if you fling the compulsory labor of four million black men into their side of the scale. . . . Abandon all the forts now garrisoned by black men, take two hundred thousand men from our side, and put them in the battlefield, or cornfield, against us, and we would be compelled to abandon the war in three weeks. . . . Will you give our enemies such military advantages as insure success and then depend upon coaxing, flattery and concession to get them back into the Union?" [13]

If Phillips had been privileged to listen in at the interview he would have been amused. The President was paraphrasing the criticism Phillips had leveled at him since the beginning of the war.

After Lincoln's death John F. Hume, St. Louis lawyer and editor who had been one of the leaders in the struggle against the pro-

[13] Henry J. Raymond: *The Life and Public Services of Abraham Lincoln.* New York, 1865, pp. 568–69.

slavery forces in his State, wrote: "If we take his official action from first to last, it is a question whether the President, owing to his extreme conservatism, was not more of an obstruction than a promoter of the Anti-Slavery cause. . . . If Mr. Lincoln had been told, when he entered on the Presidency, that before his term of office would expire he would be hailed as 'The Great Emancipator,' he would have treated the statement as equal to one of his own best jokes."

Garrison hailed the Emancipation Proclamation as "a great historic event, sublime in its magnitude, momentous and beneficent in its far-reaching consequences, and eminently just and right alike to the oppressor and the oppressed." Phillips, in touch with Congressional leaders and knowing what pressure and even threats had been required to overcome Presidential irresolution, said at Boston Music Hall: "God's hand has launched the nation on a voyage whose only port is Liberty. Neither the reluctance of the captain, nor the mutiny of the cabin-boys, will matter much. And this is why I, once a Disunionist, cling to the Union."

The Boston *Courier* gibed: "The Proclamation may lose us Kentucky, but it has given us Mr. Phillips. He will now doubtless take the field with a formidable army of twenty-five thousand adjectives."

CHAPTER II

Lincoln and Reconstruction

A FEW weeks after the appearance of the Emancipation Proclamation Phillips made a second visit to the White House. He
went as one of a committee composed of Dr. Samuel G. Howe,
George L. Stearns and others to ask for the removal of Edward
Stanly, Military Governor of North Carolina, who had ordered all
the colored schools recently established by Vincent Colyer and
others shut as "forbidden by the laws of the State"! [1] Senator Henry
Wilson of Massachusetts accompanied the committee, and they were
ushered into the Executive Chamber, from which Lincoln was
momentarily absent. A moment later he entered — tall, ungainly,
hirsute, — his lined face, his brooding eyes, suggesting a wild and
desolate autumn landscape.

The President was in a good humor, said with a chuckle that the
White House was in a "prolific" state: the cat had had kittens and
the dog, pups. Senator Wilson introduced the visitors. Lincoln
remarked he knew who the gentlemen were and bade them be
seated. He himself sat down in an armchair and crossed his legs,
displaying heavy wool hose.

Phillips expressed the joy he and his companions felt about the
Emancipation Proclamation, asked how it was working. "He [Lin-
coln] said that he doubted whether the Proclamation had not done
more harm than good; and this view he argued for some time

---

[1] "Mr. Colyer hurried on to Washington and called on Mr. Sumner, who
at once drove him to the President's. After hearing what had been done, Mr.
Lincoln excitedly exclaimed, 'Do you take me for a School-Committee-Man?'
'Not at all; I take you for President of the United States, and I come with a
case of wrong, in attending to which your predecessor, George Washington,
if alive might add to his renown.' In an instant Mr. Lincoln's tone changed, and
he heard the case patiently." C. Edward Lester, *Life and Public Services of
Charles Sumner.* (New York, 1874.) Colyer's interview with Lincoln took place
on June 2, 1862. In January, 1863, the schools were still closed.

pertinaciously," [2] he reported. To the President he said that in the opinion of many the Proclamation had been long overdue. Lincoln replied that he did not believe the country would have approved emancipation at an earlier date and bade him remember that he (Lincoln) had been elected by a minority of the people. "All I say now is that I believe the Proclamation has knocked the bottom out of slavery, though at no time I expected any sudden results from it. My own impression is that the masses of the country generally are only dissatisfied at our lack of military success. Defeat and failure make everything seem wrong."

He scanned for a moment the faces of his visitors, none of whom, he knew, altogether approved of him, then added: "Most of us here present have been long working in minorities and may have got into the habit of being dissatisfied."

Phillips made a polite remonstrance.

"At any rate," Lincoln resumed, "it has been very rare that an opportunity of 'running' this administration has been lost."

"If we see this administration earnestly working to free the country from slavery and its rebellion, we will show you how we can run it into another four years of power," Phillips assured him.

"Oh, Mr. Phillips," Lincoln said with a touch of weariness, "I have ceased to have any personal feeling or expectation in that matter — I do not say I never had any — so abused and so borne upon I have been."

"Nevertheless, what I have said is true," Phillips affirmed and then stated the object of the visit.

[2] George W. Julien, in an account of an interview with Lincoln shortly after emancipation, reported him as having said: "My proclamation was to have stirred the country; but it has done about as much harm as good." Professor J. G. Randall (*Lincoln and the South*, pp. 107–108) has written: "Inspirational aspects of the proclamation at the North — or in certain Northern circles — were tremendous. For the stirring of men's souls the war took on new meaning. Good people, Christians, humanitarians, hailed it with delight; their speeches, hosannas, and prayers had an effect upon home morale." James C. Welling, editor of the *National Intelligencer* wrote: "The anti-slavery passions of the North, which had hitherto been kicking in the traces, were now effectively yoked to the war chariot of the President. The proclamation lessened for a time the number of his supporters, but it gave to them almost the compactness of a Macedonian phalanx. It put an end to political vacillation and *atermoiement*." Compare also with Lincoln's statement to Gideon Welles, July 13, 1862, and his letter to James C. Conkling, August 26, 1864, quoted in previous chapter.

When he had finished Lincoln remarked: "Stanly can stand the Emancipation Proclamation."

"Stand it!" exclaimed one of the delegates. "Might the nation not expect in such a place a man who can not merely stand the President's policy, but rejoice in it?"

Lincoln appeared vexed. "Well, gentlemen," he said with a touch of impatience, "I have got the responsibility of this thing and must keep it."

"Yes, Mr. President," Phillips interposed, "but you must be patient with us, for if the ship goes down, it doesn't carry down you alone. We are all in it."

The argument seemed to mollify Lincoln. "Well, gentlemen, whom would you put in Stanly's place?" he queried.

Frémont was mentioned.

The President replied: "I have great respect for General Frémont, but the fact is that the pioneer in any movement is not generally the best man to carry that movement to a successful issue. It was so in old times, wasn't it? Moses began the emancipation of the Jews, but didn't take Israel to the Promised Land after all. He had to make way for Joshua to complete the work. It looks as if the first reformer of a thing has to meet such a hard opposition and gets so battered and bespattered that afterwards, when people find they have to accept this reform, they will accept it more easily from any other man."

Soon after Phillips rose to leave and his companions followed suit. Lincoln, too, had risen. Phillips thanked the President in the name of the committee for the kindly reception. Lincoln said he was happy to have met them and shook hands with each. As they were leaving he remarked: "I must bear this load which the country has entrusted to me as well as I can, and do my best."

2

To dispel prejudice against the employment of Negroes as soldiers, Phillips burnished up a lecture he had prepared some time before, dealing with the career of Toussaint Louverture, Liberator of St. Domingo, who with an army composed of Negroes and mulattoes had defeated a larger and better-equipped British force, compelling it to evacuate the island. Later his exploits against some of Napoleon's ablest generals and most seasoned troops aroused the admiration of the world. The lecture proved one of the most popular in Phillips's repertory. Many an American schooboy has since declaimed in elocution class the peroration, in which Toussaint is compared with some of the foremost leaders of the white race.

The President finally gave his consent for the recruiting of Negro volunteers, who, however, were to receive only half the pay of white soldiers. "It was not believed," Lincoln told Frederick Douglass, "that a negro could make a good soldier, as good a soldier as a white man, and hence it was thought that he should not have the same pay as a white man." However, in his message to Congress of December 7, 1863, he declared: "So far as tested, it is difficult to say they are not as good soldiers as any."

In the spring of 1863, two colored regiments — the Fifty-Fourth and Fifty-Fifth Massachusetts — went into training at Readville, near Boston. Garrison and Phillips were frequent visitors at the camp and often addressed the men, some three hundred of whom were fugitive slaves. Garrison had particular reason for being interested. His eldest son, George T. Garrison, had been offered a lieutenant's commission in the Fifty-Fifth and had accepted. Having impressed upon his children the desirability of independence of thought, Garrison took no offense at his son's rejection of the principles of non-resistance and wrote to him:

"Though I could have wished that you had been able understandingly and truly to adopt those principles of peace which are so sacred and divine to my soul, yet you will bear me witness that I have not laid a straw in your way to prevent your acting up to your highest convictions of duty; for nothing would be gained, but much lost, to have you violate these. . . . Personally, as my son, you will incur some risks at the hands of the rebels that others will not, if it is known that you are my son."

All those serving in colored regiments incurred extraordinary risk. Officers, when taken prisoner, were shot, soldiers were cruelly flogged and sold into slavery. At Fort Pillow, Tennessee, three hundred Negro prisoners and their white officers were savagely massacred by the Confederates under the command of General Nathan Bedford Forrest. The colored soldiers from Massachusetts, conscious of their worth and of the risk they were running, refused to accept any pay unless equal to that of white soldiers. Even when the Massachusetts Legislature offered to vote funds to make up the difference, they persisted in their refusal. In January, 1864, by decision of the Attorney General, they and other colored soldiers were awarded equal pay with white soldiers from the time of their enlistment.

Garrison and Phillips were guests of honor at the ceremony at the Readville camp when Governor John A. Andrew presented the State and national colors to the Fifty-Fourth, first to march off to war. There followed a review on Boston Common, after which the regiment marched through the city singing "John Brown's Body." Robert Gould Shaw, the youthful, fair-haired colonel, looked exceedingly handsome on horseback in the midst of his swarthy warriors. "As he rode at the head of his troops, the very flower of grace and chivalry, he seemed to me beautiful and awful as an angel of God come down to lead the host of freedom to victory," Whittier wrote to Mrs. Child. But ere two months had passed the Colonel and many of his men died in the assault on Fort Wagner.

Garrison was deeply moved as he watched the regiment march by, and his emotion became even greater when he noticed that he was standing on the corner of State Street and Wilson's Lane, where many years before he had been dragged on a rope by a mob. "How times have changed!" he must have thought. Yet two months later, when his son's regiment was to depart by boat for North Carolina, the review on the Common had to be abandoned for fear of a race riot. Draft riots raged in New York, where Copperhead mobs burned a Negro orphan asylum, sacked the Colored Sailors' Home, hanged Negroes on lampposts, attacked soldiers, looted, wrecked and burned scores of houses belonging to Negroes or to white men known to have favored emancipation. An attempt at a similar outbreak in Boston was suppressed with loss of life. So tense was the situation that Garrison thought it best to leave the house in Dix Place with his family until the excitement had subsided. The Fifty-Fifth Massachusetts marched to the wharf with muskets loaded. Rain fell as Garrison stood forlornly on the adjoining wharf, vainly trying to catch a glimpse of his son. "I have nothing but praise to give you that you have been faithful to your highest convictions, and, taking your life in your hands, are willing to lay it down, even like brave Col. Shaw and his associates, if need be, in the cause of freedom, and for the suppression of slavery and the rebellion," he wrote to him.

Readers of the *Liberator* could not help but notice that a change had come over the editor. He did not renounce nonresistance; but contributors who believed that, with war raging, nonresistance propaganda was particularly needful received space grudgingly, while letters from the front written by colored soldiers or their white officers were given prompt publication.

3

On December 7, 1863, President Lincoln read his Reconstruction Message to Congress. It was an overwhelmingly Republican Congress. In the Fall elections the party had more than recouped its losses of the previous year, having carried every Northern State except New Jersey. It was the Radical Republicans, critics of the Administration, who dominated the assembly. At their head was grim-faced Thaddeus Stevens, whose reconstruction program was almost identical with Phillips's, except that the Bostonian advocated from the beginning what Stevens arrived at by force of circumstances.

Unlike many of his Radical colleagues, who acted from political or selfish motives, Stevens genuinely believed in racial equality. All his life he had been a friend of the Negro. On his tombstone is this epitaph, composed by himself: "I repose in this quiet and secluded spot, not from any natural preference for solitude, but, finding other cemeteries limited by charter rules as to race, I have chosen this that I might illustrate in my death the principles which I advocated through a long life, Equality of Man before his Creator."

The victory at Gettysburg, the capture of Vicksburg, had brought the prospect of peace markedly nearer. The President hoped to bring it nearer still by offering exceedingly favorable terms to the rebels. Congress having enacted a bill confiscating the property of rebels and liberating their slaves, but leaving the power to pardon and to amnesty in the President's hands, he offered:

"A full pardon with restoration of property, except as to slaves," to all except certain categories of persons named in the Proclamation, provided they swore loyalty to the Constitution and promised to abide by Congressional enactments concerning slavery and by the Emancipation Proclamation, "so long and so far as not modified or declared void by decision of the Supreme Court."

If in any rebel State a number of legal voters not inferior to one tenth the number that had voted in the Presidential election of 1860 took the oath and established a State Government, it would be recognized as the true Government of that State. Former slaveholders were given the assurance that any provision the new State Governments found it necessary to make concerning the freedmen, "consistent . . . with their present condition as a laboring, landless and homeless class, will not be objected to by the National Executive."

The Message made no mention of a Constitutional Amendment abolishing slavery, although it was evident that the President entertained some doubt regarding the constitutionality of emancipation by any other means.

There could be no question regarding the generosity of the program as far as the former slaveholders were concerned, but to friends of the Negro it meant that the freedmen were to be turned over defenseless to the tender mercies of their former masters, with not even the self-interest that had operated under slavery to restrain the latter. To Republicans in general the program appeared appallingly reckless. What was to prevent the slaveholders from taking the oath of allegiance, joining forces with Northern Copperheads, regaining control of the Federal Government, repudiating the Union debt, assuming the Confederate debt and re-establishing slavery? The North had not sacrificed seven hundred thousand men and seven billion dollars to incur so formidable a risk. "Abraham's proclamation, take it altogether, was a silly performance," remarked Senator Fessenden. "Think of telling the rebels they may fight as long as they can, and take a pardon when they have had enough of it." Garrison wrote: "Mr. Lincoln's magnanimity is weakness, and his method of disposing of those who have been emancipated by his proclamation is that of giving the sheep over to the guardianship of wolves. This must not be tolerated."

4

In April, 1864, in a letter to Judge Stello, Phillips summed up his own reconstruction plan in these words: "The moment territory comes under our flag, reconstruct States thus: Confiscate and divide the land of rebels, extend the right of suffrage as broadly as possible to whites and blacks, let the Federal Constitution prohibit slavery throughout the Union, and forbid the States to make any distinction among their citizens on account of color or race."

His program was not only far in advance of Lincoln's, but left even Stevens far behind. Stevens did not declare himself in favor of suffrage for the freedmen until the rebel States, reconstructed by President Johnson in accordance with the plan of his predecessor,[3] had virtually restored slavery. Stevens considered suffrage of secondary importance to the freedman. "Forty acres of land and a hut would be more valuable to him than the immediate right to vote," he declared. His proposal to give land to the freedmen, which in the eyes of some historians has made him more culpable than Benedict Arnold, was made in a speech at Lancaster, Pennsylvania, in September, 1865. He proposed the following:

Seventy thousand of the chief rebels owned 394,000,000 acres of land out of a total of 465,000,000 acres in the Confederate States. If their holdings were confiscated, nine tenths of the people of the South would remain unaffected. Forty acres should be given to each adult freedman, which would dispose of 40,000,000 acres. The remaining 354,000,000 acres should be sold at an average price of $10 per acre and the $3,540,000,000 thus obtained applied mainly on the national debt, partly to pension those disabled by the war and to reimburse loyal men who had sustained property damage as a result of the hostilities. If one objected that it was inhuman to beggar seventy thousand planters, Stevens pointed to Lincoln's colonization proposal and said: "Far easier and more beneficial to exile seventy thousand proud, bloated and defiant rebels than to expatriate four million laborers, native to the soil and loyal to the government."

Phillips's land distribution plan did not differ greatly from Stevens's, except that he placed more emphasis on benefiting "the poor white, a non-slaveholder, deluded into rebellion for a system that crushes him," as well as the freedmen. Part of the confiscated acres he wished to reserve for Northern settlers: "Sell them with the guaranty of the government to the loyal Massachusetts man or New Yorker. Carry there your ploughshares, seeds, schools, sewing machines." His program aimed at rendering the leaders of the rebellion politically and economically impotent and at creating a large body of Southern voters loyal to the Union. A million landless whites and their families raised to the status of landowners by the invading Yankee could hardly have continued to regard them as their enemies. The Northern settlers were expected to introduce

---

[3] The principal and in fact the only important difference between Lincoln's and Johnson's reconstruction plan was that Johnson's required the majority of voters to swear allegiance to the Union instead of a mere 10 per cent.

better methods of agriculture and to help eliminate sectionalism. Phillips realized what few public men in the America of his time appear to have realized, that economic power was the foundation of political power — that if the land remained in the hands of the planter aristocracy, it would be only a question of time before they again ruled the South, even if the freedmen were given the vote. The rule of the planter class had proved disastrous to the people of the South, white as well as black, politically, economically and culturally. Phillips did not believe the war had changed them: "I do not believe in the efficacy of battle or a few cannon on the wrong side in changing the life-long opinions of men like Jefferson Davis and Wade Hampton. I believe, as all history shows, that adult men in the mass go to their graves with the opinions to which they have been wedded during most of their lives." Expropriation appeared to him the only guaranty against their return to power. A change so fundamental could, he believed, not be brought about in a hurry, hence he considered Lincoln's haste to restore the rebel States to their prewar status unstatesmanlike and premature. "We have," he said, "not only an army to conquer, which, being beaten, will not own it, but we have a state of mind to annihilate. . . . When England conquered the Highlands, she held them, — held them until she could educate them; and it took a generation. That is just what we have to do with the South; annihilate the old South, and put a new one there. You do not annihilate a thing by abolishing it. You must supply the vacancy."

5

Shortly after the President delivered his Message to Congress, Phillips spoke at Cooper Union, New York, to a large audience that frequently interrupted him with laughter and applause. The President's reconstruction plan, he said, was "neither wise, safe, nor feasible." But Lincoln was a man responsive to public opinion. "All honor to the growing man — all honor to the recipient intellect who loves to learn and to grow better. But how does he learn? Why did he grow? Because we watered him. Why did he advance? Because the nation pushed him on. I am here to ask you to persevere in the same effort. . . . If he were a leader, I would go to him, and not to you; should offer argument to his mind. But the President does not act simply from his own unbiased convictions. He bows to yours. He seeks to do your will. With all his merits (and they are great) with all his services (and they are momentous) the President is not a leader — never professed to be a leader. The President is the agent of public opinion. He waits to know what you will allow and what you demand that he shall do. His anxiety is North, in regard to your opinion, to know how much he may trust himself to ask.

"As commander-in-chief, he has freed slaves. I ask of the Nation to *abolish slavery*. As commander-in-chief he has done an act which the Supreme Court may reverse, and may set aside in part or wholly. Of the Nation I claim an amendment of the Constitution which that Court is sworn to obey, and in such plain terms as they cannot misconstrue.

"This nation owes the negro not merely freedom; it owes him land, and it owes him education also. It is a debt which will disgrace us before the peoples if we do not pay it. It is the first longing of the negro. His instincts are better than our laws. He knows what land means. . . . The negro has never heard of power except as associated with land, and the Confiscation Act is the jewel of Congressional policy. . . . Mr. Lincoln is anti-slavery. He does not believe in a nation being 'half slave and half free' — but he is a Colonizationist and does not believe in a nation half black and half white. Hence prejudice prevents him being fully just to the black race. . . . Give me the negro on his own soil, contented, protected, left the free use of his powers, and I will treble the cotton crop in two years."

The New York *World* commented: "Emancipation, abolition, confiscation, Southern land for landless Negroes! This is the programme. The *Tribune* will, as usual, wait six months and then follow Wendell Phillips's lead face foremost. The *Times* will wait about ten months, and then follow, as usual, back foremost."

6

Differences of opinion between Garrison and Phillips regarding the Administration's policy were becoming acute. Garrison was not uncritical of the President, but it was a benevolent criticism. "I would always rather err on the side of charitable judgment than of excessive condemnation," he was to say. The American Anti-

Slavery Society, of which he was President, and its official organ the *National Anti-Slavery Standard*, reflected his attitude; but in January, 1864, Phillips gained the upper hand in the Massachusetts Society.

The clash came as a result of a resolution offered by Phillips at the January meeting accusing the Administration of being "ready to sacrifice the interest and honor of the North to secure a sham peace, thereby risking the introduction into Congress of a strong Confederate minority to embarrass legislation, and leaving the freedmen and the Southern States under the control of the late slaveholders, embittered by their defeat in war, and entailing on the country intestine feuds for another dozen years."

That the President's reconstruction program would have the effect outlined in the resolution Garrison was willing to concede. He believed, however, that the President's proposal was an error of judgment, not a deliberate machination. "True he is open to criticism for his slowness, and needs spurring on to get more decisive action; but I am not willing to believe that he is 'ready to sacrifice the interest and honor of the North to secure a sham peace' with the rebels. That is a very grave charge." He offered an amendment substituting the words "is in danger of sacrificing" for "is ready to sacrifice."

Now, Phillips's Cooper Union speech, delivered only a few weeks earlier, made it appear as if he, too, believed in the President's good intentions. What was responsible for his change of mind? He must have reached the conclusion that Lincoln's reconstruction program was the logical result of his belief in Colonization. If it was the President's conviction that there was no room for the Negro in the United States and that ultimately he must be deported, what more natural than that he should be opposed to giving him a stake in the country? "There stands the black man," Phillips said, "naked, homeless; he does not own a handful of dust; he has no education; he has no roof to shelter him. You turn him out like the savage on the desert, to say to Europe, 'Behold our magnanimity!'"

Garrison's amendment was defeated. The importance the two Abolitionist leaders had now acquired may be judged from the fact that the clash between them was telegraphed all over the country and discussed in a multitude of newspapers and periodicals, some of which severely criticized Phillips. Garrison came loyally to his defense. "The honesty of his conviction is not to be impeached, while its soundness may be questioned without any personal feeling," he wrote.

7

Richard Henry Dana, visiting the National Capital in February and March, 1863, wrote: "As to the politics of Washington, the most striking thing is the absence of personal loyalty to the President. It does not exist. . . . If a Republican convention were to be held to-morrow, he would not get the vote of a State."

In the spring of 1864 a similar feeling prevailed. Senator Trumbull of Illinois wrote to a friend: "You would be surprised in talking with public men we meet here, to find how few when you come to get their real sentiments are for Mr. Lincoln's reëlection. There is distrust and fear that he is too undecided and inefficient ever to put down the rebellion." Congressman John B. Alley of Massachusetts wrote in 1886: "Many of the most distinguished men of the country, who were in daily intercourse with him, thought but little of his capacity as a statesman. And while entirely true, it is hardly to be believed, that those in both houses of Congress who knew him best had so little confidence in his judgment and ability to administer the government that very few of the members of the Senate and of the House were in favor of his renomination for President in 1864."

Garrison favored Lincoln's renomination, Phillips opposed it. The debate between them attracted international attention. In March, 1864, Garrison wrote in the *Liberator:* "The crisis is too solemn to justify heat or dogmatism, or even that personal preference or rivalry which, under other circumstances, would be allowable and attended with no danger. . . . Not that Mr. Lincoln is not open to criticism and censure; we have both criticized and censured him again and again. . . . Nevertheless, there is also much to rejoice over and be thankful for; and a thousand incidental errors and blunders are easily to be borne with on the part of him who, at one blow, severed the chains of three million three hundred thousand slaves — thus virtually abolishing the whole slave system."

At meetings of the American and Massachusetts Anti-Slavery Societies Phillips thus arraigned the Administration:

"My charge against the administration is that it seeks to adjourn the battle from cannon shot to the forum, from Grant to the Senate

House, and to leave the poisoned remnants of the slave system for a quarter of a century to come.

"I contend that the government has shown a willingness to let the white race and the black race remain, after the war, as nearly what they were before as possible. That is really the philosophy of the administration. What McClellan was on the battlefield — 'Do as little hurt as possible!' — that Lincoln is in civil affairs — 'Make as little change as possible!' Touch slavery the last thing; touch it as little as possible!"

The debate became increasingly personal and vehement. At a business meeting of the Massachusetts Society Phillips declared that he would sooner have "severed his right hand" than have taken Garrison's responsibility of recommending Lincoln's renomination. "There are no hundred men in this country," he said, "whose united voices would be of equal importance in determining the future of the Government and the country. A million dollars would have been a cheap purchase for the administration of the *Liberator's* article on the Presidency." Reconstruction on Lincoln's terms was, he said, "worse than disunion." To Sumner he wrote: "Lincoln is doing twice as much to-day to break the Union as Davis does. We are paying thousands of lives and millions of dollars as penalty for having a timid and ignorant President, all the more injurious because honest."

8

A political party that repudiated the man it had placed in the Presidential office condemned itself and risked apathy and defection. Only the emergence of a candidate who had captivated the popular imagination might have made it possible for the Republicans to dispense with Lincoln. No such candidate had emerged. Grant was only at the beginning of his success. Frémont had resigned in a dudgeon without any notable military achievement. The pompous Chase and the rakish Butler failed to evoke enthusiasm. "I hope we may not be compelled to push him [Lincoln] four years more," grumbled James Garfield, then a member of the House. Some favored postponing the National Convention until September in the hope that something might turn up enabling them to drop Lincoln; others spoke of getting him to withdraw voluntarily; but practical politicians became convinced that it would have to be Lincoln after all.

Congressman Owen Lovejoy, brother of the martyred editor, wrote to Garrison: "I am satisfied, as the old theologians used to say in regard to the world, that if he is not the best conceivable President, he is the best possible."

Phillips remained unconvinced. For the first time in his career he sought and obtained election as delegate to a political convention, so he might oppose Lincoln. He represented his Ward in the State Convention that was to nominate delegates to the National Convention in Baltimore. Notwithstanding his opposition the resolution endorsing the President carried by acclamation. But the convention was far from endorsing the President's policy or the make-up of his Cabinet.

In 1861, at Tremont Temple, Phillips had said of Lincoln: "A pawn on the political chess board, his value is in his position; with fair effort, we may soon change him for knight, bishop or queen." Which one of these three he considered Frémont to be in comparison with the "pawn" Lincoln we do not know. But it was the somewhat theatrical Pathfinder who was his choice for President.

On May 31, four hundred insurgent Republicans met in convention in Cleveland. Phillips did not attend, but sent a letter pledging his support and assailing Lincoln's reconstruction policy in these terms:

"To reconstruct the rebel States on that model is only continuing the war in the Senate chamber after we have closed it in the field. . . . Such reconstruction makes the freedom of the Negro a sham, and perpetuates slavery under a softer name. . . . The administration I regard as a civil and military failure, and its avowed policy ruinous to the North. Mr. Lincoln may wish the end — peace and freedom — but he is wholly unwilling to use the means which can secure that end."

The Cleveland Convention nominated Frémont, but the nomination was evidently mainly for the purpose of influencing the Baltimore Convention, for in his letter of acceptance Frémont expressed his willingness to step aside for anyone the Republicans might nominate "whose past life justified well-grounded confidence in his fidelity to our cardinal principles."

On June 7 the National Convention of the Republican Party (or National Union Party as it was to be called in that campaign) met in Baltimore. There were two rival delegations from Missouri, one of which was instructed for Grant; all other delegates were pledged to Lincoln. The vote on the question as to which delegation from Missouri was to be seated revealed to what extent Lincoln's nomination was to be a matter of expediency. The Missouri Conservatives, of whom the President had said in his interview with Taussig that they "represented his views better" and who had the endorsement of the Blair family, the President's most trusted advisers, received four votes; their opponents, the Missouri Radicals, instructed for Grant, four hundred and forty! After that no one was surprised that the speech of the President's "Lieutenant-General in politics," Henry J. Raymond, eulogizing the Administration's policy, was coldly received, while speeches advocating policies that were the exact opposite were frantically applauded. The platform adopted by the Convention repudiated the Administration's policy so decisively that acceptance of the nomination must have been embarrassing to the President. The olive branch he held out to the South (or, as Phillips claimed, to the planter oligarchy) was rudely thrust aside and unconditional surrender demanded. Dissatisfaction with the composition of his Cabinet was plainly expressed. Garrison, watching the proceedings from the gallery, wrote to his wife: "Even my friend Phillips would have been highly gratified with the tone and spirit of the Convention." Attorney General Bates, who although not impressed with the President's leadership [4] was loyal to his chief, felt aggrieved and wrote in his Diary: "It [the convention] did indeed nominate Mr. Lincoln, but in a manner and with attendant circumstances as if the object was to defeat their own nomination."

9

Theodore Tilton, poet, and editor of the *Independent*, the most widely read religious weekly in the country, thus described Garrison in the midst of the convention delegates: "All hats went off, all hands were thrust in welcome, and all hospitable honors shown — in the midst of which the bewildered man stood a modest and meek-minded conservative before those more fiery radicals on whom the new pentecost had fallen with its tongues of flame."

It was true. He whom a previous generation had called fanatic and incendiary was now considered a conservative. He had not changed,

[4] On December 31, 1861, Bates had written in his Diary: "The President is an excellent man, and in the main wise, but lacks *will* and *purpose*, and, I greatly fear, has not *the power to command*."

merely mellowed a little, but the world had moved. How conservative he was in comparison with Phillips may be judged from his reply to Professor Francis W. Newman of London, who had criticized the President for not enfranchising the Negroes of Louisiana: [5]

"If the freed blacks were admitted to the polls by Presidential fiat, I do not see any permanent advantage likely to be secured by it; for, submitted to as a necessity at the outset, as soon as the State was organized and left to manage its own affairs, the white population, with their superior intelligence, wealth, and power, would unquestionably alter the franchise in accordance with their prejudices, and exclude those thus summarily brought to the polls. Coercion would gain nothing. In other words — as in your own country, — universal suffrage will be hard to win and to hold without a general preparation of feeling and sentiment. But it will come, both at the South and with you; yet only by a struggle *on the part of the disfranchised*, and a growing conviction of its justice, 'in the good time coming.' "

Phillips's plan of providing an economic basis for popular rule in the South by dividing the land of the rebel aristocracy among freedmen and poor whites Garrison rejected as revolutionary.

10

Baltimore was full of haunting memories for the editor of the *Liberator*. Here he had lived for a while when a boy. Here his brother James had run off to sea. Here his mother had died. Here he and Lundy had published the *Genius*. Here he had had his prison experience. How the place had changed! "It has almost wholly grown out of my recollection. It is ahead of Boston in population and extent, but has not so many good residences and handsome stores," he wrote to his wife. In company with Tilton he visited the courtroom where so many years before he had been tried and convicted. The presiding judge, Hugh L. Bond, received him with open arms. He dug up the record of Garrison's trial. The paper had yellowed, the ink had faded. Eight or nine of the jurors were still liv-

---

[5] Lincoln had written to Michael Hahn, newly elected Governor of the reconstructed State: "I barely suggest for your private consideration whether some of the colored people may not be let in — as, for instance, the very intelligent, and especially those who have fought gallantly in our ranks . . . But this is only a suggestion — not to the public, but to you alone."

ing, Bond said. Should he summon them so they could make their apology? he asked with a wink. Garrison laughingly declined the offer, but said he should like to visit his old prison cell, on the walls of which he had inscribed some of his best sonnets. Ah! that was no longer possible. The old jail had been demolished and a new one erected in its place. Garrison appeared greatly disappointed.

Judge Bond had to go to Washington, and as that was Garrison's and Tilton's destination they went together "in the cars." It was Garrison's first visit to the National Capital. The unpaved streets, well-nigh impassable in spring and fall, swarmed with Negroes, soldiers, cavalrymen, carriages and convoy. Clouds of dust, whirled up by the wheels and horses' hoofs, enveloped the scene. Garrison wished to pay his respects to the President, and his two friends accompanied him. They were admitted to the Executive Chamber without difficulty and Lincoln seemed to be genuinely pleased with the visit of the famous Abolitionist. Judge Bond related how disappointed Garrison had been at being unable to visit his cell in the old Baltimore jail, and the President remarked: "So, Mr. Garrison, the difference between 1830 and 1864 appears to be this: in 1830 you could not get out, and in 1864 you could not get in." When they were leaving, Lincoln shook Garrison's hand heartily and asked him to call again on the morrow.

Senator Wilson had written to Garrison that if he visited the Capital he should not fail to call on Secretary Stanton, who had said, "there was one person whom he wished to see before he died, and that person is yourself." So Garrison went to the War Department and sent in his card to the Secretary. The bearded Stanton, brusque and irascible, seldom put people at their ease. The President himself was a little afraid of him. But to Garrison he was all amiability. They talked about Lundy, who had been his father's friend and to whom the elder Stanton had advanced the money with which to embark on his publishing venture. The Secretary related how when a small boy he had often sat on the little Quaker's knee.

Congress was in session. Garrison went to the Capitol and sent cards to Senators Sumner and Wilson. Both hastened to greet him, took him into the Senate chamber and conducted him to the seat of the absent Senator Hale. During a recess there was a veritable reception as senator after senator came to shake Garrison's hand. Senator Wilson made arrangements for Garrison and Tilton to stay at his hotel, which was fortunate, for hotels and boarding houses were crowded. That evening he entertained them at dinner. "Sumner and Wilson were exceedingly marked in their attentions," Garrison wrote to his wife.

The following day, accompanied by Tilton, he again went to the White House. The President was receiving a delegation from the Baltimore Convention, so Garrison seated himself at a desk and wrote a letter to Helen, in which he said: "I have no special desire to see him again, except that yesterday he expressed the hope that I would call again; for I know he must be bored with visitors." The visitors with whom Lincoln was particularly bored were office-seekers. Apparently he was not bored with Garrison, for he kept him over an hour. "Mr. Lincoln," Garrison said to him, "I want to tell you frankly that for every word that I have ever spoken in your favor, I have spoken ten in favor of General Frémont; but, Mr. President, from the hour that you issued the Emancipation Proclamation, and showed your purpose to stand by it, I have given you my hearty support and confidence."

Lincoln replied that the difficulties he had to contend with were very great and said he hoped the Constitutional Amendment abolishing slavery would pass. He confided to Garrison that the resolution voted by the Baltimore Convention favoring the Amendment had been prepared and introduced at his request. "There is no mistake about it in regard to Mr. Lincoln's desire to do all that he can see it right and possible for him to do to uproot slavery, and give fair-play to the emancipated," Garrison assured Helen in a letter from Philadelphia.

Tilton had remained silent during the interview. He had been opposed to Lincoln's renomination and still believed it to be a mistake. He was to join Horace Greeley and several other Republican editors in an effort to call a second National Convention, have the nomination annulled and select a new standard bearer.

That Garrison had made an excellent impression on the President became known among Republican politicians. J. M. Forbes [6] wrote to Garrison in January, 1865, asking that he use his influence with Lincoln to have Governor Andrew of Massachusetts appointed to a Cabinet post. "The President recognizes you as one of 'the Powers' — a Radical with a substratum of common sense and practical wisdom," he wrote. Garrison declined to mix into Cabinet making.

---

[6] New England industrialist and founder of The Loyal Publication Society, a pro-Union propaganda agency.

The only favor he ever asked of Lincoln was to pardon an army officer, whom he believed to be innocent. The pardon was promptly granted.

11

In the Summer of 1864 a feeling of profound discouragement settled over the North. The people were sick of war. They had lost faith in their leaders, civil and military. The government's credit was at its lowest ebb. Republican chances in the November election appeared hopeless. Lincoln himself did not expect to be re-elected. Many believed him to be principally responsible for the sorry state of affairs and considered him the party's greatest liability. Renewed efforts were made to get him to withdraw voluntarily. Some favored more forceful measures. Wade and Davis issued a manifesto against him and there was talk of impeaching him. Several Republican editors met at the house of David Dudley Field in New York to plan the calling of a second National Republican Convention that would select a new standard-bearer and force Lincoln to withdraw. "Mr. Lincoln is already beaten. He cannot be elected," Greeley wrote to George Opdyke. The editor of the New York *Tribune* favored a ticket composed of Grant, Butler or Sherman for President and Farragut for Vice President. Such a ticket, he thought, would enable the Republicans "to make a fight yet." Phillips was campaigning for Frémont. A party so divided could, it would seem, have no hope of success, but Bennett of the New York *Herald* was somewhat skeptical about Republican dissension. "Whatever they may say now," he wrote, "we venture to predict that Wade and his tail; and Bryant and his tail; and Wendell Phillips and his tail; and Weed, Barney, Chase and their tails; and Winter, Raymond, Opdyke and Forney who have no tails, will all make tracks for Old Abe's plantation, and will soon be found crowing and blowing, and vowing and writhing, and swearing and stumping."

He proved a good prophet. The Democrats were mainly responsible. At their National Convention in Chicago they nominated General McClellan on a platform written by Clement L. Vallandigham. The latter had been convicted of treason and sent into Confederate territory, but had boldly returned and was now the leader of the Northern Democrats. This was too much. Something had to be done and done quickly to unite the opposition. Zachariah Chandler went to see Lincoln. If he got Frémont to withdraw, would Lincoln promise to dismiss Montgomery Blair, *bête noire* of all the Radicals, from the Cabinet? The President agreed, whereupon Frémont withdrew, but not without declaring that Lincoln's administration "has been politically, militarily, and financially a failure, and that its necessary continuance is a cause of regret to the country."

Phillips fell into line, declaring: "Let me allow that he [Lincoln] is the only candidate in the field. As for the Confederate gunboat which anchored off Chicago, August 29, and invited McClellan to be the Captain, my only wish is it may soon meet her Kearsarge, and join her sister pirate Alabama in the ocean's depth."

In the meantime Lincoln's chances had vastly improved by Sherman's capture of Atlanta. Election day came and he won, but his popular majority of 411,428 votes was not impressive. Had all Southern States been reconstructed in accordance with his formula and allowed to participate in the election, the result might have been disastrous.

12

Richmond had fallen. The end of the war was near. Fort Sumter was again in Federal hands together with the city of Charleston. The Reverend Henry Ward Beecher, who understood the value of publicity, proposed to Secretary Stanton that on the fourth anniversary of the surrender of the Fort, Robert Anderson, now a Major General, should raise the self-same flag, which at the beginning of the war he had been forced to lower. There should be appropriate ceremony — music and speeches and flowers and cheering freedmen. And who more fitted to make the principal address than the famous pastor of Plymouth Church? Stanton fell in with the suggestion, made the necessary arrangements and invited some fourscore men of prominence to be the Government's guests. Among those invited were Garrison and his friend George Thompson, still in the United States.

The steamer *Arago,* chartered for the occasion, left New York harbor on April 8 with a distinguished company, including an Associate Justice of the Supreme Court of the United States, senators, congressmen, generals, famous divines and university professors. The principal metropolitan newspapers were represented, the Chicago

Tribune by its editor Henry M. Smith. Secretary Stanton, who had planned to go, was prevented by the press of official business.

Among the distinguished company aboard the *Arago*, Garrison was by no means the least distinguished. Many freedmen believed him principally responsible for emancipation. Hardly a freedmen's village but had its Garrison Street. In Louisiana and South Carolina several schools for colored children bore his name. In Kansas a military camp for colored soldiers had been named after the Abolitionist who still professed belief in nonresistance. But his fellow passengers on the *Arago*, with few exceptions, believed him to be behind the times. Nearly all favored suffrage for the freedmen and disagreed with Lincoln's policy of "mistaken leniency . . . to the leading actors in the horrible rebellion." Nearly all wanted no "concessions made in the reconstruction of the revolted States which would breed another explosion." Judge Joseph Holt, who had been a member of Buchanan's Cabinet, "was particularly emphatic on this point." [7]

Gaily colored pennants waved from rigging of warships and merchant vessels, cannon boomed and crowds of freedmen cheered as the *Arago* steamed into Charleston Harbor. News of Lee's surrender added to the gaiety of the occasion. The Charleston *Courier*, now in the hands of a Northern editor, had published a list of the distinguished visitors, with the result that the freedmen had come in droves to see Garrison and his friend Thompson, who had played so important a role in West Indian emancipation.

That evening there was a banquet at the Charleston Hotel at which several of the visitors spoke. In the course of his speech Garrison declared: "I am here in Charleston, South Carolina . . . I have never been her enemy, nor the enemy of the South. Nay, I have been the friend of the South, and, in the desire to save her from the great retribution, demanded in the name of the living God that every fetter should be broken, and the oppressed set free."

On the morning of April 15, Garrison, accompanied by Thompson, Tilton, Beecher and several others, went to the small cemetery opposite St. Philips's church to visit the tomb of Calhoun. On the marble slab covering the grave was chiseled, like a brusque challenge, CALHOUN — nothing more. Garrison laid his hand on the marble and said solemnly: "Down in a deeper grave than this slavery has gone and for it there is no resurrection."

[7] Garrison's letter to his wife, April 9, 1865.

While this scene was taking place in Charleston, in New York Major-General John A. Dix was reading this telegram from Secretary Stanton: "Abraham Lincoln died this morning at twenty-two minutes after seven o'clock."

The visitors knew nothing of this, nor did any one else in Charleston. A meeting had been scheduled that morning on Citadel Square, where a platform had been erected and an enormous crowd of freedmen had assembled. Garrison and his friends walked towards the square and had no sooner come in view of the crowd than a great shout went up. Stalwart Negroes lifted Garrison to their shoulders and carried him to the platform. When the cheering had subsided a freedman dressed in black, followed by two little girls in white who carried a wreath, stepped forward and addressed Garrison in these words:

"Sir, here you see stand before you your handiwork . . . I lost a dear wife, and after her death that little one [pointing to one of the girls], who is the counterpart of her mother's countenance, was taken from me. I appealed with all the love and reason of a father. The rejection came forth in these words: 'Annoy me not, or I will sell them off to another State.' I thank God that through your instrumentality, under the folds of that glorious flag which treason tried to triumph over, you have restored them to me. And I tell you it is not this heart alone, but there are mothers, there are fathers, there are sisters, and there are brothers, the pulsations of whose hearts are unimaginable. The greeting that they would give you, sir, it is almost impossible for me to express; but simply, sir, we welcome and look upon you as our saviour. We thank you for what you have done for us. Take this wreath from these children; and when you go home, never mind how faded they may be, preserve them, and keep them as a token of affection."

Garrison, almost too moved to speak, replied, in part:

"It is not on account of your complexion or race, as a people, that I espoused your cause, but because you were the children of a common Father, created in the same divine image, having the same inalienable rights, and as much entitled to liberty as the proudest slaveholder that ever walked the earth." He concluded with a statement which presaged a change of heart in his attitude towards suffrage for the freedmen: "While God gives me reason and strength I shall demand for you everything I claim for the whitest of the white in this country."

13

The Fifty-Fifth Massachusetts, in which Garrison's son was now a captain, was encamped three miles from Charleston. The regiment had been on an expedition into the interior, but returned before the departure of the *Arago*. As soon as Garrison learned of its return he hastened to the camp. After the reunion his son asked if he cared to say a few words to some twelve hundred Negro field hands the regiment had brought from the interior. They went together to the freedmen's camp and Garrison was shocked by their haggard and forlorn appearance. Hardly knowing what to say, he ventured: "Well, my friends, you are free at last, let us give three cheers for freedom!" He gave the first cheer. No response. The second and the third were received in the same manner. "They did not know how to cheer," Garrison was to comment.

Perhaps it was that, perhaps it was not. Perhaps freedom without a place to lay their heads, or a few acres of land on which to earn a living, seemed but a questionable blessing to the bewildered men and women. "When the Hebrews were emancipated," said Frederick Douglass, "they were told to take spoil from the Egyptians. When the serfs of Russia were emancipated, they were given three acres of ground upon which they could live and make a living. But not so when our slaves were emancipated. They were sent away empty-handed, without money, without friends and without a foot of land to stand upon. Old and young, sick and well, they were turned loose to the open sky, naked to their enemies."

"Their old masters will give them wages . . . and the freedmen in turn will gladly give their labor for the wages . . ." President Lincoln had predicted. What happened was that many of the old masters, in a calculated move to force the freedmen to work without wages, drove them off their plantations. "The Yankees freed you, now let the Yankees feed you," was their taunt. They expected that having experienced homelessness and starvation the freedmen would offer to work without pay. They miscalculated. The Negroes preferred to starve. Thousands died of hunger, disease and exposure. The Freedmen's Bureau, reviewing the situation in its report of October, 1869, stated that the death rate among the freedmen reached the appalling figure of 30 per cent.[8]

[8] W. E. Burghardt Du Bois, in *Souls of Black Folk* (New York, 1904), Chapter II, wrote "there was reason to believe" that four times as many Southern Negroes as Southern whites died as a result of the war and reconstruction.

CHAPTER III

Johnson and Reconstruction

GOD has graciously withheld him from any fatal misstep in the great advance, and withdrawn him at the moment when his star touched its zenith, and the nation needed a sterner hand for the work God gives it to do.

"No matter now that, unable to lead and form the nation, he was contented to be only its representative and mouthpiece; no matter that, with prejudices hanging about him, he groped his way very slowly and sometimes reluctantly forward: let us remember how patient he was of contradiction, how little obstinate in opinion, how willing, like Lord Bacon, 'to light his torch at every man's candle.' With the least possible personal hatred; with too little sectional bitterness, often forgetting justice in mercy; tender-hearted to any misery his own eyes saw; and in any deed which needed his actual sanction, if his sympathy had limits, — recollect he was human, and that he welcomed light more than most men, was more honest than his fellows, and with a truth to his own convictions such as few politicians achieve. With all his shortcomings, we point proudly to him as the natural growth of democratic institutions."

Such was Phillips's sober tribute to the fallen President, delivered in Tremont Temple, April 23, 1865. Lincoln had been opposed to vengeance and retribution; Phillips's declaration on that subject, made in the same speech, was not out of harmony with the views of the martyred President.

"The air is thick with threats of vengeance. I admire the motive which prompts these; but let us remember no cause, however infamous, was ever crushed by punishing its advocates and abettors, — all history proves this. There is no class of men base and coward enough, no matter what their views and purpose, to make the policy of vengeance successful. In bad causes, as well as good, it is still true that 'the blood of the martyrs is the seed of the Church.' We cannot prevail against this principle of human nature."

President Johnson took a different view of the matter. On April 3, 1865, after the fall of Richmond, in a speech delivered in Washington, he had demanded death by hanging for "influential" rebels:

"My notion is that treason must be made odious, and traitors must be punished and impoverished, their social power broken. They must be made to feel the penalty of their crime. . . . Hence I say this: 'The halter to intelligent, influential traitors.' But to the honest boy, to the deluded man who has been deceived into the rebel ranks, I would extend leniency; I would say return to your allegiance, renew your support to the Government, and become a good citizen; but the leaders I would hang."

After Lincoln's death, addressing a delegation from New Hampshire, he said:

"I know it is easy, gentlemen, for any one who is so disposed to acquire a reputation for clemency and mercy. But the public good imperatively requires a just discrimination in the exercise of these qualities . . . Arson and murder are crimes, the punishment of which is the loss of liberty and life. If then it is right in the sight of God to take away human life for such crimes . . . what punishment should be inflicted upon the assassins who have raised their daggers against the life of a nation, against the happiness and lives of thirty millions of people?"

These sentiments he reiterated so often and with such emphasis during the first few weeks of his term of office that even the uncompromising Benjamin F. Wade grew alarmed and entreated him to limit the number of executions "to a good round dozen and no more." Thaddeus Stevens, who as member of the Pennsylvania Legislature had opposed capital punishment, did not believe the rebel leaders could be convicted of treason under the laws then existing, and said he "would rather let every man of them run unpunished forever than to make a law now by which they could be punished."

2

Neither slavery nor involuntary servitude, except as punishment for crime, whereof the party shall have been fully convicted, shall exist within the United States, or any place subject to their jurisdiction.

Congress shall have the power to enforce this article by appropriate legislation.

So said the Thirteenth Amendment to the Constitution adopted by Congress in January, 1865, and submitted to the States for ratification. When ratified by three fourths of the States, did it signify the end of slavery in the United States or was further legislation imperatively required? Garrison held the first view, Phillips the second. The editor of the *Liberator* had abandoned his position regarding suffrage for the freedmen and now favored a Constitutional Amendment assuring suffrage to Negroes in every State of the Union. At the same time, however, he felt that since the ratification of the Thirteenth Amendment appeared certain, the object of the Anti-Slavery Society had been reached and the time had come for its dissolution. Phillips, on the other hand, felt about the Thirteenth Amendment not unlike Lincoln had felt about the Emancipation Proclamation. When Governor Edwin D. Morgan of New York had told him that most people believed the Proclamation had killed slavery, the President had replied: "I do not agree with those who say that slavery is dead. We are like whalers who have been long on chase — we have at last got the harpoon into the monster, but we must now look how we steer, or, with one 'flop' of his tail, he will send us all into eternity." When one considers that the Thirteenth Amendment was virtually nullified by the simple expedient of declaring vagrants all Negroes who failed to accept the planters' terms of employment, then one is forced to admit that the Anti-Slavery Society's task was not finished until the freedmen had been provided with some means of self-defense.

At the January meeting of the Massachusetts Society the two leaders had clashed. Both had tried not to give offense, but some of Phillips's followers had plainly intimated that Garrison had lost his usefulness as a leader and Phillips was now the standard bearer. Garrison replied with some asperity: "I cannot allow, because it is not true, that Mr. Phillips is more firmly anchored in anti-slavery principle than I am, or more inexorable in the application of that principle." He repudiated all claim to leadership and refused to acknowledge any man's right to call himself the leader of the Abolitionists. "Neither is he [Phillips] in advance, nor am I behind; neither does he lead, nor are the abolitionists led. We stand side by side, shoulder to shoulder, and march in a solid phalanx against the common foe — God alone being our leader."

His resolution to dissolve the Society having been defeated he had left the hall.

Phillips rose and said:

"Allow me, one word, which I utter with the greater pleasure and frankness because my friend Garrison has left the hall that there is nothing more unpleasant to me than any allusion to him and myself as antagonists. . . . In my experience of nigh thirty years, I have never met the anti-slavery man or woman, who had struck any effectual blow at the slave system in this country, whose action was not born out of the heart and conscience of Wm. Lloyd Garrison."

The decisive encounter took place after the death of President Lincoln, in May of that year, when the American Anti-Slavery Society held its annual meeting in New York. Garrison introduced a resolution calling for the dissolution of the national body. Phillips opposed him. The debate lasted two days. Colored leaders, including Frederick Douglass, sided with Phillips, who had the support of the younger delegates. The old guard remained loyal to Garrison. "We organized expressly for the abolition of slavery," Garrison argued; "we called our Society an Anti-Slavery Society. The other work was incidental. . . . Slavery being practically abolished . . . it seems to me that anti-slavery is, *ipso facto*, abolished also. It is an anomaly, a solecism, an absurdity, to maintain an anti-slavery society after slavery is killed."

Phillips replied that he would not abandon the Negro until absolute equality before the law and absolute civil equality had been achieved. Garrison rejoined that this could be done better by mingling "with the millions of our fellow countrymen in one common effort to establish liberty and justice for all."

When Garrison's resolution was put to a vote it was defeated by a vote of 118 to 48. He rose and said:

"I thank you, beloved friends, who have for so many years done me the honor to make me the President of the American Anti-Slavery Society. I never should have accepted that post if it had been a popular one. I took it because it was unpopular; because we, as a body, were everywhere denounced, proscribed, outlawed. To-day, it is popular to be President of the American Anti-Slavery Society. Hence, my connection with it terminates here and now, both as a member and its presiding officer. I bid you an affectionate adieu."

The nominating committee nevertheless reported his name for re-election. He declined the honor and Phillips was elected in his place.

3

When, following his resignation as President of the national body, Garrison withdrew from the Massachusetts and New England Societies, Phillips reproached him with abandoning the cause. Garrison resented the reproach and friendly intercourse between the two households ceased. "We don't see any of them, for they feel very unkindly towards us," Ann Phillips wrote to Henry C. Wright. Members of the Executive Committee and the editors of the *National Anti-Slavery Standard*, who had withdrawn together with Garrison, were voted a resolution of thanks so coldly worded that they returned it with caustic comment. Thomas Wentworth Higginson, seeing Edmund Quincy deliberately turn his back on Phillips in the lobby of the Ticknor Building, remarked: "It seemed to me the saddest thing I ever saw."

Emerson did not believe Phillips responsible for the ill-feeling. "How handsomely Mr. Phillips has behaved in his controversy with Mr. Garrison. In fact, Phillips was the same as we have always known him," he wrote. Certain it is that Phillips felt heartbroken about the turn of events. Once, when visiting Elizabeth Buffum Chace, daughter of the intrepid Quaker hatter who had been one of the founders of the society, he remarked bitterly: "Oh, I don't think there is much satisfaction to be gotten out of life."

"Thee should not say so," the Quaker woman admonished.

Tears glistened in his eyes as he said: "Half the men I worked with for thirty years will not speak to me when I meet them in the street."

Mrs. Chace's thoughts went back to the time when the Friends in solemn meeting had "disowned" her father and she said with a sigh: "That is hard, I know."

The gulf between Garrison and Phillips was destined to widen. Together with several others they served as trustees of a fund willed to the antislavery cause by Francis Jackson. When in 1868 the money became available, Garrison felt it should be devoted to freedmen's education. The majority of the trustees, including Phillips, felt it should be used to pay debts the *National Anti-Slavery*

Standard had incurred fighting for freedmen's rights. A compromise was reached, but Garrison changed his mind and the case came before the Supreme Court of Massachusetts, which decided against Phillips and his friends. In an article in the *Standard* and in private correspondence Phillips criticized the court's decision and Garrison's stand in the matter. His former friend wrote to Dr. Bowditch: "I was prepared for anything in the shape of contumacy on the part of Phillips, against the decree of the Supreme Court in regard to that bequest, because of his bitter Aspersions in the *Anti-Slavery Standard* of such of the Trustees as do not agree with his opinion."

By 1871 the breach was far from healed, but that year we find Garrison taking up the cudgels for his old friend against the latter's namesake in the Garrison family. He reminded the young man of Phillips's generosity towards the household "for more than a quarter of a century" and wrote: "Of your own indebtedness to him in the matter of your collegiate education I need not speak. Whatever you have derived, or may hereafter derive from that education, you owe to him. It was not in my power, pecuniarily, to give it to you."

4

Garrison had decided to discontinue the *Liberator* at the end of 1865 — after thirty-five years of uninterrupted publication. The paper had not benefited from the war. "To this day," the editor wrote in his valedictory, " — such is the force of prejudice — there are multitudes who cannot be induced to read a single number of it, even on the score of curiosity, though their views on the slavery question are now precisely those which it had uniformly advocated." It may well be, however, that the multitudes of followers of Phillips and Stevens now found the paper sadly behind the times. Whatever the reason, the paper still failed to pay expenses, and those who in the past had always generously come to its succor had either died or, like Phillips, were no longer interested. So, one day in December, 1865, there were gathered in the *Liberator* printing office Garrison, two of his sons, the printer and the printer's assistant. The last number of the paper was to be got ready for the press. Garrison made up the two outside pages from the galleys. Less than a column was reserved for his valedictory. He sat down to write it, handing it by installments to the printer. The last paragraph he himself put into type. Evening was falling as he stepped

to the worn composing stone, bought in the days of poor Isaac
Knapp, lifted the paragraph from the composing stick and dropped
it into the vacant space. The printer locked the form. The *Liberator*
had ceased to exist.

5

Senator Doolittle of Wisconsin, who eloquently defended the
new President against the charge of being an habitual drunkard
(he had appeared at Lincoln's second inaugural obviously under
the influence of alcohol) said at the beginning of Johnson's Administration that the difference between Lincoln's reconstruction policy
and Johnson's would be mainly that "Mr. Lincoln would have dealt
with the rebels as an indulgent father deals with erring children.
Mr. Johnson will deal with them more like a stern and incorruptible
judge. Thus in a moment the sceptre of power has passed from a
hand of flesh to a hand of iron." Somewhat worried about the President's vengeful pronouncements he added: "To Mr. Johnson I
would say while administering justice, remember mercy."

Johnson, the son of North Carolina poor whites, whom his wife
had taught to read and write, had hated and envied the planter class.
When Lincoln issued the Emancipation Proclamation, Johnson had
declared that "the emancipation of the slaves will break down an
odious and dangerous aristocracy," and "free more whites than
blacks in Tennessee." When Military Governor of Tennessee, he
had reviewed a procession of colored people at Nashville, had
promised to be their "Moses," had cried: "Remember, they who
would be free themselves must strike the blow!" and had declared
that "the great plantations must be seized and divided into small
farms and sold to honest industrious men." But Secretary Seward
had since taken him in hand, and Southern women of the planter
class, noting his monumental vanity and susceptibility to flattery,
had exercised their blandishments upon him. The results were phenomenal. Barely six weeks after his inauguration the fire-eating
"Jacobin" was referred to by the former slaveholders as the "good
President" and had promulgated a reconstruction plan differing so
little from that of his predecessor that in Congressional debates
Doolittle and others habitually were to refer to it as "the Lincoln-
Johnson reconstruction plan." Those who had interpreted Johnson's
declaration that "intelligent, influential traitors . . . must be pun-

ished and impoverished, their social power broken" to mean that the wealthy planters would lose their land and their civil rights, and would be lucky if they did not receive "the halter," were sadly disappointed. As for giving the freedmen the vote, Johnson made it plain that he had no such intention. "The question comes up," he said to a delegation of prominent Negroes, "whether those two races, situated as they were before, without preparation, without time for passion and excitement to be appeased, and without the slightest improvement, whether the one should be turned loose upon the other at the ballot box with this enmity and hate existing between them. The question comes up right here whether we do or do not commence a war of races."

As in his address to the delegation Johnson had referred to the hostility of the former slaves towards the poor white people of the South, Frederick Douglass wrote to him: "The hostility between the [poor] whites and blacks of the South is easily explained. It has its roots and sap in the relation of slavery and was incited on both sides by the cunning of the slave masters. Those masters secured their ascendancy over both the poor whites and blacks by putting enmity between them. They divided both to conquer each. . . . Slavery is abolished. The cause of this antagonism is removed."

Douglass was right in believing that relations between poor whites and Negroes were capable of improvement. During Congressional reconstruction the two classes collaborated harmoniously for a while. Claude G. Bowers, who waxes almost lyrical when extolling the virtues of Ku Klux Klan and Red Shirt leaders, indignantly tells of such reconstruction outrages as poor whites and Negroes drinking whisky out of the same bottle and white women playing the piano for the entertainment of Negro sisters. But Douglass was wrong in thinking that emancipation had destroyed the incentive of the planters to sow discord between poor whites and Negroes. On the contrary, that incentive had vastly increased. If the freedmen were given the vote and made common cause with the poor whites against the class that had oppressed and exploited both, the planters would suffer a reverse far more serious than that inflicted upon them by Northern armies.

The fact, however, was that except for Phillips, Sumner and their Abolitionist following, no one, not even Thaddeus Stevens, seriously contemplated giving suffrage to the freedmen. Not until the former rebels had practically restored slavery and had rejected the

Fourteenth Amendment — which conferred citizenship, but not suffrage, upon the Negro — did Republican leaders decide to give the freedmen the vote.

6

The former slaveholders hastened to take advantage of the opportunity the "good President" had given them. They took the oath of fealty to the Union. Their influence and experience enabled them to dominate the Constitutional Conventions that met in the rebel States and to gain control of the new State Governments. Then, with the eyes of the nation upon them, with the sword of Damocles still hanging above their heads, they did not hesitate to adopt Black Codes that restored most of the worst features of chattel slavery.

That prompt and vigorous action was necessary if the South were not to suffer complete economic collapse admits of no doubt. The freedmen had expected that land would be given them. They had a right to expect it. If not "forty acres and a mule," then at least five acres and a goat. "Confiscation is mere naked justice to the former slave," said Phillips. "Who brought the land into cultivation? Whose sweat and toil are mixed with it forever? Who cleared those forests? Who made the roads? Whose hand raised those houses? Whose wages are invested in those warehouses and towns? Of course the negro's. . . . Why should he not have a share of his inheritance?" In the Sea Islands, where General Sherman had practically divided the land among the freedmen, they went to work with a will; elsewhere, however, they exhibited little inclination to work. Who could blame them? To work for their former masters the marks of whose whips and branding irons they carried upon their bodies, who had robbed them of the fruit of their labor, had bought and sold them like cattle, had passed laws forbidding them to learn to read and write, own a bit of property or testify against a white man, no matter how brutally treated, who at the conclusion of hostilities had driven them out to starve — not if they could help it! And had they not been told that these masters were rebels and traitors? Surely the victors would not allow them to keep the land. Surely it was only a question of time before the land would be divided. In some cases they took the law into their own hands, drove away the planter and his family and divided the plantation.

Following the slave uprising in San Domingo towards the end of the eighteenth century, the Negro leader Toussaint Louverture had been confronted with an almost identical situation. The freedmen refused to work for their former masters. They expected them to be banished and their land to be divided. Toussaint realized that if the Negro population was to remain free it must be prepared to repel invasion. For this vast quantities of war material were necessary, obtainable only by the sale of export crops. The cultivation of such crops required large plantations under expert management. So, far from expelling the planters and plantation managers who had remained, he recalled many that had fled, guaranteeing them protection and a fair share of the profits. At the same time he issued an edict ordering the freedmen to resume work. They not only obeyed, but did so well that Pamphile de Lacroix, chief of staff of Napoleon's invading army, was to note with astonishment that output per laborer had more than doubled since emancipation.

What was the reason for this phenomenal success?

When Toussaint issued his edict against vagrancy he at the same time decreed that the freedmen should receive one-fourth of the value of the crop. Elaborate measures were taken so they would not be cheated. He forbade even verbal abuse of a laborer, established schools, had the children of the poor (white as well as black) reared at public expense, made surprise visits to plantations and took various other measures which left no doubt in the minds of the Negroes that he had their welfare at heart. Abuses crept in nevertheless, yet on the whole the system worked so well that he was able to arm and train practically the entire Negro population without endangering peace and order. He had only one small uprising to contend with, instigated by an ambitious Negro general who promised banishment of the planters and distribution of the land. The uprising was quickly suppressed, without white intervention.

The Southern planters, like Toussaint, passed laws against vagrancy, but while his were intended to promote the general welfare, theirs were designed to enrich the planters at the expense of the freedmen. While he took almost exaggerated precautions so the Negroes would receive their rightful share, the Southern planters left nothing undone to facilitate extortion and oppression. The Black Code of Alabama, typical of all such enactments under Presidential reconstruction, contained the following provisions:

Officers of the law were required to report to the probate courts all Negroes of less than eighteen whose parents lacked the means or inclination to support them. The courts were required to apprentice such Negro minors to masters until they became of age, the former owner being given the preference. Any one giving food, clothing or shelter to a fugitive Negro apprentice was criminally and civilly liable. Since the wages offered by the planters were twenty-five cents a day, with an allowance of a peck of corn-meal and four pounds of bacon a week, and frequently not even that, there was hardly a Negro who could not be deprived of his children on the pretense that he was unable to support them.

All Negroes over eighteen having "no lawful employment or business" were considered vagrants, subject to arrest and heavy fine. When arrested they were "hired out," preferably to the former master, to "work off" the fine. When the fine was "worked off" and they refused to continue working on the master's own terms the process was repeated.

All "persons of color" making contracts for labor were to be known as "servants" and the employers as "masters."

An act relating to the employment of freedmen provided a series of "forfeitures of rights for violation of contract" which made it virtually optional with the master whether the servant should receive any wages whatever. If the planter declared before a justice-of-the-peace that the servant was "stubborn or refractory" or that he "loitered away his time," the latter was declared a vagrant, fined and turned over to the employer to "work off" the fine.

The Legislature of Louisiana passed a bill providing that "every adult freed man or woman shall furnish themselves with a comfortable home and visible means of support within twenty days after the passage of this act," and that "any freed man or woman failing to obtain a home and support as thus provided shall be immediately arrested . . . and hired out, by public advertisement, to some citizen, being the highest bidder, for the remainder of the year." If the laborer left the employer's service without the latter's consent "he shall be arrested and assigned to labor on some public works without compensation until his employer reclaims him."

In Florida violation of a labor contract by the employer rendered him civilly liable, which in practice meant not liable at all; violation of a labor contract by a Negro was punishable with the pillory, with thirty-nine lashes across the bare back, or with a year's forced labor, at the option of the court.

To engage in any pursuit except the most menial a "person of color" had to pay a prohibitory license fee. No such fee was required of white persons or had been required of free Negroes in slavery days.

Historians, who wax indignant about unjust taxation imposed upon Southern property owners by carpetbaggers under Congressional reconstruction, are strangely silent about the disproportionate share of the tax burden imposed upon the penniless freedmen under Presidential reconstruction by means of the poll tax. Notwithstanding the destruction caused by the war, the taxable property in the State of Georgia was estimated at a quarter of a billion dollars the first year of peace. That same year the total State tax was $350,000. Of this the freedmen, who owned no property worth mentioning, paid about one fourth. If a freedman failed to pay, he was arrested, fined and "hired out" to work off tax, fine and costs, amounting to about a month's unpaid labor.

Garrison's charge, when President Lincoln first presented his reconstruction plan, that he was giving "the sheep over to the guardianship of wolves" appears to have been fully justified. James A. Garfield exclaimed on the floor of Congress that the freedom given the Negro was "a bitter mockery, a cruel delusion, and it may well be questioned whether slavery were not better." Indeed, instead of being owned by individual planters, the Negroes — those who formerly had been free as well as the freedmen — were now, to all intents and purposes, the property of the State. The planters could drive them to the limit of endurance without fear of personal loss and were relieved of all individual responsibility for the superannuated and incapacitated. Beating Negroes to death became common and was never punished. The Freedmen's Bureau was to report: "At times one was inclined to believe that the whole white population was engaged in a war of extermination against the blacks." It was as if the South meant to avenge its defeat upon the hapless Negro. In a list of grievances submitted to Congress the Bureau charged that the Black Codes "actually served to secure to the former slaveholding class the unpaid labor which they had been accustomed to enjoy before the war." These codes were passed soon after the surrender of the Southern armies, long before carpetbaggers had been heard of. They were passed while the rebel States were on their good behavior, with the victorious North jealously watching them. Was it any wonder that Republicans who had been averse to giving the freedmen the right of suffrage changed their minds about the matter? The freedmen were given the vote not merely so they might protect themselves, but so they might shield the nation from a dangerous coalition of unregenerate rebels and Northern Copperheads.

Ulysses S. Grant, in his *Personal Memoirs,* was to sum up the situation in these words: "There being a solid South on one side that was in accord with the political party in the North which had sympathized with the rebellion, it finally, in the judgment of Congress and of the majority of the legislatures of the States, became necessary to enfranchise the negro in all his ignorance. I shall not discuss the question of how far the policy of Congress proved a wise one. It became an absolute necessity, however, because of the foolhardiness of the President [Johnson] and the blindness of the Southern people to their own interest."

7

Charles Sumner in the Senate, Thaddeus Stevens in the House, Wendell Phillips from the lecture platform and in the *National Anti-Slavery Standard,* opened fire on Presidential reconstruction. Phillips was by no means the least formidable. "Mr. Wendell Phillips is perhaps a little ahead of his party, but they are traveling the same path and making for the same goal. Where Mr. Phillips stood a few months ago, the Radicals stand to-day; where he stands to-day they will doubtless be a few months hence. He is apparently the pilot fish of the political sharks," declared the New York *Daily News.* Never had his influence been greater. His lecture engagements were filled months in advance. His speeches and his editorials in the *Standard* were quoted and discussed in hundreds of newspapers. He kept in close touch with Congressional leaders. Office seekers importuned him. "What does Phillips say?" became an anxious inquiry among politicians. Having no personal ax to grind he lashed Congress and the Republican Party when he believed them to be at fault as well as the President and his Cabinet. He spoke of the "dawdling" or "swindling" Congress that "may be bought, bullied or deceived," and scoffed at its "truck and bicker policy." He reminded the Republican Party's "milk and water statesmen," that "this is not a game of jackstraws, but a war." The New York *World* declared: "Wendell Phillips does not dislike the Republican party, for it is his creature; but the Republican party dislikes Phillips, for he is its master. He whips up the host. The bummers are exasperated by the bugle call which summons them up and urges them onward." The editor of the St. Louis *Daily Dispatch* was moved to write: "Wendell Phillips has exercised a greater influence on the destinies of the country as a private man than any public man or men of his age."

He gloried in the combat. "I have great delight in taming animals. Rarey is a hero of mine," he said on one occasion.[1] The animal he apparently sought to tame, and succeeded in rendering innocuous, was Andrew Johnson, upon whom he showered an extraordinary variety of invective, calling him "Jefferson Davis Johnson," "Mobocrat of the White House," "Traitor President," "Tipsy Mountebank," "Vagabond Brawler," "Pardoner of Murderers," "Drunken Nightmare" and other names. The problem confronting the country he summed up in these words:

"The Rebellion has not ceased, it has only changed its weapons. Once it fought, now it intrigues; once it followed Lee in arms, now it follows President Johnson in guile and chicanery; once its headquarters were in Richmond, now it encamps in the White House."

He would have no half-measures:

"What I say to the American people is that we want absolute control over the Southern territory until the seeds are planted. I want the nineteenth century carried down there. Our effort should be to infect the South with the North, — the North of education and equality, — the North of toleration and self-respecting labor, — the North of books and brains. If the South had conquered us, she would have called the roll of her slaves on Bunker Hill and put her flag over Faneuil Hall. Our victory means, ought to mean, Bunker Hill in the Carolinas and Faneuil Hall in New Orleans.

"Better a renewal of the war than a surrender of the negro to the control of his old master. The real basis of reconstruction should be to concentrate all power exclusively in the hands of our friends — the loyal white man and the negro.

"A thousand men rule the rebellion — are the rebellion. . . . Banish every one of these thousand rebel leaders — every one of them, on pain of death if they ever return! Confiscate every dollar

[1] Rarey was the famous horse trainer with whom he had struck up a friendship when a young man.

and acre they own. These steps the world and their followers will see are necessary to kill the seeds of caste, dangerous States rights and secession. Banish Lee with the rest. No government should ask of the South which he has wasted, or of the North which he has murdered, such superabundant Christian patience as to tolerate in our streets the presence of a wretch whose hand upheld Libby Prison and Andersonville, and whose soul is black with sixty-four thousand deaths of prisoners by starvation and torture."

The Abolitionists, he claimed, had from the beginning been the true friends of the South:

"There have never been any friends of the Southerner in the Northern States but the Abolitionists. The Democrats deluded him; the Whigs cheated him; the Abolitionists stood on his border and said: 'It is in vain for you to fight against the thick bosses of Jehovah's buckler. You are endeavoring to sustain a system that repudiates the laws of God and the spirit of the nineteenth century. Put it away, or you will make blood and bankruptcy your guests.' But the maddened South closed its eyes and rushed on to destruction. Now we say, 'Come into line with the age, found your economy on righteousness, and then spindles will make vocal every stream and fill every valley.' "

8

President Johnson rightly regarded Phillips as one of his three most formidable opponents. On February 22, 1866, he said in a public address: "Suppose I should name to you those whom I look upon as being opposed to the fundamental principles of this government, and as now laboring to destroy them. I say Thaddeus Stevens, of Pennsylvania; I say Charles Sumner of Massachusetts; I say Wendell Phillips of Massachusetts." Realizing that they were rapidly converting the North to their viewpoint, he arranged, in the summer of 1866, a pilgrimage to the tomb of Stephen A. Douglas, combined with a "swinging round the circle" during which he meant to tell the Administration's side of the story. According to Lincoln's favorite humorist, Petroleum V. Nasby, the tour was undertaken "to arouse the people to the danger of concentrating power in the hands of Congress instead of diffusing it through one man." Seward and several other members of the Cabinet, as well as the popular heroes Grant and Farragut, were to accompany him. "In order to attract attention," Thaddeus Stevens remarked, "they took with them . . . a celebrated general; they took with them an eminent naval officer, and they chained him to the rigging so that he could not get away, though he tried to do so once or twice."

Never did a Presidential party receive a more hostile reception; never did a President behave with less regard for the dignity of his office. "I care nothing for dignity!" Johnson was to exclaim, and proved so faithful to that pronouncement that his friend and apologist Henry J. Raymond commented sorrowfully in the New York *Times:* "No matter what the people might have thought of the President's principles, they were startled and bewildered by the manner in which he advocated them." Others claimed that on several occasions he was under the influence of alcohol — though, considering the nature of the reception and his usual lack of self-control, irascibility and injured vanity were a sufficient explanation. The Governors of Pennsylvania, Ohio, Michigan, Indiana, Illinois and Missouri, through whose States he traveled, ignored him. Municipal officers of Baltimore, Philadelphia, Cincinnati, Indianapolis and Pittsburgh extended no official greeting. "The city is perfectly bare and destitute of adornment," the Philadelphia correspondent of the New York *Tribune* wired to his paper. The Union League Club took down the flag it habitually displayed. In Ohio, town after town greeted Johnson with groans and catcalls and shouted for Grant to show himself. In Cleveland, where he spoke from the balcony of the Kennard Hotel, a stone was hurled just before his appearance and he was constantly interrupted. In St. Louis hecklers disputed every statement he made.[2] In Indianapolis, where he attempted to speak from the balcony of the Bates House, the crowd grew menacing, howled for Grant, and when Johnson tried to speak, shouted: "We don't want to hear from you, Johnson! Shut up!"

A Lincoln or a Phillips might have weathered the ordeal without damage to his dignity or good humor. Johnson, however, lost his temper, exchanged epithets with the hecklers, "brought down the Presidency to the level of a grog house." In Cleveland he shouted: "Why not hang Thad Stevens and Wendell Phillips? . . .

---

[2] In the course of his St. Louis speech (September 8, 1866) Johnson said: "I have been called Judas Iscariot and all that. . . . If I have played the Judas, who has been my Christ that I have played the Judas with? Was it Thad Stevens? Was it Wendell Phillips? Was it Charles Sumner?"

He who is opposed to the restoration of this government and the reunion of the States, is as great a traitor as Jefferson Davis or Wendell Phillips!"

Times had changed. Not so many years before Phillips would have been mobbed in Cleveland, now the suggestion to hang him was received with howls of derision and his name was cheered.

Congressional elections that fall furnished indisputable proof that the reception given Andrew Johnson reflected a deep-seated distrust of Administration policies — fear that Presidential weakness or double-dealing would rob the country of every guarantee that the rebellion would not be renewed. If giving the freedmen the vote was necessary to shatter the power of the former slaveholders, whom defeat on the battlefield had apparently not in the least intimidated, the North was willing. Republican majorities were greater than they had ever been in Lincoln's time and the men elected were, with few exceptions, followers of Stevens and Phillips. Henceforth Johnson was to be a mere figurehead. No veto of his could impede the Republican program. "The people have spoken," declared Phillips, "and uttered their veto on Johnson, his policy and his adherents. They believed with Landor that 'a king should be struck but once — a mortal blow.' They mean that slavery, with all its roots, branches, suckers, parasites and dependants, shall die utterly and forever."

He had been asked to accept the Republican nomination for Congress in his district, but had declined, wishing to remain independent of party and the trammels of political office. The New York *Times* approved his decision, declaring: "The proper leader of the Radical Republican platform does better as a faithful and impartial critic of men and measures outside of legislative halls and independent of all party alliances. By virtue of his position he can proclaim in advance unwelcome truths which other men hesitate to speak."

Presidential reconstruction received its death blow on March 2, 1867, when Congress overrode Johnson's veto and passed the Reconstruction Act. The Act divided the former Confederate States (except Tennessee) into five military districts under the command of army officers. Delegates were to be elected to State Constitutional Conventions, Negroes participating. The new Constitutions had to include Negro suffrage. When new Legislatures had been elected and had adopted the Fourteenth Amendment (contemptuously rejected under Presidential reconstruction) the insurrectionary States would be admitted to the Union.

9

Phillips had little enthusiasm for Grant as a Presidential candidate. He distrusted the military mind, argued that Grant lacked experience in civil affairs and that his silence on the vital problems of the day laid him open to suspicion. Yet when after his election Grant gave his full support to Congressional reconstruction, Phillips was at times too inclined to overlook the Administration's shortcomings.

On March 30, 1870, Grant proclaimed the adoption of the Fifteenth Amendment, making Negro suffrage a constitutional obligation. Phillips, who had given up hope that land would be given to the freedmen, believed the time had now come to dissolve the Anti-Slavery Society. Formal dissolution took place on April 9, 1870, at a mass meeting in Steinway Hall, New York.[3] The hall was packed to suffocation. On the platform, against a background of flags, banners and floral pieces, sat Phillips and other officers of the society, surrounded by men and women grown gray in the anti-slavery cause. Garrison was conspicuous by his absence, and among the numerous messages and telegrams from famous men and women in all parts of the world, there was none from the society's founder. Speeches were made and warmly applauded. When finally Phillips stepped forward to deliver the valedictory address, the whole audience rose to its feet and gave him the greatest ovation of his career. He spoke feelingly of the society's work, paid tribute to its founder, and finished with these words, the significance of which did not escape those who had watched his growing interest in the labor movement:

"We will not say 'Farewell,' but 'All hail.' Welcome new duties! We sheathe no sword. We only turn the front of the army upon a new foe."

[3] At the business meeting the society decided to adjourn *sine die*.

PART FIVE

Separate Ways

"We Sheathe No Sword!"

THE Garrisons no longer lived in Dix Place. In August, 1864, they had sold the house the editor's friends and admirers had presented to him and had moved to Roxbury, where Garrison bought a house with a half acre of ground at 125 Highland Street. It was elevated by terraces thirty feet above the street level and from its upper windows commanded a view of the harbor and the surrounding country. The reason for the move was that in December of the preceding year Helen had suffered a stroke, necessitating a retired existence. The half-hour horsecar ride to Roxbury served to discourage visitors. Garrison named the new abode Rockledge, and it remained his home until the end of his life.

Since he had given up the *Liberator* he felt, as he himself expressed it, "like a hen plucked of her feathers." He would sit for hours on the sofa reading and clipping exchanges that continued to come, even though the clippings were now of little value to him. In the evening he played whist with his children and with George Thompson, who had rented a house in the neighborhood. At other times he read to Helen, whom her invalidism had not robbed of patience and good humor. She felt a little sorry for him and urged him to make a journey to Washington (where their daughter, now Mrs. Henry Villard, lived) and a short lecture tour. He did so and was showered with attentions in the National Capital. His lectures, too, were well received. Public opinion was now so favorable to him that had his health permitted it he could have had many lucrative lecture engagements. But he had suffered a fall that had severely injured his arm and shoulder and had not got over his weakness of imagining himself a prey to a variety of bodily ills.

The Boston publishing firm of Ticknor and Fields, whose imprint, according to W. D. Howells, "was a warrant of quality to the reader and of immortality to the author," made him a tempting offer for a history of the antislavery movement. He accepted provisionally and rented an office to which he moved the *Liberator* files. But he found it difficult to make a beginning. His journalistic habits and controversial turn of mind were ill suited for the work of a historian. "Be merciful!" he wrote to his son Wendell, who tried to spur him on. "I confess, I do not feel competent to the mighty task, and fear I shall make a failure of it, if I try." To Samuel J. May he wrote: "How to shape the work will be puzzling — the subject is so vast, the actors so many, the incidents so multitudinous. . . . Certainly, how to dispose of myself, without seeming egotistical by personal references on the one hand, or affectedly modest by omitting them on the other, will be a difficult and delicate task."

After more than two years of hesitation he abandoned the project.

2

Garrison's friends knew that he had saved but little and that his money could not last long. Unbeknown to him they formed a committee to solicit funds for a "National Testimonial" that would enable him to live out the remainder of his days free from financial worry. The make-up of the committee and the wording of the appeal, sent to many prominent men in the United States and to a few in Great Britain, were eloquent of the change of public opinion in his favor. The document was from the pen of Ex-Governor Andrew, chairman of the committee. Among the signatories were the Governor, Lieutenant Governor and Chief Justice of Massachusetts; all Congressional representatives of that State, and many from other States; the Chief Justice of the United States Supreme Court, and the President of the United States Senate; practically every literary man of note, including Emerson, Whittier, Longfellow, Lowell, Bryant, famous clergymen, scholars and men prominent in various other walks of life.

"The generation which immediately preceded ours," read the appeal, "regarded him only as a wild enthusiast, a fanatic, a public enemy. The present generation sees in him the bold and honest reformer, the man of original, self-poised, heroic will, inspired by a vision of universal justice made actual in the practice of nations. . . . He was the advocate of no private interest, he was the representative of no sect or party; with no hope of worldly profit to be reaped from the measures and principles he urged, he was the conspicuous, the acknowledged, the prophetic leader of the movement in behalf of the American Slave — now consummated by the Edict of Universal Emancipation."

The committee's goal had been fifty thousand dollars, and had the appeal been made to the general public there is little doubt it would have been exceeded, but being addressed to a limited number of interested persons, only some thirty-three thousand dollars were collected. The revenue from this would suffice, however, to keep Garrison and his wife in comfort, even if all other income were to cease. Over three hundred pounds were received from England. John Bright sent five pounds with the words: "I know no nobler man than Wm. Lloyd Garrison, and no man more rejoices that he lived to see the great day of freedom than I do."

In his letter to the committee accepting the "testimonial" Garrison wrote: "I accept it not as relating to any other question than that of slavery, not as an approval of all my methods of action or modes of expression (for some I should be quite sure to alter on a critical revision, now that the heat and smoke of the conflict are ended), but exactly for what it is intended to sanction and commend, to wit — the cause of universal freedom, and an unswerving advocacy of that cause, at whatever cost or peril."

3

In May, 1867, Garrison again crossed the Atlantic, the American Freedman's Union Commission having designated him as a delegate to the International Anti-Slavery Conference in Paris. It was to be his first visit to continental Europe. His youngest son, his daughter and her husband were then visiting Paris, where an International Exposition was in progress — a fortunate circumstance, since Garrison did not understand a word of French. George Thompson, after three years in the United States, had decided to return to England and was to accompany him as far as London. The esteem in which the two men were now held may be judged from the fact that when the authorities learned they were to be aboard the steamship *Cuba*, bound for Liverpool, the Revenue Cutter and the School Ship *Massachusetts* were ordered to "dress ship" and to fire a parting salute.

Garrison's visit to Paris had little significance. He arrived in the French capital at the time when Napoleon was entertaining Czar Alexander of Russia, the King of Prussia and Bismarck, and witnessed the imposing review of sixty thousand soldiers in the Bois de Boulogne, about which he wrote to Helen that "in a moral point of view," it gave him "no pleasure, but rather much pain." He then crossed over to England and in August returned to Paris for the Conference, which was a tame affair since the Emperor's Security Police would permit only the reading of papers previously approved by them, but barred all discussion. It was the interval he spent in England that has significance, since it marked the crowning of his career.

"A prophet is not without honor save in his own country." The American people were, it is true, beginning to realize the value of Garrison's contribution to the cause of liberty and democracy, but hardly to the same extent as the leaders of liberal thought in England, who considered emancipation as much his work as Lincoln's. On June 24 the London *Morning Star* announced that "a Public Breakfast in honor of William Lloyd Garrison" would be held at St. James's Hall, on Saturday, June 29, at noon, and that John Bright would preside. Over three hundred tickets (all that were available), at ten shillings each, were bought by some of the foremost men and women in the realm, while many had to be content with viewing the proceedings from the gallery. A more distinguished company could hardly have been imagined. The Duke of Argyll was Chairman of the Committee of Arrangements, which included Lord Haughton, Lord Alfred Spencer Churchill, Sir Thomas Fowler Buxton, Sir George Young, John Bright, John Stuart Mill, Professor Thomas Henry Huxley, Herbert Spencer, Frederick Harrison and many others almost equally famous. The American Ambassador, Charles Francis Adams, who had a previous engagement, expressed his regret at his inability to attend. Gladstone, unable to be present, wrote: "I should have hailed an opportunity of paying public honor to such a man as Mr. Garrison." Charles Darwin was to write that Garrison was "a man to be forever revered." The Comte de Paris, an ardent opponent of slavery, eulogized Garrison in a long communication. John Bright, the Duke of Argyll, Earl Russell, John Stuart Mill and George Thompson made the principal addresses. When it was Garrison's turn to speak, all present rose to their feet, and for several minutes he could not utter a word as men applauded and ladies waved handkerchiefs. The "son of a drunken seaman," the editor of a weekly at one time so obscure that the mayor of Boston had had difficulty locating it, the agitator on whose head there had been a prize, was deeply moved as he waited for the applause of Great Britain's immortals to subside.

More significant than the laudatory speeches were the comments of the press. The *Morning Star* declared: "Mr. Lincoln accomplished what Mr. Garrison began; but both were alike necessary to the perfect consummation of this transcendent enterprise." Most of the organs of public opinion, however, agreed with the *Daily Telegraph* that credit for emancipation belonged to Garrison rather than to Lincoln, an opinion previously expressed by the martyred President himself.[1] "So far as the fact that slavery has ceased to exist over the whole of the vast North American Continent can be attributed to the agency of any single individual," declared the *Telegraph*, "it must be ascribed to the effort of the agitator who, through good and ill repute, in season and out of season, preached the truth that all mankind has a right to freedom."

The *Times* and the *Pall Mall Gazette*, who had supported the Confederacy, sounded a discordant note, accusing him of fanaticism and of "lack of moderation and prudence." One cannot help recalling these words of Wendell Phillips: "What world-wide benefactors these 'imprudent' men are! How 'prudently' most men creep into nameless graves, while now and then one or two forget themselves into immortality."

Manchester, Newcastle, Edinburgh, Glasgow invited Garrison so they might do him honor. In Edinburgh, at a special meeting of the Town Council, the Lord Provost presiding, magistrates, members of the Council and city officials wearing their robes of office, he was solemnly presented with the freedom of the city. In Glasgow there was a public breakfast in his honor attended by the city's notables. A delegation of workingmen presented him with an address in which they assured him that his struggle for the Negro had been of incalculable benefit to the working people of England and Scotland in their battle for civil rights. "Your success won half our battle. . . . We shall ever remember, Sir, that to your labors much of our success is due."

John Stuart Mill had remarked at the London breakfast that "if you aim at something noble and succeed in it, you will generally find that you have succeeded not in that alone," but that "a hundred other good things which you have never dreamed of will have been accomplished by the way." In his fight for the Negro Garrison had

[1] See page 386.

won a victory for freedom of speech, of the press and of assembly, had purified the Church and had struck a telling blow for Woman's Rights. Now he learned that he had likewise helped British workingmen in their struggle for civil rights; and notwithstanding his attitude towards the labor movement he had done an immense service to American labor, whose progress slavery had impeded.

4

Phillips, no less than Garrison, was basking in public favor. Gone were the days when he had found it necessary to go about Boston gripping a revolver in his pocket. Boston was proud of him now. People greeted him affably on the street. Doors that had been closed to him for over a generation now opened hospitably. When he appeared at a social gathering he was the lion of the occasion. Young ladies came with their albums and begged him to inscribe a few words. He obliged amiably, usually writing:

> John Brown taught these lines to each of his children:
>   Peace if possible
>   Justice at any rate.

Soon after the war the municipal authorities had invited him to address the school children at the Festival of the Public Schools of Boston in Music Hall, and he had made a speech that delighted everyone. It really seemed as if the black sheep of the Phillips family would turn out to be a respectable sheep after all.

But in November of that same year his conservative well-wishers had received an unpleasant surprise. The workingmen of Boston held a meeting in Faneuil Hall in favor of the eight-hour day, and who should appear on the platform but Wendell Phillips. "It is twenty-nine years this month since I first stood on this platform of Faneuil Hall to address an audience of the citizens of Boston," he said. "I felt then that I was speaking for the cause of the laboring men, and if to-night I should make the last speech of my life, I would be glad that it should be in the same strain, — for laboring men and their rights."

It was not only his former proslavery critics who had been shocked by this. Abolitionists who were employers of labor heard with astonishment that "the Anti-Slavery cause was only a portion of the great struggle between Capital and Labor." The usual workday at that time being from twelve to fourteen hours, they could hardly agree that it was "a fair division to give him [the laborer] eight hours labor, eight hours for sleep and eight hours for his own, — his own to use as he pleases." Not content with this Phillips had added: "I shall not be the first to say, 'You shall not have it unless you come under bonds to use it well.' It is none of my business to say what he shall do with what is his own."

What would Arthur Tappan, first president of the American Anti-Slavery Society, have thought of that? In the days of his prosperity he had required his employees to observe the following rules:

"Total abstinence; not to visit proscribed places nor remain after ten o'clock at night; to visit a theatre, and to make the acquaintance of an actor precluded forgiveness; to attend Divine service twice on Sundays, and every Monday morning to report church attendance, name of clergyman and texts; prayer meeting twice a week, and must belong to an anti-slavery society and essay to make converts to the cause."

Phillips advised workingmen to eschew violence: "Men always lose half of what is gained by violence. What is gained by argument is gained forever. . . . When men have wrongs to complain of, they should go to the ballot-box and right them." This was well enough, but Boston politicians were far from pleased when he added: "Go into the political field, and by the voice of forty thousand workmen say, 'we mean that eight hours shall be a day's work, and no man shall go into office who opposes it' . . . Go to your next candidate for mayor, and ask him if he is in favor of the eight-hour system. If he says, Yes, let it be known that he is to have your votes. If No, let him know that he will not have them."

For some time after the war, however, Phillips was too occupied with the struggle against President Johnson and with reconstruction to make it possible for him to devote himself to labor's cause. Hence during that time his new-found popularity did not suffer greatly from his Faneuil Hall speech.

5

When the war was over and slavery officially abolished, Abolitionist leaders relaxed with a sigh of relief. Few were reformers by nature. If they had joined Garrison's crusade it was because the evil had been so monstrous, the North's complicity so flagrant, that they had found it impossible to remain silent and be at peace with their consciences. Some, like Edmund Quincy, whom a famous fellow townsman characterized as "the finest patrician type I ever met," had joined because they found "abolitionizing" a congenial pastime. In 1875 Quincy wrote to Garrison: "I had no turn for the law, and politics seemed to me beneath the notice of a gentleman. Anti-slavery was the only national and historical movement on foot — besides its humanitarian aspects." If he gave any thought to the labor movement, he assuredly must have found that, too, "beneath the notice of a gentleman." Other famous anti-slavery advocates showed as little inclination to become active in the new field. Whittier, now the nation's well-beloved poet, having reached safe harbor, had no wish to launch himself on that turbulent sea. "Like some others of the great anti-slavery men," wrote W. D. Howells, "he seemed to imagine that mankind had won itself a clear field by destroying chattel slavery, and had no sympathy with those who think that the man who may any moment be out of work is industrially a slave."[2] Alcott was enjoying the fine house his daughter Louisa had bought for him and had acquired a social philosophy in keeping with his changed circumstances. Emerson retired to his study and wrote *Society and Solitude*. Ripley, the founder of Brook Farm, "that harmless effusion of Radicalism," as Henry James called it, had no taste for mixing in the rough-and-tumble between labor and capital. Henry Ward Beecher was to express himself about the labor problem in this fashion: "Is the great working class oppressed? Yes, undoubtedly it is . . . God has intended the great to be great and the little to be little. . . . I do not say that a dollar a day is enough to support a workingman, but it is enough to support a man! . . . Not enough to support a man and five children if a man would insist on smoking and drinking beer. . . . But a man who cannot live on bread and water is not fit to live. . . . Labor unions are the worst forms of despotism that ever were bred by the human mind." Lydia Maria Child, so active and self-sacrificing in the anti-slavery cause, made this contribution to the discussion of the labor problem: "The labor question continues to seethe and grumble, like a volcano about to explode. Laborers, instead of serving their own interests by leaving off smoking and drinking, are clamoring for the expulsion of the

[2] This and other quotations from W. D. Howells are from that author's *Literary Friends and Acquaintance*. (Copyright 1900 by Harper & Brothers; copyright 1928 by Mildred Howells and John Mead Howells.)

industrious and frugal Chinese." As for Garrison, he had retired to the peace and security of Roxbury, and while giving his support to various philanthropic undertakings remained indifferent to the cause of labor. When in 1874 W. G. H. Smart attempted to interest him in "industrial reform," Garrison replied: "You ask me to 'consider the evils that now oppress society, especially the toiling masses, whose only dependence is the labor of their hands' . . . What have they to complain of in regard to constitution and laws for which they are not directly responsible? . . . Is not the government of them, by them, and for them (ostracised womanhood excepted), to be moulded as they shall judge best? Or, if in any case it is not for them, upon whom rests the responsibility but themselves? . . . Our danger lies in sensual indulgence, in a licentious perversion of liberty, in the prevalence of intemperance, and in whatever tends to the demoralization of the people."

6

Franklin H. Wentworth, speaking in Faneuil Hall in 1905, referred in these terms to Wendell Phillips: "Of all the men whom the period of the American civil war has written into history of all those who so nobly and unselfishly threw themselves into the struggle against chattel slavery, there is but one, who, when the fight was over, turned severely from the plaudits of the world his matchless eloquence had served to awaken, and, wrapping his cloak once more about him, went forth to meet a greater enemy."

In a world afflicted with self-indulgence it was an extraordinary phenomenon. It had been Phillips's youthful ambition to become a United States senator. With everything in his favor to enable him to realize that ambition, he had cast it aside to devote himself to an unpopular cause. He had lost the good will of relatives and friends, had risked confinement in an insane asylum, had made himself an outcast in society, and when not on the road lecturing had lived like a recluse. For an entire generation when walking the streets of his beloved Boston he had encountered black and hostile looks; at one time his person and his house had had to be guarded against mob violence. At last the fog had lifted. The heavens smiled upon him. He was only in his fifties, and after years of unpopularity, popular at last! His integrity and courage had finally been recognized and had gained him prestige, admiration, loyalty. There were few offices to which he could not have been elected, few posts of honor not within his reach. And what did the extraordinary man do? When the Anti-Slavery Society adjourned *sine die* he remarked to a friend: "Now that the field is won, do you sit by the camp-fire, but I will put out in the underbrush," and forthwith aligned himself with a cause more unpopular than Abolition had ever been.

The American labor movement was then in its formative stage. Many of its leaders were foreign born. Few were capable of enlightened leadership. Some were Socialists with a superficial knowledge of Socialist philosophy and tactics, others were Syndicalists or Anarchists. Still others had no philosophy to guide them, but were animated by a grim determination to meet injustice with revolt, violence with violence, conspiracy with conspiracy. In 1871 a sinister light was thrown over the labor movement of the Western world by the bold uprising of the Paris proletariat – the Communards – who hoisted the blood-red flag of social revolution above the Tuileries. In 1875 there was an epidemic of assassinations in the Pennsylvania coal fields, where reigned the Molly Maguires. With this movement of ill-repute the scion of Boston's codfish aristocracy, son of the city's first mayor, aligned himself. Rejecting Garrison's excuse for inaction he declared: "All we see at the present time is the substratum of society, heaving and tossing in angry and aimless and ignorant struggle, not knowing what it wants, nor why it suffers, nor how it can be remedied, and daily becoming angrier and more soured, and more embittered. The question is, who shall speak to it, who shall educate these conflicting interests?"

7

Phillips's biographers have claimed that he had been interested in the labor movement since 1840, a claim not justified by the evidence. In 1847, replying to the editor of the *Harbinger*, a socialistic publication, he had written:

"There are two prominent points which distinguish the worker in this country from the slaves. First, the laborers, as a class, are neither wronged nor oppressed: and secondly, if they were, they possess ample power to defend themselves by the exercise of their own acknowledged rights. Does legislation bear hard upon them? Their votes can alter it. Does capital wrong them? Economy will make them capitalists. . . . To economy, self-denial, temperance education, and moral and religious character, the laboring class and every other class in this country must owe its elevation and improvement."

As late as 1847 Phillips was therefore in full agreement with Garrison concerning labor and must share with him responsibility for a policy that failed to enlist the sympathy of wageworkers for the antislavery movement. Those who after his conversion have classed him as a Socialist are likewise mistaken. He was not a Socialist in the modern meaning of the term. He never advocated ownership and operation of industry by government. His knowledge of the Marxian philosophy was rudimentary, as was his knowledge of economics. From this Thomas Wentworth Higginson concluded that he was unfit to serve as counselor to labor. "You could not," wrote Higginson, "settle the relations of capital and labor offhand, by saying, as in the case of slavery, 'Let my people go': the matter was far more complex. It was like trying to adjust a chronometer with no other knowledge than that won by observing a sun-dial." Phillips proved his fitness by refusing to waste time pleading with capital to "Let my people go!" He jumped into the arena crying to labor to achieve its own liberation. He urged working people to join labor unions and to form their own political party. In the meantime they should vote for no man whose loyalty to labor was in the least doubtful. In April, 1872, in an address before the International Lodge of the Knights of Saint Crispin, he declared:

"If you want power in this country; if you want to make yourselves felt; if you do not want your children to wait long years before they have the bread on the table they ought to have, the leisure in their lives they ought to have, the opportunities in life they ought to have; if you don't want to wait yourselves, — write on your banner, so that every political trimmer can read it, so that every politician, no matter how short-sighted he may be, can read it, 'We never forget!' If you launch the arrow of sarcasm at labor, we never forget: if there is a division in Congress, and you throw your vote in the wrong scale, we never forget. You may go down on your knees, and say, 'I am sorry I did the act'; and he will say, 'It will avail you in heaven, but on this side of the grave never.' So that a man in taking up the Labor Question, will know he is dealing with a hair-trigger pistol, and will say, 'I am to be true to justice and to man; otherwise I am a dead duck.'"

He unceasingly urged labor to organize: "What is there against that immense preponderance of power on the part of capital? Simply organization. . . . So I welcome organization. I do not care whether it calls itself Trades-union, Crispin, International or Commune; anything that masses up the units in order that they may put in a united force to face the organization of capital, anything that does that, I say *amen* to it. . . . Only organize and stand together. Claim something together, and at once; let the nation hear a united demand from the laboring voice, and then when you have got that, go on after another; but get something. . . . Unless there is a power in your movement, industrially and politically, the last knell of democratic liberty in this Union is struck."

He refused to apologize for the violence of the laboring men, claiming it was the result of the excesses of capital: "They tell you, 'Come into the world with the white banner of peace.' Ay, we will, when you disarm. . . . Labor comes up and says, 'They have shotted their cannon to the lips; they have rough-ground their swords as in battle; they have adopted every new method; they have invented every dangerous machine, — and it is all planted like a great park of artillery against us. They have incorporated wealth; they have hidden behind banks; they have concealed themselves in currency; they have sheltered themselves in taxation; they have passed rules to govern us, — and we will improve upon the lesson they have taught us. When they disarm, we will — not before.'" He would not even repudiate so violent a manifestation of labor's discontent as the Paris Commune: "I have not a word to utter, — far be it from me! — against the grandest declaration of popular indignation which Paris wrote on the pages of history in fire and blood. . . . I for one honor Paris; but in the name of Heaven, and with the ballot in our right hands, we shall not need to write our record in fire and blood; we write it in the orderly majorities at the ballot-box."

He rejected philanthropy as a solution: "Mr. Stewart, in New York, has bought a whole town; and he is going to build model houses, and house there all the labor he can get to go into them. Yet the civilization which alone can look the New Testament in the face is a civilization where one man does not depend on the pity of another man's building him a model lodging-house; the civilization which alone can look the New Testament in the face is a civilization where one man could not build, and another would not need, that sort of refuge."

He was vague regarding the economic system that was to replace

Capitalism. It was not government ownership and operation of industry, but a loose confederation of co-operative enterprises, such as W. H. Sylvis and other labor leaders had been advocating for some time. In 1867, after a series of unsuccessful strikes, many co-operative workshops had sprung up. "At last, after years of earnest effort and patient waiting and constant preaching, co-operation is taking hold upon the minds of our members and in many places very little else is talked about," said Sylvis. In 1868 Phillips declared: "Let the passengers and employees own the railway. Let the operatives own the mill. Let the traders own the banks. Make the interests of Capital and the Community identical. In no other way shall we have free self-government in this country." And in 1871: "The ultimate thing which we aim at is co-operation, where there is no labor as such, and no capital as such, — where every man is interested proportionately in the results."

Although the State was not to be the employer it was expected to aid the development of co-operative enterprises. When in 1871 Phillips was candidate for Governor of Massachusetts on the Labor-Reform ticket, the platform, which he helped write, contained this clause: "We demand that every facility, and all encouragement, shall be given by the law to co operation in all branches of industry and trade, and that the same aid be given to co-operative efforts that has heretofore been given to railroads and other enterprises."

He advocated a system of taxation not unlike that favored by the New Deal. In October, 1871, he said in Boston Music Hall: "When we get into power, there is one thing we mean to do. If a man owns a single house, we will tax him one hundred dollars. If he owns ten houses of like value, we won't tax him one thousand dollars, but two thousand dollars; and the richer a man grows, the bigger his tax, so that when he is worth forty million dollars he will not have more than twenty thousand dollars a year to live on. .... We'll crumble up wealth by making it unprofitable to be rich."

His ideal of society was Jeffersonian: "What we need is an equalization of property, — nothing else. My ideal of civilization is a very high one; but the approach to it is a New England town of some two thousand inhabitants, with no rich man and no poor man in it, all mingling in the same society, every child at the same school, no poor-house, no beggar, opportunities equal, nobody too proud to stand aloof, nobody too humble to be shut out."

From all this it is evident that Phillips was realistic regarding labor's immediate aims and the method to achieve them, vague and uncertain regarding the ultimate goal. The system which he hoped would supplant Capitalism bears some resemblance to that advocated by Peter Kropotkin, who wished to form local co-operative and pro-ductive groups where "loving treatment, moral influence and liberty" would prevail. In more recent times the Industrial Workers of the World advocated a form of collectivism under which each industry and each local unit was to be managed by those employed in it.

8

While desiring no office, Phillips no longer kept aloof from politics and politicians. In 1869 he made a plea before the Massachusetts Legislature for the appointment of a commission to inquire into the condition of the working classes in the State. The result was the passage of a bill providing for the State Bureau of Labor Statistics. In 1871 he was the candidate for Governor of Massachusetts of the Labor-Reform and Prohibition Parties, and polled some twenty-two thousand votes, nearly one fifth of the total. His belief in Prohibition was qualified. He was opposed to the licensed saloon mainly be-cause of its corruptive influence upon politics: "There are four thousand rumshops in Boston, and taking these four thousand, and their four thousand best customers, you will have eight thousand votes, — a large number that decided any election." But he resented the activities of those who would invade the privacy of a man's home to enforce abstinence. "A Yankee's idea of hell is to mind his own business. . . . We don't care what a man does in his own parlor. He may drink champagne or whiskey and we don't care." In his address before the Knights of Saint Crispin he said: "Intemperance is the cause of poverty, I know; but there is another side to that, - poverty is the cause of intemperance." While Prohibitionists claimed that drink was the cause of crime, he believed poverty to be the main cause: "I take the thermometer of the price of English wheat for the last century, and place beside it the thermometer of crime; and find, as the wheat goes down or up, the crime increases or diminishes."

In 1871 Phillips shocked his friends by giving his support to General Benjamin F. Butler in the latter's attempt, by a direct appeal to the electorate, to force the Republican Party to nominate him for Governor of Massachusetts. The General was over-fond of women

and wine, was said to have made inordinate profits from war contracts and to have been involved in some questionable financial
transactions. During the war he had hanged a few rebels and had
earned the undying hatred of the South by his decree against the
women of New Orleans. Scornful of Southern chivalry which put
one woman on a pedestal and another on the auction block, he had
issued a decree to the effect that "when any female shall by word,
gesture or movement insult or show contempt for any officer or
soldier of the United States she shall be regarded and held liable to
be treated as a woman of the town plying her avocation."

For all his shortcomings there was much to recommend him. At
the beginning of hostilities he had endeared himself to opponents of
slavery by declaring fugitive slaves belonging to rebels "contraband
of war" and refusing to surrender them. The President had over-
ruled him, but Butler's action had done much to bring the question
to the fore. Charles A. Dana, Assistant Secretary of War, said of him:
"His intellectual resources were marvelous, his mind inclined
naturally to the cause of the poor and the weak. He was no pre-
tender and no hypocrite." Grant declared him to be "a man of great
ability . . . courage, honor and sincere conviction." In 1864 many
prominent Republicans, including Horace Greeley, had preferred
him to Lincoln as their Presidential candidate. Lincoln sent an
emissary to him to ask him to be his running mate, but Butler had
declined the honor. He used to say of himself: "God made me only
one way. I must always be with the underdog in the fight. I can't
help it; I can't change, and on the whole I don't want to."

Phillips's acquaintance with Butler dated back to the time when
after finishing Harvard Law School he had gone to work in the law
office of his former classmate Thomas Hopkinson, in Lowell. Butler,
several years his junior, had then been an impish errand boy in a
neighboring law office. He was now fifty-three, a successful lawyer,
bald, pouchy, with a drooping moustache, one drooping eyelid and
a habit of winking his other eye in a conspiratorial fashion.

Phillips was not unaware of his friend's shortcomings. "What a
splendid man he would be if he had more of the moral in him," he
had said once. In a public address he declared: "He has done a great
many things that I should not have done; he has done a great many
things that I would ask him to do differently; but I will tell you a
secret, friends. If I were Pope to-day, there is not a man among all
the candidates, Butler included, whom I would make a saint of, —

not one. If I were Pope to-morrow, there has not been a governor for fifty years that I would make a saint of. The difficulty is, saints do not come very often; and, when they do come, it is the hardest thing in the world to get them into politics. . . . I think General Butler has been charged with about every sin that can be imagined; but there is one thing (I watched very carefully, — I put my ear down to the earth, like an Indian listening) he never has been charged, even since 1861, of not doing what he said he would do. You cannot find a newspaper correspondent so utterly reckless that he will charge Butler with having broken a promise."

Butler's nomination alone would not have satisfied him. He hoped to capture the State organization of the Republican Party and make it the party of the common people: "I don't want that convention at Worcester merely to nominate General Butler; that will not satisfy me. Neither will it satisfy me if General Butler's friends go there and put a small plank labeled 'labor' in one part of the platform. I want king's post and girder, wallplate and ridge-pole, every plank and joist carved, moulded, stamped and labelled, 'Justice to MAN — MAN first — MONEY, the week after.'"

Support of Butler, whom they considered a rake and a demagogue, was more than some of Phillips's best friends were able to swallow. Emerson broke with him and Senators Sumner and Wilson issued a statement opposing the General. Butler failed to obtain the nomination, but came near enough to victory to enable Phillips to say: "He came so near succeeding that no men were more surprised than those who whipped him."

9

President Lincoln's biographers have given him undivided credit for stopping Secretary Seward from sending his bellicose dispatch to England regarding Lord John Russell's proposed reception of the representatives of the Confederacy. The wording of the dispatch was so provocative that it might have involved the United States in war with England, which under the circumstances might also have meant war with France. It does not appear unlikely that to provoke such a conflict was Seward's intention, since he labored under the illusion that a foreign war would stop the quarrel at home. The original manuscript of the dispatch shows that it was corrected by Lincoln personally. Congressman John B. Alley of Massachusetts, an admirer of both Lincoln and Sumner, has, however, assigned the major part of the credit to the latter. "Mr. Lincoln once told me," he wrote, "that he had the greatest confidence in the judgment of our Massachusetts senator in everything pertaining to foreign relations. I know, of my own personal knowledge, that Mr. Lincoln would not allow Mr. Seward to send any very important dispatch to England, until he had first shown it to Senator Sumner, who was chairman of the Committee on Foreign Relations." He went on to say that Sumner, having read the dispatch, declared it must not be sent unless considerably toned down. Seward objected, and Lincoln, acting as arbiter in the dispute, sided with Sumner. Picking up his pen, he made changes satisfactory to the Massachusetts senator. "I was told of this confidentially at the time, and never mentioned it to any one until some years afterwards," [3] wrote Alley, who also informs us that when the original draft, corrected in Lincoln's hand, was found in the archives of the State Department and shown to President Grant, the latter exclaimed: "What prudence and sound judgment this incident displays!"

Thus, unknowingly, Grant paid tribute to Sumner as well as to Lincoln, but the irony of events would have it that he should be responsible for driving Sumner from the post in which he had displayed such "prudence and sound judgment." The President and the senator had quarreled about the San Domingo treaty, which Grant favored and Sumner opposed on the ground that it meant the end of that country's independence.

Stephen A. Douglas had experienced to his sorrow what it meant to quarrel with the head of one's party. Now Sumner was in the same predicament. He was removed as party chairman and discriminated against in committee assignments. John Lothrop Motley was recalled as minister to Great Britain for no better reason than that he was Sumner's friend. Worst of all, the Senator's own State turned against him. The alleged reason was that he had introduced a bill providing that "the names of battles with fellow citizens shall not be continued in the Army Register, or placed on the regimental colors of the United States," it being "contrary to the usages of civilized nations to perpetuate the memory of civil war." The Massachusetts lawgivers, in a resolution of censure, pronounced the bill "an insult to the loyal soldiery of the nation." Hurt to the quick, the Senator replied: "It

[3] "John B. Alley," in *Reminiscences of Abraham Lincoln by Distinguished Men of His Time*, Allen Thorndike Rice, Editor. (New York, 1886.) P. 579.

was our State which led in requiring all safeguards for liberty and equality. I covet for her that other honor of leading in reconciliation."

Misfortune of a more intimate nature came to plague him. He had married late in life a woman much younger than he and the union had not proved a happy one. Now his wife deserted him and he sued for divorce.

Phillips took up the cudgels for his old friend against the President, the Secretary of State and the State Legislature. To J. B. Smith, a member of the Legislature, he wrote: "I should despise the Southerner who could march under such a [regimental] flag. Only I should despise yet more heartily a North that could ask him to do so. . . . Let such a disgraceful bunting be once borne by Carolinians and Yankees over one victorious field and the men themselves would fitly celebrate the victory by tearing such a flag to pieces and clasping generous and brave hands over its rags. . . . I hope this legislature will erase that record of intemperate haste. . . . I ask it for the honor of the Commonwealth."

It was ultimately erased.

Phillips called on Sumner at the latter's house in Lafayette Square and found an ill and embittered man. While they sat and talked a servant entered and reminded the Senator that it was time for the foot bath the doctor had prescribed. Phillips rose to leave, but Sumner begged him to stay: he would dispense with the foot bath. Phillips remarked that this would be unwise. The aging Senator who, though not older than Phillips, had only two more years to live, lifted his eyes towards him pleadingly and said: "Well, I'll take it if you don't go."

So Phillips sat down again and they talked while Sumner bathed his feet.

10

The Republican Party, both North and South, had become corrupt. Some Republicans hoped to remedy the situation by organizing a third party, although well aware that their only hope of success was an alliance with the Ku Klux Klan Democracy of the South and its Copperhead supporters in the North. In 1872, the embittered Sumner was among those who decided to support Horace Greeley, candidate of the Liberal Republicans and the Democrats, for Presi-

dent in preference to Grant. It is hardly surprising that when
Sumner made his announcement and called upon colored voters to
support Greeley, they should have been bewildered. Sumner had
been their good and faithful friend and they were aware of the
fact that their race had been shamefully betrayed by Republican
carpetbaggers and by many Republicans in Congress. At the same
time they knew defeat of the Republican Party meant that the
Fourteenth and Fifteenth Amendments would become a dead letter
in the South. Sumner's advice appeared to them like advising a man
to clean house by setting fire to it. In their perplexity they turned to
Phillips for counsel.

Phillips and Ann were at Swampscott to escape the heat of summer
when a letter arrived signed by thirty-three prominent Negroes of
Boston and vicinity requesting that he, whom they revered for his
"lifelong devotion to the cause of human rights," come and address
them on the political issues of the day. Not wishing to leave Ann
and believing he could state his views "more satisfactory in a letter
than in a public address" he sent a lengthy communication.

"Of course the first thought that occurs to you and me just now,"
he wrote, "is that one of your best, ablest and most watchful friends,
Mr. Senator Sumner, advises you to vote for Horace Greeley, and
believes that your rights will be safe only in his keeping. I touch with
reverent hand everything from Mr. Sumner. I can never forget his
measureless services to the anti-slavery cause and to your race. . . .
From such a counsellor, I venture to differ with great reluctance, and
only after mature deliberation."

He reminded his colored friends that four years before he had
vigorously opposed Grant's nomination. "The defects of his administration are no surprise to me. I may say without boasting, that
I prophesied those defects. I do not wish to hide them to-day. I
entirely agree with Mr. Sumner as to the grave fault and intolerable
insolence of the administration in the San-Domingo matter. I think
the frequent putting of relatives into office highly objectionable, and
the sad career of Webster is warning enough against any man in
public life venturing to accept gifts from living men. These and other
defects are no surprise to me. The eminent merits of Gen. Grant's
administration are, I confess, a surprise to me."

Some of the merits he enumerated were "his truly original, statesmanlike, and Christian policy toward the Indians"; his "prompt interference for justice to workingmen in defiance of those about him,

relative to the execution of the eight-hour law"; his efforts to combat the Ku Klux Klan, notwithstanding the growing indifference of his party; his services to the Fifteenth Amendment, which he had recommended in his first message to Congress.

Greeley, he wrote, was the tool and Sumner the dupe of Southern secessionists and Northern Copperheads. "Mr. Greeley's election means the negro surrendered to the hate of the Southern States, with no interference from the nation in his behalf; it means the Constitutional amendments neutralized by a copperhead Congress . . . Every man of common sense sees, that of course, if copperheads and secessionists lift Mr. Greeley into the White House, they will claim — and it is now understood that they shall have — their full share in shaping the policy, and filling the offices, of the administration. . . . This is to put in peril all the war has gained. . . . I am not ready for such an experiment. . . . We do forgive. We have forgiven. But duty to the dead and to the negro, forbids to *trust* power to any hands, without undoubted, indubitable certainty that such hands are *trustworthy*."

His opinion of Greeley was tinged with the scorn he usually displayed in personal attack: "A trimmer by nature and purpose he has abused even an American politician's privilege of trading principles for success. . . . As for his honesty — for twenty years it has been a byword with us that it would be safe to leave your open purse in the same room with him; but as for any other honesty, no one was ever witless enough to connect the idea with the name. . . . No man has known better than he, how to manufacture political and pecuniary success out of the convictions of other men. For himself he never had a conviction."

Garrison, who had disagreed with Phillips concerning Lincoln and Butler, agreed about Greeley. He wrote in the *Independent* that the editor of the New York *Tribune* was "the worst of all counselors, the most unsteady of all leaders, the most pliant of all compromisers in times of great emergency."

Phillips took the stump against Greeley and had the satisfaction of seeing him defeated. It appears probable that he and Garrison saved the day for the Republicans. Had they joined forces with Sumner they undoubtedly could have swung a considerable portion of the Negro vote to Greeley and insured his election.

11

The rule of Negroes and poor whites, led by carpetbaggers under Congressional reconstruction, was accompanied by many crying evils. It is interesting to note, however, that those who have pictured those evils in the most lurid colors are those who have depicted slavery as little short of idyllic and could see nothing wrong with its virtual restoration under Presidential reconstruction. Why were the Negroes and poor whites led by carpetbaggers? Why did not the Hills, the Lamars, the Vances, the Wade Hamptons, assume the leadership of the majority composed of Negroes and poor whites and give the South an honest administration in the interest of social justice? Was it not because they were not interested in social justice, but in restoring slavery in the form of peonage? If the politically inexperienced freed-men and poor whites fell into the hands of self-seekers and dema-gogues, who but "the South's natural leaders" were to blame? Theirs was not a battle for "honest" government. Only the most unblushing partisan could mention the word "honest" in conjunction with the robbery and oppression of the many by the few sanctioned by the Black Codes. The corruption of the carpetbaggers was a peccadillo by comparison. Nor was it a battle for "white supremacy." If all the officials elected by freedmen and poor whites had been white and paragons of virtue there would still have been a Ku Klux Klan and a White League.

What took place in the South was essentially a struggle between the landed aristocracy and the landless proletariat, white as well as black. The landless majority had discovered that they could use the taxing power to expropriate the planters and to acquire land. That they were not wholly unsuccessful may be judged from the fact that within ten years after emancipation the Negroes of Georgia managed to acquire 338,769 acres, and the poor whites did even better. The landed minority threw legality to the wind and resorted to revolu-tionary measures. To wrest control of the government from the majority it was necessary to drive a wedge between poor whites and Negroes. The Ku Klux Klan, the White League, the Red Shirts and similar organizations undertook this task with the blessings of General Lee and other famous Southern leaders.[4] The race issue was played

---

[4] The Confederate General James Longstreet in Louisiana, the Confederate War Governor Joseph E. Brown in Georgia, the Southern leader W. W. Holden in North Carolina and others sided with the Negroes and poor whites.

up as it had never been before. White men associating with Negroes were cruelly persecuted and often killed. In 1868, in Louisiana alone over one thousand murders were attributed to the Ku Klux Klan, not to mention innumerable floggings and other outrages. In that State the struggle took the form of a tug of war between Governor and Legislature. The Democrats, supported by the White League, managed to obtain control of the Legislature by parliamentary trickery. General Sheridan, Military Commander of the department, reported that martial law was imperative to protect the lives of citizens, and President Grant ordered him to intervene.

Northern Democrats and their allies the Liberal Republicans sounded the alarm. Protest meetings were held throughout the North. On January 15, 1875, a meeting was called in Faneuil Hall. Eight able speakers were on hand to express their disapproval of Grant and Sheridan.

Phillips went to the meeting and found a place in the gallery, which communicated with the platform by means of a stairway. Seated sideways on the railing he was listening to the speeches when several people recognized him and called for him to speak. The chairman ignored the calls and Phillips made no attempt to be heard. But when resolutions were read condemning Grant and Sheridan the calls became so numerous and insistent that they could no longer be ignored. Making a virtue of necessity the chairman declared: "This is Faneuil Hall — sacred to free speech. If any gentleman desires to speak, he shall be heard."

There was a burst of applause. The audience turned to the venerable figure in the gallery. There were cries demanding that he descend to the platform. He did so and was greeted by hisses as well as cheers, the former predominating. It was all he needed to arouse his fighting spirit. It was long since he had faced a hostile audience.

He spoke for half an hour, frequently interrupted by derisive laughter, hisses and cries of "That's played out!" but also by cheering and applause. As he proceeded the marks of diapprobation grew rarer and those of approval increased. "Men of Boston," he said, "if these resolutions are passed they will carry consternation and terror into the house of every Negro in Louisiana. They will carry comfort to every assassin in New Orleans. My anxiety is for the hunted, tortured, robbed, murdered population, white and black, of the Southern States whom you are going to consign to the hands of their oppressors. If you pass these resolutions, gentlemen, I say it in

*From a Steel Engraving Made in 1861
by H. Wright Smith*

the presence of God Almighty, the blood of hundreds of blacks and hundreds of whites will be on your hands before the first day of January next. . . . I should deem myself wanting in my duty as an Abolitionist and to the President of the United States, if I did not utter every word in my power against allowing a set of resolutions to go out from this hall that will make the Negro and the white Republican more exposed to danger and more defenseless."

Colonel Henry Lee and Edward Hamilton replied. The former paid a generous tribute to Phillips's oratory. "We have against us here," he said, "the most formidable orator in the United States. It is only a week since speaking to one of the most distinguished men in the city, he said to me, 'I go to hear that fellow, and in spite of my reason, in spite of my knowing he is talking something I don't agree with, he carries me off my feet at once.' One remark I want to make, and that is when he begged us not to criticize General Grant's message. It is the first time I ever knew him to abstain from criticism of any sort. I thought Mr. Phillips was nothing if he was not critical. I have always supposed that he criticized everything and everybody."

Phillips had not abstained from "criticism of any sort." He had criticized the purpose of the meeting and the resolutions of censure to such good effect that, when the latter were put to a vote, the general opinion was that they were lost. The chairman, however, declared them carried, amidst a storm of protests. The Boston newspapers spoke with admiration of Phillips's impromptu speech. The Boston *Traveller* declared that he had "completely answered some of the boldest assertions and most plausible arguments of the regular speakers." The *Daily Advertiser* recalled the orator's former triumphs over hostile crowds: "One was forcibly reminded of the scenes that occurred in the old time war meetings, amid which the same now veteran orator stood cool and undismayed. He displayed not the slightest impatience or displeasure, but calmly and determinedly waited till the excited audience had uttered its roars, and then quietly proceeded with his remarks."

CHAPTER II

Twilight

IN 1856 a writer in the New York *Independent* referred to Garrison as "an infidel of the most degraded class." He could hardly have foreseen that a dozen years later "the infidel" was to be invited to become a regular contributor to the publication and that a prominent orthodox minister was to write to the editor concerning his contributions that they "were not only specimens of fine English, but pervaded by an eminently noble and Christian spirit." So undoubtedly they were, but they were hardly worthy of the Garrison of the early days of the *Liberator*.

In an obituary of Dr. William Ellery Channing, Garrison, commenting on that clergyman's decorous protests against slavery, had written: "The sound of a ram's horn was painfully distressing to him. He was firmly persuaded that nothing but a silver trumpet was needed to cause the walls of Jericho to fall; and so he did his best upon his own." The new industrialism despoiled the land, oppressed the poor, corrupted the Government; under its lash labor strained and groaned; but he who had once sounded the ram's horn in such an ear-splitting fashion did not even do his best upon a silver trumpet. He was, as we have seen, of the opinion that it was no concern of his. Minor reforms, however, continued to occupy him. He was active in the movement for the education of the freedmen, broke many a lance for Woman's Rights and for temperance, applauded the barring of the Bible from the public schools in Cincinnati, opposed Chinese exclusion, championed free trade. He protested sternly, though hardly with the Old Testament fury of former days, against the terrorism of the Ku Klux Klan, the Red Shirts, the White League and similar organizations. In 1874 he declined to be considered as a successor to Sumner in the United States Senate, and in 1876 refused to be candidate for President of the Prohibition Party. He still believed in nonresistance, and when a Japanese student came to talk to him about the doctrine, proved so convincing that on his return to Japan the young man was imprisoned for refusing to serve in the army.

In 1873 he received a letter, signed by many prominent men and women, asking that he write his autobiography, which "would furnish the most valuable material possible, as to the matters of which it would treat, to the future historian of this country." He declined with the words: "So far as I am concerned, I feel no interest in any history that may be written. It is enough for me that every yoke is broken and every bondman set free."

Was every yoke broken? *Was* every bondman set free? "A freeman deprived of every human right is the most degraded of human beings," Thaddeus Stevens had said. Garrison lived to see the day when the freedmen, robbed of their civil rights, fled the South by the thousands to escape their white tormentors. "Those who make a revolution by half, but dig its grave," the French revolutionary Saint Just had said. Republicans who had given the freedmen civil rights, but had failed to divide the land of the principal rebels among freedmen and poor whites had but dug a fresh grave for liberty in the South.

2

In January, 1876, Helen Eliza Garrison died. Garrison himself was so ill that he was unable to attend his wife's funeral. Time had healed the breach between him and Phillips, but even if it had not, the latter would have come forward with outstretched hands in the face of such a bereavement. He was the principal speaker at the funeral, and said with feeling: "Who can forget her modest dignity — shrinkingly modest, yet ever equal to the high place events called her to? In that group of remarkable men and women which the antislavery movement drew together, she had her own niche, which no one else could have filled so perfectly or unconsciously as she did."

Garrison wrote a memorial of his wife, had it printed and sent copies to those who had known and loved her. "While writing it my head and heart were heavily oppressed," he wrote to his son Wendell; and to his daughter: "What a solitude in the house!" The solitude was to widen about him, for death was gathering its harvest among the old Abolitionists. "God's chore boy," Samuel J. May, was no more, David Lee Child, Gerritt Smith, Sarah M. Grimké and many others had died. The former leader was constantly called upon to speak at the funeral services of men and women whom he had known young, ardent, full of hope.

Garrison's children, believing an ocean voyage and a change of scene would do him good, proposed a journey to England in the company of his youngest son, Francis Jackson. He agreed, and his English friends were notified to expect him in early June, 1877, but were requested not to arrange any public appearances. On the eve of his departure death again cast its shadow across his path. One of his daughters-in-law had died, and just before boarding the steamer he learned of the passing of Edmund Quincy, that charming and witty esthete whose gentle sarcasm and sense of humor had been a welcome relief in a movement fraught with intensity.

British Abolitionists and reformers could not refrain from giving the distinguished visitor some tokens of their esteem. In London they gave a breakfast in his honor, but only some fifty people were invited and there were no lengthy speeches. Similar gatherings took place when he visited Scarborough and Newcastle. He made a short address at the London conference of the followers of Mrs. Josephine E. Butler, who advocated the repeal of the Contagious Diseases Act, which permitted the licensing of houses of prostitution in garrison towns. His closing remark was characteristic: "It is the best investment for the soul's welfare possible, to take hold of something which is righteous but unpopular. . . . As for me, I should not know how to take part in a popular movement — it would seem so weakening, so enervating. Everybody is there and there is nothing to be done, excepting to shout."

The septuagenarian had lost little of his ability to impress. Mrs. Butler wrote to his son: "I think he has a peculiar gift for awakening the conscience, and for making us all feel to what extent we have severally failed to see, or to *live up to*, the principles we profess to love." George Rolleston, Professor of Anatomy and Physiology at Oxford University, wrote that Garrison's words " 'make a man feel strong in hearing truth.' " Dr. John Brown, famous author of *Rab and His Friends*, exclaimed on seeing him: "What a beautiful face he has! It's really wonderful."

Garrison went to Westminster Abbey and meditated by the grave of Wilberforce. He made a melancholy visit to Leeds to see his friend George Thompson, who had suffered a stroke. The famous British Abolitionist was barely able to hobble about with the aid of a cane, and the once mighty voice, that had played so glorious a part in the liberation of eight hundred thousand slaves in the British colonies, now issued haltingly from the paralyzed throat. Conversation was difficult and almost painful. When it was time for Garrison to depart, Thompson sobbed aloud and his friend had difficulty to keep back the tears. It may well have been of his visit to Thompson he was thinking when he wrote to his son Wendell: "I could hope that I might pass on before my faculties are essentially impaired, or the body bowed down with hopeless infirmities."

3

October 13, 1878, was the sixtieth anniversary of Garrison's apprenticeship as a printer. He decided to celebrate the occasion (as he had his seventieth birthday) by journeying to Newburyport and trying his hand at setting type in the *Herald* office. According to the editor of the *Herald* he set up three of his own sonnets "in a time many a younger printer might emulate," and when proof was drawn it was found he had not made a single error. When he returned to Boston, the New England Franklin Club, an association of printers, gave a dinner in his honor. Quoting the wit who had said that "the greatest stand for civilization was the inkstand," Garrison declared that it was so only in conjunction with the printer's stand, without which it would have but a limited influence.

In February, 1879, a short time before his death, Garrison engaged in a spirited debate in the New York *Tribune* with Senator James G. Blaine, who favored a bill pending in Congress excluding Chinese immigrants. Nine years before, in an editorial in the *Anti-Slavery Standard,* Phillips had opposed Chinese immigration which, he claimed, was mostly contract labor: "*Importation of human freight is an unmitigated evil.* They who seek to flood us, artificially, with barbarous labor, are dragging down the American home to the level of the houseless street-herds of China. If the workingmen have not combined to prevent this, it is time they should." Garrison, basing himself on abstract right and justice, opposed Chinese exclusion. To a friend he wrote: "It is essentially the old anti-slavery issue in another form — whether one portion of mankind may rightfully claim superiority over another on account of birth, descent, or nativity, or for any other reason, and deny to them those rights and interests which pertain to our common humanity." President

Hayes, who vetoed the bill, said of Garrison's argument that it was "admirable and conclusive." Phillips was not so sure. "Theories," he remarked, "are pleasing things, and seem to get rid of all difficulties so very easily. One must begin with abstract principles, and study them. But wisdom consists in perceiving when human nature and this perverse world necessitate making exceptions to abstract truths."

Garrison was now in his seventy-fourth year and failing rapidly. When in April of that year his daughter, who now lived in New York, came to visit him, she was alarmed at the change in him. She begged him to come with her to New York and he allowed himself to be persuaded. On the tenth of May he took to his bed in his daughter's apartment in Union Square. The newspapers reported the progress of his illness and letters and telegrams streamed in. Whittier wrote to a friend: "I am greatly pained to hear of the illness of our old friend Garrison. For many years he has been an important part of our world! Much of my own life was shaped by him. It is very sad to think I shall see him no more. The next mail may bring tidings of his death."

By the twentieth of the month hope of recovery was given up and his children gathered in the apartment. A great weariness had come over the patient. Lying with eyes closed he often murmured that he wanted to "go home," by which, it was apparent, he did not mean returning to Rockledge. On the morning of the twenty-third, responding to a motion of the sick man's hand, the doctor bent over him and asked: "What do you want, Mr. Garrison?" He opened his eyes and said resolutely: "To finish it up!"

That same evening he asked his children to sing some of his favorite hymns. They gathered around the bed and sang, while he beat time with hands and feet. Shortly after he lapsed into a coma and remained in that condition for twenty-four hours. On the evening of May 24, 1879, a few minutes after eleven, he died.

4

Once a prominent divine had said: "I never speak in the pulpit of the devil or of William Lloyd Garrison." Now the pulpits of the nation rang with his praise and a chorus of eulogy rose from the columns of the newspapers. The New York *World*, which had assailed him so often and so bitterly, conceded his "simplicity, sin-

gleness of purpose and unflinching devotion to a self-imposed task."
In Boston, Philadelphia, Washington, Cincinnati, Raleigh, Atlanta
and many other cities and towns the colored people held memorial
meetings.

The remains of the famous Abolitionist were taken to Roxbury,
where on May 28 funeral services were held in the church of the
First Religious Society. The Governor, in a proclamation, spoke
of "the great citizen whose name will be forever associated with
the cause and the triumph of the contest." Flags on all public
buildings were at half-mast. Garrison had often said that he did not
regard death as an occasion for mourning. "Death was to him but
the passing from one room to another and higher one," Whittier
wrote. In conformity with this view there was an absence of gloom
at the funeral. The shutters were thrown wide open and the sun-
light was allowed to stream in unhindered upon the coffin and the
floral tributes surrounding it. Whittier, who was present, had written a poem for the occasion, but was too moved to read it and it
was read by the minister. A colored quartet sang the dead man's
favorite hymns. Phillips and Theodore D. Weld delivered the principal addresses. Forgotten were the differences that had divided the
two friends as Phillips said, for all the world to hear: "For myself,
no words can adequately tell the measureless debt I owe him, the
moral and intellectual life he opened to me. I feel like the old Greek
who, taught by Socrates, called his own scholars 'the disciples of
Socrates.' "

Garrison's significance to the cause of emancipation he summed
up in these words:

"All through the preceding century, there had been among us
scattered and single Abolitionists, earnest and able men, — sometimes, like Wythe of Virginia, in high places. The Quakers and
Covenanters had never intermitted their testimony against slavery.
But Garrison was the first man to begin a *movement* designed to
annihilate slavery. He announced the principle, arranged the method,
gathered the forces, enkindled the zeal, started the argument, and
finally marshalled the nation for and against the system in a conflict
that came near rending the Union. . . . It is true, as New Orleans
complains to-day in her journals, that this man brought upon America everything they call the disaster of the last twenty years; and
it is equally true that if you seek through the hidden causes
and unheeded events for the hand that wrote 'emancipation'

on the statute-book and on the flag, it lies still there to-day."
Garrison was buried beside his wife at Forest Hills cemetery.

On November 4, 1883, Daniel H. Chamberlain, former Governor
of South Carolina, wrote in the New York *Tribune:*
"It was my privilege once, and once only, to talk with Abraham
Lincoln, at Petersburg, Va., April 6, 1865. I spoke to him of the
country's gratitude for his great deliverance of the slaves. His sad
face beamed for a moment with happiness as he answered in exact
substance, and very nearly in words: 'I have been only an instrument. The logic and moral power of Garrison, and the anti-slavery
people of the country and the army, have done all.' "

5

How had Phillips fared in the meantime?

When in Boston he had been increasingly occupied with the care
of his wife. "The poor child has only memories left to live on —
weakness and pain and weariness make up the days now — so old
memories are the pleasantest and she lives in the past — though we
hope on," read one of his last letters to Garrison's wife. His lecture
work still occupied him a good part of the year, though the demand
for his services was not nearly as great as it had been once. He still
championed civil rights for the Negro, labor, temperance, Woman's
Rights, Ireland and various other causes. In 1877 an attempt was
made to get him to stand for governor, but he declined. "Certain
it is, that, if every man in the Commonwealth who is friendly to
Mr. Phillips should vote for him, he would carry the position by
storm," wrote a correspondent in the Boston *Commonwealth,* at the
same time remarking: "It is well known that Mr. Phillips deliberately throws his weight into the scale of the weakest side, provided
it be deserving, without much care for himself."

Impatience with the progress of fundamental reform is apt to
lead to acceptance of a panacea that promises to accomplish in one
fell stroke what years of patient labor can advance but slowly.
Phillips's lack of specialized knowledge made him particularly sus-
ceptible to the teachings of Henry Cary, who believed the root of
most social evils to be the country's faulty monetary system and advocated "Greenbackism" as the remedy. At the Radical Club in
Boston Phillips summed up Cary's panacea in these words: "Abol-

ishing all coin, and issuing two thousand million dollars (an amount equal to the national debt), based on the thirty thousand millions of property of the country, so that interest should never be more than five per cent." The results were guaranteed to be phenomenal. "This" he said, "is the last fight between wealth and the people — not between noble and serf, but between money-bags and the workingmen; between men who create wealth, and those who steal a living by the hocus-pocus of banking and the nonsense of coin. The people will now carry the Declaration of Independence into Wall Street, where it never yet penetrated; and we shall have a more honest finance than the world has yet seen."

The Radical Club, organized in 1867 and meeting more or less regularly until 1880, assembled at No. 13 Chestnut Street, in the roomy, old-fashioned residence of the Reverend John T. Sargent, whose wife took voluminous notes of the proceedings and preserved them for posterity in a volume entitled *Sketches and Reminiscences of the Radical Club*. Emerson, Longfellow, Holmes, Phillips, Henry James, John Weiss, Thomas Wentworth Higginson, Julia Ward Howe, Octavius B. Frothingham and many other celebrities belonged. Usually one of the members delivered a lecture, followed by discussion. Phillips's latest proposal to cure the evils of the social system was received with skepticism. "The next presidential election," he said at the club, "will turn, to a great extent, on the currency question. If the South can be broken into natural divisions, and brought to behave decently, the currency will be the *only* great question. The next step of the Democracy will be to establish the greenback system."

"It will be worthy of it," interrupted a Mr. Wasson amidst general laughter.

This turned the discussion to the merits of democracy as a system of government. Phillips declared: "I never said that a democracy was a *good* government. A thing may be the *best* we can get, and yet not be *good*. Democracy is not a good government, but it is the best we can get while we have only this poor, rotten human nature to work with. Governments created by the people have always been more honest and less corrupt than those originating with the aristocracy, and revolutions made by the people have generally been more merciful and less bloody than the victories of the upper classes. No student of European history can fail to see this."

Paradoxical as it may seem, Phillips was a Protectionist, in which he differed from Garrison, an ardent Free Trader. "Nations are large enough to be considered separately from each other," he said at the Club. "Internal industry should be diversified. Under free-trade rule, our country would be wholly agricultural. . . . National lines — artificial lines — trip up fine theories sadly. If all the world were under one law, and every man raised to the level of the Sermon on the Mount, free trade would be so easy and so charming. But while nations study only how to cripple their enemies, that is their neighbors . . . we must not expect the millennium."

6

Irishmen in the United States had had, as a class, little use for Abolition. Before the Civil War they were mostly wageworkers and feared that emancipation would mean an influx of Southern Negro labor and a further lowering of their standard of living. Hence the American Irish had paid little or no attention to the appeal of their countrymen that they join forces with the Abolitionists. Yet, curiously, there probably was no other American as beloved by the Irish as Wendell Phillips. Even when they had rioted against him they had admired his courage. A man who with perfect self-possession defied an infuriated crowd and boldly assailed the government was a man after an Irishman's own heart. When that same man defended labor unions and demanded an eight-hour day and higher wages for labor, Irish workmen were convinced he was their friend. Moreover, as Catholics they often suffered from intolerance, while he was more than merely tolerant and was to say: "I scorn and scout the word 'toleration'; it is an insolent term. No man, properly speaking, *tolerates* another. I do not tolerate a Catholic, neither does he tolerate me. We are equal, and acknowledge each other's rights; that is the correct statement." Last, but not least, he never lost an opportunity to speak up for Ireland and to condemn British oppression.

In 1873, James Anthony Froude, English pamphleteer and historian, came to the United States to lecture in the principal cities on Anglo–Irish relations. Public opinion in the United States at that time was not especially favorable to the Irish and Froude's sponsors hoped to solidify this sentiment. But after the lecturer's appearance in Boston, Phillips delivered a lecture in rebuttal that shattered the arguments of the Englishman and arraigned England's misrule of Ireland in a devastating manner. It was widely quoted and won him the heart of every Irishman. Its effect was such that Froude cut short his lecture tour. When two years later the Irish in New York decided to celebrate the one hundredth anniversary of the birth of Daniel O'Connell, Phillips was chosen as the orator of the occasion and delivered a speech that still further endeared him to the Irish. In February, 1881, he spoke at the Land-League meeting in Somerville, Massachusetts, on "The Crisis in Irish Affairs" and earned delirious applause by advocating "giving Ireland to the Irish. . . . So great are the difficulties in the way of union between the two islands, that that seems the only door out of the great difficulty." After this he was regarded as Ireland's foremost champion in the United States.

That same year the Irish Land League cabled Patrick Ford, editor of the *Irish World*, to try to prevail on Phillips to visit Ireland. "The League will pay all expenses." Ford sent a copy of the cable to Phillips with a letter the wording of which was eloquent of the respect and affection in which he was held by the Irish in America and in the Emerald Isle:

"I beg you, Mr. Phillips, to hearken to this as an inspiration and a call from God himself. You are the one man in America fitted for the glorious mission. All Ireland will rise to its feet to bless and cheer you. Never did Caesar receive such an ovation. Civilization will look on in admiring wonder. The good which your heroic act will effect is incalculable; and your name, consecrated in the memory of a grateful people, will live whilst time endures."

Ann's health as well as his own did not permit him to undertake the journey.

7

Among institutions of learning hostile to Abolition, Harvard College deserves a prominent place. In 1836, Dr. Charles T. Follen, Professor of German Language and Literature, failed of reappointment because of his affiliation with the Anti-Slavery Society. Long before the Civil War, Williams College, Dartmouth, Yale and Brown University had invited Phillips to address their students, but not until June 30, 1881, when the Phi Beta Kappa of Harvard College celebrated its centennial anniversary and emancipation had long ceased to be an issue, did Phillips's Alma Mater follow their example.

Phillips was now in his sixty-ninth year and it may or may not have been a coincidence that the occasion likewise marked the half-centennial of his graduation from Harvard College. He accepted and gave as the subject of his discourse "The Scholar in a Republic." Departing from his usual method, he wrote out the address in full and committed it to memory — no small feat considering that it took three hours to deliver. There was some uneasiness about what he was going to say. *Harper's New Monthly* declared after the ceremony: "On the day before, which was commencement day, there was general wonder among the Harvard men of all ages, whether the orator would regard the amenities of the occasion, and pour out his music and wit upon some purely literary theme, or seize his venerable mother by the hair, and gracefully twist it out with a smile."

Seventeen of the twenty existing chapters of Phi Beta Kappa had sent delegates. Headed by the Germania Band, members of the chapters, visiting delegates and invited guests marched in procession to Sanders theater. It was, said *Harper's*, a "long, long procession — a Phi Beta Kappa procession such as even Harvard never saw before." Except for platform and orchestra seats reserved for those in the procession the hall was already filled with a distinguished audience, among whom were many women. Joseph A. Choate of New York, President of the Society, took the chair. With him on the platform were Phillips, Oliver Wendell Holmes, George William Curtis, James Freeman Clarke, Phillips Brooks, Edward Everett Hale, Richard Grant White, President Gilman of Johns Hopkins, President Eliot of Harvard and other notables. There was music by the Germania Orchestra too, after which Dr. Peabody pronounced the invocation. Then the chairman introduced Phillips with the words: "And now I introduce to you him who, whenever and wherever he speaks, is the orator of the day."

Phillips rose, buttoned his frock coat across his white waistcoat and moved to the front of the platform.

8

Competent critics regard Phillips's Harvard oration as superior to any he ever made. His theme was the petty egotism and cowardly conservatism of university men. "Rarely," he said, " in this country have scholarly men joined, as a class, in these great popular schools n these social movements which make the great interests of society crash and jostle against each other like frigates in a storm.' " It was so in the struggle against slavery: "Amid this battle of the giants, scholarship sat dumb for thirty years until imminent deadly peril convulsed it into action, and colleges, in their despair, gave to the army that help they had refused to the market-place and the rostrum." In the struggle for woman suffrage, for reform of the criminal code, for Ireland, it was the same: "Timid scholarship either shrinks from sharing in these agitations, or denounces them as vulgar and dangerous interference by incompetent hands with matters above them."

He defended labor's right to organize ("When the easy class conspires to steal, what wonder the humbler class draws together to defend itself"), glorified the French Revolution and took up the cudgels for Russian Nihilism, which, he said, was "crushed humanity's only means of making the oppressor tremble. . . . I honor Nihilism, since it redeems human nature from the suspicion of being utterly vile, made up only of heartless oppressors and contented slaves. . . . In such a land dynamite and the dagger are the necessary and proper substitutes for Faneuil Hall and the *Daily Adveriser.*"

That the address was a remarkable feat of oratory was acknowledged by all. Thomas Wentworth Higginson commented: "He never seemed more at ease, more colloquial, and more extemporaneous; and he held an unwilling audience spellbound, while bating absolutely nothing of his radicalism. Many a respectable lawyer and divine felt his blood run cold, the next day, when he found that the fascinating orator whom he had applauded to the echo had really made the assassination of an emperor seem as trivial as the loom of a mosquito."

Phillips was surprised at the favorable reception his address had received from his Harvard audience: "I thought they would hiss me, but they showed their true education by bearing it well. Indeed, I seldom had such cheers and such a warm reception. . . . Well, I suppose they wanted me to bring myself."

9

Garrison, poor as a church mouse at the beginning of his career, during the decade preceding his death was free from financial worry

and the necessity of earning a living. Phillips, at one time in possession of a comfortable fortune, during the last ten years of his life
was plagued by money worries, and in spite of ill health forced to
keep on lecturing to provide for his modest needs. He and Ann,
while spending little on themselves, had been so open-handed that
by 1873 little remained of their fortune. That year he wrote to his
agent to sell a piece of property "for the most we can get. . . . We
must go to auction if no other way serves," and to accept "any
offer" to continue a mortgage. To a solicitation to help a philanthropic enterprise he replied: "I wish I had funds to help you labor
in that field. . . . But my means are so crippled that I have nothing
to contribute."

When in 1878 he came to New York to lecture and called on
Mrs. Buffum Chace Wyman, she remarked to him that he did not
appear well enough to be lecturing. "No," he replied, "I am not
well enough and I should not have to do it."

"Does thee have to?"

He replied with a touch of desperation in his voice: "Yes, and
it is not right that I should."

In December, 1881, he wrote to a friend: "I work hard, and battle
with snow-storms and drifts as I used to ten years ago, and hoped
I should not now. But must be what must." And to another: "Even
the few engagements I made I have been sometimes forced to break
. . . Whether another winter I lecture at all is uncertain."

It was about this time that James Redpath noticed that the lisle
thread gloves Phillips wore were darned, but he hastens to assure
us that "let him wear what he may, he never looks slovenly or
shabby."

Testimony regarding the effect his changed circumstances had
upon him is conflicting. Dr. George Edward Woodberry remembered him as "an old gray man, simple, kindly, serene; a gentleman
in every line of his fine features, in every notion, in every fibre; a
type never to be forgotten by eyes that saw him." Frank P. Stearns
found that "his temper became sharp and his mind melancholic."
Charles Eliot Norton, after hearing him lecture at Harvard, wrote
to James Russell Lowell: "His features, moving or at rest, have a
bitter and malign look, — they are not the lineaments of Gospel
Books."

Malignity was foreign to his nature, but bitterness and melancholy
were not strangers to him during that trying time. When he had

spoused the cause of labor his closest friends had abandoned him.
'It seems hard," he complained to Frank P. Stearns, "that of the
men whom I worked with for thirty or forty years, only three or
our are willing to speak to me now." He and Ann had entertained
out little at any time, now, Stearns tells us, "No company was ever
nvited to his house, and it was by the rarest chance that he went
o any entertainment." Meeting Nora Perry, the poetess, on the
street one day, Phillips asked her where she was going. "To see a
riend," she replied. "Ah," he said, "you remind me of the Frenchman who received the same answer and said: 'Take me along. I
never saw one.'"

10

The city authorities had for some time contemplated widening
Harrison Avenue, which necessitated the demolition of the house
in which Phillips and Ann had lived since 1841. He had managed
o have the work postponed, but finally the improvement could no
onger wait and in the spring of 1882 they were forced to move.
At 37 Common Street he found a house somewhat resembling the
old dwelling. The mantel and open grate from Ann's room were
installed in the chamber she was to occupy and the furniture ar-
anged as nearly as possible as it had been in their old home.

The move affected Phillips profoundly. From that time on he
prepared for death. Perhaps the fact that Longfellow and Emerson
died that year influenced his mood. Perhaps the report of the Sage
of Concord murmuring at Longfellow's funeral, "The gentleman
we have just been burying was a sweet and beautiful soul; but I
orget his name," made him wish to have done with life before his
own mind was similarly affected. Whatever the reason, thoughts of
death now intruded constantly. He told Samuel A. Green, former
Mayor of Boston, that he would not live to be seventy-four. Once,
in the company of an acquaintance, he went to where the old house
had stood and, looking sadly at the vacant space, said to his companion: "It was hard that the city would not let me stay till the
end in my home of forty years." Then, turning away, he added:
It is no matter. I am almost through with it all."

That summer he distributed his books and files of antislavery
publications among various libraries, writing to a friend: "So you
see I have acted as my own executor, to get rid of twenty-five

hundred volumes." To a woman friend he wrote some months later: "Mrs. P. for the last eleven months has been very much more ill than usual — indeed I think the shock of being flung out of our years' home is one she will never rally from. She has not stood or lifted herself from her pillow without help since . . . so I have given up lecturing — am a good boy and stay at home — cleaning up and giving away my books and pamphlets — acting as my own executor and getting ready to go."

People to whom he had loaned money had often insisted on giving him notes. There was quite an accumulation of these, some still legally collectible. He canceled all, returning them to the signatories when their addresses were known to him.

He fervently hoped that Ann might die before him, and once said to Susan B. Anthony: "I remember seeing my grandfather look out of the window at my grandmother's funeral, and hearing him say, 'I thank God I have lived to see her go first!' I did not understand his feelings then, but I know now what it was. I have lived to have every hope and desire merge itself and be lost in the one wish that I may outlive Ann."

11

W. D. Howells has written that "To value aright the affection which the old Bostonian had for Boston we must conceive of something like the patriotism of men in the times when a man's city was a man's country, something Athenian, something Florentine." It was with a feeling such as this that Phillips was saying good-by to Boston. Often in the evening he could be seen walking meditatively up Beacon Hill, and having arrived at the State House looking about him as if he were seeing the scene for the first time or meant to fix it in his memory, then slowly retracing his steps. In the afternoon he would sometimes walk down State or Washington Streets, stopping occasionally to observe the passers-by. One day Dr. Bowditch broke in upon his revery as he stood leaning against a bank building on State Street, and remarked: "Wendell, if you want these people to give you money, you must take off your hat and hold it in your hand."

Towards the end of 1883, the surviving founders of the American Anti-Slavery Society arranged a meeting in Philadelphia to commemorate the fiftieth anniversary of that event. Phillips, while no one of the founders, was invited. He was unable to go, but wrote a letter containing this plea: "Let it not be said that the old Abolitionist stopped with the negro, and was never able to see that the same principles he had advocated at such cost claimed his utmost effort to protect all labor, white and black, and to further the discussion of every claim of downtrodden humanity."

On December 26, 1883, a statue of Harriet Martineau, by Anne Whitney, was unveiled in the Old South Meeting House. Unlike so many of her compatriots who condemned slavery at home but remained discreetly silent on the subject when touring the United States for fear of losing profitable lecture engagements, Miss Martineau had refused to temporize during her visit. Phillips and William Lloyd Garrison, Jr., who addressed the audience, paid tribute to her ability, integrity and courage. "It is easy to be independent," Phillips said, "when all behind you agree with you, but the difficulty comes when nine hundred and ninety-nine of your friends think you wrong. Then it is the brave soul who stands up, one among a thousand, but remembering that one with God makes a majority."

The words applied to him even more than to the woman in whose praise they were uttered.

It was his last speech.

12

On Saturday morning, January 26, 1884, Phillips suddenly clapped his hand to his heart, his face contorted with pain, and collapsed on the bed. Dr. David Thayer, the family physician, was hastily summoned. He pronounced the attack *angina pectoris*, of which Phillips's father and three of his brothers had died. The patient grew progressively worse and by Thursday his condition was such that Thayer thought it best to inform him there was slight hope of recovery. Phillips smiled wistfully and said: "I have no fear of death. I have long foreseen this. My only regret is for poor Ann. I had hoped to close her eyes before mine were shut."

Relatives and old-time friends now crowded the house, and one, Mrs. E. F. Crosby, having been admitted to the sickroom, spoke to him of religion. He told her he had no doubt of a future life. Attacks of agonizing pain were frequent and sedatives were administered. A consultation of some of the most prominent doctors in Boston only confirmed the finding that death might be expected at any moment. On Saturday, at about four in the afternoon, the patient attempted to rise. A paroxysm of pain seized him. He fainted and was revived with difficulty. A couple of hours later, at fifteen minutes after six, February 2, 1884, he closed his eyes, "as one falling asleep," and died.

If during his lifetime opinion about him had been divided, at his death there was virtual unanimity that the country had lost one of its greatest men. The day following his death being a Sunday, there was not a pulpit in Boston from which sorrow about his passing was not expressed. On Monday the City Council met in special session and appointed a committee to make arrangements for a memorial meeting under municipal auspices. (The meeting was held on April 18 in Tremont Temple, George William Curtis delivering the eulogy.) That same Monday the Labor-Reform League met and arranged a memorial meeting at Faneuil Hall for the following evening. Joseph Cook, in his usual Monday evening lecture at Tremont Temple, spoke of Phillips and said: "Fifty years hence it will not be asked, 'What did Boston think of Wendell Phillips?' but, 'What did Wendell Phillips think of Boston?'" The Legislature of Massachusetts, in a ringing resolution, paid tribute to this man "full of the generous spirit of self-sacrifice, seeking no public honor, devoting his life and great powers to the cause of the oppressed even to his own heavy loss, standing firm against any and every injustice like the hills of his native State." Newspapers throughout the North rang with eulogies. Sad-faced crowds in New York, Philadelphia, Washington, Cleveland, Chicago and elsewhere gathered before bulletin boards announcing: "Wendell Phillips Is Dead." Even in the South — in New Orleans, Charleston and Richmond — there were men, white as well as colored, who boldly declared that he had been the friend of the common people of the South. O'Donovan Rossa voiced the sentiment of the country when he said: "Wendell Phillips of America is dead in Boston."

13

In response to numerous requests from organizations and individuals it was decided that after the religious ceremony on Wednesday morning in the Hollis Street Church the body should lie in state for several hours in Faneuil Hall. So, after the funeral service, conducted by the Reverend Samuel Longfellow, brother of the poet, and by the Reverend Samuel May, the coffin was taken to the hall through streets thronged with people. Two companies of colored militia, marching with arms reversed to the roll of muffled drums, served as a guard of honor. On the platform from which as a youth of twenty-six Phillips had rebuked the attorney-general of the Commonwealth — from which he had so often defied his fellow citizens or roused them to frenzied applause — the floral offerings of friends, admirers and organizations formed a colorful display. A mound composed of oblong bands of flowers, the word "Humanity" spelled out in violets in the center, was the tribute of the Irish National League of Boston. A flowery silver-stringed harp, one string symbolically broken and the word "Ireland" in violets on the carnation-covered base, was the gift of the Irish American Societies. On one side of the platform hung the battle flag of the Shaw Veterans, on the other the regimental flag of the colored militia. In front of the platform stood the coffin, soldiers with fixed bayonets standing guard.

Seldom, if ever, had Boston witnessed such an outpouring at the funeral of a private citizen. The city's colored population had come almost in a body to cast a last look at the face of the Boston patrician who had defended their race against the North, against the South, against "Massa Linkum" himself! The grateful Irish turned out in force. Workingmen and workingmen's delegations from neighboring towns were there, and many old-time Abolitionists. Some Boston Brahmins who remembered that, after all, he came of a great family, gained admittance before the doors were thrown open to the crowd. Notwithstanding the biting cold, the line stretching from Faneuil Hall's eastern portal seemed endless. Policemen outside and in the hall managed to keep it advancing at a reasonable pace, but George Lowell Austin, an eyewitness, has written that when the doors closed at ten minutes after four "thousands were still waiting outside."

Darkness was beginning to fall when the hearse, preceded and flanked by the military and followed by a long row of carriages and by hundreds on foot, started on its way through solemn-looking crowds down Merchants' Row, through State Street (past the spot where Phillips had seen Garrison dragged on a rope), through

Washington, School and Tremont Streets to the Phillips family plot in the Old Granary Burying Ground.

There was no service at the grave.

14

Ann survived her husband by a little over a year, dying on April 23, 1885. Barely enough was left of their combined fortune to satisfy creditors, but relatives came to the rescue and she lacked nothing. Years before, Phillips had bought a burial lot in the suburb of Milton, where he and Ann had often spent the summer. Here Ann was buried and here Phillips's remains were laid beside her. A simple slab of stone with the words ANN AND WENDELL PHILLIPS marks the grave.

Ten years after Phillips's death, the Boston City Council ordered a tablet affixed to the building erected on the spot where the Phillips homestead had stood. It bears the following inscription:

HERE
WENDELL PHILLIPS RESIDED DURING FORTY YEARS
DEVOTED BY HIM TO EFFORTS TO SECURE
THE ABOLITION OF AFRICAN SLAVERY IN THIS COUNTRY.

———

THE CHARMS OF HOME, THE ENJOYMENT OF WEALTH AND LEARNING
EVEN THE KINDLY RECOGNITION OF HIS FELLOW CITIZENS
WERE BY HIM ACCOUNTED AS NAUGHT COMPARED WITH DUTY.

———

HE LIVED TO SEE JUSTICE TRIUMPHANT, FREEDOM UNIVERSAL
AND TO RECEIVE THE TARDY PRAISES OF HIS OPPONENTS.
THE BLESSINGS OF THE POOR, THE FRIENDLESS,
AND THE OPPRESSED ENRICHED HIM.

———

IN BOSTON
HE WAS BORN 29 NOVEMBER 1811 AND DIED 2 FEBRUARY 1884.

———

THIS TABLET WAS ERECTED IN 1894 BY ORDER OF THE CITY COUNCIL OF BOSTON.

Appendix

FROM Abraham Lincoln's "House Divided" speech, delivered at Springfield, Ill., June 17, 1858:

"A house divided against itself cannot stand." I believe this government cannot endure permanently half slave and half free. I do not expect the Union to be dissolved — I do not expect the house to fall — but I do expect it will cease to be divided. It will become all one thing or all the other. Either the opponents of slavery will arrest the further spread of it, and place it where the public mind shall rest in the belief that it is in the course of ultimate extinction; or its advocates will push it forward, till it shall become alike lawful in all the States, old as well as new, North as well as South.

Have we no tendency to the latter condition?

From William Henry Seward's "Irrepressible Conflict" speech, delivered at Rochester, N. Y., October 25, 1858:

Shall I tell you what this collision [of two antagonistic systems] means? They who think that it is accidental, unnecessary, the work of interested or fanatical agitators, and therefore ephemeral, mistake the case altogether. It is an irrepressible conflict between opposing and enduring forces, and it means that the United States must and will, sooner or later, become either entirely a slaveholding nation, or entirely a free-labor nation. Either the cotton and rice fields of South Carolina and the sugar plantations of Louisiana will ultimately be tilled by free labor, and Charleston and New Orleans become marts for legitimate merchandise alone, or else the rye-fields and wheat-fields of Massachusetts and New York must again be surrendered by their farmers to slave culture and to the production of slaves, and Boston and New York become once more markets for trade in the bodies and souls of men. It is the failure to apprehend this great truth that induces so many unsuccessful attempts at final compromise between the slave and the free States, and it is the existence of this great fact that renders all such pretended compromises, when made, vain and ephemeral.

Selected Bibliography

WRITINGS AND SPEECHES OF
WILLIAM LLOYD GARRISON

THE *Liberator*, the *National Anti-Slavery Standard* and the New York *Independent* (1866–1879) are, in addition to the following, the principal sources for the study of Garrison's writings and speeches. According to Edmund Quincy, his journalistic and propagandistic output equaled in volume the writings of Voltaire.

1831 — *An address delivered before the Free People of Color, in Philadelphia, New York, etc.* Boston.

1832 — *Thoughts on African Colonization.* Boston.
An *Address on the Progress of the Abolition Cause.* Boston.

1833 — *Address delivered in Boston, New York, and Philadelphia before the Free People of Color.* New York.
Slavery in the United States of America, an Appeal to the Friends of Negro Emancipation Throughout Great Britain. London.

1834 — *A Selection of Anti-Slavery Hymns.* Preface by William Lloyd Garrison. Boston.

1836 — *Lectures of George Thompson: also A Brief History of his Connection with the Anti-Slavery Cause in England,* by William Lloyd Garrison. Boston.

1838 — *An Address in Marlboro' Chapel.* Boston.
An Address delivered at the Broadway Tabernacle, New York . . . in commemoration of the Complete Emancipation of 600,000 slaves . . . in the British West Indies. Boston.

1839 — *A Letter on the Political Obligations of Abolitionists,* by James G. Birney: with a Reply by William Lloyd Garrison. Boston.

1839 — *An Address delivered before the Old Colony Anti-Slavery Society.* Boston.
1843 — *Sonnets and Other Poems.* Boston.
 Anti-Slavery Melodies: For the Friends of Freedom. Hingham, Mass. (Hymns 3, 18, 27 and lyrics on pages 64, 70 are Garrison's.)
1846 — *Address on the Subject of American Slavery.* London.
 Proceedings of a Crowded Meeting of the Colored Population of Boston . . . for the purpose of bidding farewell to William Lloyd Garrison; with his speech on the Occasion. Dublin.
 Speeches of William Lloyd Garrison and Frederick Douglass . . . at Paisley, Scotland. Glasgow [?].
1851 — "The Great Apostate." In the *Liberty Bell.* Boston.
1852 — *Selections from the Writings and Speeches of William Lloyd Garrison.* Boston.
 Letter to Louis Kossuth. Boston.
1853 — *Principles and Mode of Action of the American Anti-Slavery Society.* London.
1854 — *No Compromise with Slavery.* New York.
 West India Emancipation. Boston.
1859 — *No Fetters in the Bay State. Speech before the Committee on Federal Relations* [of the Massachusetts Legislature]. Boston.
1860 — *The "Infidelity" of Abolitionism.* New York.
 "The New Reign of Terror" in The Slaveholding States, for 1859–60. Compiled by Garrison. New York.
1861 — *The Loyalty and Devotion of the Colored Americans in the Revolution and War of 1812.* Boston.
 Spirit of the South towards Northern Freemen and Soldiers defending the American Flag against Traitors of Deepest Dye. Boston.
1862 — *The Abolitionists and their Relations to the War.* New York.
 Three Unlike Speeches, by W. L. Garrison, G. Davis, A. H. Stephens. New York.
1867 — *Proceedings at the Public Breakfast held in Honor of William Lloyd Garrison, Esq.* (Contains speech by Garrison.) London.
1872 — *Joseph Mazzini: His Life, Writings and Political Principles.* Introduction by William Lloyd Garrison. New York.

1876 — *Helen Eliza Garrison: A Memorial*. Cambridge, Mass.
1879 [?] — *William Lloyd Garrison on State Regulation of Vice*. New York [?].
1905 — *Words of Garrison; a Centennial Selection*. Boston.

BOOKS, PAMPHLETS, ARTICLES, ABOUT WILLIAM LLOYD GARRISON

By far the most important work about William Lloyd Garrison is the four volume documentary Life written by his children: *William Lloyd Garrison, 1805–1879: the Story of his Life Told by his Children*. New York, Vol. I, II, 1885; Vol. III, IV, 1889. (New edition, 1894, Houghton Mifflin Company, Boston and New York.) Garrison's daughter, Fanny Garrison Villard, has rightly said, that the *Life* "is a quarry from which all subsequent lives have necessarily been written." The authors have allowed the documentary material to speak for itself, with but little attempt at evaluation or interpretation. Excellent as is the documentation in the *Life*, the student will want to examine the material in the Garrison and Weston Collections in the Public Library of the City of Boston and to peruse the pages of the *Liberator*, the *National Anti Slavery Standard* and the New York *Independent* (1866–1879).

Also:
AMES, ELLIS — *The Garrison Mob in Boston* (Proceedings of the Massachusetts Historical Society. February, 1881. Pp. 340–44.)
Brief Sketch of the Trial of William Lloyd Garrison for an Alleged Libel on Francis Todd, of Massachusetts, A. Baltimore, 1830 [?].
AXON, WILLIAM E. A. — *The Story of a Noble Life*. London, 1890.
CHAPMAN, JOHN J. — *William Lloyd Garrison*. New York, 1913. Second edition, revised and enlarged. Boston, 1921.
COOKE, FRANCIS E. — *An American Hero; the Story of William Lloyd Garrison*. London, 1888.
CROSBY, ERNEST HOWARD — *Garrison, the Non-Resistant*. Chicago, 1905.
GIZYCKI, GEORG — *William Lloyd Garrison*. (German translation and condensation of *The Story of his Life Told by his Children*.) Berlin, 1890.
GRIMKÉ, ARCHIBALD H. — *William Lloyd Garrison, the Abolitionist*. New York, 1891.

HOWITT, MARY — "William Lloyd Garrison." In the *People's Journal*, Sept. 12, 19, 26; Oct. 3, 1846.

JOHNSON, OLIVER — *William Lloyd Garrison and his Times*. Boston, 1881.

LYMAN, TH. 3rd. — *Papers Relating to the Garrison Mob*. Cambridge, 1870.

MARTINEAU, HARRIET — *The Martyr Age of the United States*. In *London and Westminster Review*. London, 1838.

MAY, JOSEPH — *William Lloyd Garrison; a Commemoration Discourse*. Boston, 1879.

MAY, SAMUEL J. — *Some Recollections of Our Anti-Slavery Conflict*. Boston, 1869. (Two chapters devoted to Garrison.)

Memorial of William Lloyd Garrison from the City of Boston, A. Boston, 1886.

MOORE, N. — *William Lloyd Garrison*. Boston, 1888.

National Testimonial to William Lloyd Garrison, A. Boston, 1866.

OTIS, JAMES FREDERIC — *Memoir of William Lloyd Garrison*. (n.d.)

PHILLIPS, WENDELL — "Garrison." In *North American Review*, August, 1879, pp. 141–52.

PONSONBY, ARTHUR AND DOROTHEA P. — *Rebels and Reformers*. London, 1917.

PUTNAM, A. P. — *A Discourse on William Lloyd Garrison and the Anti-Slavery Movement*. Brooklyn, N. Y., 1879.

Sketch of the Character and Defense of the Principles of William Lloyd Garrison, A. New York, 1833.

SMITH, GOLDWIN — *The Moral Crusader*. Toronto, 1892.

SWIFT, LINDSAY — *William Lloyd Garrison*. Philadelphia, 1911.

TCHERTKOFF, V. AND HOLAH, F. — *A Short Biography of William Lloyd Garrison*. Introduction by Leo Tolstoi. London, 1904.

Tributes to William Lloyd Garrison at the Funeral Services. Boston, 1879.

VILLARD, FANNY GARRISON — *William Lloyd Garrison on Non-Resistance*. New York, 1924.

WRITINGS AND SPEECHES OF
WENDELL PHILLIPS

The *Liberator*, the *National Anti-Slavery Standard* and the *Standard* should be consulted, in addition to the following:

1845 — *Can Abolitionists Vote or Take Office under the Constitution?* New York.

1847 — *Review of Lysander Spooner's Essay on the Unconstitutionality of Slavery.* Boston.

1850 — *Review of Webster's Speech on Slavery.* Boston.

1851 — "Mrs. Eliza Garnaut." In the *Liberty Bell.* Boston.

1856 — *The Constitution a Pro-Slavery Compact.* New York.

1860 — *The Philosophy of the Abolition Movement.* Boston.

1863 — *Speeches, Lectures, and Letters.* First Series. Boston.

1865 — "The Immediate Issue." *The Equality of all Men before the Law.* Boston.
        Remarks at the Mass Meeting of Workingmen in Faneuil Hall, November 2, 1865. Boston.

1871 — *The People Coming to Power!* Boston.

1875 — *Stand and Be Counted.* Boston.

1878 — *Who Shall Rule Us? Money or the People?* Boston.

1879 — "Garrison." In the *North American Review*, August, 1879, pp. 141–52.
        "The Other Side of the Woman Question." In the *North American Review*, November, 1879, pp. 439–46.

1883 — "Remarks of Wendell Phillips at the Funeral of Lydia Maria Child." October 23, 1880. *In Letters of Lydia Maria Child.* Boston, 1883.

1891 — *Speeches, Lectures and Letters.* Second Series. Boston.
        The Freedom of Speech. Boston.

1892 — "Letter to Lydia Maria Child." In *New England Magazine*, February, 1892, pp. 730–34.
        Address to the School Children of Boston. Boston.

1898 — *Speeches on the Rights of Women.* Philadelphia.

1909 — "A Bundle of Cheerful Letters." Unpublished Correspondence of Wendell Phillips. In *New England Magazine*, February, 1909, pp. 649–55; March, 1909, pp. 38–45; April, 1909, pp. 180–84.

BOOKS, PAMPHLETS, ARTICLES, AND SHORT WRITINGS ABOUT WENDELL PHILLIPS

By far the most valuable works about Wendell Phillips are the following two unpublished doctoral dissertations:

OSCAR SHERWIN — *Prophet of Liberty: A Biography of Wendell Phillips.* New York University, 1940.

JOHN WILLIAM SATTLER — *Wendell Phillips: Speaker and Agitator.* Northwestern University, 1943.

A complete list of sources of information will be found in both dissertations.

Also consult:

ALCOTT, A. BRONSON — "Wendell Phillips." In the *Radical*, September, 1867, pp. 105–10.

ALFORD (Mrs.) — *Memorial of Ann Phillips.* Library of Harvard University.

AUSTIN, GEORGE LOWELL — *The Life and Times of Wendell Phillips.* Boston, 1888.

BEECHER, HENRY WARD — *Wendell Phillips.* New York, 1884.

BENTON, JOEL — "Reminiscences of Eminent Lecturers." In *Harper's New Magazine*, March, 1898.

BRUCE, ROSCOE CONKLING — *The College Career of Wendell Phillips.* In *Harvard Illustrated Magazine*, April, 1901.

BUTTERWORTH, HEZEKIAH — "A Touch on the Arm." In the *Outlook*, January 16, 1904, pp. 179–81.

CONWAY, MONCURE D. — "Wendell Phillips." In *Fortnightly Review*, July 1, 1870, pp. 59–73.

CURTIS, GEORGE WILLIAM — *Orations and Addresses.* Vol. III. New York, 1894.

"Editor's Easy Chair" — *Harper's New Monthly Magazine.* January, 1880, pp. 307–09; April, 1884, pp. 804–05.

Exercises at the Dedication of the Statue of Wendell Phillips. Boston, 1916.

GARRISON, FRANCIS JACKSON — *Ann Phillips, A Memorial Sketch.* Cambridge, 1886.

HAGAN, H. H. — "Wendell Phillips." In the *Sewanee Review*, July, 1913, pp. 324–40.

HALE, EDWARD EVERETT — "Reminiscences of Wendell Phillips." In the *Chatauquan,* May, 1884, pp. 451–53.

HELM, T. G. — "Wendell Phillips and the Abolition Movement." In *Reformed Church Review,* Fourth Series, XX (1916), pp. 196–226.

HINTON, RICHARD J. — "Wendell Phillips: A Reminiscent Study." In the *Arena,* July, 1895, pp. 226–42.

HOFSTADTER, RICHARD — *The American Political Tradition and the Men Who Made It.* New York, 1948.

HUBBARD, ELBERT — *Little Journeys to the Homes of the Famous Orators.* East Aurora, N. Y., 1902.

HUGHES, JAMES L. — "World Leaders I Have Known." In *Canadian Magazine.* March, 1924.

JONES, JESSE H. — *His Last Battle, Wendell Phillips in Faneuil Hall on the Louisiana Difficulties.* Cambridge, 1897.

LORING, JAMES I. — *The Hundred Boston Orators.* Boston, 1853.

MARTYN, CARLOS — *Wendell Phillips, the Agitator.* New York, 1890.
"Wendell Phillips as an Orator." In the *Forum,* November, 1899, pp. 305–16.

MEAD, EDWIN D. — "A Monument to Wendell Phillips." In *New England Magazine,* December, 1890, pp. 536–39.

PARKER, EDWARD G. — *The Golden Age of American Oratory.* Boston, 1857.

PEPPER, G. W. — "Reminiscences of Wendell Phillips." In the *Independent,* October 18, 1906, pp. 931–34.

PHILLIPS, ALBERT M. — *Phillips Genealogies.* Auburn, Mass. 1885.

RUSSELL, CHARLES EDWARD — *The Story of Wendell Phillips.* Chicago, 1914.

SARGENT, MRS. JOHN T. — *Sketches and Reminiscences of the Radical Club.* Boston, 1880.

SEARS, LORENZO — *Wendell Phillips. Orator and Agitator.* New York, 1909.

SMALLEY, GEORGE W. — "Memoirs of Wendell Phillips." In *Harper's Magazine,* June, 1894, pp. 133–41.

STAFFORD, W. P. — *Wendell Phillips,* New York, 1911.

STEARNS, FRANK PRESTON — "The Career of Wendell Phillips." In *Eastern and Western Review,* November, 1916, pp. 40–47.

THOMAS, CHARLES N. — *A Personal Reminiscence of Wendell Phillips.* Boston, 1892.

VILLARD, OSWALD GARRISON — "Wendell Phillips as an Orator." In the *Nation*, February 21, 1934. "Wendell Phillips after Fifty Years." In *American Mercury*, January, 1935, pp. 93–99.

WASSON, D. A. — "Wendell Phillips as an Orator." In *Christian Examiner*, Fifth Series. November, 1863, pp. 369–409.

WELD, THEODORE D. — *Memorial Services upon the Seventy-Fourth Birthday of Wendell Phillips*. Boston, 1885.

"Wendell Phillips." Editorial in *Literary World*, February 9, 1884. Editorial in the *Nation*, Feb. 7, 1884, pp. 116–18.

"Wendell Phillips as an Orator." In *Every Saturday*, April 22, 1871, pp. 378–79.

WENTWORTH, FRANKLIN H. — *Wendell Phillips*. New York, 1907.

WHEATLEY, RICHARD — "Wendell Phillips." In *Methodist Review*, July, 1892, pp. 541–58.

WOODBERRY, GEORGE EDWARD — *Wendell Phillips, the Faith of an American*. New York, 1912.

WYMAN, LILLIE B. CHACE — "Reminiscences." In *New England Magazine*, February, 1903, pp. 725–40.
American Chivalry. Boston, 1913.

ABRAHAM LINCOLN

Principal works consulted:

ANGLE, PAUL — *New Letters and Papers of Lincoln*. Boston and New York, 1930.

BEVERIDGE, ALBERT J. — *Abraham Lincoln*. 1809–1858. Boston and New York, 1928.

CHARNWOOD, LORD — *Abraham Lincoln*. New York, 1917.

HERNDON, H. AND WEIK, JESSE — *Herndon's Lincoln*. New York, 1930.

HOFSTADTER, RICHARD — *The American Political Tradition*. New York, 1948.

LINCOLN, ABRAHAM — *Complete Works*, New York, 1922.

NICOLAY, JOHN, AND HAY, JOHN — *Abraham Lincoln, a History, Life and Writings*. Boston and New York, 1890.

RANDALL, JAMES G. — *Lincoln the President: Springfield to Gettysburg*. New York, 1945.
Lincoln and the South. Baton Rouge, 1946.
Lincoln and the Liberal Statesman. New York, 1947.

RAYMOND, HENRY J. — *The Life and Public Services of Abraham Lincoln.* New York, 1865.

RICE, ALLEN THORNDIKE (editor) — *Reminiscences of Abraham Lincoln by Distinguished Men of His Time.* New York, 1886.

TARBELL, IDA M. — *The Life of Abraham Lincoln.* New York, 1900.

TRACY, GILBERT A. — *Uncollected Letters of Abraham Lincoln.* Boston and New York, 1917.

WILBUR, HENRY W. — *Lincoln's Attitude Towards Slavery and Emancipation.* Philadelphia, 1919.

WILLIAMS, HARRY T. — *Lincoln and the Radicals.* Madison, Wis. 1941.

SOME OTHER WORKS CONSULTED

For a list of works concerning Slavery the reader is referred to the bibliography in Professor Herbert Aptheker's *American Negro Slave Revolts.* (Columbia University Press, New York, 1943.)

See also:

BANCROFT, FREDERIC — *Life of William Henry Seward.* New York, 1900.

BARNES, GILBERT HOBBS — *The Antislavery Impulse.* New York, 1933.

BEARSE, AUSTIN — *Reminiscences of Fugitive Slave Law.* Boston, 1880.

BLAINE, JAMES G. — *Twenty Years in Congress.* Norwich, Conn. 1886.

CHILD, LYDIA MARIA — *Letters.* Boston, 1883.

COMMAGER, HENRY STEELE — *Theodore Parker: Yankee Crusader.* Boston, 1936.

DU BOIS, BURGHARDT, W. E. — *Black Reconstruction.* New York, 1935.

DOUGLASS, FREDERICK — *Life and Times.* Hartford, Conn., 1882.

EATON, CLEMENT — *Freedom of Thought in the Old South.* Durham, S. C., 1940.

HART, ALBERT BUSHNELL — *Slavery and Abolition.* New York, 1906.

HIBBEN, PAXTON — *Henry Ward Beecher: An American Portrait.* New York, 1927.

HIGGINSON, THOMAS WENTWORTH — *Cheerful Yesterdays.* Boston and New York, 1899.

JAY, WILLIAM — *An Inquiry into the Character and Tendency of the American Colonization and American Anti-Slavery Societies.* New York, 1835.

JENKS, HENRY F. — *Boston Public Latin School.* Boston, 1886.

McCALL, SAMUEL W. — *Thaddeus Stevens.* Boston and New York, 1899.

McPHERSON, EDWARD — *Political History of the United States during Reconstruction.* Washington, D. C., 1871.

MAY, SAMUEL J. — *The Fugitive Slave Law and its Victims.* New York, 1861.

MILLER, ALPHONSE B. — *Thaddeus Stevens.* New York and London, 1939.

NEVINS, ALLAN — *Frémont: the West's Greatest Adventurer.* New York, 1928.

PERRY, BLISS — *The Heart of Emerson's Journals.* Boston and New York, 1926.

PICKARD, SAMUEL T. — *Life and Letters of John Greenleaf Whittier.* Boston and New York, 1894.

PIERCE, EDWARD L. — *Memoirs and Letters of Charles Sumner.* Boston, 1887–1893.

RANDALL, JAMES G. — *The Civil War and Reconstruction.* Boston, 1937.

ROSSITER, WILLIAM I. — *Days and Ways in Old Boston.* Boston, 1915.

SHEPARD, ODELL — *Pedlar's Progress: The Life of Bronson Alcott.* Boston, 1938.

STEVENS, CHARLES — *Anthony Burns.* Boston, 1856.

STROUD, GEORGE M. — *Sketch of the Laws Relating to Slavery in the Several States of the United States of America.* Philadelphia, 1827.

SUMNER, CHARLES — *The Works of Charles Sumner.* Boston, 1900.

VILLARD, OSWALD GARRISON — *John Brown.* Boston, 1910.

WELLES, GIDEON — *Diary of Gideon Welles.* Edited by John T. Morse. Boston, 1911.

WILSON, HENRY — *History of the Rise and Fall of the Slave Power.* Boston and New York, 1872.

WINSTON, ROBERT W. — *Andrew Johnson, Plebeian and Patriot.* New York, 1928.

WOODBURN, JAMES A. — *Life of Thaddeus Stevens.* Indianapolis, 1913.

Index

Index